LIMBUS

Die Aktualität der Romantik
The Actuality of Romanticism

LIMBUS

Australisches Jahrbuch für germanistische Literatur- und
Kulturwissenschaft / Australian Yearbook of German
Literary and Cultural Studies

Herausgeber / Editors
Franz-Josef Deiters, Axel Fliethmann, Birgit Lang,
Alison Lewis, Christiane Weller

Band / Volume 5

Wissenschaftlicher Beirat / Advisory Board

Jane K. Brown (University of Washington)
Alan Corkhill (The University of Queensland)
Gerhard Fischer (The University of New South Wales)
Jürgen Fohrmann (Rheinische Friedrich-Wilhelms-Universität Bonn)
Ortrud Gutjahr (Universität Hamburg)
Ulrike Landfester (Universität St. Gallen)
Sara Lennox (University of Massachusetts)
Matías Martínez (Bergische Universität Wuppertal)
Peter Morgan (The University of Sydney)
Stefan Neuhaus (Leopold Franzens-Universität Innsbruck)
Rolf Günter Renner (Albert-Ludwigs-Universität Freiburg i.Br.)
David Roberts (Monash University)
Ritchie Robertson (The University of Oxford)
Gerhard Schulz (The University of Melbourne)
Norbert Christian Wolf (Paris Lodron-Universität Salzburg)

Die Aktualität der Romantik
The Actuality of Romanticism

rombach verlag

Gedruckt mit Unterstützung der School of Languages,
Cultures and Linguistics der Monash University
und der School of Languages and Linguistics
der University of Melbourne.

Bibliografische Information der Deutschen Nationalbibliothek
Die Deutsche Nationalbibliothek verzeichnet diese Publikation in der
Deutschen Nationalbibliografie; detaillierte bibliografische Daten sind im
Internet über <http://dnb.d-nb.de> abrufbar.

© 2012. Rombach Verlag KG, Freiburg i.Br./Berlin/Wien
1. Auflage. Alle Rechte vorbehalten
Lektorat: Jenny Kühne
Umschlag: typo|grafik|design, Herbolzheim i.Br.
Satz: Martin Janz, Freiburg i.Br.
Herstellung: Rombach Druck- und Verlagshaus GmbH & Co. KG,
Freiburg i.Br.
Printed in Germany
ISSN 1869-1021
ISBN 978-3-7930-9704-4

Inhalt / Content

Vorwort / Preface 7

Aufsätze / Articles

Ritchie Robertson (The University of Oxford)
Hoffmann's *Die Elixiere des Teufels* and the
Lasting Appeal of Conspiracy Theories 11

Dale Adams (The University of Melbourne)
Wirksame Zufälle: Wahrscheinlichkeitstheorie als Erkenntnis-
und Erzähltheorie in Novalis' *Heinrich von Ofterdingen* 33

Ralf Beuthan (Myongji University)
Produktive Reflexion. Überlegungen zum
Produktionsbegriff im Ausgang von Fichte und Derrida 55

James Hodkinson (University of Warwick)
Romantic Cosmopolitanism:
On the Tensions and Topicalities of an Ideal 69

Kate Rigby (Monash University)
»Wo die Wälder rauschen so sacht«.
The Actuality of Eichendorff's Atmospheric Ecopoetics 91

Johannes F. Lehmann (Universität Duisburg-Essen)
Vom Leben und Tod der Dinge:
Zur Aktualität der romantischen Komiktheorie Stephan Schützes ... 105

Ruth Pullin (National Gallery of Victoria)
Eugen von Guérard's Romanticism Reconsidered 123

Yvonne Förster-Beuthan (Leuphana Universität Lüneburg)
The Modern Concept of Fashion and
its Origins in Romanticism 141

Andrew Benjamin (Monash University)
Hegel's Other Woman:
The Figure of Niobe in Hegel's *Lectures on Fine Art* 159

Claudia Wirsing (Friedrich-Schiller-Universität Jena)
Friedrich Schlegel's Concept of Gender in his
»Letter on Philosophy« 179

Klaus Vieweg (Friedrich-Schiller-Universität Jena)
Die romantische Kunst als ›Ende der Kunst‹ 197

Rezensionen / Reviews

Dimitris Vardoulakis. *The Doppelgänger. Literature's Philosophy.*
Reviewed by Dale Adams 217

David Roberts. *The Total Work of Art in European Modernism.*
Rezensiert von Roger Fornoff 220

Petra Rüdiger/Konrad Gross (eds.). *Translation of Cultures.*
Reviewed by Leah Gerber...................................... 228

Gaby Pailer. *Hedwig Dohm.*
Rezensiert von Birte Giesler 230

Leith Passmore. *Ulrike Meinhof and the Red Army Faction:*
Performing Terrorism. Reviewed by Michael Hau............... 234

Albrecht Dümling. *Die verschwundenen Musiker.*
Jüdische Flüchtlinge in Australien. Rezensiert von Birgit Lang............. 236

Nadine Helmi/Gerhard Fischer. *The Enemy at Home:*
German Internees in World War I Australia. Rezensiert von Glenn Nicholls ... 238

Rüdiger Görner/Angus Nicholls (eds). *In the Embrace of the Swan.*
Anglo-German Mythologies in Literature, the Visual Arts and Cultural Theory.
Reviewed by David Roberts 242

Anhang / Appendix

Richtlinien für die Gestaltung / Style Guidelines 247
Beiträger / Contributors.. 253
Herausgeber / Editors 255

Vorwort / Preface

Limbus versammelt in diesem Jahr 11 Aufsätze zur »Aktualität der Romantik«. Ein Teil von ihnen ist hervorgegangen aus Vorträgen, die im Rahmen eines Forschungsprojektes gehalten wurden, an dem Wissenschaftler und Wissenschaftlerinnen der Friedrich-Schiller-Universität Jena und der Monash University in Melbourne beteiligt waren. Finanziell großzügig unterstützt wurde diese Kooperation vom DAAD und der »Group of Eight Australia«. Darüber hinaus haben wir international ausgewiesene Experten gewinnen können, deren Beiträge den Band ergänzen.

Die Herausgeber / The Editors

Aufsätze / Articles

Ritchie Robertson *(The University of Oxford)*

Hoffmann's *Die Elixiere des Teufels* and the Lasting Appeal of Conspiracy Theories

Zusammenfassung

Ausgangspunkt dieses Beitrages ist die anhaltende Faszination, die Verschwörungstheorien und -ängste ausüben. In der jahrhundertelangen Geschichte solcher Vorstellungen markiert die Epoche der Französischen Revolution einen Höhepunkt, der dem mentalitätsgeschichtlichen Übergang von dem schon verblassenden Vorsehungsglauben zu einem aus der Aufklärung stammenden, eher soziologisch zu nennenden Versehensmuster entspricht. In dieser Übergangszeit waren welterschütternde Ereignisse wie die Französische Revolution nur durch bewusstes Handeln von Seiten internationaler Verschwörernetze zu erklären. Dieses Erklärungsmuster liegt dem Geheimbundroman und dessen romantischen Nachfolgern zu Grunde, allen voran Hoffmanns *Elixieren des Teufels*. Dort wird Medardus zum Opfer einer dreifachen Verschwörung, die teils von einer geheimnisvollen überirdischen Instanz, teils von seinem ungebändigten Triebleben, teils von der als skrupelloser Machtapparat dargestellten Katholischen Kirche herzurühren scheint.

I. Conspiracy Theories and Fiction

The legacies bequeathed by Romanticism to the present include a fascination with conspiracy theories. This term can refer both to the malign plots readily ascribed by the public to governments of every political shade, and also to the belief in an international, invisible conspiracy, organized from a hidden nerve-centre by a small group of plotters who control a network of cells and agents scattered across the world. The latter belief, which is my main concern in this paper, has usefully been called »conspiracism« (Pipes, 22). Conspiracist beliefs not only flourished in the eighteenth century but provided the foundation for a genre of fiction, the *Geheimbundroman* or secret-society novel, which in turn was adopted and transformed by Romantic writers, notably E.T.A. Hoffmann. The purpose of this paper is to take a fresh look at Hoffmann's conspiratorial masterpiece, his novel *Die Elixiere des Teufels* (1815/16), by placing it in a perspective suggested by some recent discussions of conspiracy theories.

Conspiracism may be attached to real organizations, such as the Communist International, the Catholic Church, or al-Qaeda. It detects the hand of such organizations in events, often with little or no evidence, as when terrorist acts are promptly ascribed by the media to al-Qaeda or groups linked with al-Qaeda. Conspiracism can also conjure up conspiratorial organizations which are imaginary: thus the *Protocols of the Elders of Zion*, a fabrication forged by the Tsarist police, published in Western Europe immediately after the First World War, soon discredited, yet widely current even at the present day, claim to report the plans for world domination drawn up by a secret Jewish organization comprising both right-wing capitalists and left-wing revolutionaries.

It is easy, and often right, to laugh at conspiracy theories. But our justified scepticism should not deter us from regarding conspiracism as a significant and durable cultural phenomenon. If we look back through the centuries, we find that strikingly similar fantasies have attached themselves to an astonishing variety of real and imaginary bodies. These include the Knights Templar, a military order established in 1128 but broken up, charged with devil-worship and obscene practices, and dispossessed of their wealth by Philip the Fair of France early in the fourteenth century. The witch craze which claimed, not millions of victims as sometimes alleged, but certainly thousands, in many parts of early modern Europe, often charged its victims with forming an international society. In the aftermath of the Reformation, religious sects were often represented as an international conspiracy. Thus in Catholic polemics against Protestant sects, such as Antoine Varillas's *Histoire des révolutions arrivées dans l'Europe en matière de religion* (1686), Calvinists were described as a secret society meeting at night, with passwords, and the whole of Protestantism as »une conjuration pour abolir tout ensemble la Religion Catholique et la Monarchie Françoise« (qtd. in Hofman, 164f.). Particular opprobrium was attached to the Society of Jesus, which was established on the lines of military hierarchy and discipline and soon became an instrument of the Counter-Reformation, drawing its recruits from many countries and classes; it was said to be a monolithic organization, directly subservient to the Pope, ruled by iron rationality and operating with zombie-like obedience, devoted to gaining wealth through its members' influence over the wealthy and political power through their work as confessors to kings and princes, and responsible for many political assassinations (see Peter Burke). Fear of Jesuits did not diminish when the Society was officially dissolved in 1773, for its members then became ex-Jesuits and doubly dangerous because invisible. The re-establishment of the Society in 1814 reanimated these fears, which remained powerful in many countries throughout the nineteenth century. These fears, particularly fear of Jesuits as an international conspiratorial society, provided a template for subsequent anxieties attached to Freemasons, Illuminati, international Jewry, Socialists, Communists, and many other targets (see Rogalla von Bieberstein).

The persistence and adaptability of conspiracism suggest that we should not consider it simply a series of mistaken beliefs. Rather, these mistaken beliefs are the expression of an underlying mind-set or intellectual disposition; they have the imaginative appeal and carry the emotional conviction that is characteristic of myths. Hence one of the best-known historical studies of eighteenth-century conspiracism calls secret societies the subject of a ›mythology‹. Mythologies, as Rachel Bowlby has recently said, are

> both inescapable and ubiquitous; they are the implicit explanatory stories through which we make sense of the world, and also the kinds of realistic or likely stories through which, at any one time or in any particular culture, we experience and narrate our own and others' lives (Bowlby, 8).

Mythologies are thus extended fictions, and conspiracism provides the material for much literary fiction, especially popular fiction. Jesuit and Jewish conspirators have provided material for innumerable thrillers. One of the enduring best-sellers in Germany is Gustav Freytag's *Soll und Haben* (1855), in which the stolid German hero has an evil but much more interesting shadow-self in the villainous Jew Veitel Itzig. A comparable best-seller in nineteenth century France is *Le Juif errant* (1844/45) by Eugène Sue, which, contrary to what one might expect, turns on the machinations of Jesuits. Its main character is the Jesuit Rodin whose ambition is to become Pope. By his indomitable will, power of dissimulation, and gift for psychological manipulation, he manages to induce all seven descendants of the Wandering Jew to commit suicide in the hope that the vast sum thus left without an heir will accrue to the Society of Jesus. From Victorian Britain one could mention a number of thrillers turning on Jesuits, perhaps the best being *Father Eustace: A Tale of the Jesuits* (1847) by Frances Trollope, mother of the more famous Anthony. Frances Trollope gets beyond the standard charges of villainy and gives a sympathetic psychological study of a young Jesuit's emotional condition. He falls in love with his charge, yet is obliged to persuade her to become a nun so that the Society may acquire her fortune.[1] At the present

---

[1] For these and more examples, see Robertson.

day, we may think of the popularity of Dan Brown's *The Da Vinci Code*, a page-turner which gives a highly distorted representation of the Catholic society Opus Dei as the vehicle for a millennia-old conspiracy. Beside it we may set a novel of infinitely greater sophistication and learning, Umberto Eco's *Foucault's Pendulum* (1988), which offers an enthralling tongue-in-cheek exploration of a range of conspiratorial fantasies, from the Templars to the *Protocols*; its central characters, fantasists who become obsessed with a conspiratorial fiction of their own making, eventually have to accept that what seemed a crucial document is nothing more than a medieval laundry-list. Hoffmann's *Die Elixiere des Teufels* is another, highly sophisticated conspiratorial narrative.

II. Conspiracism and the History of Mentalities

Given that conspiracy theories and conspiratorial fictions have had such a long life, what justification is there for associating either of them with Romanticism in particular? Romanticism followed a series of events which have plausibly been claimed as a watershed in the history of conspiracism. The Illuminati were a radical offshoot of Freemasonry, dedicated to spreading the atheism and materialism of such Enlightenment *philosophes* such as Helvétius, and to replacing the power of kings and aristocrats with some form of democratic government. Though these principles were indeed held by the founder of the Illuminati, Adam Weishaupt, there was no chance of their ever being put into practice: the Illuminati never had more than about 650 members and attracted few of the prominent figures of the time. Concern about their activities led the Elector of Bavaria in 1785 to forbid Illuminism and freemasonry on his territories and to order a raid on Weishaupt's premises, where some incriminating letters were found that confirmed suspicions of their subversive intentions. A widespread »moral panic« about secret societies seemed to be confirmed soon afterwards by the outbreak of the French Revolution. It was known that a leading Illuminatus, Johannes Bode, had visited Freemasons in Paris in 1787, and though the purpose of his visit was harmless, it was conjectured that German Illuminati and French masons had laid an international plot which had led straight to the Revolution. The Revolution was unmasked as the product of a world conspiracy in a series of widely-read books, of which the best-known was Augustin Barruel's five-volume *Mémoires pour servir à l'histoire du jacobinisme* (1797), which »provided a remarkably clear and well-ordered historical account, heavily and plausibly documented, which wove together almost all the existing plot theories and all the well-known events of the Revolution into one great synthesis« (Roberts, 193; see also Klausnitzer). According to Barruel, a conspiratorial organization had existed continuously since early in the Christian period; it went back to the heretic Mani, founder of the Manichaean religion, and had been carried on by the medieval Knights Templar, and then by the Freemasons; they in turn had provided the organizational basis for the Jacobins. This conspiracy theory is often claimed as the template for subsequent conspiracy theories involving Jews, socialists, anarchists, and the like, though, as I have indicated, such theories have a much longer history, and the most striking example of an international conspiratorial organization seemed to be offered by the Jesuits.

Their interest in conspiracy theories lets us place the Romantics within the historical framework proposed by a far-reaching and deservedly influential study of conspiracy theories, published by Gordon S. Wood some thirty years ago (Wood). Wood explains the rise of conspiracism by positing a sequence of explanatory models. Until the advent of modern scepticism with the Enlightenment, events could be explained by reference to divine providence. Admittedly, the notion of ›special providence‹, the belief that divine providence took a hand in individual lives and everyday events gradually came to be regarded as a self-important, possibly superstitious, certainly trivializing abuse of the concept.[2] Even if special providences were discarded, however, the concept of a general providence, governing the world on a large scale and ensuring that events would ultimately turn out for the best, remained an essential plank of natural religion. Without such a concept of providence, there could be no defence against scepticism, materialism, and naturalism, which instead posited a blind fate or a mere meaningless concatenation of natural causes. Defenders of providence, however, had to use considerable ingenuity to reconcile it with the evident existence and perhaps prevalence of evil, pain, and injustice in the world. One of the most sophisticated upholders of providence, Lessing, argued accordingly that providence was not a source of privileged insight into God's plans for the future, but could only reveal God's purposes in retrospect.[3] Thus a notorious problem in Old Testament history, God's apparent failure to inform Moses about the important doctrine of the immortality of the soul, could make sense in retrospect once enough time had passed for us to see that God doled

---

[2] For many examples, see Walsham.
[3] On Lessing's conception of providence, see now Hilliard, 86–96.

out his revelation piecemeal, entrusting relatively simple information to the child-like ancient Hebrews and reserving a more complex message for the subsequent revelation made through Jesus. Hence one should continue to trust in providence, even if its operations seemed to follow a circuitous or retrograde path:

> Geh deinen unmerklichen Schritt, ewige Vorsehung! Nur laß mich dieser Unmerklichkeit wegen an dir nicht verzweifeln. – Laß mich an dir nicht verzweifeln, wenn selbst deine Schritte mir scheinen sollten, zurückzugehen! – Es ist nicht wahr, daß die kürzeste Linie immer die gerade ist (Lessing, X, 97f.).

While many Enlightenment thinkers questioned the concept of providence as part of their hostile critique of religion, others transferred their interests to the understanding of human nature and human society as a means of ameliorating human life. »[W]hat characterised the Enlightenment from the 1740s onwards«, writes John Robertson, »was a new focus on betterment in this world, without regard for the existence or non-existence of the next«; »intellectual effort was now concentrated on understanding the means of progress in human society, not on demolishing belief in a divine counterpart« (Robertson, 8). One of the intellectual tools available to the High Enlightenment was the nascent study of statistics. With its help, the social sciences which originated at this period could explain many events with reference to social forces and statistical regularities. The history of statistics goes back to the seventeenth-century London merchant John Graunt, who in his *Natural and Political Observations* (1662) drew demographic inferences from the bills of mortality (Hacking, 16). In 1741 J.P. Süssmilch (who later had a controversy with Herder about the origins of language) published a detailed study of births, deaths and sex ratios, based on parish registers and following the example of Graunt. His work gained Süssmilch election to the Berlin Academy (Hacking, 20f.).[4] Graunt's work also provided the basis for Diderot's article »Arithmétique politique« in the *Encyclopédie* (see Lough, 327). Kant in 1784 points out that although individual actions, such as marriages, may be subject to free will, yet the annual statistics show regularities in marriages, births, and deaths which reveal underlying natural laws; similarly, the weather, though unpredictable in detail, is subject to natural regularities, and it may eventually be possible to discover an analogous »Naturabsicht« underlying human history (Kant, VI, 33). Adam

---

[4] The title of Süssmilch's work was *Die göttliche Ordnung in der Veränderung des menschlichen Geschlechts, aus der Geburt, dem Tode und der Fortpflanzung desselben erwiesen* (Berlin, 1741).

Smith, as is well known, argued that the operation of an »invisible hand« ensured that the selfish pursuit of one's individual interest was compatible with the well-being of society as a whole, and indeed more likely to benefit society than consciously public-spirited action: »By pursuing his own interest [a merchant] frequently promotes that of the society more effectually than when he really intends to promote it« (Smith, 292). Divine providence, imagined as a force external to human life, was now a superfluous concept. The internal workings of society – a term which itself signalled a new and secular focus on the study of humanity – themselves accounted for the patterns visible in human life.

Between the decline of providentialism and the rise of sociology, however, there was a period, broadly coterminous with the eighteenth century, in which political events seemed explicable only as resulting from the deliberate actions of individuals. The scientific revolution of the seventeenth century owed its success to a mechanistic logic of cause and effect. It seemed an obvious step, therefore, to apply this mechanistic logic to history, and to suppose that individual actions brought about the corresponding effects. This logic was challenged, however, by the French Revolution, which struck contemporaries as a monstrous, cataclysmic event. Writing at an early stage in the Revolution, before the execution of Louis XVI, but after the fall of the Bastille, the Declaration of the Rights of Man and the Citizen, the abolition of feudalism, and the expropriation of the Church, Edmund Burke already maintained: «All circumstances taken together, the French revolution is the most astonishing that has hitherto happened in the world« (Edmund Burke, 10). It was hard to explain this cataclysm in terms of human agency. For the mechanistic model to hold, the Revolution must result from a monstrous international conspiracy, similar to, but far exceeding, the political plots which had given rise to successive panics, for example, in British history.

> But the scale and complexity of the Revolution now required conspiratorial interpretations of an unprecedented sort. No small group of particular plotters could account for its tumult and mass movements; only elaborately organized secret societies, like the Illuminati or the Freemasons, involving thousands of individuals linked by sinister designs, could be behind the Europe-wide upheaval (Wood, 431f.).

Although the conspiracy theory of the French Revolution may not be quite such a novelty as Wood maintains (besides Hofman, see now McMahon), his scheme of successive explanatory models – providential, conspiratorial, and sociological/statistical – has considerable appeal. Less plausible is his hopeful assumption that the third model has triumphed, leaving conspiracism behind as the resource of dispossessed and simple-minded people who cannot cope with the modern world:

> In our post-industrial, scientifically saturated society, those who continue to attribute combinations of events to deliberate human design may well be peculiar sorts of persons – marginal people, perhaps, removed from the centers of power, unable to grasp the conceptions of complicated causal linkages offered by sophisticated social scientists, and unwilling to abandon the desire to make simple and clear moral judgments of events (Wood, 441).

A few minutes on the Internet will show that conspiracism is much too popular to be dismissed in this way. It is genuinely difficult to grasp the causes lying behind, for example, the international financial meltdown of 2008: hence people are ready to explain it in terms of human agency by blaming it on the greed and irresponsibility of bankers, an explanation which, though probably not false, is certainly inadequate. And, as we have seen, conspiracism has an imaginative appeal similar to that of fiction, which helps it to solidify into a mythology.

Accepting Wood's scheme, it would appear that Romanticism marks an intellectual step back from the Enlightenment. While thinkers of the Enlightenment abstract from social affairs in order to explore the underlying statistical patterns that the incipient social sciences could disclose, the Romantics objected to Enlightenment abstraction and sought to understand the world in vivid and concrete terms. Thus Novalis in *Die Christenheit oder Europa* denounced the mathematical rationalism of the Enlightenment by contrast with the charm and colour of poetry: «Reizender und farbiger steht die Poesie wie ein geschmücktes Indien dem kalten, toten Spitzbergen jenes Stubenverstandes gegenüber« (Novalis, III, 520). This concrete representation of the world is the business of imaginative literature. So in Romantic fiction we find a hankering after Wood's first explanatory model, that of providentialism; but since providentialism no longer seems truly believable, it tends to be replaced by conspiracism, which can be represented by natural and supernatural agents. A large-scale conspiracism which attributes agency to supernatural powers is accompanied by a small-scale conspiracism which acknowledges human agency in the form of plots and intrigues.

III. Conspiracism in the *Geheimbundroman*

Conspiracism is the theme of an entire genre of German fiction, the *Geheimbundroman* or secret-society novel, which was extremely popular in the late eighteenth century and served as a seed-bed for much Romantic fiction. The authors of *Geheimbundromane* were responding to the fascination with secret societies which pervaded the Germany of their time. After the establishment of the Grand Masonic Lodge in London in 1717, Freemasonry spread rapidly throughout France and Germany. By 1789 there were an estimated six hundred lodges in France alone, with between 50,000 and 100,000 members, while in Berlin alone 43 lodges were founded between 1740 and 1781. Its condemnation by the Catholic Church in 1738 strengthened its association with the Enlightenment. The Freemasons provided the template for the multitude of societies, clubs, academies and circles that sprang up in late eighteenth-century Germany to enable middle-class citizens, clerics and nobles to discuss enlightened aims and further *Bildung*. Adolph Freiherr von Knigge, briefly a leading Illuminatus, wrote in 1788: »Man wird heutzutage in allen Ständen wenig Menschen treffen, die nicht […] wenigstens eine Zeitlang Mitglieder einer solchen geheimen Verbrüderung gewesen wären« (Knigge, 391). Some measure of secrecy was usually advisable. Even in Berlin in the 1780s, the society dedicated to enlightenment, the *Mittwochsgesellschaft*, required its members to keep the matters discussed there in strict confidence and even to conceal the Society's existence.

The best-known example of the *Geheimbundroman* is probably Carl Grosse's *Der Genius* (1791–1795), which Hoffmann read enthusiastically at the age of 19.[5] In this and similar novels, secret societies admit their initiates with elaborate rituals usually held in sinister subterranean vaults and thereafter control their initiates' lives with a degree of power and omniscience that seems inexplicable. The »Verbindung« which admits Grosse's protagonist, a young Spanish nobleman, has powers extending through the whole of Spain and even beyond. Its aims appear to be enlightened, the »Vervollkommnung der ganzen Menschheit«, but in pursuit of these aims the society is prepared to sacrifice human life and to assassinate monarchs if »das Glück der Menschheit« requires such measures (Grosse, 87; 115). Any means are justified in pursuit of its exalted aims. Its initiation ceremony is particularly sinister, and apparently without parallel in its genre: an incision is made

---

[5] Letter to Hippel, 19 February 1795, in Hoffmann, *Briefwechsel*, I, 53f.

in the narrator's arm and all the assembled brothers drink his blood. This ritual of blood-drinking has no counterpart in Masonic ritual. It is in part a parody of the Eucharist, in which symbolic blood is replaced by the real thing. It can also be traced back to the ritual with which, according to the Roman historian Sallust, one of history's most notorious conspirators, Catiline, united his adherents: he made them take an oath and affirm its seriousness by drinking wine mixed with blood (Sallust, 38f.).

The concept of providence features ambiguously in Grosse's novel. His conspirators describe themselves as »gleichsam Unterbeamte der Vorsehung« (Grosse, 89). This implies that, in their pursuit of human perfection, they are simply accelerating a process which is happening anyway, in accordance with the providential design of the world. But their apparent omnipotence also suggests that despite presenting themselves as mere agents of providence, they have taken the place of providence. Such a metaphysical concept no longer has any validity or efficacy; it has been superseded by human agency. At the same time, human agency appears to have expanded beyond human understanding. The conspirators appear to be in alliance with a supernatural being, the ›Genius‹ of the title. This, however, expresses the dilemma of enlightened rationalism. Confronted with complex and mysterious events which the logic of cause and effect seems inadequate to explain, the rationalist must either overcome his scepticism and acknowledge a supernatural agency, or else posit a human agency which takes the form of a barely credible conspiracy (see Beaujean, 124f.). For much of the novel Grosse seems to be inviting the former solution, but when the ›Genius‹ is explained away, events are reduced to a human scale.

Der Genius begins with the narrator's declaration:

> Aus allen Verwickelungen von scheinbaren Zufällen blickt eine unsichtbare Hand hervor, welche vielleicht über *manchem* unter uns schwebt, ihn im Dunkeln beherrscht, und den Faden, den er in sorgloser Freiheit selbst zu weben vermeynt, oft schon lange diesem Gedanken vorausgesponnen haben mag (Grosse, 7).

At first glance, this recalls Schiller's reference to the »invisible hand of providence« in the advertisement for *Die Räuber*, promising the lesson »daß die unsichtbare Hand der Vorsicht auch den Bösewicht zu Werkzeugen ihrer Absichten und Gerichten brauchen und den verworrensten Knoten des Geschicks zum Erstaunen auflösen könne« (Schiller, I, 490). Schiller is here upholding a relatively traditional conception of providence while conceding that its workings are not readily apparent. Grosse's invisible hand, however, is not that of a supra-human providence but of human agency. His

»invisible hand« is an agent, or rather a number of human agents who have joined together in a gigantic conspiracy. But since responsibility rests with a number of individuals, Grosse is also remote from Adam Smith's use of the metaphor of the ›invisible hand‹ to signify a hidden mechanism which ensures a balance among individual and general interests. Smith's »invisible hand« has nothing to do with personal agency. The metaphor refers to a principle which can best be understood in the perspective of social science. To Grosse, however, that perspective is not yet available, and so he personalizes the occult machinations as the work of a highly organized conspiracy.

The *Geheimbundroman* tends to represent such a conspiracy as a kind of mechanical contrivance. It has little to say about the psychological motives which animate the conspirators and secure the allegiance of the initiate. Grosse's protagonist is a highly sexed young man who has little acquaintance with deeper emotions and therefore easily falls into the honey-traps set for him by the secret society, which sends amorous women to seduce him. This example confirms Marianne Thalmann's contention that the psychology of the *Geheimbundroman* is basically rationalist and mechanical (Thalmann, 70). Psychological complexity was introduced into the genre, however, by Schiller in his unfinished novel *Der Geisterseher*. Here Schiller traces the psychological development of a Prince who, brought up as a Protestant to associate religion with gloom, adopts an emotionally unsatisfying materialism. From the resulting despair he escapes by entering the Catholic Church, to which he is also attracted by the allure of a beautiful woman. Hoffmann pays tribute to it by making the narrator of *Das Majorat* call it »das Buch […], das ich, so wie damals jeder, der nur irgend dem Romantischen ergeben, in der Tasche trug« (Hoffmann, III, 207).

IV. *Die Elixiere des Teufels* as conspiratorial novel

Although Hoffmann's *Die Elixiere des Teufels* owes much to the *Geheimbundroman* genre, it differs by placing the protagonist's psychology in the foreground. Unlike Schiller, however, Hoffmann does not give his protagonist a particularly complex set of motives. The monk Medardus, like his prototype in Matthew Gregory Lewis's novel *The Monk*, is motivated principally by pride, ambition, lust, and fear.[6] From his early success as a preacher, which

---

[6] Lewis's *The Monk* (1796) is mentioned in Hoffmann's text: see Hoffmann, *Sämtliche Werke*, II,2: *Die Elixiere des Teufels*, 241. On its relation to Hoffmann's novel, see Meixner, 155–172;

he enhances by drinking the ancient wine known as the Devil's elixir, down to the extravagant public piety which he displays in Rome and his hopes of becoming confessor to the Pope, he shows an overweening vanity which is finally replaced by exemplary penitence. His story asks to be read as a psychological allegory about the splitting of the self when it is torn between contradictory impulses: for example, between Medardus's admiration for the heavenly purity embodied in Aurelie and his intense desire to enjoy her sexually. These contradictory impulses are externalized in figures – the mad monk, the *Doppelgänger* who fulfils Medardus's unconscious wish by stabbing Aurelie at the altar, the naked man who emerges from the floor of his prison cell and hands him a knife – for whose existence the novel offers only the most threadbare explanation, if any. Hence Horst Daemmrich is no doubt right to suggest that the novel should be seen »as a precursor of the modern psychological novel or a dream sequence in which Hoffmann attempts to portray the hero's psychological state« (Daemmrich, 93).[7] Not surprisingly, the novel has received psychoanalytical readings which easily detect a conflict between Medardus's incestuous desire for his mother (represented by the pure Aurelie) and the prohibitions and punishments imposed by the paternal super-ego.[8] Such readings can easily seem obvious and facile. Interpretations of Medardus's psychology need to take into account the psychological knowledge available to Hoffmann from his extensive reading in medical treatises; they also need to remember that Medardus's adventures all occur within a larger, cosmic, supernatural framework which, however we interpret it, is essential to the meaning of the novel.[9]

Nehring, 36–44. Another model, which appears not to have been noticed by commentators, is the monk Medardus in Benedikte Naubert's *Der Fischer* (1792), a criminal with the reputation of a saint. This Medardus is a painter who paints but then defaces a picture of the Virgin Mary; with the Devil's help he conducts an affair with a (willing) nun, and, when caught stealing Church treasures, is saved by the Devil, who replaces him with a double. See Naubert, III, 7–88. Guthke (33) suggests that Naubert helped to inspire *The Monk*, but does not make a connection with Hoffmann.

[7] Cf. the similar formulation by Meixner: »Hoffmann verwischt die Grenzen zwischen Einbildung und Wirklichkeit in einem Maße, daß das Geschehen wie ein ungeheurer Alptraum erscheint« (195).

[8] See e.g. the bald summary in Kremer, 156, and for a searching psychoanalytical interpretation, Wright, ch. 5.

[9] For a recent reading in the light of Hoffmann's psychological knowledge, see Hinderer. A strong case for reading the novel in the light of the psychological information available to Hoffmann is made by Dutchman-Smith, 152.

Medardus is the victim not only of his own impulses but of an overarching conspiracy, which proceeds not from mere human agency but from the scheme of sin and redemption that appears to govern the novel. It is revealed shortly before the end that Medardus is caught up in a fateful pattern of events that go back several centuries. His remote ancestor, Francesco, was a Renaissance painter who led a sinful life, worshipped the pagan goddess Venus, and, when commissioned to paint St Rosalia, painted her resembling Venus. For this sacrilegious confusion of the sacred with the profane (or rather, of the sacred and the sexual) he has been punished by having to remain on earth until his family becomes extinct. Medardus is the last of the line and must therefore, in order to satisfy Francesco, remain a monk and have no children. Hence his ancestor pursues him, appearing at intervals as a tall, gaunt man with a piercing gaze, and Medardus's many sexual misdemeanours are therefore, though he does not know it, attempts to defeat the will of his ancestor. Hence his marriage with Aurelie must be frustrated, and the double, in stabbing Aurelie, is not only acting out Medardus's innate violence but also fulfilling the demands of the family curse.

Die Elixiere thus presents itself as a religious novel in which sacrilege is punished, however many generations late, and a penitent sinner ultimately returns to the fold to die in the odour of sanctity. But how seriously is the element of Catholic religiosity to be taken? Neither Hoffmann's biography, nor the tone of the novel itself, suggests that he was writing for the edification of Catholic readers – in sharp contrast, say, to the exactly contemporary novel *Ahnung und Gegenwart* (1815), with its solemn and didactic tone, by the devout cradle Catholic Joseph von Eichendorff. Certainly the novel inquires into the relationship between human life and the supernatural world; but the latter seems to owe less to Christian theology than to the theosophical fantasies of Jakob Böhme and Gotthilf Heinrich von Schubert (see Fick). The religious atmosphere is present, not as a matter of presumed belief by either author or reader, but as a framework which gives Medardus something to rebel against and enables him to display his conflicting impulses to the full. As Horst Meixner puts it: »Die Figuren und Bilder des Christentums sind nur noch Hohlformen, die ihren Gehalt vom Ausdrucksverlangen des Subjekts empfangen« (192).

On this reading, the novel's centre of gravity lies not in its alleged spiritual or moral theme but in the fascination of Medardus's anarchic rebellion and the mysterious forces which ultimately defeat him. Medardus gains the reader's covert sympathy in his frantic transgressing of all institutional and ethical boundaries. His defeat can be ascribed only superficially to the conventional moral and religious sanctions which he has overridden; his real antagonist is a supernatural power which leads him into sin and then arranges for his punishment.

Struggling in the clutches of this power, Medardus loses his moral autonomy. At several key points in the narrative, the supernatural power takes over Medardus's will. When he preaches on St Anthony's day, in the presence of the mysterious painter, he feels impelled by an alien force (»wie von einer fremden zauberischen Gewalt getrieben«) to challenge the stranger and declare: »[I]ch bin es selbst! – ich bin der heilige Antonius!« (Hoffmann, II/2, 41). When, on arriving at the castle, he is recognized by Reinhold, he feels that an alien voice (»eine fremde Stimme im Innern«) is putting the right words into his mouth (64). When he has an extraordinary run of luck at the Prince's faro table, he feels he is the mere passive instrument of an alien force (»die fremde Macht, die in mein Wesen getreten«, 157). These and many other occasions when Medardus's will is usurped by an alien force turn him into a mere puppet, an actor following a predetermined script from which, despite his desperate efforts, he is unable to deviate. He can thus be seen as the hapless victim of a supernatural plot. Christian providentialism has been replaced by a heterodox theosophy, and while Lessing conceived providence as wise and benevolent, the power that rules Medardus's life seems mainly concerned with hunting down its victim and forcing him into sanctity.

We have, then, a conspiratorial narrative, in which Medardus is entrapped both by a cosmic and by an earthly conspiracy. While the *Geheimbundroman* ultimately reduced all apparent supernatural phenomena to mere human contrivances, Hoffmann restores the supernatural, but represents it as in many ways sinister and frightening, intent on punishment and revenge. On the earthly level, conspiracy is presented as the intrigues within the Catholic Church to which Medardus is exposed and which nearly bring about his premature death.

V.   Versions of Catholicism in *Die Elixiere*

Catholicism in *Die Elixiere* appears under three aspects: aesthetic, enlightened, and conspiratorial. In these three forms, it is presented as being of interest in its own right, and not as a mere backdrop or »Kulisse« (Saul, 408; 410). Hoffmann, like many contemporaries, was alive to the aesthetic appeal of Catholic symbolism and ritual, though he appears never to have been tempted to follow his friend Zacharias Werner into conversion.[10] As a theatre director in Bamberg, he staged Calderón's religious drama *La devoción de la cruz (Die Andacht zum Kreuz)* on 13 June 1811, appealing with great success to the Catholic population (see Sullivan, 251ff.; Steinecke, 83ff.). Catholic imagery, in Hoffmann's view, served to provide spiritual things with a vivid sensory form: he asserts that »es ganz in dem Geiste des Katholizism liegt, die Sinne bei der symbolischen Darstellung des Übersinnlichen in Anspruch zu nehmen« (Hoffmann, »Über die Aufführung der Schauspiele des Calderon de la Barca auf dem Theater in Bamberg«, I, 628). Early in the novel, Medardus describes enthusiastically the ceremonies, the High Mass and the procession celebrated at the church »zur heiligen Linde«. This church, now Swięta Lipka, near Ketrzyn in northern Poland, centres on a chapel which, having been destroyed by Protestants in the Reformation, was rebuilt and consecrated in 1619 by the Jesuits after Catholicism was once again permitted in Prussia. The church itself, a magnificent Baroque structure, was built for the Jesuits between 1687 and 1730 by the mason Georg Ertly (see DaCosta, 378). We may assume that Hoffmann knew it from his upbringing in nearby Königsberg. However, Medardus's devout enthusiasm may arouse scepticism in the reader. Hoffmann reported in a letter to his publisher Kunz, rather flippantly, that St Joseph and the Christ child would appear in the novel (»Joseph und das Christuskind erscheinen pp.«)[11], and they are no doubt to be identified with the aged pilgrim and the beautiful child who figure in Medardus's earliest recollections, though Medardus himself attributes his memories mainly to his mother's subsequent account (»unerachtet ich gewiß glaube, daß nur aus der Beschreibung meiner Mutter sich im Innern sein lebhaftes Bild erzeugt hat«, Hoffmann, II/2, 16).

Alongside this religious enthusiasm, we find a more temperate devotion being encouraged by Leonardus, the prior of the Capuchin monastery where Medardus is educated. This is surprising, since the Capuchins were a militant missionary order who rose to prominence alongside the Jesuits in the Counter-Reformation. They were energetic missioners, worked among the poor, dressed in coarse robes and went barefoot to display their own poverty, and had a reputation for ignorance, though their ranks included such famous preachers as Procopius of Templin and Marco d'Aviano. Counter-Reformation preaching tended, like that of Medardus, to describe

---

[10] Cf. Theodor's sceptical account of Werner's ›mystischer Schwärmerei‹ in *Die Serapions-Brüder*, Hoffmann, IV, 1032.
[11] Letter to Kunz, 24 March 1814, in *Briefwechsel*, I, 454.

the lives of the saints as exemplary; enlightened Catholics, however, thought that sermons should serve, as the Abbess says Medardus's should have done, »die Gemeinde zu belehren und zu frommen Betrachtungen zu entzünden« (Hoffmann, II/2, 50; cf. Saul, 104). The Catholic Enlightenment is represented by Leonardus. Besides being truly devout and an excellent theologian, he has more acquaintance with the secular world than is usual among monks; he speaks French and Italian, and has therefore been sent on many important missions. All the monks under his leadership are there because of a true spiritual vocation, and those who have sought refuge in the monastery from worldly disaster find comfort and ease after a light penance. Medardus tells us that these are »ungewöhnliche[] Tendenzen des Klosterlebens« (Hoffmann, II/2, 27). They stand in sharp contrast to the standard presentation of monastic life in Enlightenment treatises and satires, where the seclusion and routine of the monastery are said to generate discord, feuding, melancholy, and madness, and where monks are satirized for their laziness and self-indulgence (see Jäger). Leonardus has abandoned the common Counter-Reformation practice of enforcing piety through spiritual terror, vivid descriptions of hell and purgatory, and warnings about God's inexorable justice.[12] Instead, he encourages people's aspiration towards heaven: »Unerachtet der strengen Ordensregel, waren die Andachtsübungen dem Prior Leonardus mehr Bedürfnis des dem himmlischen zugewandten Geistes, als aszetische Buße für die der menschlichen Natur anklebende Sünde« (Hoffmann, II/2, 25). He shows his shrewdness by distrusting Medardus's sudden enthusiasm for entering the monastery, by questioning him discretely about sex, and by doubting his visions of St Joseph and the Christ child. Similarly, Leonardus says little about the miracles and saints' legends which were so important in Counter-Reformation piety but played down by enlightened clerics; and he takes an equally enlightened view of religious relics, considering that, though seldom genuine, they serve to inspire the devotion of believers and sometimes do bring about remarkable physical cures, not through their intrinsic qualities, but through the spiritual strength they promote in worshippers (33f.).[13]

Leonardus's enlightened piety, however, is represented as untypical of the Catholic Church as a whole. The closer we get to Rome, the more the Church corresponds to the conspiratorial fantasies characteristic

---

[12] See Delumeau, esp. part III, »La pastorale de la peur: en pays catholique«, 369–547. The Capuchin Procopius of Templin was famous for his hell-fire sermons: see Evans, 188.
[13] On the Catholic Enlightenment, see now Lehner.

of the *Geheimbundroman*. The Pope is described by Leonardus as a soft, impressionable, and credulous character who is easily manipulated by the intriguers around him.[14] Learning of Medardus's extravagant displays of devotion, the Pope summons him, hears his story, and half promises to make Medardus his personal confessor. However, the current confessor, a Dominican, forms an alliance with a Cardinal who has misappropriated revenues properly due to Medardus's convent, and between them they stage a conspiratorial intrigue modelled on those of the *Geheimbundroman*. Such novels often feature reactionary secret societies, which are typically associated with the Catholic Church. Its agents are sometimes Jesuits, since the Society of Jesus was thought to offer the paradigmatic example of a tightly structured body intent on a single goal and united by obedience to their superior, the Pope. Elsewhere the agents may be monks, for monastic orders readily serve to represent dehumanized organizations dedicated to the suppression of liberty and the spread of obscurantism. Marianne Thalmann sums up the fictional image of the monk, with unconcealed disapproval, as follows:

> Der Mönch ist sozusagen die charakteristische Type des Mittelalters, das abergläubisch und beschränkt die finstere Vorstufe zur aufgeklärten Neuzeit ist. Es ist zu betonen: *Das Mittelalter ist für den Romanschriftsteller des 18. Jahrhunderts die Zeit der Finsternis, des Aberglaubens, der Menschenknechtung*. Diese aufgeklärte Ansicht entspricht der rationalen, begrenzten Meinung der Freigeister und Atheisten aller Zeiten. Er sieht nur die Schatten einer metaphysisch ringenden und vielfach chaotischen Zeit, das Sinnenabgewandte der Mystik, die Folter der Hexe, die Unduldsamkeit der Inquisition und nirgends das Licht, um das die Dunkelheit kämpft. Daher ist der Mönch der eigennützige Betrüger, der Seelenfänger, der gewissenlose Schlemmer, der Feind freigeistiger Bewegungen, das Prototyp der geistigen Beschränktheit (Thalmann, 147).

The Dominicans who plot against Medardus fully conform to this stereotype. One of them summons Medardus to the bedside of a dying man but takes him first to an underground vault where Dominicans are seated on benches; this subterranean assembly is a staple of the *Geheimbundroman*, and also recalls the secret court or »Vehmgericht« which features regularly in historical works set in the Middle Ages (the court which pronounces sentence on

---

[14] Which Pope is meant? Hoffmann's editor, Hartmut Steinecke, assumes it is Clement XIV (reigned 1769–1774), but since Clement at least had the strength of character to abolish the Jesuits, it is more likely to be his successor, Giovanni Angelo Braschi, who ruled as Pius VI from 1775–1799 and who was worldly, spendthrift, and ineffectual; Duffy describes him as »a particularly poor specimen« (198).

Adelheid in Goethe's *Götz von Berlichingen* is a familiar example).[15] From there Medardus is led to a small chamber where he finds Cyrillus, a close associate of Leonardus and an exemplar of enlightened piety, who has come to Rome as the representative of their monastery. The Dominicans wish to dispose of Cyrillus so that their ally the Cardinal can continue to enjoy his revenues without dispute, and have persuaded the gullible Pope that Cyrillus is part of a plot to dethrone him. Cyrillus has evidently been tortured by the Dominicans, whom he describes as »die entsetzlichen Diener der Hölle«, and once Medardus has given him absolution, a Dominican takes a sword and beheads him (Hoffmann, II/2, 308). Medardus himself narrowly escapes death, for his Dominican guide then offers him wine which Medardus, recognizing it as poison, surreptitiously pours into his sleeve; soon afterwards he finds that the flesh of his arm has been eaten away by acid. Prudently, he returns to his monastery, where he finds that Leonardus is fully informed about his experiences in Rome, thanks to a network of spies which has even recorded every word of his conversation with the Pope. The Catholic Church is represented as such a hotbed of conspiracy that even an honest and devout cleric is obliged to resort to some defensive counter-conspiracy.

Where, finally, is Hoffmann's novel to be located in the sequence of mentalities described earlier in this article? Hoffmann implicitly rejects the Christian providentialism which was already proving unsustainable, but does not seek social or sociological explanations for surprising events. Instead, he goes in two directions. He attributes some events to human agency, and to provide an agent commensurable with the events, he imagines a conspiracy within the Church, thus falling back on the conspiracism of the *Geheimbundroman*. But unlike the authors of *Geheimbundromane*, such as Grosse, who generally ended up with a rationalist explanation of extraordinary events, Hoffmann resorts to the supernatural and makes Medardus the victim of a narrative of sin, suffering, and redemption, steeped in the atmosphere of Baroque Catholicism. When we penetrate this atmosphere, however, we find that the Catholicism is only aesthetic, and that Hoffmann, unlike such a contemporary as Eichendorff, is not really preaching a religious message. Rather, the novel is an exploration of mysterious but powerful forces both within the self and external to the self, and the latter can only be described in enigmatic terms which Hoffmann derived from such unorthodox and

---

[15] The reappearance of »Bundeszeremoniell« in this scene is noted by Thalmann, 260.

heterodox sources as the theosophies of Böhme and Schubert. These forces are ambivalent: they entrap the individual in wrong-doing and then compel him to undergo punishment and penance. Their relation to the individual in their power is that of a conspiracy to its victim. The victim is meanwhile being assailed not only by a supernatural but also by an earthly conspiracy, which in this novel is embodied in the agents of certain factions within the Catholic Church. Thus Hoffmann mobilizes the paranoid fantasies of his time (and later) to convey the power of human agency and confirm the status of *Die Elixiere* as a conspiratorial novel, in which a cosmic conspiracy finds a small-scale man-made counterpart in a sinister plot contrived by human agents.

Works Cited

Beaujean, Marion. *Der Trivialroman in der zweiten Hälfte des 18. Jahrhunderts*. Bonn: Bouvier, 1964.

Bowlby, Rachel. *Freudian Mythologies: Greek Tragedies and Modern Identities*. Oxford: Oxford University Press, 2007.

Burke, Edmund. *Reflections on the Revolution in France*. Ed. L.G. Mitchell. Oxford: Oxford University Press, 1993.

Burke, Peter. »The Black Legend of the Jesuits: an essay in the history of social stereotypes«. *Christianity and Community in the West: Essays for John Bossy*. Ed. Simon Ditchfield. Aldershot: Ashgate, 2001: 165–182.

DaCosta Kaufmann, Thomas. *Court, Cloister and City: The Art and Culture of Central Europe 1450-1800*. London: Weidenfeld & Nicolson, 1995.

Daemmrich, Horst S. *The Shattered Self: E.T.A. Hoffmann's Tragic Vision*. Detroit: Wayne State University Press, 1973.

Delumeau, Jean. *Le péché et la peur: La culpabilisation en Occident, XIIIe-XVIIIe siècles*. Paris: Fayard, 1983.

Duffy, Eamon. *Saints and Sinners: A History of the Popes*. New Haven/London: Yale University Press, 1997.

Dutchman-Smith, Victoria. *E.T.A. Hoffmann and Alcohol: Biography, Reception and Art*. London: Maney, 2010.

Evans, R.J.W. *The Making of the Habsburg Monarchy, 1550–1700*. Oxford: Clarendon Press, 1979.

Fick, Monika. »E.T.A. Hoffmanns Theosophie. Eine Interpretation des Romans ›Die Elixiere des Teufels‹«. *Literaturwissenschaftliches Jahrbuch* 36 (1995): 105–125.

Grosse, Carl. *Der Genius*. Afterword Günter Dammann. Frankfurt/M: Zweitausendeins, 1982.

Guthke, Karl S. *Englische Vorromantik und deutscher Sturm und Drang: M.G. Lewis' Stellung in der Geschichte der deutsch-englischen Literaturbeziehungen*. Göttingen: Vandenhoeck & Ruprecht, 1958.

Hacking, Ian. *The Taming of Chance*. Cambridge: Cambridge University Press, 1990.

Hilliard, K.F. *Freethinkers, Libertines, and ›Schwärmer‹: Heterodoxy in German Literature, 1750–1800*. London: Institute of Germanic and Romance Studies, 2011.

Hinderer, Walter. »Die poetische Psychoanalyse in E.T.A. Hoffmanns Roman ›Die Elixiere des Teufels‹«. *›Hoffmanneske Geschichte‹: Zu einer Literaturwissenschaft als Kulturwissenschaft*. Ed. Gerhard Neumann. Würzburg: Königshausen & Neumann, 2005: 43–76.

Hofman, Amos. »The Origins of the Theory of the Philosophe Conspiracy«. *French History* 2 (1988): 152–172.

Hoffmann, E.T.A. *Sämtliche Werke*. 6 vols. Eds. Wulf Segebrecht/Hartmut Steinecke. Frankfurt/M: Deutscher Klassiker Verlag, 1985–2004.

Hoffmann, E.T.A. *Briefwechsel*. 3 vols. Ed. Friedrich Schnapp. Munich: Winkler, 1967ff.

Jäger, Hans-Wolf. »Mönchskritik und Klostersatire in der deutschen Spätaufklärung«. *Katholische Aufklärung – Aufklärung im katholischen Deutschland*. Ed. Harm Klueting. Hamburg: Meiner, 1993: 192–207.

Kant, Immanuel. »Idee zu einer allgemeinen Geschichte in weltbürgerlicher Absicht«. *Werke*. 6 vols. Ed. Wilhelm Weischedel. Darmstadt: Wissenschaftliche Buchgesellschaft, 1964: IV, 33–50.

Klausnitzer, Ralf. *Poesie und Konspiration: Beziehungssinn und Zeichenökonomie von Verschwörungsszenarien in Publizistik, Literatur und Wissenschaft 1750–1850*. Berlin: de Gruyter, 2007.

Knigge, Adolph Freiherr von. *Über den Umgang mit Menschen*. Ed. by Gert Ueding. Frankfurt/M: Insel, 1977.

Kremer, Detlef (ed.). *E.T.A. Hoffmann: Leben – Werk – Wirkung*. Berlin: De Gruyter, ²2010.

Lehner, Ulrich L./Michael Printy (eds.). *A Companion to the Catholic Enlightenment*. Leiden: Brill, 2010.

Lessing, Gotthold Ephraim. *Werke und Briefe*. 12 vols. Eds. Wilfried Barner et al. Frankfurt/M: Deutscher Klassiker Verlag, 1987–1998.

Lough, John. *The ›Encyclopédie‹*. London: Longman, 1971.

McMahon, Darren. *Enemies of the Enlightenment: The French Counter-Enlightenment and the Making of Modernity*. New York: Oxford University Press, 2001.

Meixner, Horst. *Romantischer Figuralismus: Kritische Studien zu Romanen von Arnim, Eichendorff und Hoffmann*. Frankfurt/M: Athenäum, 1971.

Naubert, Christiane Benedikte Eugenie. *Neue Volksmärchen der Deutschen*. 4 vols. Eds. Marianne Henn/Paola Meyer/Anita Runge. Göttingen: Wallstein, 2001.

Novalis. *Schriften*. 5 vols. Eds. Paul Kluckhohn/Richard Samuel. Stuttgart: Kohlhammer, 1960–1988.

Nehring, Wolfgang. »Gothic Novel und Schauerroman. Tradition und Innovation in Hoffmanns ›Die Elixiere des Teufels‹«. *E.T.A. Hoffmann-Jahrbuch* 1 (1992f.): 36–47.

Pipes, Daniel. *Conspiracy: How the Paranoid Style Flourishes and Where it Comes from*. New York: Free Press, 1997.

Roberts, J.M. *The Mythology of the Secret Societies*. London: Secker & Warburg, 1972.

Robertson, John. *The Case for the Enlightenment: Scotland and Naples 1680–1760*. Cambridge: Cambridge University Press, 2005.

Robertson, Ritchie. »Jesuits, Jews, and Thugs: Myths of Conspiracy and Infiltration from Dickens to Thomas Mann«. *In the Embrace of the Swan: Anglo-German Mythologies in Literature, the Visual Arts and Cultural Theory*. Eds. Rüdiger Görner/Angus Nicholls. Berlin: de Gruyter, 2010: 126–146.

Rogalla von Bieberstein, Johannes. *Die These von der Verschwörung 1776–1945: Philosophen, Freimaurer, Juden, Liberale und Sozialisten als Verschwörer gegen die Sozialordnung*. Bern: Peter Lang, 1976.

Sallust. Tr. J.C. Rolfe. Loeb Classical Library, rev. ed. Cambridge, MA: Harvard University Press, 1931 (*Bellum Catilinae*, XXII).

Saul, Nicholas. »E.T.A. Hoffmanns erzählte Predigten«. *Euphorion* 83 (1989): 407–430.

Schiller, Friedrich. *Sämtliche Werke*. 5 vols. Eds. Gerhard Fricke/Herbert G. Göpfert. Munich: Hanser, 1958.

Smith, Adam. *An Inquiry into the Nature and Causes of the Wealth of Nations*. Ed. Kathryn Sutherland. Oxford: Oxford University Press, 1993.

Steinecke, Hartmut. *Die Kunst der Fantasie: E.T.A. Hoffmanns Leben und Werk*. Frankfurt/M: Insel, 2004.

Sullivan, Henry W. *Calderón in the German Lands and the Low Countries: His Reception and Influence, 1654–1980*. Cambridge: Cambridge University Press, 1983.

Thalmann, Marianne. *Der Trivialroman des 18. Jahrhunderts und der romantische Roman: Ein Beitrag zur Entwicklungsgeschichte der Geheimbundmystik*. Berlin: Ebering, 1923.

Walsham, Alexandra. *Providence in Early Modern England*. Oxford: Oxford University Press, 1999.

Wood, Gordon S. »Conspiracy and the Paranoid Style: Causality and Deceit in the Eighteenth Century«. *William & Mary Quarterly*, 3rd ser., 39 (1982): 401–441.

Wright, Elizabeth. *E.T.A. Hoffmann and the Rhetoric of Terror*. London: Institute of Germanic Studies, 1978.

Dale Adams *(The University of Melbourne)*

Wirksame Zufälle: Wahrscheinlichkeitstheorie als Erkenntnis- und Erzähltheorie in Novalis' *Heinrich von Ofterdingen*

Abstract

This paper examines the role of *der Zufall* (coincidence or chance event) as a narrative element in Novalis' *Heinrich von Ofterdingen* against the background of contemporaneous developments in the mathematical theory of probability. *Der Zufall*, it is argued, can be conceived of as marking subjective states of knowledge between the poles of ignorance and certainty on the one hand, and impossibility and necessity on the other. In this sense it links the external events to the inner development of the protagonist and, by perpetually indicating both the future possibilities that can be developed out of a given situation, as well as the past contingencies leading up to the same, initiates a process that can never be completed.

»Gewiß«, erzählt der junge Protagonist im ersten Kapitel von Novalis' Romanfragment *Heinrich von Ofterdingen*, »ist der Traum, den ich heute Nacht träumte, kein unwirksamer Zufall in meinem Leben gewesen, denn ich fühle es, daß er in meine Seele wie ein weites Rad hineingreift, und sie in mächtigem Schwunge forttreibt« (*NS*, I, 199).
Es ist das Attribut »(un)wirksam«, das hier dem in sich schon diffusen Begriff des *Zufalls* eine gesteigerte Ambivalenz verleiht und eine doppelte Lesart ermöglicht. Innerhalb beider werden die Kategorien des Beliebigen oder Willkürlichen negiert, doch aus jeweils anderer Perspektive. Nach der ersten wird der Traum in einen sinnstiftenden Gesamthorizont gestellt: Der Bedeutung nach, die ihm zugeschrieben wird, kann er nicht einfach Zufall gewesen sein – er muss einen Grund haben. Nach der zweiten werden *wirksame* Zufälle den *un*wirksamen gegenübergestellt. Aus einer Fülle von Einzelerscheinungen werden spezifische Ereignisse herausgehoben, indem ihnen eine bestimmte Wirkungskraft zugeschrieben wird – d.h. sie werden als Ursachen markiert. In beiden Fällen handelt es sich jedoch um reine Vermutung. Mit anderen Worten, der Traum repräsentiert für Heinrich ein Ereignis, dessen Umstände und Begleiterscheinungen eine Zukunftsprognose erlauben; und zwar eine, die (zumindest implizit) die Hypothese

einschließt, dass sich im Rückblick das Ereignis (je nach Lesart) entweder als Fügung oder als Glied einer kausalen Kette erweisen wird.

Der Traum, um den es sich handelt, ist der berühmte Traum von der blauen Blume. Für Heinrich hat er durchaus Konsequenzen insofern, als er den Jüngling in Sehnsucht erglühen lässt. Er ist allerdings auch der Anlass dafür, dass Heinrichs Vater eine bedeutende (aber bis dahin verschwiegene) Geschichte aus seinem eigenen Leben erzählt – eine Geschichte, die, wie es sich zum Erstaunen Heinrichs herausstellt, ebenfalls einen seltsamen Traum von einer wunderbaren Blume zum Inhalt hat. Der Verdacht, dem Traum müsse eine höhere Bedeutung zukommen, verstärkt sich. Diesmal wird angenommen, dass die Ähnlichkeit der beiden Träume nicht einfach Zufall sein kann. Allerdings handelt es sich weiterhin um reine Vermutung. Zwar könnte diese sich durch weitere Ereignisse erhärten, aber erst im Besitz von vollständigen Informationen wäre die Frage nach dem Status und dem Sinn des Traumes endgültig zu beantworten. Und so bleibt auch lange nach seinem eigenen Traum das Fazit des Vaters: »[…] und doch, was hat er bedeutet?« (*NS*, I, 200).

Ein anderes Wort für *vermutlich* ist jedoch *wahrscheinlich* – ein Begriff, dem seit Aristoteles eine zentrale Rolle in der Poetik zufällt und der ab ca. 1650 zum Gegenstand der Mathematik wird. Dass Novalis mit dieser Entwicklung vertraut war, geht aus seinen Notizen zu Lambert und Condorcet hervor. Bei Condorcet wird er gelesen haben, dass *Zufall* ein Wort sei, »dessen wahren Sinn« erst das Studium dieses Kalküls lehren kann (Condorcet, 255).

Der folgende Beitrag betrachtet den Zufall als Erzählprinzip und Strukturmoment im *Heinrich von Ofterdingen* vor dem Hintergrund der Entwicklung der Wahrscheinlichkeitstheorie als neuem Wissensparadigma: als *graduelles* Wissen. Wenn wahrscheinliches Wissen, so die These, als ein Kontinuum konzipiert wird, zwischen den Polen von vollkommenem *Unwissen* und absoluter *Gewissheit* auf der einen Seite und *unmöglich* und *notwendig* auf der anderen, dann lässt sich dieses Kontinuum auch als ein Erzählraum betrachten. Als Ausdruck eines bestimmten *Wissensstands* aufgefasst, markiert der Zufall Punkte innerhalb dieses Spektrums. Einerseits wird damit die Zusammensetzung der äußeren Begebenheiten an jedem beliebigen Punkt mit der inneren Entwicklung des Individuums verknüpft. Andererseits wird das Kontinuum selbst durch den Zufall *hergestellt*, indem dieser nicht nur die Möglichkeiten andeutet, die aus einer bestimmten Konstellation zu entfalten wären, sondern gleichzeitig auch auf die Voraussetzungen zurückweist, die dieselbe Konstellation bedingen. Ein solches Erzählen schließt allerdings von vornherein seine eigene Unabschließbarkeit ein.

Die Rezeption der Wahrscheinlichkeitstheorie durch die Dichtung wird zunehmend zum Forschungsgegenstand.[1] Dies schließt auch die Novalis-Forschung ein, wobei sehr unterschiedliche Ansätze gewählt worden sind. In seiner Monografie *Alea* (2009), eine Studie der »narratologischen Implikationen« einer »metaphorischen Konzeptualisierung« des Lebens als Glücksspiel (Schnyder, 9), beobachtet z.B. Peter Schnyder im ersten von Novalis' »Dialogen« (*NS*, II, 661–664) ein auffälliges Interesse für das »selbstregulierende Moment« im Kontext der explosionsartigen Zunahme von Publikationen (Schnyder, 274f.). Da es »unter den Bedingungen der Moderne keine vorgängige Norm« mehr gibt, geht es Novalis um »selbstreferentielle Variationsprozesse«, wobei im Spezialfall keine »auszugleichende Abweichung von einem Mittelwert, sondern eine Bereicherung des Möglichkeiten-Feldes« erkannt wird (276f.). In seiner Analyse der Poetik des ökonomischen Menschen, *Kalkül und Leidenschaft* (2002), diskutiert Joseph Vogl auf ähnliche Weise das Prinzip der Selbstorganisation im Kontext moderner ökonomischer Kreisläufe. Mit seiner Theorie des Wissens hat Novalis »den neuesten Stand ökonomischer Theorie eingeholt, einen Stand, der […] die Abstraktionsprozesse des Geldverkehrs, Statistik und Wahrscheinlichkeitskalkül zur Bedingung für die Selbstorganisation von Universalwissen wendet« (Vogl, 264).[2]

Eine andere Perspektive bietet Franziska Bomskis Studie *Zwischen Mathematik und Märchen. Die Darstellung des Zufalls und ihre erkenntnistheoretische Funktion bei Novalis* (2009). Die Analyse geht von einer spezifischen Differenz aus: *Subjektive Zufälle* sind Ereignisse, die der beschränkten menschlichen Wahrnehmung als »unbegründete Koinzidenzen« erscheinen, obwohl sie einer prinzipiell ermittelbaren Gesetzmäßigkeit unterliegen (Bomski, 167). Diese werden den *transzendenten Zufällen* gegenübergestellt, wie sie paradigmatisch in der Leibniz'schen Theodizee erscheinen: »Anders als der Mensch überblickt Gott alle logisch möglichen, kontingenten Welten und verwirklicht so keineswegs zufällig, sondern aus seiner allwissenden Perspektive eindeutig begründet die beste von ihnen« (168). Analog dazu unterscheidet sie »zwei Arten des Zufalls bei Novalis, zu denen der Dichter als potenzierte Form des geistigen Menschen in einem konträren Verhältnis steht«: die subjektiven

---

[1] Siehe z.B. Rüdiger Campes wichtige Studie zur frühen Wahrscheinlichkeitstheorie und Romanpoetik *Spiel der Wahrscheinlichkeit* (2002).

[2] Auch im *Ofterdingen* Roman, der »wie kein anderer Text zu einem Manifest der neuen Regulationskonzepte wird und dabei dichterische Sprache und ökonomischen Verkehr analogisiert« (Vogl, 264), lässt sich das Prinzip einer »Zirkulation« erkennen, die »feste Wertstandards auflöst und eine Destabilisierung von Referentialitätsansprüchen mit der autopoietischen Organisation des Systems kombiniert« (ebd.).

Zufälle, »die als notwendige Glieder einer teleologischen Entwicklung erwiesen werden müssen, um das Individuum von allen nicht notwendigen Beschränkungen zu befreien«, und den transzendentalen Zufall, »der gerade durch die Eliminierung des phänomenalen Kontingenten« sich »als absoluter Anfang bzw. unerreichbares Ende erweist« – d.h. als die göttliche Schöpfung, »die einzig echte Bedingung der Existenz« (185).
Die Verbindung von Wahrscheinlichkeitstheorie zu Poesie bei Novalis zeige sich am deutlichsten im *Spiel*begriff. Einerseits werde im »Spiel der Phantasie […] eine fiktive Welt geschaffen, die in der Imagination dem Subjekt vollkommen verfügbar ist«, während andererseits die Metapher des Glücksspiels eng mit der »systematisch-formalen Beschreibung des Zufalls« verbunden sei (165). Zusammen höben sie die Hierarchie von »innerweltlicher Perspektive und Transzendenz« zugunsten eines graduellen Unterschiedes auf, sodass eine »Annäherung an die metaphysische Ebene« möglich werde (174). Anhand vom Klingsohr-Märchen in *Ofterdingen* wird überzeugend dargelegt, wie die »Annäherung von endlicher Reflexion und im Unendlichen liegenden Absoluten« in der »Umschreibung vom Glücksspiel zum Schauspiel« modelliert wird – »[d]ie teleologische Struktur des Schauspiels«, die »durch eine externe Autorinstanz verbürgt« werde, sei eine »Außenperspektive«, die dem empirischen Menschen verwehrt bliebe, aber durch die Dichtung vermittelt werden könne (191).
Dieser Beitrag setzt gleichsam zwischen den obigen Perspektiven an. Denn der Blick auf den Zufall als die Markierung eines Punktes in einem Kontinuum zwischen den Polen unmöglich/notwendig und Unwissenheit/Gewissheit thematisiert sowohl die Aufmerksamkeit für die Stetigkeit selbstregulierender Kreisläufe als auch die Kontingenz der menschlichen Perspektive. Die Argumentation erfolgt in drei Schritten. Zuerst wird Novalis' Auffassung der Mathematik als ideales System zur Erzeugung neuer Wissenselemente skizziert (I.), um dann anhand seiner zwei Hauptquellen, Condorcet und Lambert, die wichtigsten Merkmale der so genannten klassischen Wahrscheinlichkeit Ende des 18. Jahrhunderts herauszuarbeiten (II.). Anschließend werden vor diesem Hintergrund die erzählerische Funktion des Zufalls und deren Reflexion durch den Erzähler in *Heinrich von Ofterdingen* analysiert (III.).

I.

Die außergewöhnliche Bedeutung der Mathematik für das Denken und Schaffen Novalis' lässt sich schon daran erkennen, dass seine intensive Beschäftigung mit ihr von seiner frühen Studienzeit in Leipzig (ab 1791)[3] über seine wichtigsten Studienjahre an der Bergakademie in Freiberg (1797–1799)[4] bis zu seinem Tode andauerte. Obwohl, wie Uerlings hervorhebt, sie damit eine Kontinuität aufweist, die sonst nur mit der Philosophie vergleichbar wäre (Uerlings, 178), bedurfte es eigentlich der Erscheinung der *Historisch-Kritischen Ausgabe* seiner Werke, um ab ca. 1960 die Abkehr von einer Novalis-Rezeption einzuleiten, die »auf Kosten des Naturwissenschaftlers den Dichter etabliert« hat und an der Tieck-Legende vom »Schöpfer der blauen Blume und schwärmerischen Jüngling« festhielt (Daiber, 44).[5] Anteil an dieser Korrektur hatte auch die erste eingehende quellenkritische Analyse seiner mathematischen Notizen: Martin Dycks heute noch maßgebende Studie *Novalis and Mathematics* (1970). Obwohl betont wird, dass die meisten Fragmente eher philosophisch verfasst sind, wird deutlich gezeigt, dass die Mathematik die Koordinaten bietet, um den Zusammenhalt im Kaleidoskop seiner Gedanken erkennen zu können (Dyck, 1f.). Die Studie zeigt die Verbindungen zu seinen wichtigsten philosophischen Einflüssen auf (Fichte, Kant und Hemsterhuis) und weist nach, dass er durchaus an der zeitgenössischen Entwicklung der Mathematik teilnahm und um ein sicheres technisches Fundament bemüht war. Obwohl die technischen Notizen auch von teilweise rhapsodischen Reflexionen zu einer zukünftigen Mathematik umrahmt werden, zeigt Hans Niels Jahnke wie Novalis, an der Schwelle des Übergangs von einer auf der Anschauung ruhenden Mathematik zum For-

---

[3] Wohl angeregt durch den Leipziger Professor Karl Friedrich Hindenburg (vgl. Dyck, 27ff.), Mitbegründer der »kombinatorischen Schule«, einer kurzlebigen, aber in Deutschland einflussreichen Forschungsrichtung (vgl. Jahnke, 33). Zur Novalis' Rezeption der kombinatorischen Analysis – der Versuch, die »Infinitesimalrechnung zu algebraisieren« und alle Funktionen als Potenzreihen zu entwickeln, die wiederum kombinatorisch begründet waren (Jahnke, 33) – siehe Dyck, 28ff., Jahnke, 33ff.

[4] In denen er neben seinen Mathematikvorlesungen auch Privatunterricht bei einem Kommilitonen nahm (vgl. Uerlings, 179).

[5] So konnte Herbert Uerlings 1990 in seinem umfassenden Forschungsbericht konstatieren, dass »die ältere Entgegensetzung von Aufklärung/Rationalität/Wissenschaft und Romantik/Irrationalität/Dichtung völlig gegenstandslos geworden« ist (Uerlings, 151) und es heute in der Forschung unstrittig sei, dass »mathematische oder aus der Mathematik entwickelte Denkmodelle für die Struktur von Hardenbergs Denken und Schreiben eine entscheidende Rolle spielen« (179).

malismus des 19. Jahrhunderts, diesen Epochenwandel mitreflektiert, sodass das Konkrete und Spekulative nicht eindeutig zu trennen sind (Jahnke, 39f.). Stark vereinfacht kann man zusammenfassen: Die Mathematik erwächst aus einer dem Menschen angeborenen Erkenntnis- und Kritikfähigkeit[6] und zeigt uns in der Anwendung die Affinität des Geistes zu den mathematischen Strukturen der Natur.[7] Sie repräsentiert sowohl ein System zur Organisation von Daten als auch eine Methode zur Wissens*generierung* in abstrakter, symbolischer Form. Sie sei, schreibt Novalis, »die *ordnende* Kraft« (*NS*, III, 459) und »ächte Wissenschaft – weil sie *gemachte Kenntnisse* enthält – Produkte geistiger Selbstthätigkeit – weil sie *methodisch genialisirt*« (*NS*, III, 473). So liefert sie das Muster für eine zukünftige Vereinigung aller Wissenschaften und soll durch Verschmelzung mit der Philosophie ein allgemeines menschliches Erkenntnissystem bereitstellen.[8] Paradigma der Abstraktion ist die Algebra, die Zahlen und Worte in unbeschränkt manipulierbare Symbole verwandelt,[9] während die Analysis die Methoden enthält, nicht nur anhand finiter, greifbarer Formeln das unendlich Große und Kleine darzustellen, sondern als Erfindungskunst (von wenigen bekannten Gliedern ausgehend) anhand von Konstruktionsformeln unbegrenzt viele weitere Produkte zu erzeugen.[10] Besondere Bedeutung fällt dabei der kombinatorischen Analysis zu, die durch freie Variation immer neue Konstellationen aus sich selbst erzeugt. So stellt die reine Mathematik nicht nur einen Prototyp bereit für die Produktionsverfahren des romantischen Künstlers,[11] sondern gibt auch ein Analogon einer romantisierten Welt:

---

[6] Vgl. »Wären wir nicht von Grund aus mathematisch, so nähmen wir keine *Unterschiede* etc. wahr« (*NS*, III, 432).
[7] Vgl. »Die Natur addirt, subtrahirt, multiplicirt, potenzirt etc. unaufhörlich. Die angew[andten] mathematischen Wissenschaften zeigen uns die Natur, als Mathematiker« (*NS*, III, 52).
[8] Vgl. *NS*, III, 50f., 593f.; *NS*, II, 600.
[9] So gilt es, deutlich zu machen, »daß es mit der Sprache wie mit den mathematischen Formeln sei – Sie machen eine Welt für sich aus – Sie spielen nur mit sich selbst, drücken nichts als ihre wunderbare Natur aus, und eben darum sind sie so ausdrucksvoll – eben darum spiegelt sich in ihnen das seltsame Verhältnißspiel der Dinge« (*NS*, II, 672). Oder noch konkreter: »Das Zahlensystem ist *Muster* eines ächten Sprachzeichensystems – Unsre Buchstaben sollen Zahlen, unsre Sprache Arythmetik werden« (*NS*, III, 50).
[10] Vgl. »In der Combinations[lehre] liegt das Princip der Vollständigkeit – so wie in der Analysis – oder d[er] Kunst aus gegebenen Datis die Unbekannten Glieder zu finden [...]« (*NS*, III, 364). Vgl. auch *NS*, III, 68, 92, 94. Vgl. auch Anmerkung 4.
[11] Prägnant heißt es: »Romantisiren ähnlich dem Algebraisiren« (*NS*, III, 242). »Die Algeber ist die *Poësie*« (*NS*, III, 309). Vgl. dazu auch Dyck, 86ff.

> Alles aus *Nichts* erschaffne *Reale*, wie z.B. die Zahlen und die abstracten Ausdrücke – hat eine wunderbare Verwandtschaft mit Dingen einer andern Welt – mit unendlichen Reihen sonderbarer Combinationen und Verhältnissen – gleichsam mit einer mathem[atischen] und abstracten Welt an sich – mit einer *poëtischen mathem[atischen] und abstracten* Welt (*NS*, III, 440f.).

Die Vorstellung, durch mathematische Operationen auf Unbekanntes schließen zu können, spiegelt sich auch paradigmatisch im folgenden Zitat wider, das Novalis fast wortwörtlich aus Condorcets *Entwurf* (vgl. Condorcet, 234) übernimmt:

> Nach Condorcet lehrt der Inf[initesimal] Calcül – die Verhältnisse der successiven Zu oder Abnahmen einer veränderlichen Größe finden, oder aus der Kenntniß dieses Verhältnisses die Größe selbst wieder auffinden – man mag nun diesen Zunahmen eine endliche Gr[öße] zuschreiben, oder deren Verh[ältnisse] nur für den Augenblick suchen, da sie verschwinden, eine Methode, die, da sie sich auf alle Combinationen veränderlicher Gr[ößen] und auf alle Hypothesen ihrer Veränderungen erstreckt, auf gleiche Weise für alle Dinge, deren Veränderungen eines bestimmten Maaßes fähig sind, entw[eder] die Verhältnisse ihrer Elemente, aus der Kenntniß der Verh[ältnisse], welche die Sachen gegen einander haben, oder die Verhältn[isse] der Sachen, wenn nur die ihrer Elemente bekannt sind, bestimmen lehrt (*NS*, III, 425).

Es geht hier allgemein um das Problem induktiven Wissens. In diesem Sinne geht es auch, wie Novalis kurz vorher notiert, um »[d]ie Gesetze des Zufalls – die *Veränderungsgesetze überhaupt* – die Gesetzreihen – der Gesetzcalcul« (*NS*, III, 425). Oder, spezifischer, um den »Probabilitaeten Calcul« (*NS*, III, 426), wie er Ende des 18. Jahrhunderts konzipiert wird.[12]

II.

Die Entstehung der Wahrscheinlichkeitstheorie bietet insofern ein »eigentümliches historisches Problem«, als im Gegensatz zu den meisten mathematischen Disziplinen, die »oft bis ins Altertum zurückverfolgt werden können« (Hauser, 9), diese erst Mitte des 17. Jahrhunderts in Erscheinung tritt. Wenn Laplace 1814 darüber staunt, »daß eine Wissenschaft, die durch

---

[12] Siehe dazu auch Bomski, 179f. Zu Condorcets und Laplaces Herleitung einiger der wichtigsten wahrscheinlichkeitstheoretischen Prinzipien als Weiterentwicklung ihrer Arbeit zur Integration und zur Theorie der Reihen siehe Gillispie, 3ff.

die Betrachtung der Spiele ihren Anfang nahm, sich bis zu den wichtigsten Gegenständen der menschlichen Erkenntniß erhoben hat« (Laplace, 206), dann bezieht er sich darauf, dass ihre Genese oft auf die Korrespondenz zwischen Pascal und Fermat im Jahre 1654 zu bestimmten Aspekten des Glücksspiels datiert wird. Um die historischen Kontexte dieser Entwicklung, die als »die bedeutendste Mutation des menschlichen Denkens seit Aristoteles« bezeichnet wurde (vgl. Kavanagh, 18f.; meine Übersetzung, D.A.), ist ein breit gefächerter Forschungskorpus entstanden. Eine der ersten dieser Arbeiten, Ian Hackings wegweisende Studie *The Emergence of Probability* (1975),[13] geht von einem Problem aus, das die Philosophie der Wahrscheinlichkeit heute noch beschäftigt. Es ist ihre inhärente Dualität, die Hacking als janusköpfig bezeichnet:

> It is notable that the probability that emerged so suddenly is Janus-faced. On the one side it is statistical, concerning itself with stochastic laws of chance processes. On the other side it is epistemological, dedicated to assessing reasonable degrees of belief in propositions quite devoid of statistical background (Hacking, 12).

Seit ihrer Axiomatisierung durch Andrei Kolmogorov im Jahre 1933, die mit beiden Interpretationen kompatibel ist, stellt die Theorie eine der kohärentesten Disziplinen der modernen Mathematik dar, sodass viele Mathematiker, wie es Jan von Plato formuliert, auf die Frage, was Wahrscheinlichkeit sei, antworten würden: »Anything that satisfies the axioms« (von Plato, 1). Die (philosophischen) Fragen, was dabei eigentlich gemessen wird, und ob die *objektiven* (oder *aleatorischen, statistischen*) und *subjektiven* (*epistemischen*) Interpretationen gegenseitig aufeinander zu reduzieren seien, werden dagegen weiterhin kontrovers diskutiert (vgl. Gillies, 1f.).

---

[13] Wie Daston es formuliert: »Hacking created a new area of inquiry by asking a new question, or, better, a new *kind* of question: What are the conceptual preconditions for the emergence of a concept so apparently simple, so useful, indeed indispensible – yet so strangely absent before circa 1650 – as the modern notion of probability?« (Daston, »History of Emergences«, 802). Dastons Aufsatz, eine Rezension der Neuausgabe von Hackings Werk von 2006, bietet eine übersichtliche Synpose von Hackings These, wonach zwei diskrete Traditionen – die durch Autorität verbürgte Meinung und die Zeichenlese im Buch der Natur, wie sie von den niederen Wissenschaften der Alchemie oder Medizin praktiziert wurden – in der Genese der modernen Probabilität verschmolzen seien, und setzt sie in den Kontext neuerer Forschung. Ihre eigene Monografie *Classical Probability in the Enlightenment* (1988) bleibt ein Standardwerk für den Zeitraum ca. 1650–1840. Zur Provenienz der mathematischen Ansätze, die der Autor als »the *coming to consciousness* of uncertain inference« beschreibt (Franklin, x), siehe James Franklins *The Science of Conjecture* (2001).

Ein wesentliches Kennzeichen der so genannten »klassischen Wahrscheinlichkeit«, wie sie Novalis Ende des 18. Jahrhunderts kennen gelernt haben wird (und die im 19. Jahrhundert durch die statistische Wahrscheinlichkeit abgelöst werden sollte), ist allerdings die Art, wie die frühen Probabilisten davon ausgingen, die subjektiven und objektiven Interpretationen, wenn nicht als identisch, dann wenigstens als weitgehend äquivalent behandeln zu können.[14] Dieser Umstand hatte zwei wesentliche Quellen. Die erste war der Glaube an die prinzipielle Einsehbarkeit von allen Ursachen und Wirkungen, die sich dem menschlichen Verstand nur durch seine Begrenztheit entzog. Die zweite war eine Art »assoziative Psychologie«, die empirische Regelmäßigkeiten mit subjektiven Wahrnehmungs- und Bewusstseinsprozessen verknüpfte (vgl. Daston, *Classical Probability*, 188–225). So galt die Theorie vielen Mathematikern als die Beschreibung der Denkprozesse, die bei einem rationalen Menschen bei der Beurteilung von Evidenz ablaufen.[15] So konnte Laplace verkünden, dass die Theorie »im Grunde nichts weiter ist, als der in Rechnung gebrachte gesunde Menschenverstand; sie lehrt das mit Genauigkeit bestimmen, was ein richtiger Verstand durch eine Art von Instinkt fühlt, ohne sich immer Rechenschaft davon geben zu können« (Laplace, 206).

Einblick in diese eigentümliche Amalgamation von Mathematik und Philosophie, von Glücksspielrechnung und früher Statistik, die als Teil der »gemischten Mathematik« auch die Grenzen zwischen Theorie und Praxis verwischten, bieten zwei Werke, die Novalis eingehend studiert hat. Diese sind Condorcets aufklärerische Hymne auf die langfristige Perfektibilität der Menschheit, *Entwurf eines historischen Gemähldes der Fortschritte des menschlichen Geistes* (1793), und Johann Heinrich Lamberts *Neues Organon* (1764), das als die »umfassendste theoretische Ausgestaltung des Gedankens einer ›mathesis universalis‹ betrachtet werden [darf], die uns in der Geschichte der Philosophie vorliegt« (Arndt, X).

---

[14] Vgl.: »This double vision, which makes the classical probabilists seem at once familiar and fanciful, is an artifact of conceptual distinctions that are the stock-in-trade of every modern probabilist, but which were rarely made by the classical probabilists – indeed, the emergence of such clear-cut distinctions spelled the end of the classical interpretation« (Daston, *Classical Probability*, xiii).

[15] Vgl. »Condillac and Condorcet described this process as a kind of ›mental calculus‹. If mental analysis was a kind of calculus, the combinatorial calculus of probabilities could be viewed as the mathematical expression of the psychological processes that guided right reasoning by a consideration of how a ›reasonable man‹ might evaluate an application of mathematical technique to a given problem« (Brown, 86f.).

Der erste Bezug dazu stellt sich durch eine unscheinbare Notiz dar: »Probabilitaeten Calcul. Über Wittwen, Waysen, Invaliden Kassen etc. Von *Kassen* überhaupt« (*NS*, III, 426). Novalis bezieht sich hier auf eine Stelle in Condorcets *Entwurf*, an der der französische Mathematiker, Philosoph und Staatstheoretiker auf die Erfolge hinweist, die die »Untersuchungen über die Dauer des menschlichen Lebens« (Condorcet, 256) schon vorzuweisen hatten. Sie ist Teil einer längeren Exposition über die neuen mathematischen Methoden, um empirische Gesetze aus Beobachtungen zu ermitteln (254). Die Passage bietet eine Art Vademekum der heterogenen Anwendungsgebiete der Wahrscheinlichkeitstheorie zu dieser Zeit. So sollte die Theorie nicht nur die Glaubwürdigkeit von außergewöhnlichen Ereignissen bestimmen können (254),[16] sondern auch die Regelmäßigkeit von Phänomenen, die keinem (anerkannten) Naturgesetz unterlagen, erklären (255). Zu diesen Anwendungen gehören einige, die erst im Verlaufe der nächsten hundert Jahre ihre heute erkennbare Form annehmen sollten. So zeigte sie z.B. auf einem Gebiet, das Condorcet besonders am Herzen lag, die Vor- und Nachteile verschiedener Wahlformen auf (255f.).[17] Es werden aber auch andere genannt, wie z.B. die Anwendung der Theorie auf Zeugenaussagen und juristische Entscheidungsprozesse (256), die schon im frühen 19. Jahrhundert als geistige Verwirrung abgeurteilt werden sollten (vgl. Daston, *Classical Probability*, xivf.).

In diesem Sinne wird diese Synopse Novalis mit der Spannung zwischen Beschreibung, Erklärung und Präskription, die der Theorie von Anfang an innewohnte, vertraut gemacht haben. Gleichzeitig exponiert sie eine ihrer zentralen Kontroversen: das Induktionsproblem oder das Verhältnis von Wahrscheinlichkeit *a priori* zu Wahrscheinlichkeit *a posteriori*. Es ging dabei (vereinfacht formuliert) um die Vermittlung von denjenigen Verfahren, die auf der Grundlage bekannter Verteilungen die Wahrscheinlichkeit zukünftiger Ereignisse berechnen, mit denjenigen, die aus Beobachtungen oder Experimenten auf die Wahrscheinlichkeit von unbekannten Wirkungen schließen. In der damaligen Terminologie, ging es im zweiten Fall um die *probabilité des causes par les événements*.[18] Besondere Bedeutung fiel der Möglich-

---

[16] Zu Condorcets eigener Formel, um die Glaubwürdigkeit von außergewöhnlichen Ereignissen zu berechnen, siehe Schlesinger, 120ff.

[17] Heute gilt Condorcet als der Pate der so genannten ›Social Choice Theorie‹. Siehe dazu McLean/Hewitt, viif., 10ff., 32–48.

[18] Der Begriff stammt von Laplace, der mit Thomas Bayes die Anerkennung für das in dieser Hinsicht wichtigste Theorem teilt (vgl. McLean/Hewitt, 12f.). Es geht im Folgenden aber nicht um das Bayes-Theorem an sich, sondern um die zwei allgemeinen Prinzipien,

keit zu, bestimmen zu können, mit welcher Wahrscheinlichkeit eine Erscheinung vom »Willen eines verständigen Wesens« abhängt oder von anderen »ihm gleichzeitigen, oder vorhergehenden Phänomenen« oder »von jener nothwendigen und unbekannten Ursache, genannt Zufall« (Condorcet, 255). Es gibt schließlich kaum einen prägnanteren Ausdruck des in einem absoluten Vernunftglauben wurzelnden Grundgedankens der Probabilität im 18. Jahrhundert als den folgenden: Die »Wissenschaften der Combinationen« (254) und das Probabilitätenkalkül lehren »die verschiedenen Grade von Gewißheit kennen, wozu wir aufzusteigen hoffen dürfen«, sowie die Bedingungen dafür, dass eine »Meinung« zur Handlungsgrundlage werden kann, »ohne gegen die Klugheit oder gegen die Gerechtigkeit anzustossen« (255).
Diese Überzeugung teilte auch Lambert, und auch er setzt sich in seinem Opus Magnum, *Neues Organon*, intensiv mit dem Grad der Gewissheit, den wir uns versprechen dürfen, sowie dem Verhältnis von *Apriori* und *Aposteriori* Wahrscheinlichkeit auseinander. Das in vier Teile untergliederte Werk widmet sich der Theorie einer Grundwissenschaft, die (nach dem Vorbild der Mathematik) ein Axiomensystem repräsentieren würde, dessen »erste Begriffe und Sätze nicht nur Herleitungsprinzipien aller aus ihnen apriorisch deduzierbaren Aussagen, sondern zugleich auch Grundprinzipien der von der menschlichen Erkenntnis erfaßten Wirklichkeit sind« (Arndt, XI). Wie Schiewer betont, muss das Werk »als eine wichtige Voraussetzung für die theoretische Fundierung des sogenannten Bibel- oder Enzyklopädie-Projektes in dem *Allgemeinen Brouillon* Novalis' betrachtet werden« (Schiewer, 14), woraus sich Verbindungen zu seiner Poetik ergeben, da das Projekt »der dichterischen Darstellung bedarf«, die wiederum wesentlich vom enzyklopädischen Konzept bestimmt wird (18).[19]
Novalis' Notizen (vgl. *NS*, III, 130–134) belegen ein intensives Interesse vor allem für den ersten Teil des Werkes (die *Dianoiologie*), in denen Lambert »die logische Form der Erkenntnis und die wissenschaftliche Beweisführung« untersucht (Arndt, XIII). Auch die Notizen, die seine Condorcet-

---

entweder von Ursachen auf Wirkungen oder von Wirkungen auf Ursachen schließen zu wollen. Für eine eingehende Diskussion der »probability of causes« siehe Daston, *Classical Probability*, 226–295.

[19] Auch Ulrich Gaier, der das Konstruktionsprinzip in *Die Lehrlinge von Sais* verfolgt, betont die Bedeutung von Lamberts Methodik »zur Gewinnung von wissenschaftlicher Erkenntnis und zur Lösung von Aufgaben aller Art« (182). Ebenso wichtig ist, dass diese Erkenntnis stets »in Zeichen umsetzbar und damit der Begriffskombinatorik zugänglich« ist (182).

Lektüre belegen, verweisen auf Lambert. Lamberts Grundlehre, heißt es direkt, sei »intellectuale Chemie« (*NS*, III, 422). Kurz vor den Notizen zur Wahrscheinlichkeitstheorie wird dann die »*Phaenomenologie*« die vielleicht »brauchbarste, und umfassendste W[issenschaft]« genannt (*NS*, III, 425). Der letzte Terminus, der von Lambert erst in die Philosophie lanciert wurde, ist auch der Titel des vierten und wohl originellsten Teils seines Werkes. Er bezieht sich bei Lambert auf den Einfluss des *Scheins*, der als der Eindruck definiert wird, »den die empfundenen Dinge in den Sinnen machen« (Lambert, 220), und dazu führt, dass wir die Wahrnehmung der Dinge oft mit den Dingen verwechseln, wie sie unabhängig davon sind (217f.). Es gilt zu bestimmen, »was in jeder Art des Scheins real und wahr ist«, und die Ursachen und Umstände zu entwickeln, »die einen Schein hervorbringen und verändern«, um daraus auf das Wahre schließen zu können (421). Der Begriff bezieht sich somit sowohl auf die theoretische Vermittlung der Mathematik und der Physik als auch auf die Kluft zwischen Erkenntnis *a priori* und *a posteriori* (vgl. Arndt, XXXf.). In diesem Zusammenhang wird (im zweitletzten Hauptstück des Werkes) die Wahrscheinlichkeitstheorie ins Spiel gebracht.[20]

Nach der Diagnose verschiedener Arten und Quellen des Scheins (sei es die Sinnestäuschung, die Einbildung oder auch die Leidenschaft) stellt sich Lambert der Aufgabe, »das Wahre und den Schein des Wahren mit der Gewißheit und ihren Graden zu vergleichen« (Lambert, 318). Der erste Schritt dazu ist die semantische Säuberung der Normalsprache. Unter den vielen Ausdrücken (vermutlich, ohne Zweifel, allem Anschein nach, usw.), die »die Art und den Grad der Versicherung angeben, mit welcher wir über eine Sache urtheilen oder denken« (318) wird w*ahrscheinlich* ausgesondert, als der Begriff, der sich auf die *Gründe* bezieht, nach welchen wir eine Sache für wahr halten (319). Da dieser jedoch nicht nur mit den anderen oft vermischt, sondern sowohl der geometrischen als auch der moralischen Gewissheit teils zur Seite und teils entgegengesetzt wird, greift Lambert

---

[20] Wie es Arndt auf den Punkt bringt, bedeutete die Betonung empirischer Quellen der Täuschung einen Bruch mit der Vorstellung, dass eine *methodus scientifica* Irrtümer prinzipiell ausschließen sollte (vgl. XIV). Es blieb der Anspruch, durch eine *Logica probabilium* (XXXII), den Grad zu finden, zu dem die Erkenntnis vom sinnlichen Schein zu lösen wäre (XXX). Wie Campe weiter hervorhebt schließt die Theorie aber ihre eigene Unabschließbarkeit ein: »Die Logik des Wahrscheinlichen ist bei Lambert also wieder Desiderat wie bei Leibniz und Projekt wie bei Jakob Bernoulli. Aber ein Desiderat, dem die Unerfüllbarkeit zumindest phänomenologisch eingeschrieben ist, und ein Projekt, dessen Unabschließbarkeit als Phänomenologie zur Theorie selbst wird« (Campe, 355).

auf die mathematische Probabilität zu, um zur »Sache selbst« kommen zu können (319f.). Er skizziert dazu zunächst die Geschichte der konzeptuellen Entwicklung der Theorie. Das Problem von Wahrscheinlichkeit *a priori* und *a posteriori* wird über die Glücksspiele fixiert. Diese haben die Besonderheit,

> daß man aus ihrer Einrichtung die möglichen Fälle abzählen, und den Grad der Möglichkeit von jedem bestimmen kann. Auf diese Art wird die Wahrscheinlichkeit jeder Fälle *a priori* berechnet. Es erhellet aber aus erstgesagtem, daß es auch *a posteriori* geschehen könnte, wenn man das Spiel lange oder unendlich vielmale wiederholte (323).

Es ist vornehmlich dieses Verhältnis, das es ermöglicht, das mathematische Modell auf die Erfahrung und die Gedächtnisvorgänge zu übertragen, wobei vorausgesetzt werden muss, dass die betrachteten Phänomene etwas Beständiges und Bestimmtes haben. Ansonsten müssen die individuellen Umstände, Beweggründe usw. in Betracht gezogen werden, um den Grad der Wahrscheinlichkeit zu schätzen, mit welcher eine Sache geschehen sei oder geschehen werde – besonders wenn die Phänomene lediglich aus der Betrachtung ihrer Folgen erschlossen werden können (328f.). Es ist aber von dieser Basis aus, dass Lambert von den »physischen Folgen« zu den logischen fortschreiten kann, die nicht länger die »Sachen selbst« darstellen, sondern »die Begriffe und Sätze, die sie uns angeben« (332).
Festzuhalten ist, dass Novalis' Lektüre ihn nicht nur in komprimierter Form mit den konzeptuellen Grundprinzipien der mathematischen Behandlung von Unsicherheit als ein neues Paradigma des Wissens und Urteilens bekannt gemacht haben wird, sondern auch mit den Hoffnungen und Ansprüchen, von denen ihre Entwicklung getragen wurde. Weiterhin wird deutlich, dass er diese innerhalb seiner Reflexionen zu einer zukünftigen Mathematik assimiliert. So kritisiert Novalis im Anschluss an Condorcet die mangelnde Systematik in der Auswertung empirischer Daten, zeigt sich fasziniert von den Regelmäßigkeiten im scheinbar Heterogenen[21] und nimmt gewissermaßen den kurz nach seinem Tode einsetzenden Aufstieg der statistischen Methode vorweg (vgl. dazu Dyck, 67). Man gehe mit »Erfahrungen und Experimenten noch viel zu sorglos um«, betrachte sie zu wenig als »Data zur Auflösung und mannichfaltigen Combinationen zum Calcül«. Man nehme

---

[21] So empfielt einer der Gesprächspartner im ersten von Novalis' *Dialogen* allen Systematikern bei der Natur in die Schule zu gehen, denn: »Die Zufälle sind die einzelnen Thatsachen – die Zusammenstellung der Zufälle – ihr Zusammentreffen ist nicht wieder Zufall, sondern Gesetz – Erfolg der tiefsinnigsten planmäßigsten Weisheit« (*NS*, II, 662).

nicht jede Erfahrung »als Function und Glied einer Reihe an« und ordne, vergleiche und vereinfache noch nicht hinreichend (*NS*, III, 427). Ebenfalls in Anlehnung an Condorcet betrachtet er diese Entwicklungen als Schritte in Richtung eines universellen Kombinationssystems, das sowohl den Denkgesetzen, als auch den wissenschaftlich ermittelbaren Gesetzlichkeiten der Natur entspricht.[22]

Diese Gedanken durchziehen Novalis' Fragmente. Einerseits geht es darum, durch die Strukturierung von Daten ihre systematischen Regelmäßigkeiten zu ergründen oder aus »zufälligen Thatsachen […] systematische Experimente« zu machen (*NS*, II, 528). Andererseits lassen sich anhand des Glücksspielmodells dieselben Prinzipien ermitteln, denn: »Spielen ist experimentiren mit dem Zufall« (*NS*, III, 574). Mit vielen Probabilisten der Zeit erscheint auch Novalis die Wahrscheinlichkeitstheorie zudem als die Kodifizierung einer dem menschlichen Intellekt immanenten Fähigkeit zum Kombinieren und Analysieren, die einerseits rationales Handeln unter der Bedingung von Unsicherheit erlaubt, sich aber andererseits auch als Instinkt und Intuition äußert.[23] Sind diese Regeln erst in mathematische Form gebracht, dann ist die Analysis »(die *Divinations*, oder) die Erfindungskunst auf Regeln gebracht« (*NS*, III, 434). Aber auch ohne ihre Formalisierung gilt: »Wer rechten Sinn für den Zufall hat, der kann alles Zufällige zur Bestimmung eines unbekannten Zufalls benutzen – er kann das Schicksal mit gleichem Glück in den Stellungen der Gestirne, als in Sandkörnern, Vogelflug und Figuren suchen« (*NS*, III, 687). In letzter Instanz bedeutet das: »Auch der Zufall ist nicht *unergründlich* – er hat *seine* Regelmäßigkeit« (*NS*, III, 414).

Ohne implizieren zu wollen, Novalis hätte spezifische mathematische Methoden direkt umgesetzt, wird im nächsten Abschnitt argumentiert, dass sein Zufallsbegriff die Entwicklung der Wahrscheinlichkeitstheorie reflektiert und zwei ihrer konzeptuellen Prinzipien in die Erzählstruktur des *Ofterdingen*-Romans einfließen lässt. Diese sind das Verhältnis zwischen Wahrscheinlichkeit *a priori* und *a posteriori* und die Tatsache, dass der Umgang mit unvollständigem Wissen stets nur partielles Wissen oder Grade des Wissens produziert und somit seine eigene Unabschließbarkeit einschließt. Oder

---

[22] Vgl. »Kalcül = Kunst, *Bestimmungen* zu *verbinden* oder *Kunst zu bestimmen überhaupt* z.B. aus gegebenen Bestimmungen nicht gegebene Bes[timmungen] zu finden. Rechnungs[lehre] = *Bestimmungsverwandtschaftslehre*« (*NS*, III, 424; vgl. dazu Condorcet, 235ff.; siehe auch die Anmerkung der Herausgeber in *NS*, III, 971).

[23] In diesem Sinne überlegt er auch, ob aus der »Identitaet der Absicht und des Zufalls« und ihrem allgemeinen Zusammenhang sich eine Möglichkeit ergibt, »die Erscheinungen des Instinkts zu erklären« (*NS*, III, 600).

wie Novalis es selbst formuliert, zeige die »Theorie der Wahrscheinlichkeit – WahrscheinlichkeitsBew[eise] und Calcül«, dass alle »Vereinigung des *Heterogénen*« ins Unendliche führt (*NS*, III, 448).

III.

In seinen Anekdoten skizziert Novalis (wahrscheinlich durch Goethes *Wilhelm Meister* angeregt; vgl. Walzel, 409ff.) einige Überlegungen zur Kompositionstechnik eines Romans anhand des Beispiels der *bouts-rimés* – ein Gesellschaftsspiel, bei dem ein Gedicht spontan nach vorgegebenen Endreimen verfasst wird. »Ein Romanschreiber«, heißt es, »macht eine Art von Bouts rimes«. Seine Kunst ist es, »aus einer gegebenen Menge von Zufällen und Situationen« eine gesetzmäßige Reihe zu machen und gezielt »Ein Individuum zu Einem Zweck durch alle diese Zufälle« hindurchzuführen (*NS*, II, 580). »Ein eigenthümliches Individuum muß er haben, das die Begebenheiten bestimmt, und von ihnen bestimmt wird. Dieser Wechsel, oder die Veränderungen Eines Individuums – in einer *continuirlichen* Reihe machen den interessanten Stoff des Romans aus« (580). Er kann dabei entweder vom Individuum oder von einer Menge Begebenheiten ausgehen, und Novalis bietet eine Art Klassifikation, wie diese miteinander zu verbinden wären. Wichtig ist, dass, sobald eine Klasse gewählt wurde, sich alles daraus rechtfertigen lässt (580f.).
Die Figur der *bouts-rimés* evoziert die Vorstellung von Verknüpfung und Variation – ein kombinatorisches Prinzip, wobei die Findigkeit des Dichters sich gerade dadurch erweist, dass sie sich innerhalb bestimmter Vorgaben entfalten muss.[24] Ebenso auffällig ist allerdings, dass das Verhältnis des Individuums zu den äußerlichen Begebenheiten anhand der gemeinhin als antithetisch aufgefassten Begriffe *Zweck* und *Zufall* thematisiert wird. Wir finden bei Novalis auch zwei verschiedene Modelle, die sich wie das Ideal einer Gesamtkomposition lesen und beide das Verhältnis des Individuums

---

[24] In diesem Sinne deutet sie Oskar Walzel als Hinweis auf eine »Variationstechnik«, bei der die »Romangestalten im Sinne von Thesis, Antithesis und Synthesis« geordnet werden (Walzel, 417), während John Neubauer das kombinatorische Prinzip betont (Neubauer, 140f.). In ihrer detaillierten Analyse der *bouts-rimés* als Lyrik- und Textform führt Erica Greber diese Interpretationen ein Stück weiter, indem sie ein Kalkül konstatiert, das »die Kategorien des strukturalistischen Modells von Propp/Lévi-Strauss/Greimas vorausdenkt: Aktanten und Funktionen – die Atome der Textgenerierung als Inventar von Kombinationen« (479).

zum Zufall thematisieren. Allerdings sind sie auf den ersten Blick nur schwer miteinander zu vereinbaren. Einerseits lesen wir im direkten Zusammenhang mit der *bouts-rimés*-Analogie:

> Das Individuum wird das Vollkommenste, das *rein Systematische* seyn, das nur durch einen *einzigen abs[oluten] Zufall* individualisirt ist – z.B. durch seine Geburt. In diesem Zufall müssen alle seine übrige Zufälle, die unendliche Reihe seiner Zustände, eingeschachtelt liegen, oder noch besser, als seine Zufälle, seine Zustände determinirt seyn. Ableitung eines individuellen Lebens aus einem einzigen Zufalle – einem einzigen Act der Willkühr (*NS*, II, 579f.).

Andererseits wird in Novalis' *Blüthenstaub* eindeutig erklärt:

> Alle Zufälle unsers Lebens sind Materialien, aus denen wir machen können, was wir wollen. Wer viel Geist hat, macht viel aus seinem Leben – Jede Bekanntschaft, jeder Vorfall wäre für den durchaus Geistigen – erstes Glied einer unendlichen Reihe – Anfang eines unendlichen Romans (*NS*, II, 437f.).

Beide Zitate konzipieren das individuelle Menschenleben als eine Reihe verketteter Ereignisse, die dem Individuum als Zufälle erscheinen – eine Reihe, die mit der Setzung eines spezifischen Zufalls anhebt. Während aber im zweiten Fall das Individuum die Zufälle aktiv und zielgerichtet verwertet, wobei ein Handlungsfreiraum impliziert wird, Zufälle als *Möglichkeiten* erkennen zu können, erscheint im ersten das Individuum weitgehend determiniert. Im zweiten Fall handelt es sich um eine unendliche *vorwärts*gerichtete Entwicklung, im ersten um die *Zurück*führung auf einen unhintergehbaren Anfangspunkt.
Wenn jedoch angenommen wird, dass der »durchaus Geistige« nicht nur seine Umstände erkennt, sondern auch sich selbst, dann lässt sich das erste Zitat in die Richtung lesen, dass im absoluten Zufall (der u.a. deswegen *absolut* ist, weil er allein sich dem Zugriff oder der unmittelbaren Erkenntnis des Individuums entzieht) alle Eigenschaften vereint liegen, deren Zusammensetzung und Entfaltung das Individuum konstituieren, und somit bestimmen, welche Zufälle er (aktiv) verwertet. In diesem Sinne ist es gerade der *Zufall*, der die Einheit der äußeren Handlung und der inneren Bildung markiert. Das Individuum, selbst niemals imstande, die unendliche Reihe seines Lebens zu überblicken, erlebt den Zufall als eine Art Momentaufnahme. Wenn der Zufall (oder die Konvergenz von mehreren Zufällen) auf diese Art als die Markierung eines bestimmten *Wissensstands* konzeptualisiert wird, so erweist er sich nicht nur als Glied einer unendlichen Reihe, sondern *stellt* diese gewissermaßen erst *her*, indem er stets gleichzeitig in zwei

Richtungen zeigt. Einerseits weist er auf alle Vorbedingungen zurück, die in einer gegebenen Situation kulminieren. Andererseits deutet er auf alle Perspektiven voraus, die sich aus derselben entwickeln lassen.

Es ist in dieser Kapazität, dass er im *Ofterdingen*-Romanfragment nicht nur als Erzählmoment eingesetzt wird, sondern als solches herausgehoben und *reflektiert* wird. Zur Erinnerung: Am Anfang des Romans äußert Heinrich (vorausblickend oder *a priori*) die Vermutung, dass sein Traum (selbst eine in sich kohärente Geschichte, die allerdings dadurch Fragment bleibt, dass Heinrich an entscheidender Stelle von der Mutter geweckt wird), der Auslöser einer großen Veränderung in seinem Leben sein wird. Nachdem der Vater seine Geschichte erzählt, entsteht die Vermutung (zurückblickend oder *a posteriori*), dass die beiden Träume in einem Zusammenhang stehen, der auf einen Grund hindeutet.

Sechs Kapitel später unterscheidet der Erzähler zwischen zwei Arten von Menschen.[25] Die ersten sind die Helden, die zum Handeln Geborenen, die »selbst im Drange großer Begebenheiten den Faden ihres Zwecks« festhalten können (*NS*, I, 266): »*Alle Zufälle werden zu Geschichten unter ihrem Einfluß*, und ihr Leben ist eine ununterbrochene Kette merkwürdiger und glänzender, verwickelter und seltsamer Ereignisse« (266; Hervorhebung D.A.). Denen werden jene ruhigen Menschen gegenübergestellt, deren »Thätigkeit die Betrachtung, deren Leben ein leises Bilden ihrer innern Kräfte ist« (266). Nur kurzzeitig treten sie in den »raschen Wirbel« der »zahllosen Erscheinungen der Welt« ein (267), wobei ihr »empfindlicher Sinn« es ihnen ermöglicht, »die überraschendsten Entdeckungen in sich selbst über das Wesen und die Bedeutung« der Welt zu machen (267). Die Dichter, die »allein den Namen eines Weisen mit Recht« (267) führen, werden eher mit dem zweiten Typus identifiziert. Heinrich, heißt es, war »von Natur zum Dichter geboren« (267). Er »sah die Welt in ihren großen und abwechselnden Verhältnissen vor sich liegen«, aber noch war sie stumm (268). »*Mannichfaltige Zufälle schienen sich zu seiner Bildung zu vereinigen*, und noch hatte nichts seine innere Regsamkeit gestört« (267f.; Hervorhebung D.A.).

Im ersten Fall geht es darum, die Möglichkeiten, die jede Situation bietet, *zweckmäßig* zu nutzen. Das heißt, rational unter den Bedingungen der Unsicherheit zu handeln, verschiedene Alternativen gegeneinander abzuwägen, die wahrscheinlich günstigsten zu bestimmen und *einer* Zukunftsperspektive allen anderen gegenüber den Vorzug zu geben. Jede Entscheidung bedingt

---

[25] An einer Stelle, die kurz darauf mit den Worten »Diese Reise war nun geendigt« (*NS*, I, 268) als eine Schlüsselstelle im Roman markiert wird.

die Umstände der nächsten, sodass sie sich (im Nachhinein) als ununterbrochene Kette erkennen lassen. Dass solche Handlungen stets auf der Basis unvollständiger Information geschehen, wird dadurch unterstrichen, dass die Ergebnisse sich als »merkwürdig« herausstellen können. Solche Etappen werden hier *Geschichten* genannt. In Heinrichs Fall wird die Blickrichtung umgekehrt. Alle Ereignisse, die zum Zeitpunkt ihres (isolierten) Auftretens als Zufälle wahrgenommen wurden, scheinen nun – das operative Wort ist *scheinen* – in der Kombination zunehmend auf einen Grund, eine unbekannte Wirkung hinzuweisen. Hervorzuheben ist auch, dass der Vorgang auf einen Zweck ausgerichtet zu sein scheint, der durch Heinrichs angeborene Veranlagung bestimmt wurde: seine Bildung zum Dichter.

Die Ähnlichkeit zu den zwei oben skizzierten Modellen ist markant – mit dem Unterschied, dass hier die beschränkte Perspektive der Figuren als Ansatz gewählt wird. Allerdings wird diese gerade dadurch markiert, dass der Erzähler sich von ihr löst und in seinem Exkurs über die Natur verschiedenartiger Menschentypen die Frage mitthematisiert, wie ihr Leben zu erzählen wäre. Im gleichen Zuge weist er auch auf die Herrschaft des Autors über die Individuen, Begebenheiten und deren Verknüpfung hin, wobei diese zumindest zu dem Grad einschränkt wird, als die Bindung an bestimmte Verknüpfungsregeln suggeriert wird.

Welche Bedeutung dem Begriff des Zufalls beigemessen werden kann, zeigt auch der Vergleich mit der Anfangskonstellation des Romans. Einerseits wird in der Verkettung von zufälligen Begebenheiten (die chronologische Erzählung der Reise von Eisenach nach Augsburg) eine lineare Progression erkennbar,[26] andererseits bleibt diese Entwicklung stets in der Schwebe zwischen einem ungewissen Endziel und einem hypothetischen Anfangsgrund. Der Zufall als ein momentaner Wissensstand wäre erst dann überwunden, wenn beide Perspektiven ineinander aufgingen. Dieser Zustand (bei dem absolute Gewissheit und Notwendigkeit gleichsam zusammenfallen würden) ist aber nie zu erreichen, solange der Prozess der Vor- und Zurückdeutung aufrechterhalten wird, sondern kann nur graduell angenähert werden.

Wie eine Auflösung aussehen könnte, wird (wie Bomski zeigt) im Klingsohr-Märchen symbolisiert. Sie wird aber auch an anderer Stelle durch die Etablierung einer weiteren Erzählinstanz fingiert. Denn durch den Roman hinweg werden immer wieder Zufälle zu Geschichten. Am deutlichsten wird dies in einer der Geschichten, die von einer Gruppe mitreisender

---

26 Die allerdings auch in der Vernetzung einer Vielzahl von Zufällen *extensive Züge vorweist*.

Kaufleute erzählt wird. Die Erzählung, die von der Vereinigung der Poesie (symbolisiert durch eine Königstochter) mit der Natur (symbolisiert durch einen im Wald lebenden Jüngling) im Reich Atlantis handelt, ähnelt in Stoff und Form einem Märchen, wird aber als *Geschichte* ausgewiesen. Und zwar als eine, die besonders geeignet wäre, um ihn »mit den Wirkungen jener wunderbaren Kunst« bekannt zu machen (*NS*, I, 213).

Auffällig ist, dass (bis weit in die Geschichte hinein) die Verhältnisse und Entscheidungen durchaus plausibel erklärt oder psychologisch motiviert werden.[27] Ebenso auffallend ist die Ausnahme dazu, nämlich »die Entwickelung [eines] sonderbaren Zufalls« (217), der vom Vater des Jünglings explizit als *Zufall* reflektiert wird. Es handelt sich um die Tatsache, dass die Prinzessin zufällig allein am Landgut des Alten vorbeigeritten ist, gerade als sie der Durst überkam. Auf diese Art begegnet sie dem Jüngling. Hieraus entwickeln sich direkt weitere Zufälle: Nach ihrem Abschied verliert sich der Jüngling im Wald und stolpert über einen Karfunkel, den die Prinzessin zufällig fallen gelassen hatte. Nach mehreren Begegnungen werden sie dann eines Tages von einem Gewitter überrascht, und »sie priesen sich beyde glücklich« (221), als sie eine Höhle entdecken, die ihnen Zuflucht verspricht. »Das Glück begünstigte ihre Wünsche« und die Höhle hält sogar Feuermaterial bereit (221).

Diese subjektive Deutung des Zufalls als *Glück* und *Gunst* wird kurz darauf explizit mit providentiellen Zügen versehen: »Eine höhere Macht«, heißt es, »schien den Knoten schneller lösen zu wollen, und brachte sie unter sonderbaren Umständen in diese romantische Lage« (221). Am nächsten Morgen erwachen sie »in einer neuen seligen Welt« (222) und der Jüngling ist um mehrere Jahre gealtert. Während sie sich gegenseitig ihre Liebe bekennen, verschiebt sich der Fokus auf den König, der glaubt, seine Tochter durch die eigene Strenge und Arroganz verloren zu haben, und seinerseits die Kontingenz weltlicher Verhältnisse weiter reflektiert, indem er sich trauernd überlegt, was möglich gewesen wäre, wenn er sich anders verhalten hätte. Erst am Schluss der Erzählung werden die zwei Protagonisten wieder eingeführt, als alle Dissonanzen im »Geist des Gesangs« (228) aufgelöst werden.

Diese Geschichte kann als die formelhafte Ausführung eines Prinzips betrachtet werden, das sich Novalis notizartig vermerkt: »Roher Zufall – *gebil-*

---

[27] Um nur ein Beispiel zu geben: Die unwahrscheinliche, aber für die Geschichte wichtige Tatsache, dass die Prinzessin weder vom Jüngling noch von seinem Vater erkannt wird, obwohl sie nahe an der Hauptstadt leben, wird dadurch erklärt, dass beide, in ihre Forschungen vertieft, das Gewühl der Menschen zu vermeiden gesucht haben (217).

deter Zufall – Harmonie« (*NS*, III, 304).[28] Sie ist allerdings selbst nur einer von den mannigfaltigen Zufällen, die sich zu Heinrichs Bildung zu vereinen scheinen, und wird als solche Instanz in den Prozess der Vor- und Zurückdeutung eingebunden. Später geschieht dies explizit, als Klingsohr vermutet, dass Heinrichs zufällige Bekanntschaften unbemerkt zu den Stimmen des Geistes der Dichtkunst geworden seien, da in der Nähe des Dichters die Poesie überall ausbricht (283). Die erzählte Auflösung wird selbst als zu deutender Zufall zum Glied eines unendlichen Romans.

IV.

In seinen Kommentaren zur dritten Auflage seiner Übersetzung von Charles Batteux' *Einschränkung der schönen Künste auf einen einzigen Grundsatz* (1770) erzürnt sich Johann Adolf Schlegel über die schwankenden Bedeutungen des Begriffes *Wahrscheinlichkeit*. Den Grund hierfür sieht er darin, dass »in der Geschichte von der Wahrscheinlichkeit eben so viel geredet wird, als in der Poesie«. Oft werden die historischen und poetischen Wahrscheinlichkeitsbegriffe undifferenziert eingesetzt und nichts könne »der poetischen Wahrscheinlichkeit [...] nachtheiliger seyn, als diese Vermischung« (cit. Scharloth, 264f.). Die zwei Konzepte, deren Kontamination hier beklagt wird, fasst Joachim Scharloth konzise zusammen: »Während die Poetik die Ähnlichkeit der Nachahmung mit der empirischen Welt oder deren Vorstellung in den Köpfen der Rezipienten zum Maßstab des Wahrscheinlichen im Sinne des *versimile* machte«, orientierte sich die Historik am Prinzip der »kausalgenetischen Herleitung« (264) bezweifelbarer Ereignisse (*probabile*). Im gleichen Zeitraum war die mathematische Wahrscheinlichkeitstheorie im Begriff, die sichere empirische Erkenntnis auf lediglich wahrscheinliches Wissen einzuschränken, strebte aber gleichzeitig danach, Verfahren bereitzustellen, um Grade der Gewissheit identifizieren, skalieren und vergleichen zu können, und so den menschlichen Umgang mit Unsicherheit zu erleichtern und zu formalisieren. Anhand seines Zufallsbegriffes vergegenwärtigt Novalis diese epochale erkenntnistheoretische Wende und macht sie zu einem Erzählprinzip, das seine eigene Unabschließbarkeit einschließt und *im* Erzählen die nicht einzuholende Unvollständigkeit des modernen Romans zum Roman macht.

---

[28] Oder in der Terminologie der Geschichte: sonderbarer Zufall – Glück/Gunst – höhere Macht/Versöhnung.

Zitierte Literatur

Arndt, Hans-Werner. »Einleitung«. *Johann Heinrich Lambert. Neues Organon. Philosophische Schriften.* Hg. Hans Werner Arndt. Bd. I. Hildesheim: Georg Olms, 1965:V–XXXVIII.

Bomski, Franziska. »Zwischen Mathematik und Märchen. Die Darstellung des Zufalls und ihre erkenntnistheoretische Funktion bei Novalis«. *Kunst und Wissen. Beziehungen zwischen Ästhetik und Erkenntnistheorie im 18. und 19. Jahrhundert.* Hg. Astrid Bauereisen/Stephan Pabst/Achim Vesper. Würzburg: Königshausen & Neumann, 2009: 163–191.

Brown, Gary I. »The Evolution of the Term ›Mixed Mathematics‹«. *Journal of the History of Ideas* 52.1 (1991): 81–102.

Campe, Rüdiger. *Spiel der Wahrscheinlichkeit. Literatur und Berechnung zwischen Pascal und Kleist.* Göttingen: Wallstein, 2002.

Condorcet, Marie-Jean-Antoine-Nicolas Caritat. *Entwurf eines historischen Gemähldes der Fortschritte des menschlichen Geistes.* Übers. Ernst Ludwig Posselt. Tübingen: Cotta, 1796 [1793].

Daiber, Jürgen. *Experimentalphysik des Geistes. Novalis und das romantische Experiment.* Göttingen: Vandenhoeck & Ruprecht, 2001.

Daston, Lorraine. *Classical Probability in the Enlightenment.* Princeton: Princeton University Press, 1988.

Daston, Lorraine. »The History of Emergences«. *Isis* 98.4 (2007): 801–808.

Dyck, Martin. *Novalis and Mathematics. A Study of Friedrich von Hardenberg's Fragments on Mathematics and its Relation to Magic, Music, Religion, Philosophy, Language, and Literature.* Chapel Hill: University of North Carolina Press, 1960.

Franklin, James. *The Science of Conjecture. Evidence and Probability before Pascal.* Baltimore/London: Johns Hopkins University Press, 2001.

Gaier, Ulrich. *Krumme Regel. Novalis' ›Konstruktionslehre des schaffenden Geistes‹ und ihre Tradition.* Tübingen: Niemeyer, 1970.

Gillies, Donald. *Philosophical Theories of Probability.* London/New York: Routledge, 2000.

Gillispie, Charles Coulston. »Probability and Politics: Laplace, Condorcet, and Turgot«. *Proceedings of the American Philosophical Society* 116.1 (1972): 1–20.

Greber, Erika. *Textile Texte. Poetologische Metaphorik und Literaturtheorie. Studien zur Tradition des Wortflechtens und der Kombinatorik.* Köln/Weimar/Wien: Böhlau, 2002.

Hacking, Ian. *The Emergence of Probability. A Philosophical Study of Early Ideas about Probability, Induction and Statistical Inference.* London/New York: Cambridge University Press, 1975.

Hauser, Walter. *Die Wurzeln der Wahrscheinlichkeitsrechnung. Die Verbindung von Glücksspieltheorie und statistischer Praxis vor Laplace.* Stuttgart: Steiner, 1997.

Jahnke, Hans Niels. »Mathematik und Romantik. Die Aphorismen des Novalis zur Mathematik«. *Unikate* 33 (2008): 30–41.

Kavanagh, Thomas M. »Chance and Probability in the Enlightenment«. *French Forum* 15.1 (1990): 5–24.

Lambert, Johann Heinrich. *Neues Organon. 2. Band. Philosophische Schriften.* Hg. Hans-Werner Arndt. Bd. II. Hildesheim: Georg Olms, 1965 [1764].

Laplace, Simon Pierre. *Philosophischer Versuch über Wahrscheinlichkeiten.* Hg. Karl Christian Langsdorf. Nach der dritten Pariser Auflage. Übers. Friedrich Wilhelm Tönnies. Heidelberg: Groos, 1819 [1814].

McLean, Iain/Fiona Hewitt (Hg.). *Condorcet. Foundations of Social Choice and Political Theory.* Aldershot/Brookfield: Edward Elgar, 1994.

Neubauer, John. *Symbolismus und symbolische Logik. Die Idee der ars combinatoria in der Entwicklung der modernen Dichtung.* München: Fink, 1978.

Novalis. *Schriften. Die Werke Friedrich von Hardenbergs. Historisch-kritische Ausgabe in vier Bänden und einem Begleitband.* Hg. Paul Kluckhohn/Richard Samuel. 3. Auflage. Stuttgart/Berlin/Köln/Mainz: Kohlhammer, 1977ff. (*NS*)

Plato, Jan von. *Creating Modern Probability. Its Mathematics, Physics and Philosophy in Historical Perspective.* Cambridge/New York: Cambridge University Press, 1994.

Scharloth, Joachim: »Evidenz und Wahrscheinlichkeit. Wahlverwandtschaften zwischen Romanpoetik und Historik in der Spätaufklärung«. *Literatur und Geschichte. Ein Kompendium zu ihrem Verhältnis von der Aufklärung bis zur Gegenwart.* Hg. Daniel Fulda/Silvia Serena Tschopp. Berlin/New York: de Gruyter, 2002: 247–275.

Schlesinger, George N. »The Credibility of Extraordinary Events«. *Analysis* 51.3 (1991): 120–126.

Schiewer, Gesine Lenore. *Cognitio symbolica. Lamberts semiotische Wissenschaft und ihre Diskussion bei Herder, Jean-Paul und Novalis.* Tübingen: Niemeyer, 1996.

Schnyder, Peter. *Alea. Zählen und Erzählen im Zeichen des Glücksspiels 1650–1850.* Göttingen: Wallstein, 2009.

Uerlings, Herbert. *Friedrich von Hardenberg, genannt Novalis. Werk und Forschung.* Stuttgart: Metzler, 1991.

Vogl, Joseph. *Kalkül und Leidenschaft. Poetik des ökonomischen Menschen.* München: Sequenzia, 2002.

Walzel, Oskar. »Die Formkunst von Hardenbergs ›Heinrich von Ofterdingen‹«. *Germanisch-Romanische Monatsschrift* 7 (1915–1919): 403–444; 465–479.

Ralf Beuthan *(Myongji University)*

Produktive Reflexion. Überlegungen zum Produktionsbegriff im Ausgang von Fichte und Derrida

Abstract

The basic claim of this paper is that the idea of ›work‹ not only finds itself in a crisis these days but also represents a paradigm shift in the contemporary way of thinking within modern philosophy. The article will focus on this paradigm shift concerning the idea of ›productivity‹. In a conceptual montage of Fichte's proto-Romantic idea of subjectivity and Derrida's anti-romantic critique of subjectivity, I will argue that we may conceive the change within the modern and the common idea of a fundamental productivity as a shift from the principle of reflexivity to the principle of media.

I. Vorbemerkung: Arbeit und Produktion

Es ist ein für unser Selbstverständnis und unsere Zeit interessantes Indiz, dass ein Leitbegriff moderner Gesellschaften westlichen Zuschnitts in die Krise geraten scheint, nämlich der Begriff der ›Arbeit‹. Arbeit, so könnte man sagen, basiert nicht nur auf dem Verbrauch von Energieressourcen, von denen sich manche dramatisch verknappen, sondern erscheint im gesellschaftlich-ökonomischen Leben selbst als eine knappe Ressource – mit zum Teil verheerenden Konsequenzen für die Menschen und ihre sogenannten ›Erwerbsbiographien‹. Arbeit ist nicht nur aus externen, materiellen Gründen, sondern vor allem aufgrund ihrer Verflechtung mit der Ordnung des Ökonomischen krisenanfällig. Die ökonomischen, technologischen und gesellschaftspolitischen Ursachen und Folgen des Rückgangs institutionell gesicherter und bezahlter Arbeit werden breit diskutiert. Ich möchte mit den folgenden Überlegungen nicht – oder zumindest nicht direkt – etwas zu dieser Diskussion beitragen. Vielmehr möchte ich eine für den Arbeitsbegriff, wie ich meine, maßgebende begriffliche Komponente fokussieren: den Gedanken der ›Produktion‹. Dieser Gedanke ist zweifelsohne auch in unserem alltäglichen Verständnis von Arbeit enthalten, insofern wir mit Arbeit fast immer so etwas wie ein ›Hervorbringen‹ und ›Formieren von etwas‹ verbinden. Der Gedanke der Produktion markiert aber auch ein zentrales Motiv der modernen Geistesgeschichte – insbesondere im Horizont der Romantik –, welches in verschiedenen ästhetischen und theoretischen Formen reflektiert wird. Anhand zweier theoretisch radikaler Positionen will ich versuchen, den systematischen Stellenwert des Produktionsbegriffs, aber auch einen signifikanten Wandel im Produktions-Denken zu beleuchten. Nur am Schluss, nach diesem Umweg über den Begriff der Produktion, will ich ausblickhaft versuchen, einige kurze Bemerkungen zur Krise des Arbeitsbegriffs zu machen.

Meine Überlegungen zum Produktions-Denken sind eher als eine Art ›Entdeckungsreise‹, denn als bündig durchargumentierte Konstruktion eines Konzepts zu verstehen. Es geht darum, im Rahmen eines Experiments gedankliche Motive freizulegen, die mit dem Produktions-Denken verbunden sind; und es geht darum, Bruchlinien innerhalb des modernen Produktionskonzepts zu sondieren. Für dieses Experiment habe ich zwei Autoren gewählt, deren Denkstile unterschiedlicher kaum sein könnten: Fichte und Derrida – d.h. zum einen den Denker, der im Anschluss an Kant wegweisend ebenso für den Deutschen Idealismus (und andere Letztbegründungsphilosophien) wie für die romantische Innerlichkeit und Subjektivitätsphilosophien war, und zum anderen einen Denker, der als ein Schlüsseldenker der Postmoderne und als raffiniertester Kritiker von Letztbegründungsphilosophien und Subjektivitätstheorien gelten kann. Fichte und Derrida in einer Art Kontrastmontage zusammenzustellen, ohne den Übergang etwa durch eine Einflussgeschichte zu ›legitimieren‹, mag an jene surreale »Begegnung eines Regenschirms mit einer Nähmaschine auf dem Seziertisch« (Lautréamont) erinnern. Nur ist der Anspruch natürlich nicht der, dass dieses Zusammentreffen schön, sondern nur, dass es philosophisch interessant sein möge, sprich: dass sich hier auf einer konzeptionellen Ebene etwas entdecken lassen möge.

Die Annahme, dass diese experimentelle Zusammenstellung von Fichte und Derrida interessant sein könnte, hat – das will ich wenigstens andeuten – damit zu tun, dass beide Denker trotz der sehr unterschiedlichen Denkstile und Aufgabenstellungen mindestens in einer Hinsicht konvergieren: Beide konfrontieren die philosophische Reflexion mit den Grenzen des Denkbaren; beide thematisieren mit begrifflichen Mitteln etwas Unbegreifliches. Und der systematische Kern dessen, was jeweils als ein Unbegreifliches theoretisch umkreist wird, ist – so meine These – der Gedanke einer fundamentalen Produktivität. Fundamental ist die Produktivität – das wird zu zeigen sein –, weil sie unser Selbstverhältnis, unser Weltverhältnis sowie die Welt selbst überhaupt erst zu ermöglichen scheint.

II. Fichte: Von der Selbsttätigkeit zur Produktivität

Fichte als Kantianer. Transzendentalphilosophie und Praxisprimat

Wenden wir uns zunächst Fichte zu. Fichtes Theorie erscheint als durchaus ambivalent. Einerseits radikalisiert er das Kant'sche Letztbegründungsunternehmen; andererseits entwickelt er eben dazu einen Gedanken, der sich wie ein Sprengsatz auf die Systemansprüche auswirken konnte. In Umkehrung eines vielzitierten Wortes könnte man sagen: »Wo die Rettung ist, wächst die Gefahr«.
Woher diese Ambivalenz? Um dies zu verstehen, ist zunächst zu sehen, dass Fichte in doppelter Weise an Kant anschließt. Zum einen folgt er der transzendentalen Aufgabenstellung: der Analyse der ›Bedingungen der Möglichkeit von Erkenntnis‹. Die darin enthaltene Theorie der Subjektivität und Begründung einer gesetzlich geregelten Totalität von Objekten (= Natur) fasst Fichte lakonisch zu der »Frage nach der Objektivität der Welt« (*WLnm*, 4)[1] zusammen. Mit dieser Frage markiert er sogleich seine Nähe zu Kant und seinen Abstand zu den Romantikern. Fichte wird sie entschieden zugunsten der Objektivität und d.h. zugunsten ›objektiver Erkenntnis‹ beantworten. Die skeptischen Einreden gegen ›objektive Erkenntnis‹ und die romantischen Vorstellungen einer sich unendlich ausdehnenden Innerlichkeit werden durch seine transzendentalphilosophische Begründung von Objektivität in ihre Grenzen gewiesen.
Zum andern folgt Fichte Kant nicht nur darin, dass er die epistemologische Grundthese (Objektivität) und den argumentativen Ansatz (Transzendentalphilosophie) übernimmt, sondern vielmehr auch darin, dass er Kants Primat der Praxis und seine Freiheitsidee weiterdenkt. Dabei wird unser theoretischer Weltzugang gerade so konzipiert, dass Freiheit – selbstbestimmtes Handeln aus Gründen – als möglich gedacht werden kann.
Doch wäre es nur so, dass unser theoretisches Weltverhältnis Freiheit nicht ausschließen darf, dann wäre Fichte wohl nur ein Kant-Epigone geblieben. Er geht jedoch einen entscheidenden Schritt weiter und macht *prima facie* Ernst mit Kants Primat einer praktischen Vernunft gegenüber der theoretischen.

---

[1] Hier wie im Folgenden beziehe ich mich vor allem auf Fichtes *Wissenschaftslehre nova methodo* (1798/99) (*WLnm*), die im Wesentlichen keine Abweichung von seiner berühmten *Grundlage der gesamten Wissenschaftslehre* (1794) darstellt, aber gegenüber dieser den Gedanken der Produktivität deutlicher herausarbeitet. Vgl. dazu den sehr aufschlussreichen Aufsatz von Loock, »Fichtes Wechselwirkung und der implizite Hörer der ›Wissenschaftslehre nova methodo‹«.

Der springende Punkt ist der, dass Fichte den Freiheitsgedanken an die Spitze seiner Theorie stellt und aus ihm unser theoretisches Weltverhältnis herleitet. Um diesen Schritt über Kant hinaus deutlich werden zu lassen, möchte ich es so formulieren: Kant konzipierte unser erkennendes Weltverhältnis so, dass Freiheit theoretisch möglich ist; Fichte hingegen entwickelt den Sachzusammenhang von theoretischer und praktischer Vernunft mit einer anderen Stoßrichtung, nämlich so, dass Objektivität möglich ist, weil Freiheit in uns wirklich ist. Diese Wendung hat tiefgreifende Konsequenzen, unter anderem jene Ambivalenz, die Fichte sowohl als Kantianer als auch als Romantiker erscheinen lässt.

Fichtes These. Vom Primat des Tuns gegenüber dem Sein. Übergang zum Produktionsdenken

Fichte geht also zunächst im Anschluss an Kant von einem Praxisprimat innerhalb der Architektonik der Vernunft aus und radikalisiert diesen. »Freiheit«, so lautet seine These, »ist [...] der erste Grund und die erste Bedingung alles Seins und alles Bewusstseins« (*WLnm*, 46). Es ist hier freilich nicht der Ort, den daraus resultierenden äußerst komplizierten Argumentationsgang auch nur annäherungsweise nachzuzeichnen. Einige mit dieser These verknüpfte Grundgedanken sollen an dieser Stelle reichen:
(i) Die für den Theorieaufbau zentrale Freiheitsthese enthält die anti-dogmatistische Überzeugung, dass das Begründungsfundament ein freies Tun (= Handeln) sein muss. Der Ausgang von einem *Tun*, statt von einem *Sein*, und die Ableitung des Seins aus einem ursprünglichen Tun heraus – dies charakterisiert den Praxisprimat des Fichte'schen Ansatzes.
(ii) Doch warum kommt diesem Tun das Prädikat ›frei‹ zu? – Fichtes Grundgedanke ist: Das ursprüngliche (= allem Sein logisch vorausgehende) Tun ist frei, weil es *selbstbestimmt* (autonom) ist. Der für die Fichte'sche Theorie entscheidende Punkt ist der, wie der Gedanke der *Selbstbestimmung* konzeptionalisiert werden kann. Dies ist der Dreh- und Angelpunkt seiner gesamten Theorie.[2] Das leitende Problem kommt hier noch überhaupt nicht in den Blick, wenn man Selbstbestimmung denkt als ›nicht von außen bestimmt‹. Dann wäre z.B. Freiheit auch als ›Nicht-bestimmt-Sein‹ oder als Indifferenz denkbar. Doch das ist eben nicht Fichtes These. Freiheit heißt für ihn Selbst-

---

[2] Vgl. dazu die detaillierte Untersuchung von Schwabe, *Individuelles und transindividuelles Ich*. – Schwabe entwickelt Fichtes Theorie sehr überzeugend auf der Folie einer »Theorie des Bestimmens« (vgl. insbes. 177ff.).

bestimmung, und die leitende Frage ist, wie hier überhaupt Bestimmtheit, und d.h. auch: Unterschied, gedacht werden kann, wenn die Bestimmung nicht von außen (= Fremdbestimmung) kommen soll.
(iii) Fichtes Entdeckung ist, dass die Strukturmomente der Selbstbestimmung in einem ursprünglichen, d.h. vorbewussten, Tun beschlossen sind, welches uns allerdings durch eine kleine, aber entscheidende Umlenkung der Aufmerksamkeit bewusst werden kann. Wir müssen nur, so Fichtes Überzeugung, unsere Aufmerksamkeit von dem abziehen, worauf sie üblicherweise gerichtet ist – nämlich Gegenstände –, und müssen stattdessen unsere Aufmerksamkeit auf unser Denken selbst im Erfassen der Gegenstände lenken. Indem wir unsere Denktätigkeit nicht auf externe Inhalte richten, sondern auf sich selbst zurückwenden, haben wir eben in diesem Tun einen Zugang zu dem ursprünglichen Tun gewonnen, das im Weiteren als Theoriefundament dienen soll. Dass dieses Tun – die *in sich selbst zurücklaufende Denktätigkeit* – dann als Modell für die Gewinnung der Strukturmomente der Selbstbestimmung fungieren kann, wird deutlich, wenn man sich auf die dabei gewonnene Grundstruktur besinnt: Es ist die Struktur einer in sich zurückgebogenen Tätigkeit, oder kurz: die Struktur »*reiner Reflexion*« (*WLnm*, 34). Und Fichtes subjektivitätstheoretische Pointe lautet: Dieses Tun ist nichts anderes als das Ich selbst. Und das Ich ist nichts anderes als eine solche in sich zurücklaufende Tätigkeit.
(iv) Welche Strukturmomente ergeben sich daraus für ein Konzept der Selbstbestimmung? Beziehungsweise: Wie kommt Bestimmtheit in die Selbstbestimmung? – Halten wir zunächst die beiden begrifflichen Komponenten fest, die gerade genannt wurden: Die gesuchte Struktur wird generiert durch eine *Tätigkeit,* eine »Agilität« (*WLnm*, 32), die nur insofern bestimmt ist, als sie sich nur auf sich selbst bezieht. Wenn man so will, könnte man sagen: Die Substanz dieser Struktur ist nichts als reine Tätigkeit. Und die Struktur als solche ist die Struktur der *Reflexion,* d.h. eine Relation der Selbstbeziehung. *Agilität* und *Reflexivität* sind also die ersten beiden Komponenten, die zu berücksichtigen sind. Darin zeichnet sich bereits eine Antwort auf die Frage nach der Bestimmtheit ab: Bestimmtheit kommt ins Spiel, weil hier eine tätige Beziehung zu denken ist, die zwar bis dato kein externes Relat, aber dennoch mindestens ein Relat erkennen lässt, nämlich sich selbst. Das bedeutet, diese Beziehung ist nicht ganz unbestimmt, da sie eben ein bestimmtes Relat hat. Und es hat eine gewisse Plausibilität, wenn Fichte uns zu verstehen geben will, dass diese reine Selbstbeziehung, deren Bestimmtheit nur als Resultat der Selbstbeziehung gedacht werden soll, den Kern dessen ausmacht, was wir ein ›Ich‹ nennen.

(v) Doch eine entscheidende, besser noch: die eigentlich Fichte'sche, Komponente ist damit noch nicht benannt. Fichte betont nämlich, dass die angedeutete Bestimmtheit wesentlich als ein *Produkt* zu denken ist. Die Bestimmtheit, ein Ich zu sein, ist allererst durch die tätige Selbstbeziehung produziert. Das heißt, sie ist erst durch diese Tätigkeit ›hervorgebracht‹, sie hat kein ›Bestehen‹ vor der Tätigkeit, sondern *ist* erst durch die reflexive Tätigkeit, ist deren Resultat. Insofern die Bestimmtheit aber nicht nur durch die reflexive Tätigkeit produziert wird – Fichte spricht hier immer von einem »Setzen« –, sondern eben auch nichts anderes ist als diese reflexive Tätigkeit, kommt es zu einer Struktur besonderer Art: Das Ich ist nämlich eben die Struktur, in der *Produktion* und *Produkt* schlechthin identisch sind. Fichte nennt diesen Sachverhalt, in der die freie Tätigkeit (= Handlung) und das Produkt dieser Tätigkeit identisch sind, bekanntermaßen »Tathandlung«. Die Pointe seiner Theorie macht also nicht einfach der Gedanke aus, dass das Ich etwas ist, was mit sich identisch ist, sondern der, dass das Ich etwas ist, das sich hervorgebracht hat. Und das bedeutet eben auch: Bestimmtheit wird hier wesentlich als Resultat eines Produktionsprozesses, kurz: als Produkt, gedacht. Die für den Gedanken der Bestimmtheit notwendige Differenz wird also im Rahmen der Idee absoluter (unbeschränkter) Selbstbestimmung vor allem durch den Unterschied zwischen Produktion und Produkt (mit Fichte gesprochen: zwischen »Setzen« und »Gesetztsein«) gewonnen.

(vi) Indem Fichte das Ich bzw. die Selbstbestimmung, also die *produktive Reflexion*, zum Prinzip seiner Theorie gemacht hat, lässt sich bereits erahnen, dass der Gedanke der Produktivität auf das damit Prinzipierte durchschlägt. Und tatsächlich: Der Strukturzusammenhang von Produktion und Produkt spielt in der Deduktion sowohl des praktischen als auch des theoretischen Weltverhältnisses eine zentrale Rolle. Dabei ist zunächst zu sehen, dass Fichte in der *Wissenschaftslehre nova methodo* – anders als noch vier Jahre zuvor in der *Grundlage* – grundsätzlich nicht mehr das Theoretische vom Praktischen trennt. Fichte unterscheidet freilich noch den *theoretischen Bezug* auf einen gegebenen Gegenstand von einem *praktischen Weltverhältnis*, dem Realisieren eines nur gedachten Zwecks, aber er entwickelt das Theoretische und Praktische nicht mehr getrennt. Mehr noch, er denkt beides als wesentlich nicht voneinander trennbar. Praktisches und theoretisches Weltverhältnis bedingen sich wechselseitig. – Das Prinzip der produktiven Reflexion kommt dabei vor allem in drei Hinsichten zum Tragen: (1) Die Produktivität der Selbstbestimmung zeigt sich innerhalb des Beweisgangs zunächst sinnfällig in der Konstruktion unseres praktischen Weltverhältnisses, insofern die Selbstbestimmung des Ich für Fichte das *Hervorbringen eines Zweckbegriffs* und ferner das Realisieren eines Zweckbegriffs impliziert. Unser Weltverhältnis erweist sich insofern im Kern als ein ›Machen‹. Diese *Primordialität des Hervorbringens gegenüber dem Finden* betont Fichte zum Beispiel, wenn er sagt: »Es ist kein Objekt als Objekt unmittelbar Gegenstand des Bewusstseins, sondern nur das Machen, die Freiheit« (*WLnm*, 50). Wenig später heißt es dann lapidar: »Vor dem Akte der Freiheit ist nichts, mit ihm wird alles, was da ist« (*WLnm*, 50). Dabei wird deutlich, dass Fichte – anders als Kant – den praktischen Grundzug unseres Weltbezugs bereits in ein produktives Weltverhältnis transformiert hat. (2) Diese Produktivität schlägt durch den konstitutiven Zusammenhang von Theorie und Praxis bzw. von Finden und Tun unmittelbar durch auf unseren Objektbegriff, oder allgemeiner: auf die Gestalt der Welt. Fichtes gleichsam ›idealistischer Pragmatismus‹ enthält nämlich die These, dass die Erscheinung der Objekte bedingt ist durch unsere Zweckbegriffe bzw. durch den Wert, den sie für unser Handeln haben. Beides gehört – entsprechend der These vom konstitutiven Zusammenhang von Theorie und Praxis – für ihn untrennbar zusammen: »Das Denken eines Zwecks und das eines Objekts sind eigentlich dasselbe« (*WLnm*, 183). Darin liegt zugleich die Idee, dass unsere Zwecksetzungen und -realisierungen nicht nur unsere Praxis leiten, sondern eben auch eine *theoretische, welterschließende Funktion* haben. Es gibt, so die Fichte'sche These, keine Objektbegriffe ohne Zweckbegriffe. Oder anders: Es gibt keine Objekte ohne Praxis. Doch diese pragmatistische Seite Fichtes darf nicht vergessen lassen, dass sie auf der Idee wesentlich freier Zwecksetzungen basiert, d.h., dass dieser Pragmatismus nur eine Konsequenz der produktiven Reflexion ist.[3] (3) Fichtes zentrale Idee, dass letztlich praktische (zwecksetzende) und theoretische (objektfindende) Vernunft nicht zu trennen sind, ist vor allem eine Reaktion auf ein fundamentales Problem Kants, nämlich die Frage, wie die Einheit der Vernunft bzw. die Einheit von Freiheit und sinnlicher Welt gedacht werden kann. Fichtes Kritik an Kant markiert sogleich den ganzen Unterschied: die Entdeckung der Produktivität im praktischen und theoretischen Weltverhältnis. Fichtes Problemdiagnose kulminiert in der These, dass Kant die Produktivität des Ich nicht hinreichend gesehen hatte. Er konnte, so Fichtes Überzeugung, die Kluft zwischen dem Reich der Freiheit und dem Reich der Natur nicht schließen, weil er »in der Kritik der reinen Vernunft das Ich einseitig und nur als das Mannigfaltige *ordnend*, nicht aber

---

[3] Vgl. *WLnm*, 200f.: »Der Zweckbegriff ist nichts gegebenes, sondern er ist mit meinem Wissen durch mich selbst hervorgebracht; dies mein Hervorbringen ist das eigentliche Objekt meines Bewusstseins«.

als *produzierend* dachte« (*WLnm*, 124; Hervorhebung R.B.). Fichtes eigene Theorie versucht, diesen Mangel zu beheben, indem er einen zentralen Terminus Kants aufgreift und radikalisiert: den Begriff der »produktiven Einbildungskraft« (*WLnm*, 199ff.). Der springende Punkt ist hier der, dass Fichte die Produktivität der Einbildungskraft neu fasst: Die Einbildungskraft sichert nicht mehr nur die Anwendbarkeit unserer Kategorien auf sinnlich Gegebenes (durch die Verzeitlichung der Kategorien), sondern sie produziert selbst auch die Materie, auf die die Kategorien angewandt werden können. Mit dieser radikalen Erweiterung der Funktion produktiver Einbildungskraft hat Fichte mit einem Schlage den Gedanken des »Dings an sich« verabschiedet und zugleich Kants Praxisprimat im Prinzip in einen Primat der Produktivität verwandelt. Der Gedanke der »produktiven Einbildungskraft« ist ohne Frage ein Schlüsselbegriff der Fichte'schen Theorie und nicht zuletzt ob seiner fundamentalen Rolle ein schwer zu fassender Begriff. Die nähere Erläuterung dieses Konzepts würde den Rahmen hier sprengen.[4]

Fichtes Protoromantik

Die vorangegangene Skizze einiger Fichte'scher Grundgedanken sollte vor allem verdeutlichen, wie sich hier im Anschluss an Kants Idee einer freien Vernunft ein für die nach-Kant'sche Moderne wegweisendes gedankliches Motiv entwickelt hat: das Motiv einer allen Oppositionen vorausgehenden, sie erzeugenden und übergreifenden Produktivität. Dieses Motiv markiert sogleich einen kritischen Punkt innerhalb seiner Theorie, mehr noch: innerhalb der nach-Kantischen Moderne. Es ermöglicht nämlich zwei grundsätzlich unterschiedene Theorieprogramme: einerseits eine Vertiefung der Transzendentalphilosophie in Richtung eines Systemdenkens,[5] andererseits die Demontage des Systemdenkens. Fichte, so sollte deutlich geworden sein, entwickelt das Motiv zugunsten der ersten Richtung. Doch die Ironie der Geschichte ist, dass er mit der Entdeckung jener ursprünglichen Produktivität (welche im selbstbestimmten Ich beschlossen ist) zugleich einen Gedanken für seine Zeitgenossen in die Welt gebracht hatte, der ausgerechnet wegweisend für eine Tendenz werden konnte, die später als romantische Systemkritik Epoche machen sollte.

---

[4] Vgl. dazu die umfangreiche und meines Wissens beste Monographie zu diesem Thema von Loock, *Schwebende Einbildungskraft*.
[5] Fichte selbst verfolgt diese Richtung, Schelling und Hegel werden sie auf die Spitze treiben.

Fichte selbst sieht freilich diese Ambivalenz, die eigentümliche Spannung zwischen dem Transparenzprinzip, dem Sich-durchsichtig-Sein des selbstbestimmten Ich und einer zuletzt opaken Produktivität. Beides gehört zu seinem Prinzip der Selbstbestimmung (qua produktiver Reflexion). Dass er mit dem Gedanken der Produktivität den Boden für die Romantik bereitet hat, kündigt sich an, wenn er z.B. nicht nur sagt: »[D]ieses Sich-Bestimmen ist der absolute Anfang alles Lebens und Bewusstseins [...]« – d.h. eben das Prinzip, dem nichts vorausgeht und aus dem vielmehr alles andere folgt –, sondern ergänzend anmerkt: »[...] eben deshalb ist es *unbegreiflich*« (*WLnm*, 208; Hervorhebung R.B.). Die Betonung der Unbegreiflichkeit jener ursprünglichen Produktivität lässt eben das gedankliche Motiv hervortreten, welches zu einem Topos romantischer Systemkritik werden konnte. Fichte selbst hat es, wie angedeutet, im Rahmen seines Argumentationszusammenhangs zwar gesehen, aber zu revozieren versucht. In diesem Sinne möchte ich ihn als einen Protoromantiker bezeichnen: Er erfand gleichsam den philosophischen Kern der Romantik, ohne selbst Romantiker sein zu wollen. Doch die frühen Romantiker erkannten schnell den romantischen Geist, der in Fiches Theorie wehte. Philosophieren wurde für sie zum »fichtisieren«.[6]

III. Derridas Postromantik

Ich möchte jetzt versuchen, Fichtes Protoromantik mit einer Derrida'schen *Postromantik* zu kontrastieren. In welchem Sinne ich Derrida einen Postromantiker nennen möchte, wird sich dabei zeigen. Ich werde mich nur schlaglichtartig auf zwei Aspekte beziehen, welche für Fichte von zentraler Bedeutung sind: *Subjektivität* und *Produktivität*. Auch wenn Fichte für Derrida kaum eine Rolle gespielt hat (und damit gewissermaßen jenes Missverständnis zu bestätigen scheint, dass Fichte nur eine Übergangsgestalt zwischen Kant und Hegel war) – der mit Fichte in einzigartiger Weise in die Welt gebrachte Zusammenhang zwischen Subjektivität und Produktivität ist auch für Derrida ein Schlüsselthema. Nur sieht die Sache jetzt deutlich anders aus – und es könnte uns auf eine geschichtliche Differenz aufmerksam machen. Derridas Referenzautor ist in dieser Sache Husserl. Husserl ist natürlich nicht einfach mit Fichte gleichzusetzen, aber es kommt hier auch nicht auf Husserl an, sondern nur darauf, wie der Zusammenhang zwischen Subjek-

---

6 So Friedrich Schlegel in einen Brief an Novalis (Schlegel, 363).

tivität und Produktivität von Derrida gedacht wird. In seinem frühen Text *Die Stimme und das Phänomen* (1967) werden wir dazu fündig:
(i) Auch hier bestätigt sich zunächst, was gemeinhin bekannt ist: Derrida ist ein Kritiker von Subjektivitätstheorien. Er kritisiert anhand von Husserl die These, dass wir in unserem Selbstbezug, im Inneren unseres Bewusstseins, auf eine Sphäre absoluter Transparenz stoßen, die dann als Erklärungsfundament für unser Gegenstandsbewusstsein und für Objektivität dienen könnte. – Schauen wir aber vor dem skizzierten Fichte-Hintergrund noch einmal genauer hin. Sogleich fällt dann auf, dass Derrida genau das Motiv infrage stellt, das es Fichte unmöglich machte, ein Romantiker zu werden, und ihn stattdessen vom theoretischen Ansatz her als Kantianer erscheinen ließ: nämlich die Überzeugung, dass Philosophie die Möglichkeit von Objektivität begründen soll. Denn obwohl Fichtes Theorie sowohl pragmatistische als auch romantisch-produktionistische Züge trägt – den Anspruch ›objektiver Erkenntnis‹ hat er gerade nicht preisgegeben. Derrida wird demgegenüber herauszuarbeiten suchen, dass bereits dieser Erkenntnis- und Wahrheitsanspruch den Zugang zu uns selbst und der Welt in einer Weise normiert, die entscheidende Dimensionen ausblendet, ja gleichsam wegrationalisiert. Derrida moniert dabei aber nicht die *transzendentale Reflexion* (auf die Bedingungen der Möglichkeit von Bewusstsein und Gegenständen), sondern nur deren *Restriktion* des Komplexes ›Bewusstsein/Gegenstände‹ auf *Erkenntnis*.
(ii) Doch welche entscheidende Dimension sollte dabei ausgeblendet worden sein? – Um es kurz zu machen: Ausgeblendet wird, nach Derrida, eine Dimension ursprünglicher Produktivität. Doch dann ist zu fragen, warum die transzendentale Reflexion auf ein bewusstseinsimmanentes Begründungsfundament die ursprüngliche Produktivität ausblenden kann, während sie umgekehrt Fichte geradewegs zur Einsicht in eine solche Produktivität führte. Die Antwort liegt darin, dass Husserls Reflexions- bzw. Selbstbewusstseinsbegriff ein vollkommen anderer ist. Zumal Husserls frühe Konzeption auf einer – aus Fichte'scher Perspektive stark verkürzten – Vorstellung von dem basiert, was ein Selbstbewusstsein ist, nämlich eine Reflexion auf sich als etwas unmittelbar Gegebenes. Derrida sieht sehr richtig, dass Selbstbewusstsein bzw. Ichbegriff hier im Kern auf eine Vorstellung unmittelbarer »Selbstgegenwart« (*SuPh*, 82) reduziert ist. Leitend ist bei Husserl, wie Derrida hervorhebt, »die Identität des im selben Augenblick sich selbst gegenwärtigen Erlebnisses« (*SuPh*, 83). Letztlich spielen hier also die beiden für Fichte maßgebenden Merkmale des Ich gar keine Rolle. Weder *Reflexivität* noch *Produktivität* kennzeichnen die Husserl'sche Idee der

»Selbstgegenwärtigkeit« (*SuPh*, 83). Was hier vielmehr gedacht wird, ist das Erlebnis einer »absoluten Nähe zu sich« (*SuPh*, 81) in einem vermeintlich ungeteilten Gegenwartspunkt. Während also Fichte noch die Identität als Resultat einer produktiven Reflexion denkt, wird sie bei Husserl zu einer Art unmittelbarem Identitätserlebnis. Genau besehen zeigt Derridas Kritik also, dass Husserls Fundierungsinstanz der »Selbstgegenwart« nicht nur die Produktivität, sondern auch die Reflexivität, nämlich die in jeder Gegenwart (Unmittelbarkeit) mitzudenkende Vermittlungsstruktur, ausblendet.

(iii) Derridas – an Husserl orientierte – Kritik des Subjektivitätsparadigmas lenkt unsere Aufmerksamkeit anhand bestimmter Inkonsistenzen[7] auf eine der vermeintlichen Fundierungsinstanz logisch vorgeordnete Dimension. Entscheidend, und vielleicht auch nicht mehr so überraschend, ist, dass die der Subjektivität vorgeordnete Dimension nicht einfach nur dunkel ist. Sie ist vielmehr genau durch die Merkmale geprägt, die Husserl aus der Subjektivität um ihres Prinzipienstatus Willen auszuschließen bemüht war: Es ist nämlich eine Dimension, die nicht auf ›Letztgegebenheiten‹ gründet, sondern die durch eine unbedingte (= auf kein Gegebenes zurückführbare) *Vermittlungsbewegung* (vgl. Fichtes Reflexivität) gekennzeichnet ist, die allen positiven Instanzen vorgeordnet ist. Und es ist eine Dimension, deren Prozessualität erst die Identität des Selbst *hervorbringt* (vgl. *SuPh*, 112), die im Erlebnis der Selbstgegenwart unmittelbar gegeben scheint. Es ist also genau die Dimension, der die vermeintlich unmittelbare Selbstgegenwart entspringt. Da Derrida aber bereits mit Husserl davon ausgeht, dass der Subjektbegriff im Kern als unmittelbare Selbstidentität – und nicht etwa als produktive Reflexion – zu denken ist, muss er die ursprüngliche Produktion weitgehend vom Selbstbewusstseinsbegriff abkoppeln. – Damit haben wir zugleich einen signifikanten Unterschied zu Fichte markiert: Während Fichte, wie gesehen, jene ursprüngliche Produktivität als Herzstück der Subjektivität begreift, versucht Derrida, diese Produktivität gerade nicht mehr von der Subjektivität her zu denken. Dieser Unterschied schlägt sich in der Verschiedenheit der Leitbegriffe nieder: Fichte denkt die ursprüngliche Produktivität von der Idee der Freiheit (Selbstbestimmung) her und nennt sie »*Ich*«; Derrida denkt die ursprüngliche Produktivität als eine dem Ich vorgeordnete Dimension und nennt sie, um dabei die Vermittlungsstruktur von der Reflexivität des Ich unterscheiden zu können, »*différance*« (*SuPh*, 112).

---

[7] Vgl. letztlich Derridas Aufweis von Vermittlungsstrukturen in der behaupteten ungeteilten Einheit der Selbstgegenwart; Husserls Unmittelbarkeit »originärer Intuition« erweist sich dabei nur als eine nicht zu Ende gedachte Vermittlung.

(iv) Für Fichte und Derrida gilt aber, dass unser Bewusstsein und seine Ansprüche auf objektives Wissen insgesamt als ein Produkt einer logisch früheren, ›ursprünglichen Produktion‹ aufzufassen ist. Beide haben damit ein analoges Problem: Die ursprüngliche Produktion verdunkelt sich für das daraus entspringende reflexive Bewusstsein zu einer präreflexiven Ursprungsdimension. Doch anders als bei Fichte fällt Derridas Problemlösung salopp gesagt ganz und gar ›unromantisch‹ aus. Denn Fichte entwickelte die ursprüngliche Produktivität noch anhand des Subjektivitäts- und Reflexivitätsparadigmas und gewann damit die für die Romantiker so aufregende Idee einer ins Unendliche über sich hinaustreibenden Reflexionsbewegung. Derridas nüchterne Analyse lässt jedoch im vormaligen Pathos einer erhabenen Bewegtheit unserer Subjektivität eine ganz andere, nicht durch das Subjektivitätsparadigma definierte Bewegtheit erkennen: Das für die Ursprungsdimension konstitutive Vermittlungsgeschehen wird von der Idee einer Reflexionsbewegung losgelöst und als offene Verweisungsstruktur ausgelegt. Dieser zunächst unscheinbare Unterschied hat erhebliche Konsequenzen. Denn der Produktionsbegriff enthält zwar notwendig den Gedanken der Differenz (nur so sind Produktion und Produkt unterscheidbar), aber die Frage ist, wie die notwendige Differenz jeweils gedacht wird. Und es ist zu sehen, dass sich der Gedanke der Differenz bei Fichte und Derrida jeweils ganz unterschiedlichen Prinzipien verdankt: Fichte gewinnt die notwendige Differenz (und letztlich alle Differenzen) durch den Begriff der Reflexion; Derrida – durch Husserls rigorose Verkürzung auf andere Wege gebracht – denkt hingegen eine basale Differenz, die nicht durch die Reflexion erbracht ist, sondern durch die eigentümliche Verweisungsstruktur von Zeichen. In der Analyse dieser Verweisungsstruktur entdeckt er einen Differenzierungsprozess eigener Art: eine mediale Differenzierung. – Um es zusammenzufassen: Fichte entdeckt und konzipiert die ursprüngliche Produktivität vom *Reflexionsprinzip* aus. Damit ist er ein Protoromantiker. Derrida entdeckt die ursprüngliche Produktivität neu, gleichsam ›unter‹ einem verkürzten Subjektbegriff, und konzipiert sie vom *Prinzip der Medialität* aus. D.h., er konzipiert die produktiven Differenzen nicht mehr nach Maßgabe der Subjektivität, sondern anhand medialer Differenzen. Damit ist er ein Postromantiker.

IV. Ausblick: Verändertes Produktionsparadigma und Folgen für den Arbeitsbegriff

Ich habe mit meinem kleinen ›surrealistischen Experiment‹ das Produktions-Denken ins Zentrum gestellt. Es konnte dabei, so hoffe ich, schlaglichtartig deutlich werden, dass das Produktionsdenken in der modernen Geistesgeschichte eine zentrale systematische Rolle spielt und signifikante Veränderung erfährt. Die Geschichte des Wandels des Produktionsdenkens von einem transzendentalphilosophisch geprägten Reflexionsprinzip zu einem subjektkritischen Medialitätsprinzip konnte hier freilich nicht nachgezeichnet werden. Für das Verständnis dieser Geschichte dürften – einmal abgesehen von Fichte und Derrida – Denker wie Schelling, Hegel, Schopenhauer, Marx, Nietzsche, Husserl, Heidegger und Merleau-Ponty meines Erachtens allerdings sehr hilfreich sein. Aber dies steht hier nicht zur Debatte. Ich möchte abschließend versuchen, noch einmal eine Brücke zu schlagen zum gegenwärtig so dringlichen Thema ›Arbeit‹. Dass der Zusammenhang zwischen einer Konzeption ursprünglicher Produktion und dem Begriff der Arbeit nicht so handgreiflich ist, dass man sich bei Nichtbeachtung an ihm stoßen könnte, wird gerne eingeräumt. Dass aber ein Zusammenhang besteht, sei wenigstens mit einer Schlussüberlegung angedeutet.

Das Fichte'sche Denken – so fern es uns auch manchmal scheinen mag – ist uns mit einigen Grundintuitionen immer noch sehr nah: Es geht z.B. davon aus, dass unser Tun und die daraus entspringenden Taten etwas mit uns zu tun haben, so sehr, dass wir uns letztlich nicht selbst erfahren oder bestimmen könnten, ohne eben etwas hervorzubringen. Die dabei also leitende Intuition ist, dass Arbeit zuletzt nicht einfach der Subsistenzsicherung dient, sondern eine konstitutive Funktion für unser Selbstverständnis bekommt, mehr noch: für die Entwicklung unserer personalen Identität. Selbst noch die Sphäre der Objektwelt wird uns, das haben wir bei Fichte gesehen, erst über unseren tätigen Bezug zugänglich. Damit werden aber zugleich einige Konsequenzen des oben skizzierten Paradigmenwechsels erahnbar: Das Medialitätsprinzip begreift die produktiven Differenzen nicht im Horizont von Subjektivität. Das heißt vor allem, dass weder das Subjekt noch die in diesem Prozess generierten Objektbegriffe sich an der Logik der Selbstbestimmung bemessen lassen. Nicht einmal das Subjekt im Verhältnis zu sich selbst folgt dieser Logik, sondern erfährt sich allenfalls als ein in divergente Rollen und Identitäten auseinanderdriftendes Ichfeld. Doch weniger die Pluralisierung des Ich im postmodernen Spiel der Identitäten ist das Problem, als vielmehr die Frage, wie sich das Subjekt im gesellschaftlichen

Spiel und Zuspiel von Rollen noch als selbstbestimmtes Subjekt soll geltend machen können, wenn die identitätsstiftende Funktion und Möglichkeit klarer Zuschreibungen seiner Tätigkeiten an Bedeutung verloren haben sollte. Extrapoliert man aus dem fröhlichen Treiben der sogenannten ›digital natives‹, den Experten im Überschreiten medialer Grenzen und ihrer Camouflage verschiedener Identitäten, dann kann man zu dem Gedanken kommen, dass zwar nicht Tätigkeit überhaupt, aber eben doch (in ihrem Resultat, in ihrer Bedeutung für den Einzelnen und die soziale Gemeinschaft) ›belastbare‹ Tätigkeiten, wie sie ehemals Arbeit genannt wurden, an Bedeutung für unser Selbstverständnis zu verlieren scheinen. Ungeachtet solcher bereits sichtbarer Szenarien: Arbeit, verstanden als identitätsstiftendes und zuschreibbares, ›verdienstvolles‹ Tun, kommt nicht nur als ›knappe Ressource‹, sondern auch konzeptionell in die Krise, wenn Subjektivität und Produktivität als prinzipiell entkoppelt gedacht werden.

Zitierte Literatur

Derrida, Jacques. *Die Stimme und das Phänomen. Einführung in das Problem des Zeichens in der Phänomenologie Husserls*. Hg. Hans-Dieter Gondek. Frankfurt a.M.: Suhrkamp, 2003. (*SuPh*)

Fichte, Johann Gottlieb. *Wissenschaftslehre nova methodo. Kollegnachschrift K. Chr. Krause 1798/99*. Hg. Erich Fuchs. Hamburg: Meiner, 1994. (*WLnm*)

Loock, Reinhard. »Fichtes Wechselwirkung und der implizite Hörer der ›Wissenschaftslehre nova methodo‹«. *Fichte-Studien* 16 (1999): 69–89.

Loock, Reinhard. *Schwebende Einbildungskraft. Konzeptionen theoretischer Freiheit in der Philosophie Kants, Fichtes und Schellings*. Würzburg: Königshausen & Neumann, 2007.

Schlegel, Friedrich. *Kritische Ausgabe seiner Werke*. Hg. Ernst Behler. Bd. 23. Paderborn: Schöningh, 1987.

Schwabe, Ulrich. *Individuelles und transindividuelles Ich. Die Selbstindividuation reiner Subjektivität und Fichtes Wissenschaftslehre*. Paderborn: Schöningh, 2007.

James Hodkinson *(University of Warwick)*

Romantic Cosmopolitanism:
On the Tensions and Topicalities of an Ideal

Zusammenfassung

In den letzten zwei Jahrzehnten ist sowohl in der Soziologie wie auch in der Politik- und Literaturwissenschaft immer wieder die Debatte um den Begriff ›Kosmopolitismus‹ entflammt (zeitgenössisch wie auch historisch verstanden). Dabei wurde der vor allem in der Aufklärung und Romantik getätigte Versuch, einen Menschheitsbegriff zu entwerfen, der über kulturelle und ethnische Grenzen hinausgeht, immer wieder als ein westlich-koloniales Projekt entlarvt, das die Bedürfnisse und Selbstbestimmung von nicht-europäischen Kulturen ignoriert. Vor diesem Hintergrund widmet sich der vorliegende Aufsatz der romantischen Auffassung des Kosmopolitischen oder ›Weltbürgerlichen‹. Im letzten Jahrzehnt erschienen mehrfach Studien zum Thema: Während diese oft differenzierten und aufschlussreichen Arbeiten die frappierende Gleichzeitigkeit von kosmopolitischen und nationalistischen Impulsen in romantischen Texten wahrnehmen, wird der eurozentrischen Dimension dieser Texte, also der Frage, ob sich die Romantiker ernsthaft Gedanken über die Folgen ihrer Ideen für die nicht-europäische Welt gemacht haben, weniger nachgegangen. Anhand der Lektüre romantischer Texte, Fragmente und Prosa, vor allem Hardenbergs *Europa* (1799) und Schlegels *Über das Studium der Griechischen Poesie* (1795–1797), wird in diesem Beitrag ergänzend untersucht, wie diese Texte zwischen nationalistisch-essentiellen, eurozentrischen und global-kosmopolitischen Impulsen schweben. Die Aktualität romantischer Texte liegt weder in der Idealisierung dieser Texte als glänzende Beispiele kosmopolitischen Denkens noch in deren Reduktion auf reine Produkte kolonialer Ideologie, sondern in den ambivalenten Aussagen zu diesen Themen, die in einem analogen Verhältnis zu den Ambivalenzen der zeitgenössischen Debatte stehen.

I.

Cosmopolitan social theory is a collective endeavour to build a science of society founded on a claim to universalism. Its basic presupposition is that the human species can be understood only if it is treated as a single subject, within which all forms of difference are recognized and respected but conceptualized as internal to the substantive unity of all human beings (Fine, x).

> It has been one of the tensions internal to Enlightenment and post-Enlightenment Cosmopolitanism […] to attempt to grasp the unity of mankind without working through the relationship of the part to the whole (Bhahba, 41).

Twentieth-century attempts by scholars to present German Romanticism as a field of ongoing contemporary relevance have been plentiful in number (see for instance Behler/Hörisch), though have often run the risk of de-historicizing the period.[1] This essay seeks to avoid such pitfalls by examining the Romantic reception of a key idea that was as topical around 1800 as it is today: that of cosmopolitanism. In recent times, the idea has been rejuvenated in the contemporary political sciences and cultural studies and has, as it ever was, been hotly disputed. This discussion opens with two quotations from contemporary theorists, both of whom deal with cosmopolitan thought and writing from around 1800, in an attempt to rehabilitate or critique the concept. The first is taken from Robert Fine's admirably concise study of cosmopolitanism, and presents the concept as the powerfully transformative idea, applicable to law, politics, social and cultural theory, that humanity must be conceived of as part of a single, universal community. Cultural, ethnic or other markers of difference that subdivide the species are not quashed – indeed they are to be »recognised and respected« – though they must never take precedence in determining relationships between groups, individuals and the laws that govern them. The second quotation is taken from the postcolonial theorist Homi K. Bhabha: Bhabha invokes Frantz Fanon's plea of some forty years earlier for the continued scrutiny

---

[1] The late 1980s and early 90s saw a wave of enthusiasm for the *Frühromantik* of Novalis, Friedrich Schlegel and Friedrich Schleiermacher. Language was now understood to be the medium for the self-reflexive construction of Romantic subjectivity. Consequently, for many scholars Romantic writing now bore certain hallmarks of poststructuralism and was seen to pre-figure many of its writing strategies (cf. Kuzniar, *Delayed Endings*). Eventually the discussion became more measured, for Romantic thought was still, after all, predicated on the metaphysical absolutes that were anathema to poststructuralism (Neubauer, 207–220; Uerlings, 615–625).

of and resistance to colonialism in its varied forms.² This forms the ideological basis for Bhabha's take on cosmopolitanism: part of his approach is to critique historical forms of the European ideal for not having thought through how the »part« relates to the »whole«. The metaphor implies that the cosmopolitans of Europe (the part), however universal in their ambition, have traditionally predicated their discourse upon largely European needs, values, ideals, and have thus failed to recognize the diversity and the political-cultural agency of the world beyond Europe (the whole), and rendered this form of cosmopolitanism ›vernacular‹, essentially a mode of colonial thought. Of relevance for this essay is the central question generated by this contemporary disagreement: to what extent can we simply accept Romantic cosmopolitanism at face value, as a historical ideal that can enrich contemporary issues of cultural difference, and to what extent must it be treated with critical scepticism for its proximity to parochial, nationalist or Eurocentric values and practices.

II.

Many of the recent attempts to rejuvenate historical cosmopolitanisms for the contemporary context have been provided by scholars of the so-called new sociology, or by philosophers in the wider sense, and have centred on Enlightenment incarnations of the ideal.³ There is, however, a long tradition of scholarship that has examined the idea's transition into and transformations within German Romanticism.⁴ Interest has been particularly resurgent in the last decade,⁵ with the most sustained treatment given by Andrea

---

[2] In particular, Bhabha makes reference to Fanon's seminal work *Les Damnés de la Terre* (1961).
[3] Re-readings of Kant's writing on cosmopolitanism have been a point of particular focus here – a representative list of studies would include Hannah Arendt, *Lectures on Kant's Political Philosophy* (1992); Ulrich Beck, *Der kosmopolitische Blick* (2004); Robert Fine, *Cosmopolitanism* (2007); and Pauline Kleingeld, *Kant and Cosmopolitanism* (2012). One unfortunate side-effect of these developments has been to re-enforce old misconceptions amongst non-specialists about cosmopolitanism as a purely Enlightenment phenomenon.
[4] Take for instance Kuno Francke, *Weltbürgertum in der deutschen Literatur von Herder bis Nietzsche* (1928), which was an extension of an earlier essay in English »Cosmopolitanism in German Romantic Thought« (1927).
[5] Wohlgemut published a book-length study of Romantic cosmopolitanism in Anglophone traditions (Wohlgemut), for instance, whilst another collection of essays (Perkins/Liebscher) sought to map out the complex dialogue between cosmopolitan and nationalist discourses through case studies of particular German writers and texts from the late Enlightenment until 1914.

Albrecht (Albrecht), whose monograph charts the Romantic reception of the cosmopolitan ideal and its increasing embroilment in issues of nationalism and patriotism in Germany, with a look forward to the first half of the nineteenth century.[6]

One point of consensus amongst critics is that Romantic cosmopolitan writing is inextricably bound up with apparent counter-discourses, which seek to define or even promote models of national identity and national cultures. Crucial to understanding this complexity is the recognition of a paradigmatic shift that occurred in German thinking about nation and culture around 1800, one best represented and in some ways instigated by Johann Gottfried Herder. Herder's *Ideen zur Philosophie einer Geschichte der Menschheit* (1784–1791) sought to understand humanity precisely in terms of its internal differences, be they negatively or positively connoted.[7] In this text, Herder worked from a model of humanity's biological unity, held no polygenic views on ethnicity,[8] and has even been rated as a cosmopolitan, albeit in other writings.[9] Nonetheless, his vision of the historical process was of an on-going revelation of the essential cultural characteristics of peoples in terms of mutual differences – differences that arose from the topography and climate in which a *Volk* developed and were expressed, ultimately, in its distinctive culture and language. This mode of thinking both defined the historiographical method and drove the quest for the distinctive literary voice of Germany for which Herder became known; and it is this mode of thinking that arguably conflicts with cosmopolitan ideals (see Whitton, 146–168). Of course, these discourses evolved alongside historical events that strained

---

[6] Albrecht's study is historically well-grounded and nuanced in its discussion of how ostensibly cosmopolitan texts veer towards nationalist tendencies. She does not, however, critically pursue the Eurocentric nature of Romantic cosmopolitan writing as critiqued in this essay.

[7] On the controversies surrounding the precise nature of Herder's essentialism see Barnard and Löchte.

[8] See Herder's *Ideen*, where the first subsection of the seventh book is tellingly entitled: »In so verschiedenen Formen das Menschengeschlecht auf der Erde erscheint: so ists doch überall ein und dieselbe Menschengattung« (Herder, II, 7, I, 251ff.).

[9] Forster writes against the injustice of labelling Herder a German nationalist, referring to his avowed concern for all humanity as expressed in the *Humanitätsbriefe* and calling him a »cosmopolitan«: in sharp contrast to Kant, Herder wrote against ideologically loaded racial prejudice and his definition and promotion of nations is, for Forster, mitigated by his belief in the equality of all nations, in a rejection of colonialism and international conflict and predicated on his dismissal of the possibility and desirability of a total homogenization of humanity (Forster, xxxi–xxxii). Forster's position does not, however, preclude a reading of Herder in terms of the influential model, prevalent in the *Ideen*, of humanity's internal subdivisions as marked out by linguistic difference.

or at least modified the cosmopolitan beliefs of many German intellectuals: following the French Revolution of 1789, which came increasingly to represent a powerful form of transnational republicanism, even the more committed republicans amongst the early German Romantics harboured an increasing distrust of the »cosmopolitan« project of extending the revolution East of the Rhine, especially in the wake of the Jacobin *Terrorherrschaft* of the 1790s. So if Romantic cosmopolitanism is interspersed with identifiable stirrings of German national feeling, however benign they might appear, as well as theoretical discourses of national self-definition, we must remain aware of these contradictory impulses as we turn to read Romantic texts.

Bearing in mind such concerns, the discussion will first survey the Early German Romantic treatment of cosmopolitanism, discussing key, representative essayistic and fragmentary texts by Novalis (Friedrich von Hardenberg) and Friedrich Schlegel, and with a brief final glance at Schlegel's later lectures from 1830's Vienna, which serve to illustrate his ›final word‹ on cosmopolitanism. In so doing the essay does not seek to characterize texts as *either* cosmopolitan *or* essentialist in outlook, but recognizes their locus within a field of tension between the two tendencies. A number of specific questions arise: is the Romantic representation of cultural and national difference simply the recognition of such difference, or more a celebration of its importance? Is this writing still firmly ensconced in an universally inclusive vision of humanity, which is seen as genuinely transformative and desirable, or does its essentialism veer towards a more orthodox Herderian position, or even beyond, paradoxically, towards overt nationalism? And given that the immediate context for Romantic writing – the decade following the French Revolution – the question arises as to whether Romantic cosmopolitanism is limited to an idea of Europe, be it a Europe of nations or a Europe aspiring to transnationalism, or whether these ideals extended beyond Europe, however tentatively, to the so-called Orient and beyond, thus offering a cosmopolitan perspective that was truly global, not from a contemporary perspective, but on its own historical terms?

III.

Novalis (Friedrich von Hardenberg, 1772–1801) has often been thought of as the ›poster boy‹ for Early German Romanticism. His works have been co-opted to be exemplars of all manner of methodologies and ideologies, from Jacobin politics to proto-fascism, from irrational mysticism to proto-modern linguistics (see Uerlings, 521–614). The last fifty of those years have seen a process of largely consensual revision (Mähl; Frank; Molnár; Uerlings; O'Brien), whereby the poet's corpus of works is now seen to derive from a core set of philosophical reflections. Writing in 1796/97, in reaction to Fichte's *Wissenschaftslehre* (1794/95), Novalis defines his notion of *Poësie* as an enterprise of ironized, aesthetic transcendentalism. The nature of identity remains a dark unknown, and both subject and object are only present to consciousness as constructions in language, effectively as ›signs‹.[10] The poet recognizes the »fictionality« or merely referential nature of these signs, and their fluid relationship to the deeper truths they signify. This, in turn, makes it possible for poetry to change the self and the world through language by re-assigning those signs. *Poësie* seeks to encourage change by introducing provocative possibilities, figured within language, into the linguistically bound discourses of our world – be they political, religious, literary or scientific. The poet is no anarchist, but rather one who strategically generates ›new possibilities‹ in the hope that they will interact dialectically with the *status quo*, eliciting a tendency towards change.[11]

What, though, are the implications of this for Novalis's cosmopolitanism? Novalis's politics have represented one of the most contentious areas in scholarship: a number of commentators have pointed out that the iconic blue flower from the novel *Heinrich von Ofterdingen* (1801) has been seen to display many »other colours« over the years (see Mahoney, 83–100). The most significant text for this discussion is probably Novalis's essay *Europa* (1799),[12] though this, as we shall see, must be viewed in the context of his collected writings. Did he display some form of cosmopolitan Jacobin politics that welcomed the transnational revolution from West of the Rhine; did he react against the French Revolution by reverting to a brand of German nationalism; did he think about the cosmopolitan project in more universal terms, or is the truth, as it often is the case with Novalis, more complex? Whilst Novalis's writing on cosmopolitanism has eluded certain studies, it has been given fairly substantial treatment by others. Kleingeld (»Roman-

---

[10] In his *Fichte-Studien* Novalis writes: »Das Wesen der Identität läßt sich nur in einem Scheinsatz aufstellen. Wir verlassen das Identische um es darzustellen« (*N*, II, 104:1), and later »Die Nothwendigkeit der Beziehung eines Zeichens auf ein Bezeichnetes soll in einem Bezeichnenden liegen. In *diesem* aber wird beydes frey gesetzt« (*N*, II, 109:11).

[11] Uerlings writes of the »narrative Konstruktion einer erhofften Tendenz« (see the chapter of the same name, 609–613).

[12] The name *Die Christenheit oder Europa: Ein Fragment* is thought to have been applied to the text posthumously by Novalis's early editors (*N*, III, 502f.).

tic Cosmopolitanism«, 269–284; *Kant and Cosmopolitanism*, 149–160) rightly shows Novalis to reject more literally political forms of cosmopolitanism – such as the discourse of social contract in the French and German Enlightenments – in favour of an ideal of spiritual union, promoted through religion and poetry, which was to bring forward the perfection of humanity as a universal society transcending conventional national borders. There is much to speak for this approach. In his enigmatic and provocative political collection of aphorisms, *Glauben und Liebe* (1798), Novalis makes what appears to be a condescending aside at Kant's major work on cosmopolitanism, *Zum ewigen Frieden* (1795), as well as the so-called cosmopolitans of the day. The aphorism in question envisions a utopian moment, a time of *truly* perpetual peace, in which the paper-bound discourse upon which Enlightened social contract was written (that which currently functioned as the social adhesive between people in society for Novalis) turns to dust and is replaced by a genuine spirit of unity that binds people together – to use the poet's analogy – as a pair of lovers:

> Wie würden unsre Kosmopoliten erstaunen, wenn ihnen die Zeit des ewigen Friedens erschiene und sie die höchste gebildetste Menschheit in monarchischer Form erblickten? Zerstäubt wird dann der papierne Kitt seyn, der jetzt die Menschen zusammenkleistert und der Geist wird die Gespenster, die statt seiner in Buchstaben erschienen und von Federn und Pressen zerstückelt ausgingen, verscheuchen, und alle Menschen wie ein paar Liebende zusammen schmelzen (*N*, II, 488:16).

One of Novalis's most important contributions to Romantic cosmopolitanism comes in the form of his address *Europa* (1799), which was as controversial at the time he wrote it, as it has been since in scholarship (see O'Brien, 227–245). The text has been shifted across the political spectrum, and read variously as a proto-fascist manifesto for a European super-state with Christian Germany at its centre, as well as a proto-leftist, anti-authoritarian tract – a number of studies chart these fluctuations (Kurzke; Uerlings). The text offers both a history of Christian Europe and a vision for its future,[13] discerning the classic triadic structure of Christian eschatological thought across the epochs: the text constructs first an edenic state, identifiable with pre-Reformation Christian Europe; this is subsequently lost through the

---

[13] Through close and critical examination of Novalis's use of historical sources Kasperowski shows the text not to be an abstract ideal of the Middle Ages, but also a contribution to serious historiography of the time, and one not out of keeping with other works of the period (Kasperowski).

ideological, religious and geo-political schisms arising from Luther's Reformation, the Enlightenment and the French Revolution; and history is finally ›completed‹ with a vision of future redemption, of a burgeoning *neue Welt*, a new spirit of unity, whose first green shoots are to be found in Germany, derived from the spirit inherent in the Christian religion (cf. O'Brien, 232). The text, though, has long been seen as anything but a call for the literal restoration of a German-led Christian Europe, a latter-day Holy Roman Empire (see Uerlings, 569–578). Of course, *Europa* begins by eulogizing about pre-Reformation Christendom, recalling the »schöne glänzende Zeiten, wo Europa ein christliches Land war, wo *Eine* Christenheit diesen menschlich gestalteten Welttheil bewohnte« (*N*, III, 507) – a phrase emphasizing the oneness of Europeans as united by their religion. Novalis writes, furthermore, with disdain about those historical movements and events that sundered that unity: »Mit der Reformation wars um die Christenheit getan« (*N*, III, 513) he contends, for Luther had made the mistake of reducing religion to a philology of the Bible, which had been »höchst verderblich« to Europe's sense of religion (*N*, III, 512). And yet, *Europa* also appears to undercut its own apparent judgements on historical instances of unity and division. The feeling of »love«, derived from spiritual unity that apparently bound together pre-Reformation Europe, is subsequently downgraded to »eine erste Liebe« (*N*, III, 509), a mere first love. In this earlier epoch, humanity was, effectively, an adolescent entity »für dieses herrliche Reich nicht reif, nicht gebildet genug« (*N*, III, 509). In a sense, Reformation and Revolution represent a necessary if painful sequence of transitions for Europe: whilst the Reformation shattered the naive communality of Early Christianity, in the process subordinating religion to the temporal rule of princes, the French Revolution separated religion from the secular republic, »In Frankreich hat man viel für die Religion gemacht, indem man ihr das Bürgerrecht genommen […] hat« (*N*, III, 518), and in so doing left a spiritual and political anarchy. Precisely this chaos, though, provides in 1799 the context for what Novalis sees as religion's return in a higher sense, as the spiritual bond for a new world: »Wahrhafte Anarchie ist das Zeugungselement der Religion. Aus der Vernichtung alles Positiven hebt sie ihr glorreiches Haupt als neue Weltstifterin empor« (*N*, III, 517).

Scholarship has concluded that *Europa* is not ultimately reducible to a single empirical statement on specific historical periods, to events such as Reformation or Revolution or even to a particular confessional stance. Whilst critics pointed to the self-reflexive nature of the narrative (Malsch), others have over several decades read the text as a Romantic allegory of historiography, of the process of writing and reading history (Saul; Kuzniar, *Delayed Endings*). Part of the text's self-reflexivity flows from its identification of itself as language, as comprising ›signs‹ in the Romantic sense discussed above. Thus, phrases such as »Die Reformation war ein Zeichen der Zeit gewesen« (*N*, III, 515) are to be read not as the text's recourse to (clichéd) idiom, but as its exposition of history as a readable narrative, an object of hermeneutic investigation. The nature of that interpretative process is also outlined in the text by the (dialogically inclined) first-person narrative voice: »An die Geschichte verweise ich Euch, forscht in ihrem belehrenden Zusammenhang, und lernt den Zauberstab der Analogie gebrauchen« (*N*, III, 518). From the perspective of the present, the ›text‹ of history is to be used in conjunction with the ›magic wand‹ of analogy: only by seeing history in terms of its analogous relationship to our present and future, will it be truly instructive. The narrator is filled with a degree of hope about his audience's ability to make such use of history, for »[j]etzt stehn wir hoch genug um auch jenen oberwähnten, vorhergegangenen Zeiten freundlich zuzulächeln und auch in jenen wunderlichen Thorheiten merkwürdige Konstellationen des historischen Stoffs zu erkennen« (*N*, III, 520). Given its critical distance from the events discussed, the text's audience will doubtless discern new patterns within history, the »strange constellations« to which the narrative voice refers. In other words, the process of reading history, as exemplified by *Europa*, has revealed newly emergent tendencies, which are gathering momentum and are to be further promoted by the essay itself.[14] Specifically, it is the inkling of a new spirit of unity born of a new Romantic religiosity, one transcending all manner of borders, »eine gewaltige Ahndung der schöpferischen Willkühr, der Grenzenlosigkeit […]« (*N*, III, 519), that is the foundation of, and will further propagate, the new cosmopolitanism. So, in teaching its readership ›how‹ to read history in this way, outlining explicit lessons, via analogy, about Europe's childhood, adolescence and coming of age, and guided by the utopian ideal of a new age that looks beyond nations, *Europa* seems geared to preaching Romantic cosmopolitanism.

Yet, can an essay on the role of Christianity in Europe's history and future offer a vision that embraces all humanity, all continents, faiths and ideologies? Firstly, in *Europa* Europe's unified future is to be derived from the spirit of only *one* religion: Christianity. Novalis does, however state that

---

[14] Uerlings contended that the arresting utopian fictions Novalis produced were designed as narrative constructions of tendencies to be encouraged, as images that were to engage dialectically with the *status quo* (Uerlings, 609ff).

»Christenthum ist dreifacher Gestalt« (*N*, III, 523). This refers not to the Holy Trinity but to three modes of Christianity, one of these is the orthodox belief in Christ and the Virgin Mary, the other two forms relate to »Mittlerthum überhaupt«, that is to all religions that involve the mediation of divinity through self-reflexive symbolism (this understanding of religion was only *exemplified by* and not *limited to* Christianity), and also to the »Zeugungselement der Religion«, the »Freude an aller Religion« (*N*, III, 523), which is, quite simply, the positively transformative power of religion. According to Kleingeld, it is Romantic religiosity in a trans-confessional sense, rather than Christianity in a restrictive, doctrinal sense, to which Novalis looks for the force that will, in the future, bring together nations.[15]

Secondly, though, what of nations within this cosmopolitanism, what of Germany's future role as a nation, and what, finally, of Europe's relationship to the rest of the world? Novalis's text does use the apparently inclusive and universal term *Menschheit*. The main focus, though, is on the German *part* of the human species, »ein Theil des Geschlechts«, which is to lead the way to a cosmopolitan future. And what is that cosmopolitanism to embrace? Quite naturally, *Europa* spends much of its time on matters European, and it is in largely European terms that the state of cosmopolitan ideal is discussed: »Deutschland geht einen langsamen aber sichern Gang vor den übrigen europäischen Ländern voraus« (*N*, III, 519). One of the most abiding images of cosmopolitanism is of a »Staat der Staaten« (*N*, III, 522), a consensual and non-hierarchical coming together of nations, as each surrenders its borders to a greater »whole« (Kleingeld, »Romantic Cosmopolitansim«, 283). This »state of states«, though, is constructed under European horizons as the product of a »nähere und mannigfaltigere Connexion und Berührung der europäischen Staaten« (*N*, III, 522). At this point in the text, there is scant mention of the non-European world, little more in fact than a brief anecdotal reference to »Mohamedaner und Heiden« (*N*, III, 513), who appeared at certain points in history less divided from both Catholics and Protestants collectively, than the two halves of Christianity did from each other. Only in the fourth-to-last paragraph is mention made of the rest of the world: »Die andern Welttheile warten auf Europas Versöhnung und Auferstehung, um

---

[15] This resonates with Novalis's modern, self-reflexive model of religion as a process of mediation. In the *Blüthenstaub Fragmenten* he writes: »Nichts ist zur wahren Religiosität unentbehrlicher als ein Mittelglied – das uns mit der Gottheit verbindet. [...] In der Wahl dieses Mittelglieds muß der Mensch durchaus frey seyn. [...] Es ist ein Götzendienst im weitern Sinn, wenn ich diesen Mittler für Gott selbst ansehe. [...] Wahre Religion ist, die jenen Mittler als Mittler annimmt [...]« (*N*, II, 441ff.:74).

sich anzuschließen und Mitbürger des Himmelreichs zu werden« (*N*, III, 524). Is the implication here that the rest of the world is waiting in a spirit of world-citizenship for the nations of this troubled continent to unite, catch up and join with them as equal partners in a new global community? Or is it more the case that these parts of the world remain something of a blindspot for Novalis, figuring as an homogenous, indistinct and passive other, at best waiting to be led by Germany towards a Europe-centred future? In other words, is the charge levelled by Bhabha against historical European traditions applicable to Novalis – does he fail to work through »the relationship of the part to the whole«?

A brief glance at other texts will place this concern in context and complete our discussion of Novalis. Anything approaching a full discussion of the novel *Heinrich von Ofterdingen* (1801) is beyond the scope of this essay. However, the novel's fourth chapter does contain an encounter between Europe and the so-called Orient, which Heinrich meets in the form of the female slave Zulima. The novel has been read as something more than a Romantic *Bildungsroman* centred on the experiences and needs of a single (male, German) poetic subject, in fact as a narrative which cultivates the participation of other voices of women and non-Europeans (Kuzniar; »Hearing Women's Voices«; Hodkinson, *Women and Writing*, 134–167). The encounter appears to place the German poet in a hierarchical relationship with Zulima (underwritten by a seemingly conventional gender dualism). The dualisms of gender and poetic agency soon blur however, with Zulima taking the lead in a discursive exchange across the apparent dualism of Occidental and Oriental culture. Her monologues offer an alternative account of the crusades, calling them »einen fürchterlichen, unnützen Krieg« (*N*, I, 237), worsened by the fact that the re-conquest of Jerusalem was in many ways unnecessary: Christians had been honoured guests when visiting Christ's grave in the city, a policy derived from the fact that Muslims also venerate Jesus as a prophet of their own (Hodkinson, »Der Islam im Dichten und Denken der deutschen Romantik,« 69–72). Having already distanced himself from the politics of the Crusaders who enslaved Zulima, Heinrich leaves the encounter wishing that he could in some way be Zulima's saviour, though not quite knowing how. In a sense, the young German poet appears to take on, in an admittedly idealistic and overly ambitious manner, the role of the future mediator between Christendom and Islam, Europe and the East, and the new relationship between the two figures seems thus to represent a »gentler German cosmopolitanism« (Kontje, 99).

However, the text is perhaps not quite so clear cut. Arguably, as Heinrich moves on in his journey, leaving behind the captive Zulima and desiring to be her »Retter«, a raft of dualisms resurfaces, which contrasts an active, male German (Europe) with a passive, feminine Orient. The episode ends ambiguously, expressing both the drive to define a (leading) role for the German nation on the world stage: the seemingly paradoxical role is that of the future champion of world citizenship, the cosmopolitan who acts on behalf of other cultures. Elsewhere, in his fragments, Novalis continues to hover provocatively between an ideal cosmopolitanism and a discourse that, whilst it avoids the crasser sentiments of ›Deutschtümelei‹, or the more essentialist modes of Herder's thought, nevertheless seeks to define and promote a German national-cultural identity and, in so doing, participates in a mode of thought that it also seeks to overcome.[16] The young Romantic's seemingly paradoxical position is summed up nicely by an enigmatic phrase in a letter to A.W. Schlegel of 1797, in which he defines German national character as a form of cosmopolitanism, though one peppered with a potent sense of individuality: »Deutschheit ist Kosmopolitismus mit der kräftigsten Individualität gemischt« (*N*, IV, 270ff.).

---

[16] The *Blüthenstaub Fragmente* (1798) contain a series of reflections on the topic: »Der Deutsche ist lange das Hänschen gewesen. Er dürfte aber wohl der Hans aller Hänse werden. Es geht ihm, wie es vielen dummen Kindern gehn soll – er wird leben und klug seyn, wenn seine frühklugen Geschwister längst vermodert sind, und er nun allein Herr im Hause ist« (*N*, II, 436:60). Having looked with some scorn at Germany's past role as the naive child or »Hänschen« of Europe, this excerpt relishes the golden future that awaits Germany – in sharp contrast to the cultural decline and (quite literal) decay he envisages for other European nations. Arguably there is something playful about the tone of such statements and they are not to be taken as literal *Schadenfreude*. Novalis further mitigates the position at another point, noting that German national character is »so wenig, wie Romanitaet, Graecitaet, oder Brittannitaet auf einen besondern Staat eingeschränckt – Es sind allgemeine Menschencharaktere – die nur hie und da vorzüglich allgemein geworden sind« (*N*, II, 438:66). Kleingeld suggests that Novalis sees nations, national cultures and nationalism as things to be overcome, though as necessary stages in the development towards a cosmopolitan world (Kleingeld, *Kant and Cosmopolitanism*, 157), which is evidenced by the following excerpt from the so-called *Ergänzungen zu den Teplitzer Fragmenten* (1798): »Der Europaer ist so hoch über den Deutschen, wie dieser über den Sachsen – der Sachse über den Leipziger. Über ihn ist der Weltbürger. Alles Nationale, Temporelle, Locale, Individuelle läßt sich universalisiren, und so canonisiren und allgemein machen« (*N*, II, 616:5). The fragment appears to look beyond national identity and reflect upon a universal notion of humanity – though its starting point is provincial Germany.

IV.

In the mid-1790s, Friedrich Schlegel[17] was very much a writer with republican sympathies. His *Versuch über den Begriff des Republikanismus* (1796) marks a contribution to political philosophy and a direct critical engagement with cosmopolitan discourse opened out by Kant in his essay *Zum ewigen Frieden* (1795). Kant had offered a vision of a federation of freely self-determining states, connected through their subscription to certain basic international human rights, and promising, amongst other things, a right of hospitality to citizens of one nation abroad within the borders of another. Schlegel's far more radical solution was to reject such »*partiellen* Republikanismus« (*S*, VII, 22) and propose rather a »Weltrepublik«. This world republic was to express transnational cosmopolitanism, made up of a »Vielzahl selbstbewußter nationaler Republiken« (*S*, VII, 25), which were to be autonomous and equal within the confederation; he writes of the »*Autonomie jedes einzelnen Staats*« and the »*Isonomie aller*« (*S*, VII, 22) – though this autonomy was to be checked by the »*Polizierung aller Nationen*« (*S*, VII, 22). Friedrich's republicanism also requires the democracy of states, calling for a »majesty of the people« (»Volksmajestät« *S*, VII, 21) and – through a complex synthesis of anthropology, post-Fichtean philosophy and proto-psychology – discusses how the ideal of a collective identity will both grow from and be inculcated in the individual subjects that make up nations.[18] Whilst the ideal of a world republic appears in theory to embrace all nations and cultures, quite what Schlegel's explicit view of the position of the Orient, Africa and the so-called New World would be within this ideal realm of realms remains unclear.

The *Versuch* does not mark the end of Friedrich's interest in *republicanism per se* (again see Deiters), though his *cosmopolitan* thinking continues elsewhere, and does so in a more literary vein. Whilst there is a less explicit, terminological reference to cosmopolitan ideas in the aesthetic writings, the essay *Über das Studium der Griechischen Poesie* (1795–1797) marks a major contribution nonetheless. This is both a study of Greek art but also a vision of the »Wiederherstellung der echten schönen Kunst« (*S*, I, 354). This restoration does not simply call for a return to the mechanical appreciation, execution

---

[17] Both the brothers Schlegel, Friedrich and August Wilhelm, engaged with cosmopolitan ideals in their writing from the 1790s onwards. A.W. Schlegel's writing on the topic is more sporadic than that of his brother and has been treated elsewhere, cf. Albrecht (2005).

[18] For a full discussion of Schlegel's republicanism essay, including his anthropological definition of humanity and its elevation beyond a plurality of individual subjects into a unified community, see Deiters.

and mastery of the rules and techniques of classical poetry, drama and sculpture, as in the French neo-classical tradition (S, I, 363), but rather the creation of a new kind of modern art – one that is European. In the first ›diagnostically‹ inclined section of the essay, »Von dem Zustande der modernen Dichkunst«, Schlegel concedes modern art in Europe to appear divided, with the mutual cultural differences between nations causing such division. However, he also points to the fact that European cultures tend to be referred to collectively, to belong together, on the basis of undeniable forms of common heritage:

> Es ist wahr, bei aller Eigentümlichkeit und Verschiedenheit der einzelnen Nationen verrät das Europäische Völkersystem dennoch durch einen auffallend ähnlichen Geist der Sprache, der Verfassungen, Gebräuche und Einrichtungen, in vielen übrig gebliebenen Spuren der frühern Zeit, den gleichartigen und gemeinschaftlichen Ursprung ihrer Kultur. Dazu kommt noch eine gemeinschaftliche von allen übrigen sehr abweichende Religion (S, I, 225).

The gradual diminution of internal European divisions between nations is further driven by the dynamic tendency amongst the continent's modern cultures both to transmit their own, and absorb and imitate each other's traditions, a tendency towards »stete *Wechselnachahmung*« (S, I, 226). Even this model, according to Schlegel, runs the risk of overstating cultural differences, given that »die verschiedenen urspünglichen Eigentümlichkeiten« of national cultures (ibid.) have so much in common that they appear as »Zweige eines Stammes« (ibid.). Modern European culture, then, bears the hallmarks of mutual difference that both drive and inform change, though also carry the trace of common heritage, which directs that change teleologically towards a cosmopolitan definition of European culture.

What, though, is it about European art that Schlegel believes will both express and encourage this drive towards a shared European cultural identity? For him, European aesthetic modernity can largely be characterized as a constant »Streit der *subjektiven Anlage*, und der objektiven Tendenz des ästhetischen Vermögens und des allmählichen Übergewicht des leztern« (S, I, 355), a struggle not simply between epistemological constructs of subjectivity and objectivity, but between aesthetic paradigms that are limited by national cultures and those that tend towards a more universal concept of beauty. Schlegel sees cultural modernity as falling into several phases: firstly, a period of overtly conflicting national cultures prior to the re-birth of classical art; secondly a »Blütezeit« of classical reawakening that had, however, been limited by the fact that neo-classical art became the property of individual national cultures; and thirdly, a final phase which had in some respects already begun for Schlegel, and would yet witness the advent of new European art (*S*, I, 355f.). Prefiguring in some ways Novalis's comments on religiosity, history and European communality in *Europa*, Schlegel sees that only out of this anarchy within art could »eine wichtige Revolution der ästhetischen Bildung« (*S*, I, 356) come to pass such cultural coalescence. The modern, transnational culture of Europe will not naively imitate classical art, but will evolve to produce a new art, founded upon a consensus on the nature of beauty that reaches beyond national parochialism as Greek art had done for the ancients.

Where again, though, does the German nation figure in this thinking? Schlegel already detects the »*unverkennbare[n] Anfänge objektiver Kunst und objektiven Geschmacks*« in Europe – does Germany have any particular part to play in these developments? Once again, the Germans are initially shown as the belated children amongst European nations (*S*, I, 259), indeed reference is made to the emptiness of German character, and the ›charakterlose Deutsche‹ appears too slow and clumsy in his thoughts to keep up with the »leichten Spielen der freien Kunst« (228). This so-called »Charakterlosigkeit der Deutschen« (259), however, is quickly reconfigured to put the Germans ahead of other nations in the context of emerging European culture, for it marks an aspiration to cultural pluralism and self-cultivation, which is »dem manirierten Charakter andrer Nationen weit vorzuziehen« (259). Other nations will catch up with Germany in this respect only once their art and aesthetics have lost their one-sidedly national characteristics: »[E]rst, wenn die nationale Einseitigkeit ihrer ästhetischen Bildung mehr verwischt, und berechtigt sein wird, können sie sich zu der höhern Stufe jener Vielseitigkeit erheben« (259). Once more, Schlegel weaves a thread of national pride into a cosmopolitan discourse. Once more, though, he arguably eludes charges of chauvinistic nationalism, on the basis that his concept of German national character is defined precisely in terms of its openness to other cultural influences. This interpretation is placed under a degree of strain, however, by Schlegel's reflections on the achievements of different national literatures in the fifth and final section of the essay. Of all art it is drama, he writes, which demands most to be completely freed from »nationellen Schranken, Eigenschaften, von denen die Franzosen sehr weit entfernt sind« (362). However, it is not merely the French who are seen to be lacking a cosmopolitan view of drama or the arts generally:

> Ohnehin fehlt es den Franzosen wie den Engländern und Italienern […] an objektiver Theorie […]. Um nur auf die Spur zu kommen, wie sie den Weg dahin finden könnten, würden sie bei den Deutschen in die Schule gehn müssen. Eine Sache, zu der sie sich wohl schwerlich entschließen werden! (*S*, I, 363)

Reflecting on the relatively advanced state of German culture, scholarship and education at the dawn of the nineteenth century, it still seems somewhat paradoxical that Schlegel chooses to locate these comments within a text which posits as its ideal the transcendence of national cultures through art. The irony is intensified, perhaps, by Schlegel's comment that other nations will not readily look to Germany as their superiors for reasons of national pride.

Much of what Schlegel writes about in this essay is centred on Germany and Europe. Several years later, during a journey to Paris in 1803, he completed plans for and first published the successor to the *Athenäum*, which was to be the magazine *Europa*. Together with its title, the »Vorrede« to the first edition heralds a publication seemingly dedicated to cosmopolitan culture,[19] at least in the European context.[20] However, the stay in Paris also gave him occasion to immerse himself in the study of the so-called Orient, particularly Persian and Indic language and culture. Would these dual interests combine to produce a cosmopolitan outlook that embraced more than just Europe? Schlegel's account and reflections in his *Reise nach Frankreich* (1803) tell something of his attitudes. Here he contends that the conception of European unity remains underdeveloped, with northern and southern Europe appearing as two separate entities. In contrast to this divided Europe is Schlegel's vision of the Orient, a region of harmony and unity, whose characteristics are needed in Europe: »Was im Oriente alles in Einem mit ungeteilter Kraft aus der Quelle springt, das sollte hier sich mannigfach teilen und künstlicher entfalten« (*S*, VII, 73). In the closing paragraph of the text, Schlegel envisages the globe of the Earth and considers the task of re-connecting Europe, referred to as »der Norden« and the Orient (78). Before this can happen, however, Europe must complete its own development and attain unity: »[W]ir selbst sollten mitwirken, die tellurischen Kräfte in Einheit und

---

[19] Schlegel wrote: »Diese Zeitschrift ist bestimmt, an allem Antheil zu nehmen, was die Ausbildung des menschlichen Geistes am nächsten angeht, und das Licht der Schönheit und der Wahrheit so weit als möglich zu verbreiten« (*Europa*, 3).

[20] Behler (*S*, VII, XLI) believes that Schlegel starts thinking of Europe as a »Romanisch-Germanische Einheit«, with Paris as a new centre, in this 1803 text. The text does, however, also contend a huge sense of division, especially between northern and southern Europe, which figure effectively as two different »halves« (73).

Harmonie zu bringen, wir sollen die Eisenkraft des Nordens, und die Lichtglut des Orients in mächtigen Strömen überall um uns her verbreiten« (78). Rather like Novalis, the notion of re-connecting Occident and Orient appears to be a future goal. For Schlegel though, the primary function of the Orient in the text is to embody a place of light, harmony and unity, to serve as a template for qualities that Europe must incorporate and arguably improve upon before it can look beyond itself. It seems that Schlegel is, at this point in his writing, more interested in what the Orient represents to Europe, than with any serious thoughts of a world culture embracing all continents on an egalitarian footing.

Taking into consideration his whole career, in 1803 Schlegel's oriental studies were in their relative infancy. His first great work in the area, *Über die Sprache und Weisheit der Indier*, did not appear until 1808. By the time this work went into print Schlegel's cultural politics had moved with the reactionary currents in the German-speaking world. In his *Gedanken* (1808/09) Schlegel now wrote in open rejection of cosmopolitan politics: »Wie elend ist doch das was man von Kosmopolitismus redet, gegen diesen Weltgeist der Deutschen und (vollends) gegen die ehemalige christliche Einheit der Völker« (*S*, XIX, 280). Critics point rightly to the fact that any genuine cosmopolitanism had been supplanted by a far more limited transnationalism, namely a model of a united, Pan-German Christian »Reich« (Albrecht, 316f.). It is, though, towards the end of his career that both the full range of his Oriental learning and his repudiation of universal cosmopolitan becomes apparent.

In his *Philosophie der Geschichte* which he first gave as a series of lectures in Vienna in spring 1828, Schlegel unfolds across eighteen chapters his reflections on this history of many cultures, including those of the Arabian Peninsula and Far-East Asia. Far from working from any form of cosmopolitan standpoint, Schlegel now writes as a cultural essentialist working in an unflinchingly Christian-centred mode. The lectures present non-Christian cultures in terms of whether or not they have received God's revelation, and to what extent their cultures mark a departure from, or a perversion of it. Thus, in the »Dritte Vorlesung«[21] he seeks to explain Chinese culture as a corruption of Christianity: The symbol of the fallen dragon in the ancient Chinese text of *Yijing* (now thought to have originated between two and

---

21 »Dritte Vorlesung. Von der chinesischen Staatseinrichtung und äußern Landes- und Sittenkultur; dann von der chinesischen Geistesbildung und wissenschaftlichen Richtung« (*S*, IX, 58–81).

three millennia before Christ) denoted for Schlegel the fallen Angel of the Bible: the Chinese had received the word of God, but distorted the story and appropriated it as part of this foundational text. Schlegel writes how in China »dem Monarchen fast eine eigentliche Anbetung gezollt wird« (*S*, IX, 77); Chinese emperors, who (albeit naively) took the fallen dragon as their symbol in effect usurped divine status from the true Christian God (77; see also Bernier, 271f.). Similarly, in the »Zwölfte Vorlesung«[22] he explains the Islamic prohibition of alcohol not as an act of moral progress, but as the refusal of Muslims to take part in the sacrament of Holy Communion. Turning to oppose diametrically Novalis's view on the matter, he blames Islam for thus erecting an impenetrable wall of separation, an »unübersteigliche Scheidewand« (*S*, IX, 276), between itself and Christianity (cf. Hodkinson, »Der Islam im Dichten und Denken der deutschen Romantik«, 79f.).

V.

Novalis, then, offers us a vision of cosmopolitanism driven by the goal of transnational unity, which is in turn derived from an ideal of shared spirituality. Although he represents this spirituality in terms of the Christian religion, he relativizes his position and ascribes that unifying power to all religions or religiosity *per se*. He also flirts with national-cultural essentialism, casting the Germans as the leading cosmopolitans of a new century, though undercuts those statements by playing disruptive semantic games with definitions of who or what can be called German, and subsequently constructs a Romantic ideal that appears to look beyond national allegiances. There is no doubt that he subscribes to a form of utopian Romantic cosmopolitanism and that he is no chauvinistic nationalist. Yet he spills a fair amount of ink in writing about Germany's national-cultural specificity in a manner that seems at odds with his own ideals. In this he appears both to have been living up to his own anti-dogmatic ideal of a system of »Systemlosigkeit« (*N*, II, 289), and also, to some extent, to have been hedging his bets as the eighteenth century neared its end. In the mid-1790s Schlegel's cosmopolitan republicanism dovetails with a more culturally oriented vision of a transcultural consensus on what constitutes beauty within aesthetic theory and

---

[22] »Zwölfte Vorlesung. Charakterschilderung des Mahomet und seiner Religion, so wie der arabischen Weltherrschaft. Neue Gestaltung des europäischen Abendlandes und Wiederherstellung des christlichen Kaisertums« (S, IX, 269–290).

practice, though such sympathies all but disappear by the close of the new century's first decade: whereas Novalis died in 1801, Schlegel lived through a massive change of political climate, as the Napoleonic wars swept across Europe, accompanied by waves of nationalism and reaction in the German speaking territories. Most significantly for this essay, both Romantics show an awareness of the extra-European implications of cosmopolitanism and move from a solely Eurocentric cosmopolitan focus to consider Europe's (re-)connection to the Orient: in so doing, however, they run the risk – Schlegel somewhat more than Novalis – of reducing the Orient to a passive spectator, which waits either to reconnect with Europe in some ideal future, or to function as a template of the »ideal other«, whilst Europe engages in a self-preoccupied quest for its own unity. The continuing thread of Schlegel's Oriental studies becomes increasingly incriminating: it is perhaps ironic that, during the period in which he was writing in cosmopolitan mode, he worked with so reductive an image of the Orient, and that by the time he had extended and enriched his Oriental learning, he was no longer writing as a cosmopolitan and adapted his knowledge to serve his Germano-Christian centred world view.

When writing from a postcolonial perspective, particularly the older Friedrich Schlegel has become something of a popular and easy target:[23] this essay does seek to use his work in this way. Neither, though, has the discussion sought to be wholly approving: many contemporary theorists appear to be quite forgiving in their readings of historical incarnations of the ideal, calling for the postcolonial reader to allow cosmopolitanisms to be ›of their time‹, to recognize the different and period-specific frameworks in which they operated, and call for us to emphasize the ›gains‹ they made in challenging parochial national thinking of their time, rather than their ›failure‹ to measure up to contemporary norms (cf. Pollock et al., 1–14). Yet both Novalis and Schlegel remained aware of the extra-European implications of cosmopolitan thinking, and of the limitations of nationalist thinking. Both Romantics also spoke a language of national particularism and in so doing ran the risk of succumbing to it. This kind of historically grounded discussion of the complexities and contradictions in Romantic cosmopolitan thinking can resonate usefully with the contemporary reader. It is not the case that this is a debate lost to the present – one that only the Romantic

---

[23] Whilst Lucie Bernier's essay »Christianity and the Other« is justified in exposing the bias involved in Schlegel's oriental writing, her essay does focus solely on the cultural politics of the later works.

can re-supply. Neither does this material allow us simply to project our postcolonial chagrin retrospectively onto an earlier epoch. The topicality of this theme derives from the fact that the Romantics faced a series of conflicting choices. Those choices pull us between aspirations to an ideal that appears to guide a divided humanity towards a shared sense of community on the one hand, and on the other, the inclination to define oneself, particularly at times of intercultural conflict and trauma, in terms of that which is local and familiar: the more tangible things we feel we have in common with those who appear to share our more immediate origins. So if we can accept Novalis's idea that history is most informative when taken as an analogy to our present situation, then we can begin to recognize that these seemingly Romantic dilemmas are actually much like our own.

Works Cited

Albrecht, Andrea. *Kosmopolitismus: Weltbürgerdiskurse in Literatur, Philosophie und Publizistik um 1800*. Berlin/New York: de Gruyter, 2005.
Arendt, Hannah. *Lectures on Kant's Political Philosophy*. Ed. with an interpretative essay by Ronald Beiner. Chicago: Chicago University Press, 1992.
Barnard, Frederick M. *Herder on Nationality, Humanity, and History*. Montreal: McGill-Queen's University Press, 2004.
Beck, Ulrich. *Der kosmopolitische Blick oder: Krieg ist Frieden*. Frankfurt/M: Suhrkamp, 2004.
Behler, Ernst/Jochen Hörisch (eds.). *Die Aktualität der Frühromantik*. Paderborn: Ferdinand Schöningh, 1987.
Bernier, Lucie. »Christianity and the Other: Friedrich Schlegel's and F.W.J. Schelling's Interpretation of China«. *International Journal of Asian Studies* 2.2 (2005): 265–273.
Bhabha, Homi K. »Unsatisfied: Notes on Vernacular Cosmopolitanism«. *Postcolonial Discourses: An Anthology*. Ed. Gregory Castle. Oxford/Malden, MA: Blackwell, 2001: 38–52.
Deiters, Franz-Josef. »›Die Poesie ist eine Republikanische Rede‹ – Friedrich Schlegels Konzept einer selbstreferentiellen Dichtung als Vollendung der Politischen Philosophie der europäischen Aufklärung«. *Deutsche Vierteljahrsschrift für Literaturwissenschaft und Geistesgeschichte* 81.1 (2007): 3–20.
Fanon, Frantz. *Les Damnés de la Terre*. Paris: Maspero, 1961.
Fine, Robert. *Cosmopolitanism*. London/New York: Routledge, 2007.
Forster, Michael N. (ed.). *Johann Gottfried Herder. Philosophical Writings*. Cambridge: Cambridge University Press, 2004.

Francke, Kuno. »Cosmopolitanism in German Romantic Thought«. *Proceedings of the American Philosophical Society* 66 (1927): 183–190.
Francke, Kuno. *Weltbürgertum in der deutschen Literatur von Herder bis Nietzsche.* Berlin: Weidmannsche Buchhandlung, 1928.
Frank, Manfred. *Das Problem ›Zeit‹ in der deutschen Romantik: Zeitbewußtsein und Bewußtsein von Zeitlichkeit in der frühromantischen Philosophie und in Tiecks Dichtung.* Paderborn: Winkler, 1972.
Herder, Johann Gottfried. *Werke in zehn Bänden.* Ed. Martin Bollacher et al. Frankfurt/M: Deutscher Klassiker Verlag, 1989ff.
Hodkinson, James. »Der Islam im Dichten und Denken der deutschen Romantik: zwischen Kosmopolitismus und Orientalismus«. *Islam in der deutschen und türkischen Literatur.* Eds. Michael Hofmann/Klaus von Stosch. Paderborn: Ferdinand Schöningh, 2012: 61–80.
Hodkinson, James. *Women and Writing in the Works of Novalis: Transformation beyond measure?* Rochester/New York: Camden House, 2007.
Kasperowski, Ira. *Mittelalterrezeption im Werk des Novalis.* Tübingen: Max Niemeyer, 1994.
Kleingeld, Pauline. »Romantic Cosmopolitanism: Novalis's ›Christianity or Europe‹«. *Journal of the History of Philosophy* 46.2 (2008): 269–284.
Kleingeld, Pauline. *Kant and Cosmopolitanism: The Philosophical Ideal of World Citizenship.* Cambridge: Cambridge University Press, 2012.
Kontje, Todd. *German Orientalisms.* Ann Arbor: University of Michigan Press, 2004.
Kurzke, Hermann. *Romantik und Konservatismus. Das ›politische‹ Werk Friedrich von Hardenbergs (Novalis) im Horizont seiner Wirkungsgeschichte.* Munich: Fink, 1983.
Kuzniar, Alice. »Hearing Women's Voices in *Heinrich von Ofterdingen*«. *PMLA* 107.5 (1992): 1196–1208.
Kuzniar, Alice. *Delayed Endings: Nonclosure in Novalis and Hölderlin.* Athens/London: Georgia University Press, 1987.
Löchte, Anne. *Johann Gottfried Herder. Kulturtheorie und Humanitätsidee der ›Ideen‹, ›Humanitätsbriefe‹ und ›Adrastea‹.* Würzburg: Königshausen & Neumann, 2005.
Mähl, Hans-Joachim. *Die Idee des Goldnen Zeitalters im Werk des Novalis. Studien zur Wesensbestimmung der frühromantischen Utopie und zu ihren ideengeschichtlichen Voraussetzungen.* Heidelberg: Carl Winter, 1965.
Mahoney, Denis. *The Critical Fortunes of a Romantic Novel: Novalis's ›Heinrich von Ofterdingen‹.* Columbia: Camden House, 1994.
Malsch, Wilfried. *›Europa‹. Poetische Rede des Novalis. Deutung und Reflexion auf die Poesie in der Geschichte.* Stuttgart: J.B. Metzler, 1965.
Molnár, Géza von. *Novalis' Fichte Studies. The Foundations of his Aesthetics.* The Hague: Mouton, 1970.
Müller-Funk, Wolfgang/Schuh, Franz (eds.). *Nationalismus und Romantik.* Vienna: Turia & Kant, 1999.

Neubauer, John. »Novalis und der Postmodernismus«. *Geschichtlichkeit und Aktualität. Studien zur deutschen Literatur seit der Romantik. Festschrift für Hans-Joachim Mähl zum 65. Geburtstag*. Eds. K. Müller et al. Tübingen: Max Niemeyer, 1988: 207-220.
Novalis. Schriften. Die Werke Friedrich von Hardenbergs. Eds. Paul Kluckhohn/Richard Samuel/Heinz Ritter/Hans-Joachim Mähl/Gerhard Schulz. 3rd edition, 6 vols. Stuttgart: Kohlhammer, 1977ff. (*N*)
O'Brien, William A. *Novalis. Signs of Revolution*. London/Durham: Duke University Press, 1995.
Oesterle, Günter. »Friedrich Schlegel in Paris oder die romantische Gegenrevolution«. http://www.goethezeitportal.de/fileadmin/PDF/db/wiss/schlegel_fr/oesterle_revolution.pdf
Perkins, Mary Ann/Martin Liebscher. *Nationalism versus Cosmopolitanism in German Thought and Culture, 1789–1914: Essays on the Emergence of Europe*. Lampeter: Edward Mellen, 2006.
Pollock, Sheldon/Homi K. Bhabha/Carol A. Breckenridge/Dipesh Chakrabarty. »Cosmopolitanisms«. *Cosmopolitanism*. Eds. Pollock, Sheldon/Homi K. Bhabha/Carol A. Breckenridge/Dipesh Chakrabarty. Durham, NC/London: Millennial Quartet Books, 2002: 1–14.
Saul, Nicholas. *History and Poetry in Novalis in the Tradition of the German Enlightenment*. London: Institute of Germanic Studies, 1984.
Schlegel, Friedrich (ed.). *Europa. Eine Zeitschrift*. Frankfurt/M: F. Wilmans, 1803.
Schlegel, Friedrich. *Kritische-Friedrich-Schlegel-Ausgabe*. Eds. Jean-Jacques Anstett/Ernst Behler/Hans Eichner. 35 vols. Paderborn/Vienna/Zurich: Schöningh, 1958ff. (*S*)
Uerlings, Herbert. *Friedrich von Hardenberg, genannt Novalis. Werk und Forschung*. Stuttgart: J.B. Metzler, 1991.
Whitton, Brian J. »Herder's critique of the Enlightenment: Cultural Community vs. Cosmopolitan Nationalism«. *History and Theory* 27 (1988): 146–168.
Wohlgemut, Esther. *Romantic Cosmopolitanism*. London/New York: Palgrave Macmillan, 2009.

Kate Rigby (*Monash University*)

»Wo die Wälder rauschen so sacht«.
The Actuality of Eichendorff's Atmospheric Ecopoetics

Zusammenfassung

Dieser Aufsatz befasst sich mit der Frage nach der Aktualität der Romantik aus ökologischer Perspektive unter Heranziehung von Gernot Böhmes neuer Ästhetik von ›Atmosphären‹. Die Erfahrung von Atmosphären, die durch Naturphänomene hervorgerufen werden, spielt eine wichtige Rolle in der Literatur der Romantik. Diese romantische Naturästhetik richtet sich implizit gegen dualistische Auffassungen von ›Mensch und Natur‹, ›Geist und Körper‹, ›Ich und Nicht-Ich‹, indem sie menschliche Existenz als umweltbedingt, leiblich und intersubjektiv enthüllt. Gleichzeitig aber hat die romantische Ästhetisierung der Natur zur Entstehung des bürgerlichen Konsumverhaltens beigetragen. Diese zweideutige Aktualität der romantischen Naturästhetik wird hier am Beispiel von Eichendorffs Poetik der akustischen Atmosphären untersucht, die sich allerdings einer bürgerlichen Vereinnahmung der Natur betont widersetzt.

While Romantic understandings of literary authorship and interpretation, such as those pioneered by William Wordsworth and Samuel Taylor Coleridge in *The Lyrical Ballads* (1798, 1800, 1802) and by the Jena circle in the magazine *Athenäum* (1798–1800), proved pivotal in the emergence of the modern discipline of literary studies, literary critics have in turn made of Romanticism a kind of touchstone, upon which successive generations of scholars have tried out their favoured theories and approaches. As Jonathan Bate observes, »Romanticism has remained a living legacy because, like a fit Darwinian organism, it has proved singularly adaptable to a succession of new environments, whether Victorian medievalism, *fin de siècle* aestheticism, new critical Urn-wrighting, Hartmanesque phenomenology, or the counter-reading of 1980s ideologism« (»Living with the Weather«, 433). The biological simile that Bate deploys here is indicative of the revisionary angle from which he himself was returning to Romanticism, as was the title that he gave to the special issue of *Studies in Romanticism* (1996) from which this quote is taken: *Green Romanticism*.

The ecocritical approach to Romanticism that was pioneered by Bate in his earlier monograph, *Romantic Ecology: Wordsworth and the Environmental Tradition* (1991), like that of Karl Kroeber in *Ecological Literary Criticism: Romantic Imagining and the Biology of Mind* (1994), locates the actuality of English Romantic literature in the proto-ecological understanding of natural systems and human subjectivity that a new generation of environmentally aware scholars was eager to trace historically. Supported by extensive research into Romantic natural history and natural philosophy (see e.g. Cunningham/Jardine; Poggi/Bossi; Heringman; Nichols), the case for Romanticism's »green« credentials – not only in Britain, but also in the German region – is by now well established. Not only is it possible to discern within German and English Romanticism around 1800 the emergence of a modern (or possibly even postmodern) understanding of the natural world as a profoundly complex, dynamically interactive and historically evolving network of biotic and abiotic entities and processes; there is also evidence of a dawning awareness of the dangers posed to both natural environments and human wellbeing by the industrialization process then underway, above all in Britain, and of a new ethical, as well as aesthetic, sensibility towards other-than-human beings. While a series of ecocritical publications following Bate's and Kroeber's (e.g. Morton, *Shelley and the Revolution in Taste*; McKusick; Lussier; Oerlemans; Hutchings, *Imagining Nature*) continued and deepened their broadly sympathetic exploration of »romantic ecology«, Greg Garrard's more cautious view of the Romantic legacy as »both vital and ambiguous« (129) has been borne out in the later studies of Rigby (*Topographies of the Sacred*), Morton (*Ecology without Nature*) and Hutchings (*Romantic Ecologies*).[1] In this article, I propose to extend this ecocritical consideration of the ambiguous actuality of Romanticism to an examination of Eichendorff's ecopoetics, as seen through the lens of Gernot Böhme's »ecological aesthetics of nature« and my own theory of »negative ecopoetics«.

As Tim Chandler and I explain in the introduction to our translation of his essay *Atmosphärisches in der Erfahrung der Natur*, Böhme is a leading figure in the contemporary renaissance of German *Naturphilosophie*, in the guise of a renovated Critical Theory of social-natural relations, interweaving (post-)Marxist social critique and the new phenomenology of Hermann

---

[1] See Hutchings' overview of »Ecocriticism in British Romanticism Studies« (up until 2006) and Rigby, »Romanticism« (forthcoming).

Schmitz.[2] Böhme's work is underwritten by the sober recognition that »we no longer stand on the brink of environmental catastrophe: we are in the midst of it« (*Die Natur vor uns*, 261). Under these circumstances, Böhme calls for a pragmatically oriented *Naturphilosophie*, which, like the older Critical Theory as defined by Max Horkheimer, would be »driven by the interest in reasonable conditions«, while nonetheless recognizing that what constitutes »reasonableness« with regard to social-natural relations cannot be presupposed, but must be communicatively elucidated over time, and oriented toward safeguarding the reproduction of natural systems as the necessary foundation for human society. The urgent need for such a critical theory of social-natural relations arises from the increasingly anthropogenic character of our earthly environs, or »the nature that we are not«, coupled with the growing technologization of the human body, or »the nature that we ourselves are«.

Böhme acknowledges that the transformation of our industrially degraded earthly environs into a flourishing and humane social-ecological living space requires the guidance of the natural and technical sciences. Scientific and technical knowledge, he argues, is nonetheless insufficient to the task of grounding an ethical relationship with other-than-human nature, let alone an ecological aesthetics: science might be able to define limit conditions for healthy environments, but it cannot tell us why we might desire to share our living space with a diversity of plants and animals, or why we should treat them with respect in their own right. If we are to reposition ourselves as allies rather than conquerors of nature in the production of a newly »habitable earth«, to recall the utopian vision of Shelley's *Queen Mab* (1, 122), we need to supplement the sciences with a different type of knowledge, premised not on objectification, but on recognition: this would be a carnal kind of knowing, whereby we come to understand the other, if never fully, on the basis of a relationality that is given in and through our shared physical existence. In this way, the discovery of other-than-human nature is necessarily conjoined with the recovery of our own naturality. And that is where aesthetics comes in.

In order to answer the question as to what kind of nature we wish to inhabit and embody, we need to begin by ascertaining what ›nature‹ means to us from a non-instrumental perspective. On one level, as Simon Schama has

---

[2] For a more detailed introduction to Böhme's thought as it pertains in particular to ecopoetics and ecocriticism, see Rigby, »Gernot Böhme's Ecological Aesthetics of Atmosphere«. The following four paragraphs are drawn from parts of this essay.

demonstrated in *Landscape and Memory*, this is a question for the cultural historian who traces the ways in which stories, books, and paintings invest certain entities and places with meaning, and inscribe them in our affections. What is it, though, about roses for examples, that has invited the symbolic significance that European culture, for one, has ascribed to them? For Böhme, this is a question for the phenomenologist, for it concerns the way in which things manifest themselves to human perception in potentially mood-altering ways. Somatics, in other words, precedes semantics. Corresponding to the project of transforming the »nature that we ourselves are not« into a humane living space, Böhme thus identifies the cultivation of the »nature that we ourselves are« as an ethical »task« (*Leibsein als Aufgabe*): one oriented towards overcoming the mind-body dualism that haunts the modern Cartesian subject, in tandem with the culture-nature dualism that has blighted our relations with the nonhuman world. Recognizing that ethical questions, and the answers we give them, are to some degree historically contingent, Böhme argues that while it was formerly considered virtuous to exercise control over the wayward flesh, today we need to make a virtue out of heeding our bodily states and sensations (*leibliches Spüren*). The articulation and theorization of this attentive sensing of one's own bodily state of being, or disposition, in the presence of other people, things, and places constitutes the core concern of Böhme's ecological aesthetics.

The key concept of this new aesthetics comes from Schmitz: namely, »atmosphere«. Atmospheres are »affective powers of feeling, spatial bearers of moods« (Böhme, *Atmosphäre,* 119), and they constitute what Böhme terms the »space of feeling« or »mood« (*Gefühlsraum*). While Schmitz discusses aesthetics, he does not relate it to atmosphere. In order to do so, Böhme corrects Schmitz's view of atmosphere as uncoupled from things and unlocalizable in space by drawing on Aristotle's notion of *ekstasis:* how things go forth from themselves, giving themselves to perception through particular qualities, for instance, of size, shape, colour, smell or sound. Such self-disclosure always involves an element of self-concealment: no other is ever fully present to us, and we wrong the other that we take to be so. Being, according to Böhme's neo-Aristotelian ontology, is nonetheless always being-for-another, which is to say, being-in-communication (*Atmosphäre*, 183–186). In their »ecstasies«, people, things, and places »tincture« the environment in which they are perceived, and in so doing, generate »atmospheres«:

> Conceived in this fashion, atmospheres are neither something objective, that is, qualities possessed by things, and yet they are something thinglike, belonging to the thing in that things articulate their presence through qualities – conceived as ecstasies. Nor are atmospheres something subjective, for example, determinations of a psychic state. And yet they are subjectlike, belonging to subjects in that they are sensed in bodily presence by human beings and this sensing is at the same time a bodily state of being of subjects in space (»Atmosphere as the Fundamental Concept«, 122).

While Böhme's concept of atmosphere takes aesthetics »beyond the frame« of the work of art, as I put it in an earlier article (*Beyond the Frame*), and into such varied fields as landscape architecture, urban planning, interior design, and the critique of the »aesthetic economy«, it also offers an ecocritically valuable perspective on the arts, including literature. For Böhme, the particular value of the work of art lies in its capacity not only to represent and generate particular atmospheres, but also to draw attention to the phenomenon of atmosphere per se as a fundamental dimension of human bodily being in the world, or ecological selfhood. In my assessment, this potential of the work of art became particularly important within Western culture in response to the perceived deficits of rationalist reductionism: namely, within that strand of Romantic ecopoetics which seeks to foster an attunement to »the moods/ Of time and season, to the moral power,/The affections and the spirit of the place«, as Wordsworth puts it in *The Prelude* (235f.). Romantic painting, music, and literature frequently foreground the phenomenon of atmosphere, which also found an early theoretical articulation, as Böhme observes, in Baumgarten's aesthetics of sensual experience, Goethe's research into the »sensual-ethical« effects of colour, and Alexander von Humboldt's concept of the »physiognomy« of landscape (*Atmosphäre*, 101–152). As far as the literary work of art is concerned, lyrical language holds a privileged place in Böhme's ecological aesthetics. In its use of metaphor, metonymy, rhythm and rhyme, alliteration, and assonance, poetry is a particularly effective medium not only for the depiction of atmosphere, but also for its production: namely, in the bodily and affective responses of readers. In this way, the »space of poetry« itself constitutes a *Gefühlsraum*, not so much through the detailed description of any putative ›real‹ place, but through the use of figurative language and phonetic effects to inflect the reader's state-of-feeling. Among German Romantic writers, the master-craftsman of poetic atmospheres is undoubtedly Eichendorff. What is perhaps most characteristic of the Eichendorffian *Stimmungsgedicht*, moreover, is the privilege it accords to sound in the generation of the atmospheres it invokes. In his discussion of the phenomenon of »acoustic atmospheres«, Böhme explains how sounds modify the space in which they are heard, informing the listener's disposition, sometimes reaching »directly into his or her corporeal economy« (»Acoustic Atmospheres«, 16). Particular combinations of sounds contribute to the acoustic character of specific lifeworlds, »be they natural ones, like the sea, the forest or other landscapes, or be they the life worlds of cities and villages« (16).

When we find ourselves out-of-doors, or even indoors, but listening to what's leaking in from outside, some of the sounds that assail us are likely to be weather-borne. To go outside is to enter what Tim Ingold terms the »weather-world«, a world not of static objects, but of »comings and goings«, of »formative and transformative *processes*« (117), in which, as we move through it, we are corporeally caught up – and which, ensconced in our air-conditioned interiors, we forget at our peril. »As an experience of light, sound and feeling that suffuses our awareness«, Ingold writes, »the weather is not so much an *object* of perception as what we perceive *in*, underwriting our very capacities to see, to hear and to touch« (127). Drawing on Böhme, Ingold notes also that in the weather-world, the aesthetic and meteorological meanings of ›atmosphere‹ come together. Acoustic atmospheres, whether weather-borne or otherwise, Ingold stresses, should not be thought of as ›soundscapes‹, which implies objectification rather than immersion. In attending to the audible ecstasies of the phenomena around us we are, in a sense, taken out of ourselves and beyond the confines of a fixed location:

> Sound flows, as wind blows, along irregular and winding paths, and the places it describes are like eddies, formed by a circular movement *around* rather than a fixed location *within*. To follow sound, that is to listen, is to wander the same paths. Attentive listening, as opposed to passive hearing, surely entails the very opposite of emplacement (139).

As Böhme observes:

> Human beings who listen in this way are dangerously open; they release themselves into the world and can therefore be struck by acoustic events. Lovely tunes can lead them astray, thunderclaps can shatter them, scratching noises can threaten them, a cutting tone can damage them. Listening is a being-beside-yourself [*Außer sich sein*]; it can be the joyful experience of discovering oneself to be alive (»Acoustic Atmospheres«, 18).

This doubly ecstatic dimension of sound is brought to the fore in Eichendorff's writing. Sound figures significantly throughout his work as a verbal means of confirming the perceptibility of a material reality that transcends individual consciousness and has the power to impose itself on the lived experience of the perceiving subject at the level of mood. In this way, as Uwe Steiner has argued, Eichendorff sought to contest the subjective idealism that had gained popularity among some of the early German Romantics, according to which the perceived world existed only in the eye of the sovereign I (as argued in particular by Johann Gottlieb Fichte in his *Theory of Knowledge* of 1794). For Eichendorff, this idealist philosophy of human consciousness effectively condemned us to a nightmarish condition of solipsistic self-enclosure, severing us from the more-than-human materiality of the circumambient world; a world, moreover, that was for him, as a practicing Catholic with romantically panentheistic leanings, suffused with the trace of the divine (Schilson). Resisting the solipsistic and even sacrilegious implications of Fichtean idealism, Eichendorff dethrones the sovereign self by showing how external entities, and in particular, things that we cannot even see, manifesting themselves to us only as non-localizable sounds, have the capacity to interrupt our intellections, altering our psycho-physical state of being, and reconnecting us with a material reality beyond the self. Herein, then, lies a key aspect of the actuality of Eichendorff's atmospheric ecopoetics: the disclosure of human subjectivity as corporeal, affective and environmentally inflected. In his lyrical use of language, moreover, Eichendorff's writing does to the reader what it shows happening to his lyrical subjects: in its sonorous musicality, no less than in the associations that it summons semantically, Eichendorff's verse draws attention to the somatic and affective force of sound.

Consider, for example, the role of acoustic atmospheres in generating that most paradigmatic of Romantic moods – longing – in Eichendorff's poem of that name. What I find particularly striking in *Sehnsucht*, and so characteristic of Eichendorff, is that while the poem begins by alluding to the visible realm (*Es schienen so golden die Sterne*), the speaker's attention is swiftly deflected from the starlit sky to the space that is opened up by what he hears. It is, in the first place, the distant sound of the posthorn penetrating the stillness, silence or quietude (*still* can mean all of these and more) of the nocturnal countryside that summons the sense of longing named in the title. That this is interpreted by the speaker as a desire to »go roving« cannot be attributed solely to the sound qua sound, however, but is inevitably inflected also by the cultural connotations of the posthorn, an instrument traditionally blown to announce the arrival of news from afar, signifying metonymically also the roving existence of those who convey it. As such, the posthorn, which echoes across so much of Eichendorff's verse, could be read as a metaphor for the poetic voice, calling the reader to attention: hey, listen up, I've got a missive for you!

This displacement of the visual by the auditory is repeated in the second stanza, where the image of two companions walking a mountain trail is immediately eclipsed by the sound of their singing as they traverse the peaceful terrain. In the song within the song this pattern is twice repeated. In the second stanza, a landscape is briefly visualized – *Sie sangen von schwindelnden Felsenschlüften* – which is immediately rendered acoustically – *wo die Wälder rauschen so sacht* – and while the sound of the mountain springs is not described, it is hinted at phonetically in the tinkling alliteration and broken metre of the lines that describe them (*Von Quellen, die von den Klüften/ Sich stürzen in die Waldesnacht*: note also how the precipitous fall of the water, literally throwing itself down the rockface, is echoed in the enjambement of this clause). Then, in the last stanza, we are again invited to visualize a locale, but one that is primarily characterized by its acoustic atmosphere: that which is said to be experienced by the girls listening at the palace window – somewhat queerly, these are evidently identification figures for the solitary speaker listening at his window – who have themselves, it seems, been awakened by the sound of an awakening lute (*Wann der Lautenklang erwacht*). This arousing lute music is in turn said to mingle with the drowsy sound of the fountains or springs, which *verschlafen rauschen* in the »glorious summer's night« summoned up in the speaker's imagination by the walkers' song, this »glorious summer's night« (*Werke und Schriften*, vol. 1, 35).

Importantly, *Sehnsucht* not only instantiates the phenomenon of acoustic atmosphere: it can also be read as issuing an implicit warning about the risk of being carried away, and potentially led astray, by the power of the poetic word. Just as the speaker is dislocated from his own immediate environs by the fantasy of an exotic, erotic other world evoked by the wayfarers' song, one that draws the trajectory of his desire down from the blessed intimation of divine presence in the starlit sky above to the blissed-out burbling of waters welling up from below ground, so too might the reader be swept up in the atmosphere of longing engendered by the poet's words. What Tim Morton refers to as the ambient ecomimesis of Romantic poetry can itself function as a form of idealist seduction, and one that is intimately entangled, as he observes, with the birth of bourgeois consumerism (*Ecology without Nature*, 82, 110). Eichendorff too was alert to the narcissistic lure of consumeristic ecomimesis, as revealed, for example, in the fashion for constructing artificial wildernesses in privately owned woodland that he targets in »Der Adel und die Revolution«. In the third book of *Ahnung und Gegenwart*, Friedrich and Leontin are dismayed to stumble upon a folly of this kind, a carefully landscaped English garden fenced off from the surrounding forest, and disoriented by the hall of mirrors in which they find themselves in the nearby »surrogate-temple« (*Werke und Schriften*, vol. 2, 248). The description of this experience implicitly links the taste for nature-faking with the idolatry of sovereign selfhood – this is nothing less than a temple to the solipsistic human ego – which is in turn indexed to a privileging of the visual over the auditory:

> Wände und Decke bestanden daselbst aus künstlich geschliffenen Spiegeln, die ihre Gestalten auf einmal ins Unendliche vervielfältigten. Ihr Kopf war ganz überfüllt und verwirrt von dem Gesehenen. Kein Mensch war in der weiten Runde zu hören, es grauste ihnen fast, länger in dieser Verrückung so einsam zu verweilen und sie begaben sich daher schnell wieder ins Freie (249).

Once outside this crazy-making realm of endless self-reflection, they are eventually returned to their bodily being-with-others (including their trusty steeds), in the lively midst of the more-than-human weather-world, by following the path of a freely-flowing stream back into the sounding forest,

> dessen Rauschen gegen die unruhig phantastische Spielerei der Gartenanlage fast schmerzlich abstach, so daß die beiden Freunde überrascht stillstanden. Sie sehnten sich recht in die große, ruhige, kühle Pracht hinaus und atmeten erst frei, als sie wirklich wieder zu Pferde saßen (249f.).

In Steiner's assessment, »[d]ie Klanglandschaften Eichendorffs beschreiben demnach Figuren der Immersion, die sich der Selbstbezüglichkeit, der Zirkularität monadischer Introversion widersetzen« (115).

While I am in agreement with this reading of Eichendorff's deployment of *Rauschen* as key to his anti-idealist, one might even say theo-materialist atmospheric ecopoetics, it is important to note that with the advent of auditory recording devices, the acoustic atmosphere of the forest too can be faked and made available for aesthetic consumption, as can be seen in today's thriving eco-muzak industry (typically marketed under the label of ›ambient‹ music). The repeated use of the onomatopoeia *Rauschen*, a verbal form of ecomimesis, in the song-within-the-song of *Sehnsucht* might be seen to partially prefigure this consumerist and, for Eichendorff, idolatrous, replication and appropriation of natural sounds. Elsewhere in Eichendorff's verse, however, this consumerist tendency is at least partially disrupted by the uncanny alterity that is shown to attend the experience of the audible rustling of the more-than-human world. Whether it is occasioned by wind billowing in the trees, springs burbling up from below ground, or waterways making their winding way across the land, *Rauschen* conveys an impression of movement, indicating that something invisible and unlocalizable is stirring: in the forest, it sets the trees in motion; giving them voice, as it were, it engenders a mood of excitement or expectation in the human hearer. Yet the arousal occasioned by *Rauschen* is variously inflected in Eichendorff's verse: *Rauschen* itself is a moody phenomenon.

In *Mondnacht*, for example, the softly rustling forests bear witness not only to the movement of air, but also, perhaps, to the breath of God, conveying a sense of divine presence that is hinted at in the opening lines in the image of a hypothetical heavenly kiss. Less theologically, we might say with Tim Ingold, that the sound of the swirling passage of wind through a forest in the weather-world discloses the mutual implication of earth and sky (119). This intermingling is not always so felicitous, however. Elsewhere, it conjures the stirring of something unsettling, uncanny, even foreboding, as in *Der Abend*:

> Schweigt der Menschen laute Lust:
> Rauscht die Erde wie in Träumen
> Wunderbar mit allen Bäumen,
> Was dem Herzen kaum bewußt,
> Alte Zeiten, linde Trauer,
> Und es schweifen leise Schauer
> Wetterleuchtend durch die Brust.
> (*Werke und Schriften*, vol. 1, 37).

Tellingly, earth's vespertine *Rauschen* is said to be audible here only when human noise is stilled. This is an acoustic environment in which the human is decentred, the dominion of instrumental reason overthrown, and we discover that we are in some sense strangers to ourselves, called into being-with-others by things beyond our grasp. As such, it might be read as a manifestation of what Keats termed the »material sublime«, in which the human subject realizes that consciousness »cannot fully represent the material order (which is truly ›other‹), but that it is the ground for being« (Oerlemans, 5). As I have observed elsewhere, Eichendorff's ecopoetics manifests an impulse towards *kenosis*, or self-emptying, »a longing to go radically astray: to renounce the dominion of the ego over the psyche, and, by extension, of man over nature. As Adorno puts it [in his essay *In Memory of Eichendorff*], ›this poetry never knows where ›I‹ am, because the ego squanders itself on what it is whispering about« (Rigby, *Topographies*, 227f.). This kenotic impulse surfaces most strikingly in another of Eichendorff's many poems of the night, *Nachts*, in which the nightsong of the earth unmoors the subject's thoughts, infusing his own song with a trace of that reality which subtends and exceeds human consciousness:

> O wunderbarer Nachtgesang:
> Von fern im Land der Ströme Gang,
> Leis Schauern in den dunklen Bäumen –
> Mein irres Singen hier
> Ist wie ein Rufen nur aus Träumen.
> (Werke und Schriften, vol. 1, 12).

For ecocritics favouring realistic description, Eichendorff is bound to be a disappointment. Greg Garrard, for example, criticizes his verse for its paucity of »concrete content« (128). But this is really a category error, because Eichendorff's way of affirming the autonomy of material reality is precisely to refuse to image it literally: to do so would be to betray the materiality of things as they are given to bodily experience for a mere verbal simulacrum, and, as we have seen, he had no time for nature-faking. So, the somewhat paradoxical thought with which I wish to conclude is that Eichendorff's *Rauschen*, even while it echoes the rustling weather-world to which it refers, simultaneously signals the irreducibility of the watery and wooded earth to human words. Legible, as Ralf Simon has argued, as a figure of *différance*, it is central to the »negative ecopoetics« (Rigby, »Earth, World, Text«) of Eichendorff's verse, the positive value of which is to turn our attention towards the more-than-human world beyond the page by foregrounding the nonidentity of words and things, signs and their infamously slippery referents. At a time when woodlands and forests around the world are being silenced at an unprecedented rate, waterways sullied by industrial pollutants and, in some cases, desiccated by anthropogenic climate change, while wired-up people of privilege retreat ever further into simulacral worlds of human making, an ecopoetics that recalls, without replicating, the unspeakable ecstasy of air passing through tangled boughs in the weather-world and of free-flowing waters making their winding way across the land, acquires a new significance, and a further dimension of actuality. *Rauschen*, in this sense, is the sound of silence, or at least, of wordlessness, arising from that which cannot be fully grasped and adequately named within human systems of cognition and signification, but which nonetheless flows around and even through the speaking subject, subtly recomposing, or radically discomposing, their bodily disposition and state of mind.

As an audible trace of the mobile material phenomena of the weather-world, this uncanny *Rauschen* might also be seen as disclosing the affectedness of the local by the global: the inevitable susceptibility of particular places to planetary forces, including unruly wind systems and changeable water flows, but also acid rain and global warming, all of which have no respect for humanly-instituted terrestrial boundaries. From an environmental justice perspective, moreover, it is important to recall that the negative impacts of those environmental and climatic changes wrought by industrial modernity's onslaught upon the planet – earth conceived reductively as a standing reserve of »resources« rather than as an interdependent collective of more-than-human life – tend to get passed on to the poor, who suffer disproportionately from such environmental ills as toxic pollutants, increased vulnerability to weather extremes, and the depressingly grey atmosphere of monotone urban slums. In this context, Eichendorff's *Rauschen* not only conjures an acoustic atmosphere: it might also read as constituting an appeal, calling for a politico-ethical no less than an aesthetic-affective response.

To finish, then, a final word from Eichendorff, this time explicitly in hortatory mode, from a poem that hints at the potentially life-defeating implications of the suppression, or disruption, of the atmospheric ecstasies of earth and sky in the service of creating artificial paradises for the rich and powerful:

> Prinz Rokokko hat die Gassen
> Abgezirkelt fein mit Bäumen,
> Und die Bäume scheren lassen,
> Daß sie nicht vom Wald mehr träumen.
>
> [...]
>
> Quellen, die sich unterfingen,
> Durch die Waldesnacht zu tosen,
> Läßt du als Fontänen springen
> Und mit goldnen Bällen kosen,
>
> [...]
>
> Laß die Wälder ungeschoren:
> Anders rauscht's, als du gedacht,
> Sie sind mit dem Lenz verschworen,
> Und der Lenz kommt über Nacht.
> (*Werke und Schriften*, vol. 1, 176).

Works Cited

Bate, Jonathan. *Romantic Ecology: Wordsworth and the Environmental Tradition.* London: Routledge, 1991.
Bate, Jonathan. »Living with the Weather«. *Green Romanticism.* Ed. J. Bate. Special issue of *Studies in Romanticism* 55.3 (1996): 431–448.
Bate, Jonathan. *The Song of the Earth.* Cambridge, Mass.: Harvard University Press, 2000.
Böhme, Gernot. *Für eine ökologische Naturästhetik.* Frankfurt/M: Suhrkamp, 1989.
Böhme, Gernot. »Atmosphere as the Fundamental Concept of a New Aesthetics«. *Thesis Eleven* 36 (1993): 113–126.
Böhme, Gernot. *Atmosphäre: Essays zur neuen Ästhetik.* Frankfurt/M: Suhrkamp, 1995.
Böhme, Gernot. »Acoustic Atmospheres: A Contribution to the Study of Ecological Aesthetics«. Tr. Norbert Ruebsaat. *Soundscape* 1.1 (Spring 2000): 14–18.
Böhme, Gernot. *Die Natur vor uns: Naturphilosophie in pragmatischer Hinsicht.* Kusterdingen: Graue Edition, 2002.
Böhme, Gernot. *Leibsein als Aufgabe: Leibphilosophie in pragmatischer Hinsicht.* Kusterdingen: Die Graue Edition, 2003.
Böhme, Gernot. »Contribution to the Critique of the Aesthetic Economy«. *Thesis Eleven* 73 (May 2003): 71–82.
Böhme, Gernot. »Driven by the Interest in Reasonable Conditions«. *Thesis Eleven* 81 (May 2005): 80–90.
Böhme, Gernot. »The Atmospheric in the Experience of Nature« (1995). Tr. and intro. Timothy Chandler/Kate Rigby. *Nach der Nature/After Nature. Limbus* 3 (2010): 67–88.
Cunningham, Andrew/Nicholas Jardine (eds.). *Romanticism and the Sciences.* Cambridge: Cambridge University Press, 1990.
Eichendorff, Joseph Freiherr von. *Werke und Schriften.* Eds. Gerhart Baumann/Siegfried Grosse. Stuttgart: Cotta, 1957.
Garrard, Greg. »The Romantics' View of Nature«. *Spirit of the Environment: Religion, Value and Environmental Concern.* Eds. D.E. Cooper/J.A. Palmer. London: Routledge, 1998: 113–130.
Heringman, Noah. *Romantic Rocks, Aesthetic Geology.* Ithaca/London: Cornell University Press, 2004.
Hutchings, Kevin. *Imagining Nature: Blake's Environmental Poetics.* Montreal/Kingston: McGill-Queen's University Press, 2002.
Hutchings, Kevin. »Ecocriticism in British Romanticism Studies«. *Literature Compass* 4.1 (2007): 172–202.
Hutchings, Kevin. *Romantic Ecologies and Colonial Cultures in the British Atlantic World 1770–1850.* Montreal/Kingston: McGill-Queen's University Press, 2009.
Ingold, Tim. *Being Alive: Essays on Movement, Knowledge and Description.* Abingdon: Routledge, 2011.

Kroeber, Karl. *Ecological Literary Criticism. Romantic Imagining and the Biology of Mind.* New York: Columbia University Press, 1994.

Lussier, Mark. *Romantic Dynamics: The Poetics of Physicality.* Basingstoke: Macmillan, 2000.

McKusick, James. *Green Writing: Romanticism and Ecology.* New York: St. Martin's Place, 2000.

Morton, Timothy. *Shelley and the Revolution in Taste: The Body and the Natural World.* Cambridge: Cambridge University Press, 1994.

Morton, Timothy. *Ecology without Nature: Rethinking Environmental Aesthetics.* Cambridge, Mass.: Harvard University Press, 2007.

Oerlemans, Onno. *Romanticism and the Materiality of Nature.* Toronto: Toronto University Press, 2002.

Poggi, Stefano/Bossi, Maurizio (eds.). *Romanticism in Science: Science in Europe, 1790–1840.* Dordrecht: Kliewer Academic Publishers, 1994.

Nichols, Ashton. *Romantic Natural Histories: William Wordsworth, Charles Darwin, and Others.* Boston: Haughton, 2004.

Rigby, Kate. »Beyond the Frame: Art, Ecology and the Aesthetics of Nature«. *Thesis Eleven* 32 (1992): 114–128.

Rigby, Kate. »Earth, World, Text: On the (Im)possibility of Ecopoiesis«. *New Literary History* 35.3 (Summer 2004): 427–442.

Rigby, Kate. *Topographies of the Sacred: The Poetics of Place in European Romanticism.* Charlottesville: University of Virginia Press, 2004.

Rigby, Kate. »Gernot Böhme's Ecological Aesthetics of Atmosphere«. *Ecocritical Theory: New European Perspectives.* Eds. Axel Goodbody/Kate Rigby. Charlottesville: University of Virginia Press, 2011: 139–142.

Rigby, Kate. »Romanticism«. *The Oxford Handbook of Ecocriticism.* Ed. Greg Garrard. Oxford: Oxford University Press (forthcoming).

Schama, Simon. *Landscape and Memory.* London: Harper Perennial, 1996.

Schilson, Arno. »Romantische Religiosität? Religion als Thema im Werk Eichendorffs«. *Eichendorffs Modernität.* Eds. Michael Kessler/Helmut Koopmann. Tübingen: Stauffenberg, 1989: 121–139.

Shelley, Percy Bysshe. *The Complete Works of Shelley.* Eds. Roger Ingpen/Walter E. Peck. New York: Gordion, 1965.

Simon, Ralf. »Der Baum der Sprache. Zum lyrischen Bild bei Eichendorff«. ›*Du kritische Seele‹ Eichendorff: Epistemologien des Dichtens.* Ed. Daniel Müller Nielaba. Würzburg: Königshausen & Neumann, 2008: 51–62.

Steiner, Uwe C. »Spiegelfluchten und Soundscapes. Eichendorffs Dinge und Nichtdinge«. ›*Du kritische Seele‹ Eichendorff: Epistemologien des Dichtens.* Ed. Daniel Müller Nielaba. Würzburg: Königshausen & Neumann, 2008: 109–125.

Wordsworth, William. *The Fourteen-Book Prelude.* Ed. W.J.B. Owen. Ithaca: Stanford University Press, 1985.

Johannes F. Lehmann (*Universität Duisburg-Essen*)

Vom Leben und Tod der Dinge:
Zur Aktualität der romantischen Komiktheorie
Stephan Schützes

Abstract

Between 1810 and 1817 Stephan Schütze developed a theory of the comic which focuses primarily on the connection between action and objects. He observed that while dead objects seem to be animated by their capability to resist human will and thereby obtain agency, agents seem to become machines (»Maschinen zu werden scheinen«). It is exactly this incorporation of objects and objectivity into the concept of action that accounts for the topicality of Schütze's theory which has largely been neglected in research and which also becomes essential in the technical-philosophical and sociological works of Bruno Latour. By using historical discourse this paper reflects on how the applied oppositions such as life and death or organism and mechanism, which are also important in Henry Bergson's vitalistic *Laughter: An Essay on the Meaning of the Comic*, are placed in the context of life sciences around 1800. Taking into consideration this theoretical background this article will show that especially romantic and literary fairy tales regarded the connection between action and objects as a central theme, at the same time as Schütze developed his theory.

I.

In seinem 1817 publizierten *Versuch einer Theorie des Komischen* formuliert Stephan Schütze (1771–1839) erstmals eine Komiktheorie, die zentral die Sphäre der toten Dinge und ihr *Als ob* des lebendigen Handelns zur Grundlage des Komischen macht: »Zur Lächerlichkeit des Menschen gehört durchaus die Abhängigkeit seines Geistes von der Körperwelt und das Widerstreben derselben« (*VK*, 52f.). Eben dieses Widerstreben der Materie erscheint als lebendiger, intentionaler Akt: »In diesem Sinne erscheint die beschränkende Körperwelt wieder als belebt, als ein handelnder Geist [...]« (*VK*, 77). Lange vor Henri Bergson und noch länger vor Bruno Latour gerät so im Feld der Komiktheorie das anthropologisch und technisch intrikate Verhältnis des Menschen zu den Dingen in den Blick. Ich will im Folgenden zum einen die Aktualität dieser (von der Forschung völlig vergessenen) Schütze'schen Theorie des Komischen vor dem Hintergrund heutiger Kulturtheorien herausarbeiten und zum anderen zeigen, dass es insbesondere Märchen und Kunstmärchen der Romantik sind, die vom Tod und Leben der Dinge auf dem Niveau der Schütze'schen Komiktheorie erzählen.

II.

Bruno Latour ist kein Komiktheoretiker. Aber da er sich seit rund zwei Jahrzehnten mit dem Verhältnis des Menschen zu den Dingen beschäftigt, mit einer »symmetrischen Anthropologie« (Latour, *Wir sind nie*) bzw. einer »Akteur-Netzwerk-Theorie« (Latour, *Eine neue Soziologie*), die jene »Große Trennung« (Latour, *Wir sind nie*, 77) zwischen menschlichen Handlungssubjekten und toten Dingen, d.h. die prätendierte Modernität eines hierarchischen Subjekt-Objekt-Verhältnisses unterminiert und in beide »Kollektive« (Latour, *Das Parlament*) überführt,[1] überrascht es nicht, dass er bei der philosophischen und soziologischen Analyse der komplexen Mensch-Ding-Interaktionen auch auf das Feld des Komischen, ja des Comics gerät. In einem Beitrag zu seinem Band *Der Berliner Schlüssel* mit dem Titel *Porträt von Gaston Lagaffe als Technikphilosoph* analysiert Latour ausführlich einen kurzen Comicstrip von Gaston. In ihm geht es um das Handlungsensemble zwischen dem Menschen, einer Katze, einer Möwe und einer Tür. Prunelle, der Vorgesetzte Gastons, ist wütend, da er permanent aufstehen und der Katze die Tür aufmachen muss, wenn diese, so wie es Katzen tun, kommt und geht, wie es ihr gefällt. Die Freiheit der Katze, so zeigt Latour in seiner Deutung des Comics, verwandelt Prunelle, der Zugwind hasst und daher auf einer immer wieder zu schließenden Tür besteht, in »eine Maschine« bzw. in einen »Roboter« im Dienst der Katze (Latour, *Porträt*, 17). Die Tür kann entweder geöffnet sein, dann ist es gut für die Katze, aber schlecht für Prunelle (Zugwind), oder geschlossen, dann aber schreit die Katze, weil sie nicht hinaus kann, und stört damit Prunelle. Die Tür mit ihrer Binarität von offen versus geschlossen stört also hier das Zusammenleben von Mensch und Tier. Da kommt Gaston auf die Idee, in die Tür eine Katzenklappe einzubauen, die nun mit ihren Scharnieren das permanente mechanische Türöffnen Prunelles übernimmt und dennoch vor Zugluft schützt. Das

---

[1] Vgl. hierzu auch: Kneer.

kostet zwar die Integrität der Tür, die nun ein Loch und damit eine neue Funktion hat, verändert aber das Zusammenleben von Mensch und Tier, insofern nun auch die Tür (als Ding) »handelt«, indem sie sich nun von selbst öffnet und schließt. Die Komik des Comics liegt nun darin, dass die ebenfalls im Büro mitlebende Möwe angesichts der Katzentür eifersüchtig wird und Gaston nun auch den oberen Rand der Tür absägt, damit auch die Möwe herein und hinaus fliegen kann, wie sie will.

Latour zeigt an diesem Beispiel, dass Mensch und Technik keinen Gegensatz bilden, sondern einen Handlungs- und Aushandlungszusammenhang: »Für Dinge und Menschen gibt es nur eine einzige Syntax und eine einzige Semantik« (26). Den Menschen mit seinen Erfindungen aus den Beziehungen, die er mit Dingen und Tieren bildet, herauslösen zu wollen, bezeichnet Latour abschließend als eine »barbarische Tortur, die hoffentlich nicht mehr unter dem schönen Namen Humanismus paradieren wird« (27).[2]

Die Dinge (und auch die Tiere) derart als Mitspieler und als Handelnde wahrzunehmen, die Handlungen der Menschen übernehmen, geht über eine Theoriebildung des Komischen weit hinaus. Gleichwohl ist die hier in Frage stehende Anthropologie und die Aufmerksamkeit auf die Dinge als Aktanten in den Handlungskreisen der Menschen ein für die moderne Komiktheorie zentrales Feld. Es waren insbesondere Theodor Friedrich Vischer und Henri Bergson, die auf zugleich ähnliche und verschiedene Weisen die Dinge im Feld des Komischen theoretisch geltend gemacht haben. Sprichwörtlich geworden ist die »Tücke des Objekts«, von der Vischer in seinem 1878 in erster Fassung erschienenen Roman *Auch einer. Eine Reisebekanntschaft* erzählt und die er zugleich in seiner Ästhetiktheorie als Problem des Zufalls und der Frage seiner ästhetischen Darstellbarkeit reflektiert. Wo immer nämlich sich die Dingwelt mit ihrer Widerständigkeit und Eigensinnigkeit gleichsam handelnd in die Handlungskreise menschlicher Subjekte einmischt, handelt es sich nach Vischer um einen Zufall: Wenn etwa ein Held einen Kampf verliert, weil der Regen die Waffen unbrauchbar gemacht hat (Vischer, *Ästhetik*, I, 119), oder wenn ein Held stirbt, weil ihm ein Ziegelstein auf den Kopf fällt (365). Während solche »rohen Zufälle« für Vischer in der Tragödie unstatthaft sind, finden sie umso mehr ihren Ort im Komischen, wenn etwa der Hosenträger reißt oder der Hemdknopf sich unter einer silbernen Platte verhakt, so dass »der ganze Plunder, den

---

2 Vgl. im selben Band auch den Aufsatz: *Ein Türschließer streikt*.

sie trug, Saucen, Eingemachtes aller Art, zum Teil dunkelrote Flüssigkeit«, über den Tisch »rollt, rumpelt, fließt« (Vischer, *Auch einer*, 22).
Der Mensch ist hier nicht mehr allein Handlungssubjekt, sondern zugleich Umwelt für Ding-Ding-Kausalitäten, die auf den Menschen keine Rücksicht nehmen. Zur Voraussetzung der Rede von der »Tücke des Objekts« wie auch von Vischers Theorie des Komischen gehört nun aber auch, dass den Objekten, die sich derart einmischen, eine – mit Latour gesprochen – *agency* zugeschrieben wird, kurz: dass die Dinge erscheinen, als ob sie Leben und (böse) Absicht hätten. Wir leihen ihnen, so Vischer, ein Bewusstsein; wir können nicht anders als dem Stein, über den wir stolpern, die Absicht zu unterstellen, uns absichtlich zu Fall gebracht zu haben, denn: »Es sieht ja auch gerade aus, als stecke ein Kobold dahinter; der Stein, an dem Einer strauchelt, scheint ihm aufgelauert« (Vischer, *Ästhetik*, I, 420) zu haben.
Der Mensch ist nach Vischer be-*dingt* von dreierlei Dingen: den Dingen der Außenwelt, dem Ding, das sein Körper ist, und dem Unbewussten. Komisch wird er, weil er im Zusammenstoß mit den widerständigen Dingen diese einerseits unwillkürlich belebt und in beidem – im Zusammenstoß und in der Belebung – jenes Dinghafte zum Vorschein kommt, das der Mensch selber ist, das er aber in seinem Selbstbewusstsein zugleich transzendiert. In einem *re-entry* des Gegensatzes von Selbstbewusstsein und Ding findet sich dieser Gegensatz auf der Seite des Selbstbewusstseins selbst. Denn schon das Nicht-anders-Können, als den Zufällen der Dingwelt, »hingerissen von dem Scheine einer planmäßigen Störung« (419), Leben und Absicht zu unterstellen, ist eine Art Unbewusstes bzw. eine Mechanik des Selbstbewusstseins, das nämlich nicht umhin kann, sich selbst auf alles außer ihm zu projizieren: Vischer spricht von dem im Menschen »selbst wirkenden Bestreben des Selbstbewußtseins, sich über das Weltganze zu erweitern« (419).
Abstrahiert man die Opposition, mit der Vischer das Komische aus dem Zusammenstoß zwischen dem menschlichen Bewusstsein und den Dingen entwickelt, erhält man den Gegensatz von Tod und Leben, von Mechanismus und Organismus. Es sind die toten Dinge, denen man als Beobachter »Leben« und Absicht leiht, d.h. Handlungen zuspricht, und dieses Leihen wiederum erscheint als ein Mechanismus im Bewusstsein. Auf der einen Seite steht so als Figuration des autopoietischen und organischen Lebens das Selbstbewusstsein des Menschen. Auf der anderen Seite ist alles andere, man könnte sagen die Kontingenz aller Ereignisse, die den Organismus betreffen, oder noch einfacher: die Umwelt, die aber bis ins Mechanische des Bewusstseins hineinreicht. Der lebendige Organismus steht so den Zufällen der Außenwelt gegenüber, auf die er reagieren muss. Der Zufall wirkt, so

Vischer, im Sinne »einer fortdauernden Wechselbeziehung« (96) zwischen dem Individuum und seiner Umwelt als »Lebensreiz« (96). »Das Lebendige wählt« (97), d.h., es verarbeitet nach Maßgabe der eigenen Gattungsstruktur die Umweltereignisse. »Leben«, so definiert Vischer, »ist ein ständiges Verarbeiten des Zufalls« (144). Dass Vischer die Tücke des Objekts erfinden und das Stolpern über Alltagsdinge ins Zentrum der Komiktheorie rücken kann, liegt exakt daran, dass er mit einem organischen Lebensbegriff arbeitet, dem das Mechanische als die tote Sphäre der Dinge und der Zufälle gegenübersteht, die dennoch den Anschein des Lebens gewinnen kann.

Es ist exakt diese Opposition von Leben und Tod, Organischem und Mechanischem, die Vischers Theorie des Komischwerdens der Dinge mit der 50 Jahre später formulierten Komiktheorie Henri Bergsons verbindet. Auch hier ist die Opposition zwischen Mechanischem und Organischem vor dem Hintergrund eines emphatischen Begriffs des Lebens der Horizont, in den Phänomene des Komischen eingestellt werden. Bis auf die Ebene der einzelnen Beispiele finden sich hier Korrespondenzen zwischen Vischer und Bergson. Damit ist aber Vischer nicht einfach ein Vorläufer von Bergson, sondern beide – Vischer wie Bergson – folgen einem Paradigma des Lebens, das in der Romantik formuliert wird. Die zentralen Gedanken seiner Komiktheorie hat Vischer den Schriften des Publizisten, Schriftstellers und Komiktheoretikers Stephan Schütze entnommen. Der alte Schütze hatte noch in seinem vorletzten Lebensjahr Vischers 1837 erschienene Schrift *Ueber das Erhabene und das Komische* positiv rezensiert.[3] Dadurch spätestens mag Vischer auf Schütze und dessen eigene Theorie des Komischen, die er in seiner Rezension auch erwähnt, gestoßen sein. Vischer jedenfalls bedankt sich für die positive Aufnahme seiner Theorie durch Schütze damit, dass er Schütze in seiner Ästhetik ausgiebig und fast immer zustimmend zitiert.

III.

Stephan Schütze, seit 1804 tätig in Weimar als Schriftsteller, Reisebegleiter Goethes und Publizist, etwa als Herausgeber des *Journals des Luxus und der Moden* und des *Taschenbuchs der Liebe und Freundschaft*, für das E.T.A. Hoffmann schrieb, veröffentlichte 1810 und 1812 zwei kurze Aufsätze zum Komischen, die er dann zu seinem umfangreichen »unserm Göthe« gewidmeten *Versuch*

---

[3] Jenaische Allgemeine Literatur-Zeitung Nr. 176 und 177, September 1838, Sp. 441-451.

einer Theorie des Komischen erweiterte, aber erst 1817 publizierte. Sein Buch folgt in seinem zentralen Theoriekapitel in der Struktur seiner Anlage den Schelling'schen Oppositionstermen von Freiheit und Notwendigkeit, von »Willkühr und Naturhandlung« (*VK*, 24). Im ersten Teil geht es um die Freiheit des Menschen (*VK*, 35–70), im zweiten um die Natur (*VK*, 70–79), die der Freiheit des Menschen als »handelnde Gegenwirkung« (*VK*, 70) auch und gerade in Form der Dinge gegenübersteht. Einerseits handelt der (freie) Mensch, andererseits begibt er sich, um zu handeln, notwendig in die Sphäre materieller Körper und Dinge: Der Mensch muss, »um eine Art von freyer Handlung auszuüben, sich der Körperwelt, sich der Arme und Beine bedienen« (*VK*, 227). Diese »Körperwelt« erscheint, wenn sie die Handlungen des Menschen tangiert oder stört, ihrerseits als handelnd, sie erscheint als »handelnde Gegenwirkung«. Da Handlungen immer ein intelligibles Moment enthalten, eine Absicht, sie aber auch ein materielles Moment enthalten, um realisiert zu werden, kommt der Begriff der Handlung sowohl auf der Seite der »Freiheit« wie auf der Seite der »Natur« vor. Hieraus erwächst nach Schütze das Komische.

Komisch ist, dass der Mensch »in und mit den Dingen Absichten zu erreichen sucht« (*VK*, 55) und dabei in Abhängigkeit eben dieser Dinge gerät: »Ein Strang, der zerreißt, ein Tropfen, der einen Funken auslöscht, ein Schall, ein Unterschied von einer Minute, tausend Kleinigkeiten können den Plan des Menschen vereiteln« (*VK*, 55). Die Dinge geraten deshalb ins Zentrum des Komischen, da sie – wie die Handlungen, die ihnen zugeschrieben werden – sowohl auf der Seite der Freiheit wie auf der der Natur vorkommen. Zwar sind Dinge zum einen »Geistes-Instrumente« (*VK*, 73) und also Werkzeuge des freien Willens und seiner Handlungen, zum anderen aber sind sie mögliche Hindernisse und gehören auf die Seite des Bedingten und Bedingenden. »So schwebt das Komische immer zwischen Körper und Geist, zwischen dem Bedingten und Unbedingten, zwischen der Natur und der Freyheit« (*VK*, 79).

Das Komische, das im Kampf des Menschen mit den Dingen entsteht, liegt nun darin begründet, dass die unbelebten Dinge, wenn sie sich als tote dem Menschen in den Weg stellen, gerade deshalb als belebt erscheinen. Das »Komische romantischer Art« wirkt »durch den Zufall todter Gegenstände, welche für den Augenblick selbst vernünftig scheinen« (*VK*, 29). Im Kern des Komischen »romantischer Art« liegt somit ein Akt der Verlebendigung, insofern der Mensch in der Interaktion mit den toten Gegenständen diese belebt, indem er ihnen Handlungen zurechnet. So fundiert Schütze das Komische im Spiel mit der Opposition von Leben und Tod:

> Das Todte liegt nur in so fern außer dem Kreise des Lächerlichen, als es nicht handelnd und mit Verstand begabt erscheinen kann, es paßt aber dafür, in so fern es überhaupt ist. Für die höhere Ansicht giebt es nemlich kein todtes Seyn, sondern dieses wird als Theil und Mittel von etwas Lebendigem und Handelnden betrachtet, und kann damit in Verbindung gestellt werden (*VK*, 37f.).

Indem wir den toten Dingen Absicht und das heißt Handlungen zurechnen, halten wir sie folgerichtig für lebendig. »Personifikationen von todten Gegenständen« (*VK*, 40) gehören nach Schütze ebenso ins Feld des Komischen wie die redende Verlebendigung von Leichen bei Aristophanes (*VK*, 40). Die rhetorische Figur des Komischen »romantischer Art« ist somit die Prosopopöie.

Das Komische entsteht aber nicht nur, wenn toten Dingen Handlung, d.h. Absicht (freie Wahl) und folglich Leben, zugerechnet wird, sondern auch umgekehrt, wenn die Handlungen des Menschen nicht als frei, sondern als von den Dingen, seinem Körper und dessen Mechanismus geprägt erscheinen. Die Körperwelt, die der Mensch mit seinem freien Willen als Geistesinstrument nutzt, reicht gleichsam in ihn und seine Freiheit hinein: »Der Geist findet die Gegenstände seiner Thätigkeit in der Außenwelt, aber auf dem Wege zu ihnen hinüber muß er Hände, Füße, Worte, Blicke u.s.w. gebrauchen, und sie in Bewegung setzen« (*VK*, 64). Als Geist initiiert der Mensch freie Handlungen, für die er seinen Körper braucht, als Körper aber gerät er selbst in die Mechanik der dinglichen Bewegungsabläufe. Damit ist bereits – ähnlich wie später bei Vischer und bei Bergson – das Mechanische des Körpers als ein Dingliches angesprochen, das bereits selbst komisch ist: »Gehen, stehen, sprechen, essen, trinken, jede Bewegung eines Gliedes hat schon von Natur seinen komischen Theil, der den völlig freien Geist zum Lachen reitzen kann« (Schütze, »Ueber das Komische«, 294).

Explizit verweist Schütze, wie später Bergson, auf die Struktur von »Wiederholungen, durch welche die Natur wie instinctartig fortwirkt« (*VK*, 125). Und er gibt hierfür Beispiele, die dann später in Vischers Roman (und in Bergsons Theorie) konkret wieder auftauchen, wie etwa das Husten und Niesen in der Rede: »Das Niesen wird komisch, wenn die Natur wider den Willen des Menschen dadurch mithandelnd erscheint (nach der Definition), z.B. durch das Plötzliche bey dem wichtigsten Wort der Rede, durch einen besonderen Ton, und durch unablässige Wiederkehr in einer größeren Versammlung« (*VK*, 124).[4]

---

[4] Der Katarrh der Hauptfigur von Vischers Roman, A.E., sein ständiges Niesen und Husten, vor allem auch in Situationen, in denen er als politischer Redner auftritt, sind Legion.

Die Abhängigkeit des Menschen von seinem Körper und seine Tendenz, in Bewegungsmechanik und Wiederholung zur Maschine zu werden, verknüpft Schütze mit der Sphäre der Arbeit und des Ökonomischen, ja der Notwendigkeit der Arbeitsteilung. In ihr nämlich kommt die unhintergehbare Verwiesenheit des Menschen auf seine Physis am stärksten zum Ausdruck. Das Komische konterkariert das Ideal des ganzen, gebildeten Menschen:

> Die Menschen, in dem vergeblichen Bestreben, Alles zu seyn, haben für nöthig gefunden, sich für das praktische Leben eine engere Bestimmung zuzumessen, und zur Wohlfahrt des Ganzen, wie zur Befriedigung des Einzelnen, sich in die Geschäfte getheilt. Diese Selbstbeschränkung wird für das Komische aber wieder eine große Bereicherung. – Jeder Stand an und für sich giebt schon jedem Menschen durch das bestimmte Gepräge, das er ihm aufdrückt, eine lächerliche Seite. [...] Die Arbeit, das Geschäft, der Umgang, die Art zu leben prägt sich auf seinem Gesicht, in Mienen und Gebehrden, im Ton der Stimme, in Stellung, Gang und jeder Bewegung, ja sogar in der Kleidung aus (*VK*, 86).[5]

Immer wieder macht Schütze auf das Komische des Standes aufmerksam, darauf, dass sich jenseits des Anspruchs des Menschen, unbeschränkt bzw. ganz zu sein, seine Beschränkung durch die Ausübung seines jeweiligen Berufs physisch niederschlägt, sich seinem Körper einschreibt als ein Etwas, das seine Freiheit unterminiert, so dass er »an das Physische zurückfällt«: »Es ist, als hätten ihm neckende Buben etwas angehängt, womit er lustig herumspringt, ohne die Posse zu ahnen« (*VK*, 87).

Das Mechanische, das dem Organischen gegenübersteht und ihm doch unhintergehbar einwohnt, ist so die zentrale und die fundamentale Quelle des Komischen. Komische Wirkung hat alles, »*was den Menschen zur Sache zu machen scheint*, und die Ahnung von einem Mechanismus giebt« (*VK*, 125). Komisch ist bereits der Anblick, »wie sich unsere Maschinerie in Bewegung setzt, wie wir gehen und stehen, essen und trinken [...]« (*VK*, 123). Komisch ist, wenn die Menschen »Maschinen zu werden scheinen« (*VK*, 126). Aufgrund dieser Tendenz des Menschen, als Mechanismus bzw. als Maschine zu erscheinen, folgert Schütze, dass es auf der Bühne bereits komisch wirke, »wenn viele Personen schnell einer nach dem anderen abgehen« (*VK*, 126) oder wenn viele Personen »blos, um eine Reihe zu bilden, hinter einander gehen« (*VK*, 126).

---

5 Vgl. auch *VK*, 151ff.

Wenn 30 Jahre später Vischer behauptet, komisch sei es, wenn die Bewegungen des Menschen, die eigentlich organisch gesteuert werden sollten, »dem Mechanischen« (Vischer, *Ästhetik*, I, 381) verfallen oder ins »Maschinenartige« (381)[6] sinken, und 80 Jahre später Bergson sagt, dass das Komische dem Ineinander der Vorstellungen von Mensch und Mechanismus entspringe,[7] dann ist Stephan Schütze ihr eigentlicher Ahnherr.

IV.

Indem Schütze das Komische in einem Begriff der Handlung fundiert, der aus Freiheit und Natur, bzw. aus der immateriellen Absicht, die »Leben« impliziert, und der Verwiesenheit auf Körper und Dinge, die »Tod« implizieren, zusammengesetzt ist, bewegt er sich vor dem diskursiven Horizont der Bestimmung des Lebens und des Organischen im Unterschied zum Anorganischen bzw. zum Tod um 1800. Es war hier nämlich genau die Frage, worin sich der lebende Organismus vom toten unterscheidet. Die Irritabilität, d.h. Reizbarkeit und Bewegungsreaktion, wie sie seit Albrecht von Haller – neben der Sensibilität – als zentrale Eigenschaft des Lebendigen diskutiert wurde (vgl. Haller), konnte hier keine eindeutige Antwort liefern, da sie auch bei bereits toten Lebewesen noch eine Zeitlang funktioniert: »Frösche mit abgehauenem Kopf hüpfen davon, als wäre ihnen eine unnütze Last genommen, Schildkröten bewegen sich mit ausgerissenem Herzen und abgenommenem Kopfe noch viele Tage fort« (Kielmeyer, 22). Und auf die Sensibilität, die Fähigkeit Schmerz zu empfinden und Vorstellungen zu haben, kann man von außen nur dann schließen, wenn sich das Lebewesen auf einen Reiz als Reaktion *bewegt*. Um 1800 wurde daher versucht, das Dilemma einer Erklärung des Lebens durch den Begriff der »Lebenskraft« zu lösen.[8] Sie sorgt dafür, dass der Organismus, solange er lebt, ein Stück weit von den physikalischen und chemischen Naturgesetzen befreit ist, so dass er zum Beispiel nicht verwest: »[D]ie Lebenskraft ist der Materie eigen und würkt den physischen Kräften der Verwandtschaft, Anziehung u.s.w. *entgegen*. Kein organischer Körper gährt also oder fault, so lange er lebt,

---

6 Vgl. auch 423: »Das Komische ist hier das Eindringen eines Mechanischen […]«.
7 Bergson, 28. Vgl. auch 21: »Stellungen, Gebärden, Bewegungen des menschlichen Körpers sind in dem Maße komisch, als uns dieser Körper dabei an einen bloßen Mechanismus erinnert«.
8 Vgl. zu dieser Debatte ausführlich Thüring.

gährt aber gewiß, sobald er todt ist« (Brandis, 18). Als Körper ist der Organismus den Naturgesetzen unterworfen (»den Gesetzen der Natur entläuft kein Körper«; 20), als lebender Organismus ist er durch die Lebenskraft dennoch von ihnen suspendiert, indem er eine organische Eigengesetzlichkeit ausbildet, erkennbar etwa an seiner relativ gleichbleibenden Temperatur. Das Leben bildet so eine inklusive Opposition von Leben und Tod, insofern der lebende Organismus zwar aus Materie besteht, aber allein die Lebenskraft verhindert, dass die Naturgesetze auf diese Materie unmittelbar durchgreifen können. Damit kann aber nun der Begriff der Lebenskraft allein das Leben nicht erklären, es muss zugleich eine Art Gegenkraft geben, gegen die sich die Lebenskraft manifestieren kann. Der französische Biologe Francois Xavier Bichat definiert daher bündig: »Das Leben ist der Inbegriff der Functionen, welche dem Tod widerstehen« (Bichat, 1).[9] Ähnlich formuliert Schelling diesen Gedanken einer notwendigen Gegenüberstellung von Kräften: »Das Leben, wo es zu Stande kommt, kommt gleichsam wider den Willen der äußeren Natur (invita natura externa), durch Losreißen von ihr, zu Stande« (Schelling, *Erster Entwurf*, 126). Es war vor allen Dingen Schelling, der derlei naturwissenschaftliche Debatten über den Unterschied zwischen Leben und Tod naturphilosophisch gewendet und in ein dialektisches Begriffsspiel von Freiheit (Organismus) und Natur (Mechanismus, Naturgesetze), von Geist und Materie verwandelt hat.[10] »Die Natur soll in ihrer blinden Gesetzmäßigkeit frei: und umgekehrt in ihrer vollen Freiheit gesetzmäßig seyn, in dieser Vereinigung allein liegt der Begriff der Organisation« (Schelling, *Weltseele*, 581).
In seiner Schrift *Vom Wesen der Komödie* legt Schelling nun das Verhältnis von Notwendigkeit und Freiheit auch für eine Theorie des Komischen zugrunde, wobei normalerweise »die Nothwendigkeit als das Objekt, die Freiheit als das Subjekt erscheint« (539). Das Komische besteht nun nach Schelling in der Umkehrung dieses Verhältnisses, also darin, dass das Objekt selbst als frei handelndes Subjekt erscheint. Das Komische ist nach Schelling da, »wo ein allgemeiner Gegensatz der Freiheit und Notwendigkeit ist, aber so,

---

[9] Vgl. hierzu Borgards, 125.
[10] »Wenn ein Theil derselben [der Naturforscher, J.L.] eine besondere Lebenskraft annimmt, die als eine magische Gewalt alle Wirkungen der Naturgesetze im belebten Wesen aufhebt, so heben sie eben damit alle Möglichkeit die Organisation physikalisch zu erklären auf. Wenn dagegen andere den Ursprung aller Organisation aus todten chemischen Kräften erklären, so heben sie eben damit alle Freiheit der Natur im Bilden und Organisieren auf. Beides aber soll vereinigt werden« (Schelling, »Weltseele«, 580f.). Vgl. hierzu Jantzen; Thüring.

daß diese in das Subjekt, jene ins Objekt fällt« (540). Was hier lediglich in einer abstrakten begrifflichen Struktur gefasst wird, übersetzt Schütze ins Konkrete, indem er die bei Schelling eingerichtete Systemstelle der ›Natur‹ bzw. der ›Notwendigkeit‹ tatsächlich mit Dingen (und gerade mit Dingen des Alltags) und dem Mechanischen des eigenen Körpers besetzt. So enthält der Gegensatz von Freiheit und Notwendigkeit, den Schütze von Schellings Theorie der Komödie übernimmt, zwei zentrale Achsen, eine innere und eine äußere: »Das Materiale, der Mechanismus der Welt, worin er [der Mensch, J.L.] mit seinem Geiste schwebt, kommt hier noch besonders in Betrachtung. Diese bestimmende Welt ist sowohl in ihm als außer ihm, und trägt überall dieselben Kennzeichen« (*VK*, 79f.): Zum einen die Achse zwischen dem Menschen und den toten, aber belebt scheinenden handlungsmächtigen Dingen außer ihm, die er als Behelf benötigt und in deren Abhängigkeit er steht, und zum anderen die Achse zwischen dem Organismus des Menschen und seiner eigenen mechanischen Körperlichkeit als seiner konstitutiven Rückseite, die ebenfalls dafür sorgt, dass der Mensch mit seiner Freiheit immer zugleich an das Physische zurückfallen muss. So wie die Dinge als Handelnde den Anschein des Lebens gewinnen, so erscheint zugleich das Leben als Mechanismus. Nur wenn man diese Doppelbewegung berücksichtigt, versteht man das »Komische romantischer Art« in vollem Umfang. Dem eigentlich romantischen Akt der Verlebendigung des Dinglichen korrespondiert die Mechanisierung des Lebendigen.

V.

Es sind die Volkslieder und die Volksmärchen, wie sie zu Beginn des 19. Jahrhunderts von Achim von Arnim und Clemens Brentano einerseits sowie von Jacob und Wilhelm Grimm andererseits gesammelt, bearbeitet und publiziert wurden, die – vor dem Hintergrund der Sphäre der Arbeit bzw. der zumeist handwerklichen Erwerbswelt – Gegenstände des Alltags in ihrer potentiellen Widerständigkeit wie in ihrer Handlungsmächtigkeit thematisieren. In dem berühmten Kinderlied *Das bucklige Männlein* aus dem dritten Band der Sammlung *Des Knaben Wunderhorn* stört oder stiehlt das bucklige Männlein die Arbeitsdinge des sprechenden Mädchens, so als ob es in den Dingen stecke oder mit ihnen magisch verbunden sei: Das Männlein zerbricht das »Töpflein«, es stiehlt das »Hölzlein«, es schnappt den »Krug« weg und es lässt das »Rad« nicht laufen. Und auch als Körper stört das Männlein das Mädchen, mit seinem Niesen und Lachen (Arnim, 1136). In den Grimm'schen Märchen, in der ersten Auflage publiziert 1812 und 1815, kommen ebenfalls Dinge des Alltags vor, die leben, wie zum Beispiel in dem komischen Märchen *Das Lumpengesindel* (KHM, 10) oder in *Herr Korbes* (KHM, 41).[11] Auch die Widerständigkeit der Dinge wird thematisiert. In dem Märchen *Der Nagel* (KHM, 184) etwa ist es der titelgebende Hufnagel, der sich löst, weil der Reiter sich keine Zeit nimmt, ihn festzuklopfen, so dass das Pferd den Huf verliert, stolpert, sich schließlich das Bein bricht und der Reiter nun zu Fuß nach Hause gehen muss. Mit der Thematisierung der Dinge bilden die Märchen nach einer Formulierung von Gabriele Brandstetter und Gerhard Neumann einen »ambivalenten Realismus«, betreiben sie eine »Brechung des Realen ins Phantastische« (Brandstetter/Neumann, 20). Es ist vor diesem Hintergrund das Kunstmärchen, das darüber hinaus den Zusammenhang zwischen der Konfrontation des Menschen mit den (belebt scheinenden) Dingen und der Mechanik (und der mechanischen Simulierbarkeit) des Lebens aufzeigt. Und hier ist es vor allem E.T.A. Hoffmann, der die Komiktheorie Schützes nutzt. Die Komik, die sich aus dem »Vorhandenseyn der Körperwelt« (VK, 80) und aus der Widerständigkeit der Dinge ergibt, hat er weidlich ausgeschlachtet, wie aber auch – als deren Kehrseite – die Unhintergehbarkeit des Körpers und die katastrophische Schreckphantasie seiner Fragmentierung.

Widerständige Alltagsdinge, das Stolpern und Hinfallen und das schallende Gelächter über die Stolpernden begegnen einem allenthalben und sind jeweils verknüpft mit einem unerlösten Zustand der so Verlachten. Das gilt zum Beispiel für Anselmus aus *Der goldene Topf*, der von den widerständigen Dingen als seinem »Unstern« geplagt wird (HW, 1, 280). Ähnliches gilt für Ludwig aus *Der Zusammenhang der Dinge*, der sich angesichts platzender Strumpfmaschen und abspringender Westenknöpfe von der »Tücke des feindlichen Schicksals« (HW, 4, 480) verfolgt wähnt. Und es gilt für Giglio Fava aus *Die Prinzessin Brambilla*, wo etwa eigens beschrieben wird, wie mühsam die phantastische und prätentiöse Feder mit Draht an dem Hut befestigt wird.[12] Eben diese Sichtbarkeit des mühseligen Kampfes mit dem widerständigen Ding, das sich nur schwer fügt, markiert nicht nur Giglios Armut, sondern zugleich seine Unerlöstheit und seinen Selbstzerfall

---

11 Vgl. hierzu Brüggemann.
12 »Dabei wird, unerachtet alles sauber gehalten, doch eine gewisse Armseligkeit sichtbar; man merkt's der Spitzenkrause an, daß zum Wechseln nur noch eine vorhanden, und den Federn, womit der schief auf den Kopf gedrückte Hut phantastisch geschmückt, daß sie mühsam mit Draht und Nadel zusammengehalten« (HW, 5, 609).

in Wunsch und Wirklichkeit. An ihm wird sichtbar, dass der Mensch »der Mangelhaftigkeit des Behelfs ausgesetzt« ist: »Wie er auch das Kleid, worin er sich hüllt, ziehen und rücken mag, nirgends reicht es zu, ihn ganz zu bedecken, bald kommt hier, bald dort eine Blösse zum Vorschein« (Schütze, »Ueber das Komische«, 294f.). Hoffmann greift das in *Die Prinzessin Brambilla* fast wörtlich auf, indem er – wiederum ganz im Sinne Schützes – das Kleid selbst zur Metapher des Körpers macht: »[D]er Geist trägt den Körper wie ein unbequemes Kleid, das überall zu breit, zu lang, zu ungefügig ist« (*HW*, 5, 628). Genau deshalb ist auch oft der Zusammenstoß des Körpers mit den Dingen verknüpft mit dem Verlust der eigenen Körperintegrität. Missgeschick, so in *Nussknacker und Mäusekönig*, reimt sich auf Missgestalt. Umgekehrt ist der ideale Zustand der erfüllten Wünsche, das Prinzessinnensein, gerade damit verknüpft, dass hier nun die Dinge von helfenden Geistern bewohnt erscheinen und an die Stelle des Kampfes mit dem widerständigen Ding ihr sich fügender Gehorsam tritt. Ein Gehorsam, der sich zugleich auch im Körperbild und der eigenen Identität widerspiegelt: »Als sie [die alte Beatrice, J.L.] nun dem Mädchen das prächtige Kleid anlegte, war es, als ständen ihr unsichtbare Geister bei. Alles fügte und schickte sich, jede Nadel saß im Augenblick recht, jede Falte legte sich wie von selbst« (*HW*, 5, 608), so dass Giacinta sich durch das so gut passende Kleid in eine Prinzessin verwandelt.

Wenn es im Komischen nach Schütze um die Dinge geht, die der Mensch als Behelf braucht, die sich aber seinem Geist in den Weg stellen, so dass eben dieser Geist selbst den Anschein des Mechanischen und Dinglichen gewinnt, dann kann von dieser Komiktheorie auch ein Licht auf die Thematisierung der mechanischen Simulation des Lebens bei Hoffmann geworfen werden. Widerständige Dinge, die das Mechanische des Menschen hervortreiben, und die mechanische Simulation des Lebens in Puppen, Automaten und Marionetten erscheinen vor dem Hintergrund der Komiktheorie als zwei Seiten desselben komischen Zusammenhangs. Die Dinge der Außenwelt, die das Leben des Menschen bedingen, rücken bei Hoffmann in dem Maße in den Blick, wie der Mensch selbst als körperliches Ding und sein Leben als mechanisch Supplementierbares und Simulierbares erscheint.

Das kann man abschließend an *Die Prinzessin Brambilla* zeigen. Giglio Fava wird durchgehend als Schauspieler dem maschinenhaften künstlichen Leben angenähert. Man könne zwar Giglio für »Fleisch und Bein« (*HW*, 5, 633) halten, erkenne aber dann, dass er nur »eine leblose Puppe ist, die an künstlichen Drähten von außen her gezogen« (*HW*, 5, 634) wird. Als Giglio schließlich anscheinend im Duell stirbt, ist erstens unklar, ob er wirklich tot

ist, und zweitens, ob der, der getötet wurde, wirklich gelebt hat, denn von seinem »vermeintlichen Leichnam« wird als von einem »aus Pappendeckel geformte[n] Modell« gesprochen, das nicht wirklich »Fleisch und Blut« hatte. Vielmehr heißt es bei der Obduktion der Leiche, dass er voller »Rollen aus den Trauerspielen des Abbate Chiari gefunden wurde« (*HW*, 5, 728).[13]
Dass das Leben technisch simulierbar ist – über Mechanik, Maschinen, Puppen oder Marionetten –, ist zugleich das Thema des in den Text eingelagerten Märchens vom Urdarsee, insofern der gestorbene König Ophioch als Leiche in eine Marionette umfunktioniert wird, die Leben vortäuscht. Und genau in dieser Szene zeigt sich nun der Zusammenhang der Komik widerständiger Dinge, des *slapstick,* mit der mechanischen Simulation des Lebens. Als das Holzgestell der toten Königsmarionette vom Holzwurm zerfressen zusammenbricht, reißt auch die Schnur, von der das Zepter bewegt wird: »Ich selbst großer Magus, zog gerade die Zepterschnure, welche als die Majestät umstülpte, mir im Zerreißen dermaßen ins Gesicht schnellte, daß ich dergleichen Schnurziehen auf zeitlebens satt bekommen« (*HW*, 5, 698). Die technisch-mechanische Simulation des Lebens bedarf der toten Dinge, die ihrerseits Ding-Ding-Kausalketten bilden, die im Fall, sei es Unfall oder Zufall, den Anschein des Lebens gewinnen. Die dynamische Mechanik der zerreißenden Schnur und ihres Rückschlags kehrt die Verhältnisse um, so dass nun nicht der Marionettenspieler die Marionette am Geistesinstrument der Schnur führt, sondern die Schnur als materielles Ding den Schein von Handlung und Leben gewinnt und den Körper des Spielers trifft. Erst im Fall lebt das tote Ding wieder auf, womit König Ophioch noch als Leiche bestätigt, was er als Lebender gesagt hatte, nämlich dass erst beim Umfallen das wahre Ich aufstehe, nämlich als eines, das unhintergehbar in seinen Handlungen an den Körper und die mithandelnden Dinge gebunden ist. Literarisch wird hier bereits jene gemeinsame Syntax und Semantik von Mensch und Ding, von der Bruno Latour spricht und die Stephan Schütze seiner Komiktheorie zugrunde gelegt hat, ausbuchstabiert. Die philosophische Dialektik zwischen Geist und Materie, Freiheit und Notwendigkeit, wie sie Schelling entwickelt und wie sie nach Latour den Graben der großen Trennung zwischen Subjekt und Objekt durch Vermittlungsfiguren nur immer weiter vertieft (Latour, *Wir sind nie*, 79), ist in der Komiktheorie Schützes und in der komischen Literatur Hoffmanns überführt in eine Reflexion und eine Darstellung, die die Trennung – im Medium des Komischen und des

---

[13] Brambilla/Giacinta spricht an anderer Stelle davon, dass sie sich Giglio, »ist er auch zurzeit auseinandergenommen, immer wieder zusammennähen lassen kann« (*HW*, 5, 740).

Phantastischen – aufhebt. Diese Aufhebung bleibt aber einerseits, gerade weil sie ›nur‹ im Medium des Komischen geschieht, zugleich in Gefahr als bloß komisch marginalisiert zu werden. Das wird besonders deutlich in Vischers Umsetzung der Schütze'schen Theorie, zeigt Vischer doch seine Hauptfigur A.E. mit seiner Wut über die Handlungsmächtigkeit der Dinge nur aus der sicheren Distanz von Groteske und Komik. Andererseits reicht die Theorie des Komischen »romantischer Art«, wie sie Schütze entwickelt und wie sie über Vischer, Bergson und Heimito von Doderer[14] bis hin zu Peter L. Berger (vgl. Berger) weiter getragen wird, doch bis in die Gegenwart. Die Agency der Dinge und die Dinge als nicht-menschliche Mitspieler, wie Latour es tut, auch außerhalb des Komischen zu denken, zeugt von der Aktualität der Romantik.

Zitierte Literatur

Arnim, Achim von. *Des Knaben Wunderhorn. Alte deutsche Lieder gesammelt von Achim von Arnim und Clemens Brentano.* Hg. Heinz Rölleke. Frankfurt a.M./Leipzig: Insel, 2003.

Berger, Peter L. *Erlösendes Lachen. Das Komische in der menschlichen Erfahrung.* Aus dem Amerikanischen von Joachim Kalka. Berlin/New York: de Gruyter, 1998.

Bergson, Henri. *Das Lachen. Ein Essay über die Bedeutung des Komischen.* Zürich: Die Arche, 1972.

Bichat, Xavier. *Physiologische Untersuchungen über Leben und Tod.* Aus dem Französischen frey übersetzt. Tübingen 1802.

Borgards, Roland. *Poetik des Schmerzes. Physiologie und Literatur von Brockes bis Büchner.* München: Fink, 2007.

Brandis, Joachim Dietrich. *Versuch über die Lebenskraft.* Hannover: Hahn'sche Buchhandlung, 1795.

Brandtsetter, Gabriele/Gerhard Neumann. »Gaben. Märchen in der Romantik«. *Romantik und Exil. Festschrift für Konrad Feilchenfeldt.* Hg. Claudia Christophersen/Ursula Hudson-Wiedemann in Zusammenarbeit mit Brigitte Schillbach. Würzburg: Königshausen & Neumann, 2004: 17–38.

---

14 In seinem grotesk-komischen Roman *Die Merowinger oder die totale Familie* (1962) zitiert Doderer mehrfach Vischers Roman *Auch einer* und dessen Thematisierung der »Tücke des Objekts«.

Brüggemann, Heinz. »Mitgespielt. Vom Handeln und Sprechen der Dinge. Thema mit Variationen in Texten der Romantik«. *Schläft ein Lied in allen Dingen? Romantische Dingpoetik*. Hg. Christiane Holm/Günter Oesterle. Würzburg: Königshausen & Neumann, 2011: 97–119.

Grimm, Jacob/Wilhelm Grimm. *Kinder- und Hausmärchen*. Ausgabe letzter Hand. Mit einem Anhang sämtlicher, nicht in allen Auflagen veröffentlichten Märchen und Herkunftsnachweisen Hg. Heinz Rölleke. 3 Bde. Stuttgart: Reclam, 1984. (*KHM*)

Haller, Albrecht von. *Abhandlung von den empfindlichen und reizbaren Theilen des menschlichen Leibes*. Hg. und eingeleitet von Karl Sudhoff. Leipzig 1922 [1756].

Hoffmann, E.T.A. *Poetische Werke in sechs Bänden*. Berlin: Aufbau Verlag, 1958. (*HW*)

Jantzen, Jörg: »Theorien der Lebenskraft«. *Friedrich Wilhelm Schelling: Ergänzungsband zu Werke Bd. V bis IX. Wissenschaftshistorischer Bericht zu Schellings Naturphilosophischen Schriften 1797–1800*. Hg. Michael Baumgartner et al. Stuttgart: Frommann-Holzboog, 1994: 498–565.

Kielmeyer, D. Carl Friedrich. *Ueber die Verhältniße der organischen Kräfte unter einander in der Reihe der verschiedenen Organisationen. Eine Rede, den 11. Februar 1793*. Tübingen: Osiander, 1814.

Kneer, Georg/Schroer, Markus/Schüttpelz, Erhard (Hg.): *Bruno Latours Kollektive*. Frankfurt a.M.: Suhrkamp, 2008.

Latour, Bruno. *Eine neue Soziologie für eine neue Gesellschaft. Einführung in die Akteur-Netzwerk-Theorie*. Aus dem Englischen von Gustav Roßler. Frankfurt a.M.: Suhrkamp, 2007.

Latour, Bruno. »Porträt von Gaston Lagaffe als Technikphilosoph«. *Der Berliner Schlüssel. Erkundungen eines Liebhabers der Wissenschaften*. Aus dem Französischen von Gustav Roßler. Berlin: Akademie Verlag, 1996: 17–27.

Latour, Bruno. *Wir sind nie modern gewesen. Versuch einer symmetrischen Anthropologie*. Berlin: Akademie Verlag, 1995.

Latour, Bruno. *Das Parlament der Dinge. Für eine politische Moderne*. Aus dem Französischen von Gustav Roßler. Frankfurt a.M.: Suhrkamp, 2001.

Schelling, Friedrich Wilhelm Joseph. »Erster Entwurf eines Systems der Naturphilosophie«. Hg. Wilhelm G. Jacobs/Paul Ziche. *Historisch-kritische Ausgabe*. Hg. Hans Michael Baumgartner et al. Reihe I. *Werke*. Bd. 7. Stuttgart: Frommann-Holzboog, 2001.

Schelling, Friedrich Wilhelm Joseph: »Von der Weltseele, eine Hypothese der höheren Physik zur Erklärung des allgemeinen Organismus«. *Ausgewählte Werke. Schriften von 1794–1798*. Darmstadt: Wissenschaftliche Buchgesellschaft, 1967: 399–637.

Schelling, Friedrich Wilhelm Joseph. »Vom Wesen der Komödie«. *Philosophie der Kunst (1802/1803). Ausgewählte Schriften in 6 Bänden*. Hg. Manfred Frank. Bd. 2: *Schriften 1801–1803*. Frankfurt a.M.: Suhrkamp, ²1995: 539–654.

Schütze, Stephan. *Versuch einer Theorie des Komischen*. Leipzig: Hartknoch, 1817. (*VK*)

Schütze, Stephan. »Ueber das Komische«. *Gedanken und Einfälle über Leben und Kunst*. Leipzig: Gleditsch, 1810: 278–296.

Thüring, Hubert. *Das neue Leben. Studien zum biopolitischen Lebensbegriff in der modernen Literatur 1750 bis 1938*. München: Fink, 2012.

Vischer, Theodor Friedrich. *Ästhetik oder Wissenschaft des Schönen*. Hg. Robert Vischer. Band I/II: *Die Metaphysik des Schönen*. Nachdruck der Ausgabe 2. Aufl. München 1922. Hildesheim/New York: Georg Olms Verlag, 1975.

Vischer, Theodor Friedrich. *Auch einer. Eine Reisebekanntschaft*. Mit einem Nachwort von Otto Borst. Frankfurt a.M.: Insel, 1987.

Ruth Pullin *(National Gallery of Victoria)*

Eugen von Guérard's Romanticism Reconsidered

Abstract

Der Text untersucht die Aktualität der Romantik im Werk des deutsch-australischen Landschaftsmalers Eugen von Guérard (1811–1901). Vor dem Hintergrund seiner von ihm ausdrücklich bekannten Ehrfurcht vor den Narazenern und Mitchell B. Franks Neu-Definition der deutschen romantischen Malerei wird die Auffassung der kunsthistorischen Orthodoxie überprüft, welche von Guérards Romantik grundsätzlich im Rahmen einer am Werk Caspar David Friedrichs orientierten Romantikauffassung betrachtet. Auf die Analyse der Bedeutung der Schule der Nazarener für von Guérard folgt eine Neubewertung von Aspekten des romantischen Denkens und seiner Praktiken, die von Guérards Perspektive auf Natur und die Landschaften Australiens geformt haben.

> It was in the beginning of the nineteenth century that the great German Artists Cornelius, Overbeck, Schadow, Veit, Schnorr, Reinhard, Koch and others met in Rome and drawing a parallel between the state of the fine arts in the time of Michale Angelo Buonarotti and Raphael with that of their own time recognized the necessity to begin with a totally new course of studies […]. More than all the others it was Peter Cornelius which [sic] tried to raise the art of drawing and painting […]. (Guérard, »Reply on the critic«)

So wrote Eugen von Guérard (1811–1901) in an impassioned letter penned in response to criticisms levelled at him by his erstwhile champion and friend, the art critic James Smith, in a review published in the Melbourne newspaper, the *Argus*. Today it may seem strange that von Guérard did not, as might be expected, invoke the names of the great landscape painters now regarded as the quintessential German Romantics, Caspar David Friedrich and Phillip Otto Runge. Rather, in order to defend himself against Smith's stinging criticisms, von Guérard drew on the authority of artists associated with the Brotherhood of St Luke, or as they became known, the Nazarenes, many of whom, he emphasized, he had »the honour to know personally«. Von Guérard's identification with the Nazarenes (and his silence on Friedrich) must be considered within its nineteenth-century context, when, as Mitchell B. Frank argues in *German Romantic Painting Redefined,* it was the

Nazarenes with whom German Romanticism was most closely identified. Not only were they »regarded as the prime movers in the revival of a modern and specifically German painting«, but according to »almost all nineteenth-century histories Overbeck's and Cornelius's contributions to Romanticism were much more significant than Friedrich's and Runge's« (Frank, 143). This perception prevailed with equal force outside Germany: in the 1830s »nobody thought of Friedrich and Runge. German art was identified with the Nazarenes« (Grewe, 77).[1] The shift towards a concept of German Romanticism centred on Friedrich and Runge emerged only at the beginning of the twentieth century and was signalled by the inclusion of their work in the Centennial Exhibition of German Art in Berlin in 1906. In invoking the names of the Nazarene painters von Guérard aligned himself with the artists who were regarded as the great German artists of their age and who were understood to epitomize German Romanticism. In the twentieth-century literature on von Guérard, however, most of which postdates the 1970s when art historical interest in von Guerard's landscape painting was revived after almost a century of critical neglect, it is with reference to Caspar David Friedrich that his work has frequently been understood.[2] This paper is an exploration of the precise nature of von Guérard's Romanticism. It begins with an analysis of the significance of the Nazarene artists for von Guérard and then, through a series of case studies, considers the ways in which German Romantic thought and practice informed the artist's vision of the Australian landscape.

I. Von Guérard and the Nazarenes

Eugen von Guérard was born in Vienna in 1811 where his father, Bernard von Guérard (1771–1836), a Düsseldorf-born painter of portrait miniatures, held a prestigious position in the royal court of Franz I. Through his private business as a supplier of pigments and artists' materials Bernard came into contact with the wider artistic community in Vienna and in this way he may have met, or at least would have been aware of, the students who, in

---

[1] »Als man in Frankreich zu Beginn der 1830er endlich von einer ›école allemande‹ zu sprechen begann, dachte zunächst kaum jemand an die heute so geliebten Caspar David Friedrich oder Philipp Otto Runge. Und so verzeichnete mancher Zeitgenosse mit Ärger, dass ›deutsch‹ zunächst ›nazarenisch‹ meinte – wenigstens für eine Weile«.

[2] For example, Candice Bruce/Edward Comstock/Frank McDonald. *Eugene von Guérard: a German Romantic in the Antipodes 1811–1901*. Martinborough, N.Z.: Alister Tayler, 1982.

1809 and as a result of their dissatisfaction with the Academy, formed the *Lukasbund* or the Brotherhood of St Luke. In 1810 Friedrich Overbeck and Franz Pforr, the leaders of the group, along with two colleagues, left Vienna for Rome where they established themselves, initially in the Villa Malta and later in the secularised monastery of Sant' Isidoro. Twenty years later, in 1830, Bernard von Guérard and his nineteen-year-old son arrived in Rome. There, the young von Guérard came into contact with some of the greatest artists in Europe, including the then famous Nazarene artists.

Although the Brotherhood of St Luke had formally disbanded by the time the von Guérards arrived in Rome, individual members, notably Overbeck, Philipp Veit, Peter Cornelius and others associated with the group, including Joseph Anton Koch and Johann Christian Reinhart, lived, worked and remained a vital presence in the city. The von Guérards found lodgings within the German artist's quarter, at Via Pinciana 8, one of the streets that fans out from the top of the Spanish Steps. They were close to the Villa Malta, on the Via di Porta Pinciana, and Sant' Isidoro on the Via degli Artisti. In 1830 Reinhart was working at the Villa Malta, painting his famous *Four Views of Rome from the Villa Malta* (1829–1835)[3], and Overbeck lived just down the road in the Palazzo Guarnieri at Via di Porta Pinciana 37; the von Guérards may have numbered amongst Overbeck's many foreign visitors (Frank, 5).[4] In the 1830s the community of German, Danish and Austrian artists in Rome was vibrant, close knit and inclusive and the meeting places, most famously the Café Greco located on the Via Condotti at the bottom of the Spanish Steps, provided opportunities for new arrivals such as the von Guérards to meet the established German-speaking artists working in the city.

Eugen's career as a landscape painter began in Rome when he studied under Giambattista Bassi, the foremost Italian landscape painter then working in the city. However, it was not Bassi but the great German landscape painters Joseph Anton Koch (1768–1839) and Johann Christian Reinhart (1761–1847) to whom von Guérard referred in the letter written in defence of his art in 1870. Koch and Reinhart were each closely associated with the Nazarenes: Koch had worked on the project described as »the Nazarenes' most important artistic endeavor while in Rome« (Frank, 26), the frescoes

---

[3] Johann Christian Reinhart. *Four Views of Rome from the Villa Malta* (1829–1835), oil on four canvases. Neue Pinakothek, Munich.

[4] The von Guérards' Catholic faith should be noted in relation to their connections with the Nazarenes.

for the Casa Bartholdy completed in 1816/17. Undoubtedly, Eugen and his father joined the visitors who flocked to see the famous frescoes in the Casa on the Via Sistina.

Koch and Reinhart were each senior and charismatic figures within the *Deutsch-Römer*; Koch in particular was known for his mentorship of younger artists. Each offered models for landscape painting that proved to be significant for von Guérard. While they drew on the classical landscape traditions of Gaspard Dughet, Nicholas Poussin and Claude Lorrain, their respective practices reveal an increasing concern with Naturalism and specificity. Reinhart attempted to find a balance between the conventions of the ideal landscape tradition and, for example, the accurate depiction of particular tree species. Koch had a serious interest in the new science of geology (Holst, 24). He produced illustrations for Alexander von Humboldt's *Atlas pittoresque* (1810) and his understanding of Humboldt's vision of the interconnectedness of natural phenomena informs his heroic *Der Schmadribachfall* 1821.[5] At a formative stage in his career, von Guérard was exposed to the example of two great German landscape painters, artists who recognized the new relevance of the natural sciences to landscape painting while remaining true to a vision that aspired to a higher ideal.

The Nazarenes were not primarily landscape painters but they were deeply interested in nature as the meticulous, intimate studies of humble plants, leaves and grasses produced by Julius Schnorr von Carolsfeld, the Olivier brothers and others reveal. Such studies were a response to the renewed interest in German Renaissance artists such as Albrecht Dürer, Martin Schongauer and Albrecht Altdorfer, an interest encouraged by Goethe, Ludwig Tieck and Wilhelm Heinrich Wackenroder and one that was vital to the development of German Romanticism (Hargraves, 72). The close observation of the minutiae of nature became a defining element of von Guérard's landscape painting, from his portrayal of riverbank plants growing on the banks of the Düssel in oil studies such as *Speckermönch* 1841 to the faithful depiction of, it seems, each individual blade of grass in the lush pasture foreground of *View of the Gippsland Alps, Bushy Park* (1860).[6] This attitude to nature reflects the enduring influence of his father, the miniaturist,

---

[5] Joseph Anton Koch. *Der Schmadribachfall* (1821/22), oil on canvas, 131.8 x 110 cm. Neue Pinakothek, Munich.

[6] Eugen von Guérard. *Speckermönch* (1841), oil on paper, 19.5 x 26.0. Private collection, Canberra; Eugen von Guérard. *View of the Gippsland Alps, from Bushy Park on the River Avon* (1861), oil on canvas, (a-b) 36.1 x 94.1 cm (overall). Rex Nan Kivell Collection, National Library of Australia, Canberra, and National Gallery of Australia, Canberra.

and, importantly, it was aligned with the clarity and detail found in studies produced by the Nazarenes. The precision and delicate linearity that characterizes their drawings was typically achieved with the use of a fine, hard pencil on paper, the lines sometimes worked over in ink. The centrality of drawing in von Guérard's practice reflects the privileging of draughtsmanship in Nazarene practice.

The significance of the Nazarenes for the young von Guérard lies as much in the model of the lives they lived as artists, in their sense of vocation and their identity as artists, as in the example of their art. The founding members of the Brotherhood had set out to revive a new true German art, inspired by the examples of Raphael and Dürer and, in literature, Wackenroder's *Confessions from the Heart of an Art-Loving Friar*, published by Ludwig Tieck in 1798 (Frank, 13). In the pure and monastic way of life pursued at Sant' Isidoro the artist's life and his work were integrated. Franz Pforr held that »in order to be great, the painter must be not just a painter but a man […] that the way to become a truly great painter is identical with the path of virtue« (qtd. Wesenberg, 117). In a similar vein the Melbourne art critic, James Smith, writing in 1860, linked von Guérard's exemplary life as a man with his achievements as »decidedly the landscape painter of Australia«, describing the artist as »faithful to his high calling, and reflecting honour upon it, not only by his genius as a painter, but by his sterling worth and genuine unworldliness as a man«.

In von Guérard's case the identification between art and life – and with it the realization of the self, essential for »authenticity« which, as Frank argues, was »one of the unifying factors of German Romantic painting« (38) – was played out, not in a monastic setting, but on long and often difficult expeditions into the most rugged and remote areas of Australia's southeastern colonies. As for the Nazarenes, von Guérard's practice as an artist was a vocation, one inspired by a sense of the higher purpose of art and one in which his commitment to his vision of landscape painting did not waver even when, in the 1870s, it was out of step with the times.

II. Von Guérard in Düsseldorf

In the winter of 1830, the year that the von Guérards arrived in Rome, the director of the Düsseldorf Academy, Wilhelm von Schadow, led a group of teachers and students from the Academy, the Düsseldorf Compagnie, to the »›Promised Land‹ of art« (Sitt, 233). Their presence in the city was significant for von Guérard and his future studies in Düsseldorf: as a signatory to the Brotherhood's *Letter of Association* in 1813, and still committed to their principles, Schadow represented the pivotal link between the Nazarenes and Düsseldorf for the young artist.

In May 1838, von Guérard left Italy for Düsseldorf. He had spent the previous six years in Naples and in 1836 lost his beloved father in the cholera epidemic that swept the city. Düsseldorf, the home of his father's family, was also the home of one of the most highly regarded academies in Europe and one, significantly, with a strong and progressive school of landscape painting. Von Guérard arrived in August 1838. It seems that he was immediately accepted into the ranks of the Düsseldorfer Malerschule as his portrait was painted by Friedrich Boser just a few months later, in November 1838, for inclusion in his monumental work, *57 Einzelporträts, überwiegend Künstler der Düsseldorfer Malerschule* (1835–1845).[7] Von Guérard's portrait sits alongside those of such eminent Düsseldorf painters as Wilhelm von Schadow, Carl Friedrich Lessing and Hans Gude. It has the distinction of being one of only a few to bear an inscription on the verso, a poetic dedication to friendship that concludes with the lines: »Let our friendship remain firm, near and far, until at life's end we meet again on the other side«. Friendship, artistic brotherhood and respect for individual autonomy within a community were qualities that lay at the very heart of the Nazarene brotherhood: they found their most moving and eloquent expression in the deeply personal paintings that Franz Pforr and Friedrich Overbeck painted for each other, Pforr's *Sulamith and Maria* (1811)[8] and Overbeck's *Italia and Germania* (1828).[9] They are qualities that distinguished artistic life in Düsseldorf in the 1830s and 40s, where a sense of community, close friendships, camaraderie and a lively social life flourished both within and outside the Academy.

---

[7] Friedrich Boser. *57 Einzelporträts, überwiegend Künstler der Düsseldorfer Malerschule*, 1835–1845, 59.5 x 284.0 cm. Stadtmuseum Düsseldorf, on loan from the Kunst Palast Düsseldorf, B382.

[8] Franz Pforr. *Sulamith and Maria* (1811), oil on canvas, 34.5 x 32 cm. Georg Schäfer Collection, Schweinfurt.

[9] Friedrich Overbeck. *Italia and Germania* (1828), oil on canvas, 94.4 x 104.7 cm. Neue Pinakothek, Munich.

Friedrich Boser (attrib. to). *Eugen von Guérard* (1838–40), oil on canvas, 16.6 x 12.8 cm. National Gallery of Victoria, Melbourne.

Wilhelm von Schadow, from 1826 onwards the Director of the Düsseldorf Academy, played a key role in nurturing this atmosphere, founded on principles enshrined by the Nazarenes, that made Düsseldorf one of the most successful academies in Europe. In a recent essay Cordula Grewe explores the influence of von Schadow's Nazarene painting practice in Düsseldorf (78). While it exists she argues that his influence as a teacher and director, with a commitment to Nazarene ideals, was more far reaching. His fostering of an atmosphere of tolerance and his encouragement of individual talent saw Düsseldorf take the lead in the schools of genre painting and landscape, areas that did not necessarily reflect his own artistic interests or direction.[10] Von Guérard's teacher, the landscape painter Johann Wilhelm Schirmer, recalled that von Schadow treated his students »only with loving care, only with understanding and gentle consideration«[11] (qtd. Baumgärtel, 19), responding to the special gift of each individual. He introduced the master class, a one-to-one relationship between student and teacher modelled on the teacher-pupil relationship practiced by the Nazarenes (Hoopes, 20). An article published in the London weekly *Saturday Review* in 1868 recognized the special atmosphere that prevailed at the Academy in Düsseldorf:

> More worthy of remark is the mutual culture and relation of brotherhood maintained between professors and pupils. While other academies may be compared to monarchies or oligarchies, that of Düsseldorf is, by its liberty and equality, like a republic. The Director does not constitute himself a dictator; no one mind, no exclusive art-manner, dominates. Thus, during half a century, Düsseldorf, the ascendancy of the so-called spiritual or Christian school, has given equal rights and privileges to all styles, including, of course, the naturalistic (qtd. Grewe, 87).

While von Guérard did not study directly under Wilhelm von Schadow, his respect for the Director is recorded in the sketches he made of von Schadow's house immediately prior to his departure for Australia in 1851[12] and in his contribution of a watercolour to the Schadow-Album (cf. Bott), a collection of 69 works by Düsseldorf artists presented to the Director on the occasion of his 25th anniversary as Director of the Academy.

Outside the Academy the idea of a brotherly community of artists was realized in the art associations that flourished in the city, most strikingly in the Künstlerverein Malkasten.[13] Von Guérard was one of the 112 founding members of the Künstlerverein Malkasten which formed on the evening of August 6th 1848, following a theatrical demonstration for national unity staged by the citizens of Düsseldorf. Just as the Nazarene community formed in »the wake of the Napoleonic upheaval« (Frank, 37), the Malkasten may have offered artists an environment in which their democratic tendencies could be expressed. When the principles of the Künstlerverein were finally

---

[10] By contrast landscape painting was not encouraged at the Munich Academy under the directorship of the Nazarene Peter Cornelius.
[11] »Nur liebevolle Sorgfalt, nur das Verständnis und Schonung.«
[12] Eugen von Guérard. Sketchbook XV (1843), Dixson Galleries, State Library of New South Wales, DGB14, vol. 5, f. 64.
[13] Other associations include the Landschaftliche Componiervereine, small associations of artists which met regularly for discussion of their own and others' landscape compositions.

codified, they emphasized its social, non-partisan character and in particular its tolerance of the free expression of artistic direction. The name, Malkasten (paint box), was intended to express the way in which the painters would stand by one another, just as the different colours in the artist's paint-box lie next to each other (Hütt, 196).

While von Guérard's reference to the Nazarene painters in his letter of 1870 reflects his experience and understanding of the Romanticism that prevailed in Germany in the 1830s and 40s, his sketchbooks reveal that during those years he was also absorbing a Romantic visual language that was ultimately derived from the example of Caspar David Friedrich (1774–1840). Although the Dresden-based Friedrich had achieved considerable recognition earlier in his career, by the end of his life he had been virtually forgotten outside his immediate circle. His influence, however, continued to be felt and the most direct way in which it was transmitted to Düsseldorf was through the landscape and history painter Carl Friedrich Lessing (1808–1882), who, as a student in Berlin, had been deeply influenced by Friedrich's painting, to the extent that contemporary critics referred to him as »Friedrich's successor« (Hütt, 117). The archetypal motifs of German Romantic painting – Gothic ruins, gnarled oak trees and castles on cliff tops – that appear in von Guérard's German sketchbooks are almost certainly a response to works such as Lessing's *Cloister in the Snow* (1828).[14] Von Guérard's engagement with the themes and language of German Romanticism emerges most strongly in his sketchbook of compositions ›drawn on winter evenings‹ between 1847 and 1851.[15] In one, a traveller rests against a stone cross below the animated and expressive arching branches of an ancient oak tree; in its convergence of religion and nature it echoes Friedrich's seminal *The Cross in the Mountains (The Tetschen Altar)* of 1808.[16]

Von Guérard's involvement in the practice of *Freilichtmalerei* that flourished in Düsseldorf in the 1830s and 40s has emerged recently with research related to a group of previously unknown oil sketches (Pullin, 2007, 2009, 2011). An expression of the intense focus on nature that characterized Romanticism, it was informed by a literary and philosophical tradition that included Goethe, Novalis, and Schelling. Carl Gustav Carus, in his *Nine*

---

[14] Carl Friedrich Lessing. *Cloister in the Snow* (c. 1829), oil on canvas, 61 x 75 cm. Wallraf-Richartz-Museum, Cologne.
[15] Eugen von Guérard. Sketchbook XVIII (1847–1851). Dixson Galleries, State Library of New South Wales, DGB14, vol. 7, f. 21.
[16] Caspar David Friedrich. *The Cross in the Mountains* (1808), oil on canvas, 115 x 110.5 cm. Staatliche Kunstsammlungen, Gemäldegalerie Neue Meister, Dresden.

Letters on Landscape Painting, saw nature as a source of emotional and spiritual enlightenment; the later letters, reflecting the influence of Goethe's essay on Luke Howard's classification system for clouds, are premised on the belief that through science art could penetrate nature's mysteries. Both attitudes – a deeply emotional reverence for nature and the penetrating, informed observation of nature – were expressed in the *Freilichtmalerei* of Johann Wilhelm Schirmer and his students at the Düsseldorf Academy.

In the 1840s von Guérard joined the Düsseldorf landscape painters who trekked out to favoured sites – Grafenberg, the Neandertal, Erkrath, Bilker Busch and the Eifel – to paint directly from nature. His oil sketch *Rabenstein* (1843) with its focus on the profusion and diversity of plants growing on the banks of the River Düssel in the Neander Valley, painted at close range and from a ground level viewpoint, is the quintessential Düsseldorf study.[17] Schirmer's advice to his students to paint with an »obedient, natural sense, that everything seen should be seen as it is, always with open eyes and a warm heart«[18] (qtd. Eggerath, 63) conveyed both Carus's requirement for scientific accuracy and a deeply emotional attitude to nature. Von Guérard's intimate connection with the fragment of nature portrayed in *Rabenstein*, where he looked into »the true and wondrous life of nature« (Carus, 30), was, in the Wordsworthian sense, profoundly Romantic.[19]

III. Von Guérard in Australia

Von Guérard arrived in Australia in December 1852, a few years after the publication of the first two volumes of Alexander von Humboldt's *Cosmos: A Sketch of a Physical Description of the Universe*,[20] one of the most influential texts of the age. Humboldt's views on landscape painting and the role of the artist permeate his texts and he devoted an entire chapter of the second volume of *Cosmos* to the subject. In it he encouraged landscape painters to pass »the narrow limits of the Mediterranean« to regions where he hoped

---

[17] Eugen von Guérard. *Rabenstein* (1841), oil on paper, 32.5 x 44.0 irreg. Private collection, Coates, England.
[18] »Ein kindlich natürlicher Sinn, der jedes Ding so ansieht, wie was ist, der also immer offene Augen und ein warmes Herz mitbringen muß […]«.
[19] In *Lines Composed a few miles above Tintern Abbey, On Revisiting the Banks of the Wye during a Tour. July 13, 1798,* William Wordsworth wrote of seeing »into the life of things«.
[20] Volume I was first published in Germany in 1845 and volume II in 1847.

they could seize »on the true image of the varied forms of nature« (*Cosmos*, v. 2, 452). Von Guérard's response was to travel to the New World of Australia where, informed by Humboldt's vision of nature and in the context of the generation of German Humboldtian scientists who arrived in Melbourne in the 1850s, he painted its landscapes, its flora and its geology. Humboldt's conception of the interconnectedness of all natural phenomena was a profound scientific achievement. With its premise, echoing Schelling's »world soul«, that »one sole and indissoluble chain binds together all nature« (*Cosmos*, v. 1, 5), it was also intensely Romantic. It shaped von Guérard's response to the Australian landscape and although this is not the argument pursued here as it is presented elsewhere (Pullin, 2007, 2011), it must be registered as it underpins von Guérard's vision of nature. Here, in three case studies, the significance of specific aspects of German Romantic landscape painting for von Guérard's Australian career are considered.

a. The ›ruin metaphor‹: *Castle Rock, Cape Schanck* (1865)

Eugen von Guérard. *Castle Rock, Cape Schanck* (1865), oil on canvas, 61.0 x 91.3 cm. Art Gallery of South Australia, Adelaide.

Von Guérard first saw Cape Schanck, on the Victorian coast, from a steamer on his 1855 journey to Tasmania. He visited the site three years later in 1858 and again in 1863. On the basis of sketches made on the latter expedition, he painted *Castle Rock, Cape Schanck* (1865), a work described as »›capital R‹ Romantic« for its subject, »a rocky shore, a sun setting over a calm sea, a lonely lighthouse« (Bruce, 1).[21]

The eminent geologist Ferdinand von Hochstetter was impressed when he saw von Guérard's lithograph of this subject in Vienna in 1870 (Hochstetter, 157) and contemporary geologists have since confirmed the accuracy of von Guérard's portrayal of the successive basalt flows and the sandstone strata of the exposed cliff face.[22] In its concentration on the geology of the site and, by inference, to the geological processes and time involved in its formation (its ›history‹), the work constitutes what Carus described as a *geognostic* landscape.

In *Castle Rock* the historical dimension of the geological subject was made explicit by the association of the rock formation with a ruined castle: geological history was signified, and made comprehensible, by reference to the weathering of man-made edifices. Carus had used the ›ruin metaphor‹ in geognostic works such as *Die Dreisteine im Riesengebirge* (1826);[23] in von Guérard's composition the focus on the ›castle‹ and its vertical form is heightened by the verticality of the reflections of the setting sun on the water and the tiny lighthouse on the cliff top. Depicted at sunset, the formation is dramatically back-lit in a way that recalls Lessing's treatment of the convergence of rock and castle in his great romantic landscape *Das Felsenschloss* (1828)[24], a composition that von Guérard had responded to in his sketchbook of ›Compositions drawn on winter evenings‹.

---

[21] For Mary Mackay von Guérard's coastal landscapes are examples of the »geological sublime‹ (compare 342–349).

[22] For example Ross Cayley, Geologist, GeoScience Victoria, Department of Primary Industries 2006.

[23] Carl Gustav Carus. *Die Dreisteine im Riesengebirge* (1826), oil on canvas, 64 x 92.5 cm. Galerie Neue Meister, Staatliche Kunstsammlungen Dresden.

[24] Carl Friedrich Lessing. *Das Felsenschloss (Schottische Landschaft, Bergschloss, Schloss Lochleven, Ritterburg*, 1828), oil on canvas, 138 x 194 cm. On loan from the Staatlichen Museen zu Berlin, Nationalgalerie, Kunstmuseum Düsseldorf, Düsseldorf.

b. The Romantic Tree: *Mount Kosciusko, seen from the Victorian border (Mount Hope Ranges*, 1866)

Eugen von Guérard. *Mount Kosciusko seen from the Victorian Border* (*Mount Hope Ranges*, 1866), oil on canvas, 108.2 x 153,3 cm. National Gallery of Victoria, Melbourne.

»For the Romantics«, observed Matthew Hargraves in his recent study, *Varieties of Romantic Experience,* »trees reigned supreme as the most revered elements of landscape« (90). One of the most evocative of all the trees in von Guérard's painted repertoire is the magisterial dead tree that leans across the canvas in *Mount Kosciusko, seen from the Victorian border (Mount Hope Ranges,* 1866). It reaches from the dark, fern-covered floor of the foreground to over the tops of the distant snow-clad mountains, symbolically uniting, according to a Humboldtian world view, the successive vegetation zones of the landscape. Von Guérard travelled through this landscape in November 1862 on an expedition led by the German geophysicist Georg von Neumayer, one of ten undertaken by the scientist as part of his magnetic survey of the colony of Victoria. The party reached View Point, the vantage point for this composition, on November 16th 1862 and at 3 pm von Guérard settled down to sketch the view.

The dead tree in von Guérard's *Mount Kosciusko* unquestionably refers to an actual tree observed by the artist at Mt. Hope: although it does not appear in the drawing it was recorded in the artist's small sketchbook on the same day. And yet, by virtue of its significance to the composition and the way it reaches towards the light – the bleached surfaces of its trunk and branches washed in the exquisite pinks of late afternoon light – it asks to be read as a symbol of something more, something beyond itself. Like many great Romantic paintings it evokes multiple associations.[25] Does the tree symbolize the heroic undertaking of the expedition party, linking as it does the adventurers camped at its base, with the distant snow-clad mountains, their destination? Does it refer to the cycle of life and death in nature? Or is it a more universal metaphor for the transience of life? Like the gnarled dead tree in Friedrich's *Eichbaum in Schnee* (1829)[26] or the angular branches of the oak tree in Lessing's *Die tausendjährige Eiche* (1837)[27], this tree communicates an essential humanity; its branches reach out like hands to receive the rays of setting sun, symbolizing, in Schelling's terms, the bond between the soul and nature offered by art (see Busch, 278).

c. The ›Rückenfigur‹: *North-east view from the northern top of Mount Kosciusko* (1863)

Eugen von Guérard. *North-east view from the northern top of Mount Kosciusko* (1863), oil on canvas, 66.5 x 116.8 cm. National Gallery of Australia, Canberra.

[25] Schelling observed that every true work of art is »capable of an infinity of interpretations [...] and yet one can never say whether this infinity resided in the artist or whether it simply resides in the work« (qtd. Busch, 279).
[26] Caspar David Friedrich. *Eichbaum im Schnee* (1829), oil on canvas, 71 x 48 cm. Nationalgalerie, Berlin.
[27] Carl Friedrich Lessing. *Die tausendjährige Eiche* (1837), oil on canvas, 123 x 165.7 cm. Städel Museum, Frankfurt am Main.

Von Guérard used the motif of the Rückenfigur, a figure seen from the back looking into the pictorial space of the canvas, to spectacular effect in *North-east view from the northern top of Mount Kosciusko*. The identification of this motif with Caspar David Friedrich, »its undoubted master« (Hargraves, 198), may at least in part explain the comparisons that have so frequently been drawn between von Guérard and Friedrich.

Von Guérard's *North-east view from the northern top of Mount Kosciusko* captures the moment when the artist and Georg von Neumayer's scientific party scaled what they believed to be the highest peak in Australia.[28] The intensity of the experience, given dramatic frisson by the approaching storm, is concentrated in the figure, probably the artist, in his wind-swept cloak, his arm outstretched towards the vast, majestic and awe-inspiring mountain ranges in front of him.

The Rückenfigur typically plays the role of intermediary between the viewer and the scene depicted in the painting. Von Guérard's cloaked figure, in whom the heightened emotions of the moment are so expressively invested, directs the viewer's gaze deep into the painting, where, on the basis of sketches made on the day, the physical landscape is depicted with topographic precision. By contrast, when we attempt to read the landscape viewed by the Rückenfigur in Friedrich's *The Traveller Above a Sea of Fog* (c. 1818)[29] we are confounded. Drifts of fog obscure the physical landscape making its scale and distances ambiguous and difficult to assess. In Friedrich's work, the Rückenfigur constitutes the »site of both our identification with, and our isolation from, the painted landscape« (Koerner, 217). The making of studies from nature was essential for Friedrich but it was the inner, ›spiritual‹ eye that was, for him, paramount.[30] »While Friedrich's paintings are so detailed and carefully executed that they do seem to engage the ›outer eye‹, in fact they elicit an internal exploration«, argues Frank. Various »obstacles confine the painted figures and viewers to their own solitary realm« leading to »a conflict between expectation and fulfillment« (Frank, 126). By contrast, our

---

[28] The painting depicts the view from the top of Mt Townsend, another peak on the Kosciuszko plateau, rather than Kosciuszko itself, which the party had climbed earlier on the same day.

[29] Caspar David Friedrich. *The Traveller Above a Sea of Fog* (c. 1818), oil on canvas, 74.8 x 94.8 cm. Kunsthalle, Hamburg.

[30] Friedrich famously advised the painter to »close your bodily eye so that you may see your picture first with the spiritual eye. Then bring to the light of day that which you have seen in the darkness so that it may react upon others from the outside inwards« (qtd. Vaughan, *German Romantic Painting*, 68).

expectation is fulfilled in von Guérard's painting as a landscape of unrivalled topographical, geological and spatial accuracy opens up for the viewer, as for the exultant cloaked figure in the painting. With its topographically accurate landscape, its references to the actual events that unfolded on the Kosciuszko plateau on November 19th 1862 and its portrayal of scientists taking readings and their guides clambering over the mountainous terrain, von Guérard's *Kosciusko* may be more akin to the works of Caspar Wolf than those of Caspar David Friedrich.

IV. Epilogue

Von Guérard absorbed the language of Romanticism. A solitary eagle soaring high above the Earth, skies of exceptional luminosity, a rocky coastline radiated by the intense light of the setting sun or a contemplative figure gazing across a still and timeless landscape – all seem to be intimations of a transcendent spirituality in nature. At the same time von Guérard's portrayal of such phenomena reflects the reality of his experience: he observed the eagles in the Grampian Ranges, he sketched Cape Schanck at sunset and he saw the enigmatic dead tree, so apparently redolent with symbolism, at Mt Hope on November 16th 1862. While he recognized the language of German Romantic painting in the landscape itself his ›true‹ Romanticism is to be found in his deep response to nature.

Von Guérard's Romanticism, while it reflects many aspects of German Romantic thought and practice, was in the final analysis, his own vision. His deep engagement with nature was intensely Romantic. He depicted the minutiae of nature at a microscopic level, at times painting under magnification. In his penetrating observation of phenomena – of, for example, a mountain range – he was able to grasp, in Schelling's terms, »the essence of Nature by bringing out what is *characteristic*« (qtd. Busch, 278). In his panoramic landscapes, lifted beyond the realm of description by the wondrous, transparent luminosity of their skies and the purity of their compositional geometry, there is an intimation of something beyond the literal, a sense of the indissoluble chain that Humboldt understood »binds together all nature«. His dedication to the pursuit of »truth« to nature did not waver throughout his long career. In his life and his art von Guérard exemplified the integrity and commitment to a higher purpose he had recognized in the Nazarene painters he met in Rome in his youth.

Works Cited

Baumgärtel, Bettina. »Naturstudie und landschaftliche Komposition«. *Johann Wilhelm Schirmer in seiner Zeit*. Ed. Siegmar Holsten. Heidelberg: Kehrer, 2002: 17–23.
Bott, Katharina. *Das Schadow-Album. Der Düsseldorfer Akademieschüler von 1851*. Hanau: CoCon-Verlag, 2009.
Bruce, Candice. »Eugene von Guérard. Castle Rock, Cape Schanck 1865«. *Landscapes of the Mornington Peninsula*. Mornington: Mornington Peninsula Regional Gallery, 2009.
Busch, Werner. »Empirical Studies of Nature«. *The Romantic Spirit in German Art 1790–1990*. Eds. Keith Hartley/Henry Meyric Hughes/Peter-Klaus Schuster/William Vaughan. London: Thames and Hudson, 1994: 278–282.
Carus, Carl Gustav. *Nine Letters on Landscape Painting, written in the years 1815–1824; with a letter from Goethe by way of introduction*. Tr. David Britt. Los Angeles: The J. Paul Getty Trust, 2002.
Eggerath, Hanna. »Die Geschichte des Neandertals«. *Bewegte Landschaften: Die Düsseldorfer Malerschule*. Eds. Bettina Baumgärtel/Klaus Thelen. Heidelberg: Edition Braus, 2003: 60–106.
Frank, Mitchell Benjamin. *German Romantic Painting Redefined: Nazarene Tradition and the Narratives of Romanticism*. London: Ashgate, 2001.
Grewe, Cordula. »Nazarenisch oder nicht? Überlegungen zum Religiösen in der Düsseldorfer Malerschule«. *Die Düsseldorfer Malerschule und ihre internationale Ausstrahlung 1819–1918*. Vol. 1. Ed. Bettina Baumgärtel. Düsseldorf/Petersburg: Museum Kunstpalast/Michael Imhof, 2011.
Guérard, Eugen von. »Reply on the critic of Eugene von Guérard's painting of the north Grampians«. Unpublished letter to the *Argus*, Melbourne, July 1870, reproduced in: Candice Bruce. *Eugen von Guérard*. Canberra: Australian Gallery Directors Council and Australian National Gallery, 1980: 134f.
Hargraves, Matthew. *Varieties of Romantic Experience. British, Danish, Dutch, French and German Drawings from the Collection of Charles Ryskamp*. New Haven, Connecticut: Yale Centre for British Art, 2010.
Hochstetter, Ferdinand von. »Eugen von Guérard's australische Landschaften«. *Mitteilungen der Kaiserlich-Königlichen Geographischen Gesellschaft* 27 (1884): 154–158.
Holst, Christian von. *Joseph Anton Koch. Ansichten der Natur*, Stuttgart: Staatsgalerie Stuttgart/Edition Cantz, 1989.
Hoopes, Donelson F. »The Düsseldorf Academy and the Americans«. *The Düsseldorf Academy and the Americans: An Exhibition of Drawings and Watercolours*. Atlanta: High Museum of Art, 1972: 19–34.
Humboldt, Alexander von. *Cosmos: A Sketch of a Physical Description of the Universe*. London: Henry G. Bohn, 1849–1858 [1845].

Hütt, Wolfgang. *Die Düsseldorfer Malerschule 1819-1869*. Leipzig: E.A. Seemann, 1995.
Koerner, Joseph Leo. *Caspar David Friedrich and the Subject of Landscape*. London: Reaktion, 1990.
Mackay, Mary. »All that mighty mass of rock: the geological Sublime«. *Art and Australia* (March 1994): 342–349.
Pullin, Ruth. *Eugene von Guérard: Nature Revealed*. Melbourne: National Gallery of Victoria, 2011.
Pullin, Ruth. »The Vulkaneifel and Victoria's Western District: Eugene von Guérard and the Geognostic Landscape«. *Europe and Australia. Melbourne Art Journal 11/12*. Ed. David Marshall. Melbourne: The Fine Arts Network, 2009: 6–50.
Pullin, Ruth. *Eugene von Guérard and the Science of Landscape Painting. PhD dissertation*. Melbourne: The University of Melbourne, 2007.
Smith, James. »The Essayist«. *Examiner, and Melbourne Weekly News*. 8.09.1860: 8.
Sitt, Martina. »The Düsseldorf ›Compagnie‹ in Rome 1830–1860. In Goethe's Footsteps«. *Goethe, Boerner, and the Artists of their Time*. Ed. C.G. Boerner. Düsseldorf: C. G. Boerner, 1999: 223–272.
Vaughan, William. *German Romantic Painting*. New Haven/London: Yale University Press, 1994.
Wesenberg, Angelika. »Origin and Archetype: The Dream of a New Start«. Tr. David Britt. *The Romantic Spirit in German Art 1790-1990*. Eds. Keith Hartley/Henry Meyric Hughes/Peter-Klaus Schuster/William Vaughan. London: Thames and Hudson, 1994: 115–121.

Images

1. Friedrich Boser (attrib.). *Eugen von Guérard* (1838–40), oil on canvas, 17.2 x 13.3 cm. National Gallery of Victoria, Melbourne.
2. Eugen von Guérard. *Castle Rock, Cape Schanck* (1865), oil on canvas, 61.0 x 91.3 cm. Art Gallery of South Australia, Adelaide.
3. Eugen von Guérard. *Mount Kosciusko, seen from the Victorian Border (Mount Hope Ranges*, 1866), oil on canvas, 108.2 x 153.3 cm. National Gallery of Victoria, Melbourne.
4. Eugen von Guérard. *North-east view from the northern top of Mount Kosciusko* (1863), oil on canvas, 66.5 x 116.8 cm. National Gallery of Australia, Canberra.

Yvonne Förster-Beuthan (*Leuphana Universität Lüneburg*)

The Modern Concept of Fashion and its Origins in Romanticism[1]

Zusammenfassung

In diesem Essay werden zentrale Aspekte des modernen Modebegriffs überblicksartig dargestellt, die um 1800 sowohl in der Debatte um Mode selbst als auch im Denken der Romantik relevant werden. Für die Moderne besonders maßgeblich ist dabei der Gedanke, dass Mode ein Medium der Individualität und jene ihrerseits als Merkmal aufgeklärter Bürgerlichkeit zivilgesellschaftlich bedeutsam wird. Diese Entwicklung weg von der Verurteilung von Mode als reiner Oberflächlichkeit, hin zu einer funktionalen Neudefinition vor dem Hintergrund politischer und ökonomischer Erwägungen wird im ersten Teil des Aufsatzes dargestellt. Daran anschließend wird ein zweiter Schlüsselbegriff im Konzept der Mode vorgestellt: Zeitlichkeit ist sowohl für Mode überhaupt als auch für das aktuelle Modegeschehen im Besonderen entscheidend. Zum einen stellt die Wahrnehmung der Zeitlichkeit und zeitlichen Abfolge des Modegeschehens die Bedingung dafür dar, Mode konzeptuell erfassen zu können. Zum anderen ist für das moderne Modeschaffen Zeitlichkeit zentral, denn Zeit wird an den Produkten der Mode selbst sichtbar gemacht. Dabei soll deutlich werden, dass diese ›Verzeitlichung‹ der Mode selbst Parallelen zu zentralen Begriffen der Romantik, vor allem der romantischen Ironie aufweist.

I. Introduction

At first sight, there seems to be no relation between Romanticism and the concept of fashion, although during the ›Goethe era‹[2] it was a topic of discussion which reflected an anthropological perspective on fashion. It also seems to be an interesting coincidence that the first fashion magazines were published at roughly the same time as Romanticism in literature and philosophy appeared. This historical period was also the cradle of modern

---

[1] This study has been supported by a scholarship granted by the Klassik Stiftung Weimar.
[2] For an overview on fashion in Goethe's time see Purdy, *The Tyranny of Elegance in the Era of Goethe*.

life, in which the first forms of industrialization, ideas about democracy and the rise of the middle classes, the so-called *Bürgertum* [bourgeoisie], emerged. Some of the most important concepts of modernity, such as *Bildung*, ›labour‹ and ›production‹, were reflected in Romantic thinking. These concepts, together with the science of economics and free markets, evolved around 1800. Romanticism took a critical stance toward economics as the dominant social paradigm, which might be worth recalling in the crisis it is facing today. Although fashion was not a central topic amongst Romantic writers, the historical coincidence of Romanticism and the flourishing discussion about fashion is worth a second look.

In this paper I begin by investigating the relationship between fashion and economics, since it is a conceptual link to Romanticism. I then consider the concept of art in fashion and Romanticism. The idea of art as something self-referential and universal, as in transcendental poetry, is central to the modern notion of literature (see Behler) and originated in Romantic thought. I will attempt to show how economics and art related to fashion at the turn of the 19th century and consequently how a modern concept of fashion arose. In the second part of this paper I will consider temporality, a central element of the modern concept of fashion, indeed its necessary condition. I will analyse this development in order to show how the Romantic concept of irony has returned within fashion over the past 30 years.

II. Fashion and the Economy

In 1786, Friedrich Justin Bertuch, an editor in Weimar and a friend of Goethe, published with an explicitly commercial goal one of the first and most famous fashion magazines, the *Journal des Luxus und der Moden* (*JLM*). In his introduction to the first issue, he discussed the role of luxury and fashion, knowing that he would have to defend himself against accusations of endorsing extravagance and superficiality. It should be remembered that at this time Germany was still largely an agrarian society and showed poor industrial potential. To publish a fashion journal then must have seemed a strange if not pretentious undertaking. But Bertuch knew that there was a growing number of readers in the expanding middle class who were embracing enlightened values. If it were possible to stimulate their interest in fashion, then that would lead to growth in the industrial and economic sector. Besides this economic perspective, Bertuch conceived of fashion as a deeply rooted anthropological phenomenon. This combination of an anthropological perspective with an economic one is shown in the following quotation from the introduction of the first issue:

> Wohlleben will und kann jeder Mensch auf der ganzen weiten Erde, so bald er sich etwas mehr, als seine ersten nothwendigen Bedürfnisse des Lebens erwerben kann; und eben der heiße Wunsch dahin zu kommen, und sich güthlich zu tun, ist die mächtigste Triebfeder der Industrie, der Künste, der Erfindungen und des Geschmacks, kurz des größten Theils der menschlichen Thätigkeit (JLM, 1, 24).[3]

If fashion was to become the motor of the national economy, it would not be enough for people to become interested in the latest fashion, they would also have to be interested in buying goods produced domestically. This was a further goal of Bertuch and he encouraged the readers of his journal to buy German products. But fashion was usually imported from Paris or London, the two cities that then ruled the world of fashion. In Britain, where industrialization had already begun and mass production left its mark, dress at that time was guided by simplicity and practical considerations. France on the other hand was known for more extravagant dress, both before and after the Revolution. English and French styles not only had great influence on German consumers, but the cloth and fabric to make them were also imported from these countries. At the same time, the idea of a national costume was discussed in Germany and in other countries throughout Europe. In 1791, Samuel Simon Witte, a German theologian and philosopher, wrote an answer to a query of the Danish Academy as to whether or not a national dress code should be established (see Witte, 72–78). Interestingly, Witte's answer was negative – although such an enterprise could have led to an increase in national production and consumption – as he was convinced that for citizens of a modern state, clothing was an important means of expressing their individuality. Although a potential consequence of an obligatory national dress code would be the development of a stronger national identity, he argued that the citizens of a country should be attached to their nationality by their free will and rational arguments. This idea of national unity was becoming increasingly important in Germany at that

---

[3] »The good life is something that every man on earth wants and is able to achieve once he can afford something more than what is needed to satisfy his primary needs. The burning wish to arrive at this state and enjoy oneself is the most powerful mainspring of industry, art, invention and taste; in short: it is central to the greatest part of human activity.« Note that Bertuch chose a synonym for ›luxury‹ in order to avoid its negative connotation. He used »Wohlleben« (good life) instead, a word which has a more modest sound to it in German.

time, since the German territory was still fragmented into various dukedoms and principalities. Witte argued against the idea of a national costume by pointing out that fashion is a means of communication and social contact. In an Aristotelian manner he remarked: »[F]inery and dress, like music in another regard, are generally a good means of diverting the passions in a harmless way for society« (Witte, 77). A bourgeois government, he claimed, as opposed to a national government needed its people to be individuals able to express themselves freely if a public life were to be established. »The existence of the public and the existence of the public personality tied to it is also the existence of taste« (Witte, 78). The formation of a modern society where the individual could contribute to society in a free and responsible way also required, according to Witte, self-expression by means of outer appearance. Outer appearance is the first and most direct way in which individuals perceive each other; the choice of clothes and accessories is not arbitrary, but rather constitutes a realm of communication that finds its own conventions and signs. Similarly in 1792 Christian Garve argued in favour of fashion when he pointed out that »as long as man has existed there have been fashions among them« (Garve, 67). He also took fashion as a means not only of constituting personal identities but also those of social class and nation. In a seemingly modern twist he observed that fashion simultaneously divides and unifies people. It gives them the opportunity to understand and present themselves as individuals as well as members of a social group or a particular lifestyle. Garve presented a number of arguments as to why fashion should be regarded as a positive force in constituting a nation, amongst them the notion that continuously changing fashion styles become an economic factor.

This discourse on fashion around 1800 had two sides. The first was the simple description found in numerous magazines of the latest styles and luxury goods. As the presentation of fashion was often seen as amoral and vain, this discourse needed to be justified. And it was here that the second side of the discourse on fashion came into play and made two pragmatic arguments. Firstly, it claimed that there were profits to be earned from fashion and that the chief reason for promoting fashion were its potential benefits for industry and the national economy. Secondly, the other argument adopted an anthropological perspective, arguing that the human desire to shape his or her outer appearance is a ›natural‹ desire and should be cultivated in a bourgeois society, not only in order to enhance social communication and as a means of inoculating passions. It is obvious that the discourse on fashion and the discourse of economics are in a positive and reciprocal relationship.

III. Romanticism and the Economy

Beyond the discourse on fashion, Romanticism took a more critical perspective on the economy, with Romantic writers distancing themselves from the economization of society. Various processes of modernization had set in, most importantly the political changes in the wake of the French Revolution, the beginning of industrialization and the increase of trade and exchange of goods. These processes were accompanied by a particularization of society into different spheres of work, trade and life, all seeming to coexist alongside each other with no bond whatsoever between them. Moreover, neither religion nor science nor indeed any other cultural practice seemed able to unite these different social spaces as they all appeared to contain their own set of values and follow their own rules, with no independent standpoint from which one could express universal values and rules.

As Dirk von Petersdorff points out, this situation is reflected in Novalis's *Heinrich von Ofterdingen*. Although Novalis had set his plot in medieval times, what he described fits the society of that time, with a strong notion of unity being developed to counteract the particularization found in actual life. The tendency to value things only by their economic potential is criticized in a passage in *Heinrich von Ofterdingen* in which the separation of art and commerce is being discussed by merchants. Art, in their opinion, serves only as a form of distraction and relaxation for people after work. That is precisely the opposite of the Romantic view, where art figures as the highest form of insight. There, science and art form a unity, where in fact science becomes art and vice versa. Productive thinking is a form of art that leads to scientific knowledge.

In this discourse on fashion, political and economic considerations legitimate the wish for self-expression and luxury goods. Social communication is enhanced by self-expression through fashion. Here the underlying goal was to encourage people to consider themselves as free citizens in a modern state. And increasing the consumption of luxury goods would increase trade and help to develop national industry. Romanticism on the other hand saw the challenges that come with such developments. When Romantic thinkers spoke about productivity they focussed on something completely different from industrial growth. Productivity for them meant an original kind of relation which constituted the self and its counterpart, the world. These notions of unity, productivity and relation will be central in the following discussion. I will now attempt to show that, apart from its critical assessment of economics, in Romanticism there are similar motifs to be found in the discourses on fashion. If nothing else, the making and use of fashion is an aesthetic practice and therefore cannot develop detached from the intellectual climate of its time. One example of art's influence on fashion is Goethe's novel *Werther*, which was responsible for many young men adopting a style of clothing they imagined the protagonist to have worn and imitating his behaviour, even in extreme cases to the point of committing emulation suicide (Landfester, 122ff.). Without going into detail into the ›Werther cult‹, I argue that art, which is central to Romantic thinking, serves as a linking concept between fashion and Romanticism. The question will be how the term applies to fashion. In the following section I will discuss the semiotic character of fashion and then turn to the notion of ›transcendental poetry‹.

IV. The Semiotic Character of Fashion

Clothing has a semiotic character because it not only serves to cover the body but is also a sign of gender, social rank and an expression of individual taste. Johann Gottfried Herder, who was always very suspicious of fashion, considered the semiotic capacity of clothing to have a stronger necessity than linguistic signs, which in his view are always arbitrary. The primary function of clothing in human society, according to Herder, is the restriction of sexuality. Clothing for Herder represented a »sensual economy« (qtd. Landfester, 47), regulating sexual desire, which also means that clothing is not only hiding the body but also denoting it as a sexual object. Clothing is certainly able to express more than that. But what is interesting in Herder is the dialectic between concealment and disclosure. This tension becomes important in *directoire* and Empire styles in fashion in the wake of the French Revolution.

Although men's fashion was mainly influenced by trends in Britain, pre-revolutionary Paris was generally considered to be Europe's leading fashion centre. Fashion at that time largely meant the fashion at court, that is the clothing worn by the royals and the aristocracy. It was an expression of power and rank and as such developed bizarre forms of artifice. Whole landscapes for example were constructed in a woman's coiffure while hooped dresses had such wide hips that their wearers needed specially made chairs if they were to sit down. Clothing as a sign clearly denotes something exterior to the bearer, primarily wealth and power, but not any kind inner of qualities. Such tailoring gave the body an outrageously artificial form and this would soon become an object of criticism. Courtly extravagance became synonymous with decadence, as one can see in Jean-Jacques Rousseau's writing on fashion (Rousseau, 38f.). After the monarchy was discredited during the revolution, the call for a more natural beauty to replace the courtly artifice became louder. And it was in the Romantic era that a new concept of fashion developed, one that I would argue is the first that can be thought of as modern. This development only becomes apparent when examining the illustrations of clothing and their commentary in fashion magazines together with current philosophical concepts of the time.

From the very beginning of the 19th century, the new styles of dress known as *directoire* and *à l'antique* (elements of both entered the later Empire style and were in sharp contrast to the stiff and capricious Rococo styles) exhibited a different semiotic character. *À l'antique* is a style in which the gown is meant to resemble the loose draping on Greek statues. It was a style which Hegel, in his reflections on sculpture, admired (Hegel, 145f.). This draping effect establishes, as these clothes gain their form through the movements of the body, a different relation between the subject and its appearance. Hegel thought that this kind of draping exhibited the human body in the most appropriate way: covering enough of the natural body so that the human figure is perceived as restrained while still revealing enough to show its beauty. In the Greek manner of clothing that was idealized at the turn of the century (not exactly copied but similar to Greek dress) there is an intimate relation between the body and the form of dress. The dress signifies the body in a dynamic way by exhibiting its form indirectly through movement in contrast to the pre-revolutionary dress that is more a static space of representation.

The most important characteristic of dress (mainly women's) during early Romanticism was its dynamic form. Clothing no longer strived to give the body an artificial form, confined within boned corsets, but instead it flowed over the natural human form. Dresses now had a much simpler cut and were often transparent, reminiscent of a veil, which is a common literary motif. The dialectics of concealing and disclosing is a recurring theme not only in fashion but also in poetry, which is directed towards the subject's inner life. As in poetry, the internal life and the mind find expression in a new direction, with dress giving more freedom to fashion design and allowing a stronger sense of individuality, which becomes a central topic in modernity. The change in the semiotic direction of fashion in this era can be described as a movement from the external to the internal sphere of the subject. A similar change can be noted in poetry since in Romanticism literary production is not about external reference but about self-referentiality and original production.[4] In the next sections of this paper, I would like to apply the concept of self-referentiality to fashion.

V. Fashion and Literature

To compare fashion and literature means to regard fashion as art, as for example Herder did in his *Ideas for the Philosophy of History of Humanity*. Fashion can belong to the realm of art in two different ways. It can be produced *as* a work of art (for example the performances of the Viktor & Rolf fashion house), or it can be an *artful* expression of the subject. Around 1800 it was clearly not meant to be art in the first sense, although it was treated in a way that comes close to art. The many hand-painted images in the journals for example treat clothing as if they were pieces of art. The discussions about different items and forms resemble interpretations of artworks. This is possible because dress is not a mere object but also a sign for something else; clothing in this sense resembles a language.

Romanticism conceptualizes literature as a form of art that is not obliged to represent something external. Literature is conceived of as self-referential; its meaning is constituted by literary reflection itself and not by external reference (see Deiters). The concept of subjectivity is also a central topic and related to self-referentiality, because self-consciousness clearly implies a relation to oneself. Subjectivity and self-referentiality both require reflection, an active relation to oneself. The self is not thought of as something given, but is instead the result of an original production.[5] What comes into play here is an original form of relation, what could be called a primordial reflexivity. This reflexive process produces the self. Production and product come to be identical. These are in short the motifs of Romanticism on which I rely in my enquiry into fashion.

The question is now whether Romantic thought has left its traces on the concept of fashion. Around 1800 countless journals on fashion were published all across Europe. Half a century earlier fashion had still only been communicated by means of dolls that were transported from court to court. Only the gentry had the possibility of viewing and developing an opinion

---

[4] On the notion of production see Deiters.
[5] On the problem of the self and the notion of production in Johann Gottlieb Fichte's philosophy see Ralf Beuthan's contribution in this volume.

about the latest fashion. This situation had completely changed by the dawn of the 19th century. It is not only the information about new and fashionable clothing that spread quickly amongst a far more extensive group of people, but also the means of production changed dramatically. From factories full of young women sewing by hand, clothes were cut in a way that permitted their mass production, with the sewing machine about to be invented. The Industrial Revolution, its progress driven by specialization, lay ahead – followed by the Romantic critique of economics, science, rationalism and the particularization of society and thought. As a unifying and universal principle, Romanticism proposed a concept of art that in its production of significance dispensed with external reference; the world should become romanticized (Novalis). Science and philosophy were thought of as forms of poetry. In this way self-referential significance became universal, that is became transcendental poetry.

The opposition of nature and artifice was present in discussions of fashion. Natural beauty, at least in women, was regarded as an ideal and while fashion should contribute to beauty, it was not a means to artificially gain beauty. With Romanticism, a new sense of artificiality was put forward. Artificiality in Romanticism did not mean the opposite of natural; it meant being *gebildet* or cultivated. And this concept became universalized. In fashion magazines the realm of aesthetic cultivation was not restricted to fashion and clothing but was extended to furniture and everyday objects. The cultivation of outer appearance was regarded as an important factor in a modern society. The idea that personal identity depends on appearance turned fashion into an anthropological topic.

It is interesting that in his story *The Sandman* E.T.A. Hoffmann depicts the clear-minded Clara, a young woman that loves the protagonist Nathanael, as well-proportioned but not really beautiful, whereas Olimpia, whom Nathanael falls in love with, is in fact an automaton, and praised for her beauty. In a description of her clothes several details are considered beautiful. Although her character has something uncanny about it, she is not seen as a mechanical monster. In this story it is instead the human characters such as Coppelius that seem monstrous. Without going into detail, it is obvious that the Romantic perspective on the artificial is ambivalent. On the one hand, it stands for mechanical objects that represent the economic sphere; on the other, there is the positive connotation of art and poetry. That is why an artificial being can also be beautiful. Ironically the one aspect of Olimpia's clothes that is criticized is her too tight corset (a recurring topic for discussion in fashion magazines). The beauty of the automaton does not vanish once Nathanael has discovered that she is not a human being.[6]

This complex view of the artificial is central: Artificiality does not necessarily stand in contrast to nature, but can figure as an anthropological universal, because the self is only present and perceivable by others as mediated through appearance. When our outer appearance is a means of communication and of producing identity, then it is not alien to the inner self. Originary production is central to Romantic thought and it plays a decisive role in the concept of fashion.

VI. Fashion and Temporality

Since the Romantic era, fashion has undergone a significant change, which has led it away from Romanticism in one respect, yet has brought it closer in another. The historical development of styles is clearly a temporal one. The other comes with the changing temporal characteristics of fashion and concerns its relation to art. The concept of fashion in a modern sense arises when there is a perception of clothing as temporally changing objects of taste. As I have already shown, such debates started around 1800 with the publication of fashion journals. Fashion is linked to a special form of temporal experience; it is an experience that consists first and foremost in the recognition of transience. The temporal character of fashion materializes in the various journals on fashion, amongst them the *JLM*, with styles being described in contrast to former styles. Fashion is thus not only the creating of transient aesthetic preferences but it is also a technique of memory. What is fashionable can be recognized by its difference to what is unfashionable. It is essential to the awareness of fashion to have a *memory* of what has just passed or what is being revived. In the *JLM* one finds for example illustrations contrasting styles of different periods of time to explain how clothing had evolved. With the appearance of these journals, historical thinking – that is, thinking in historical categories – is extended to fashion. Fashion only exists if there is a culture of memory of clothing and decoration. This aspect of memory is often only implicit in theories on fashion. It is its transience and focus on the present that creates the nimbus

---

[6] A playful thought: When the self is not pre-given, there might be several ways it can be constituted. Maybe the automaton can become a self because she has a bodily presence and therefore is regarded as a self by others.

of fashion and makes it an object of conspicuous consumption, as Thorstein Veblen put it in 1899 (Veblen, 261f.).

While the concept of fashion as temporal change in clothing is seen as a modern phenomenon, Hegel considered the ancient Greek way of dressing as timeless (see Hegel, 145f.). Although researchers have yet to agree on the exact point in time when one can speak of fashion as we understand it today, in *Fashion-ology* Yuniiya Kawamura proposes that modern fashion begins with the establishment of a ›Parisian fashion system‹ in 1868. Clothing and fashion seem to be two different concepts, as speaking about clothing does not necessarily imply the concept of fashion (this is a rather contested issue, but a discussion of it may be reserved for another occasion). Suffice it to say that clothing becomes fashion when its temporality is acknowledged. This is a rather simple but fundamental point, which is however not meant to replace other definitions of the concept of fashion.

In short, fashion only exists when changes in clothing are recognized. The central question of the second aspect of fashion's change since the Romantic period is: How are these changes perceived and what kind of temporal experience accompanies this perception? My hypothesis is that the way in which fashion figures as a temporal experience is a temporal development in itself. Currently the temporal experience initiated by fashion is itself changing. This process of change has resulted, according to Barbara Vinken, in the end of the era of fashion and the beginning of a post-fashion era (Vinken, 61f.). I will return to this point later on. According to Vinken, the era of fashion – that is the era in which fashion as a concept developed and flourished continuously – lasted from the late 18th century until the end of the 20th century. Whether or not the term post-fashion is fitting to describe the state of fashion today is another question, perhaps a question of theoretical taste.

Roughly 200 years ago fashion began its ascendance because journals were published that focussed on the changes in clothing and accessories. The popular readership of these journals was fairly large, mainly women, but, as can be seen in the work of Rousseau and Hegel, fashion also was discussed in philosophy. With the recognition that styles in clothing change over time, a sense of fashion's contemporaneous presence was established. Fashion is widely regarded as a transient phenomenon that exists only in the glamorous present moment and fades soon after. What remains unsaid is the condition of possibility of that very sense, the recognition of differences between the fashionable and its past – former styles of clothing. Clearly, this is not a sufficient condition for fashion – but it is a necessary one. A current style of clothing must not only be recognized as new but also as desirable; only then can it be called fashionable. For the time being, I will limit my considerations to its temporal aspect. As I have already pointed out, this became manifest with the appearance of fashion journals, a medium which has been successful until today in communicating the latest fashions (now only rivalled by the internet).

The specific temporal experience that accompanies fashion had been quite stable until the end of the 20th century. During the last 200 years fashion has been seen as a means of distinction – be it of social rank, class, gender or social function. Most theories of fashion work along the lines of a concept of distinction as developed by, for example, Georg Simmel or Thorstein Veblen. This is also then evidence of the present-centred view of fashion, which I propose is a characteristic feature of fashion now undergoing a change. If fashion has the function of distinguishing in some way its wearer (and therefore, as Georg Simmel [1957, 291] maintains, also a means of identification), then one can speak of a process that centres on presence – of the wearer and his or her surroundings against which distinction and identity can be gained. This process is a creative one and not only adaptive. Even though the trickle-down theory of fashion (Veblen) for example focussed on adaptation, if styles are being adapted from other people or a different social strata, it is still a creative process because the choices one makes concerning the outer appearance shape one's identity. The interaction of the individual body with a styling of its form precludes the use of fashion as a mere adaptive process. Clothing – as Hegel puts it in his lecture on sculpture – is animated by body and spirit.

It is because our outer appearance is so intimately tied to our identity and therefore what we take as our inner self that our way of clothing ourselves (at least since its changes have been recognized as fashions) becomes part of our experience of time. Fashion shapes our temporal perception of the cultural world in a distinctive way. This is due to memory, and our memory is enhanced by medial objectification in the form of images. In this way fashion is a creative process of representation of identity, which is doubled by medial images of the wearer.[7] Speaking of fashion one cannot be oblivious of its presentation in the form of images, whether they be in paintings, journals or private photography. These objectifications play a central role in

---

[7] I am aware that the issue of self-portrait as part of identity formation opens a large field of questions which I am unable to discuss in the context of this article.

the way we perceive fashion as a temporal form because they are a means of registering changes over time; they stabilize the impression of change.

VII. Changing Temporal Experiences

It was around 1800 that fashion started to be reflected in the print medium; it was around 1900 that the Paris fashion system was developed and individual designers moved into the spotlight. By then, industrial production allowed for standardized mass production. The rapidly evolving industry shaped the face of cities and society. The turn of the 19th century is associated with dandyism and decadence, and thus artificiality. The upcoming 20th century then celebrated grand designers and every decade was characterized by a new form and silhouette of clothing. The style of the 20th century was characterized by the passing of the decades – until the 1980s. With the dawn of the new millennium that rhythm does not seem to hold anymore. What has become the new paradigm in fashion is the blending of styles and the visibility of temporality in its objects. More provocatively, we can say that fashion has become self-reflexive. What it finds in this self-reflection is time, or temporality. Barbara Vinken calls this new era post-fashion. There are three characteristics of fashion-making that are closely related with temporality and memory and aim at exhibiting these. Firstly, it is the technique of prewashing clothes in order to make them look pre-worn. The Japanese fashion-designer Yohji Yamamoto was one of the first to start this in the 1970s. Interestingly, this practice dates back to dandyism, as Vinken points out that »Coco Chanel reported that the Earl of Winchester, the richest man in the world, never gave the impression of wearing new clothes« (Vinken, 69). Secondly, it had once been the pride of designers to hide the signs of production, the seams and stitches. But for some time now it has become a common practice to exhibit the signs of production in the finished product. There seems to be no longer an imperative to hide these signs; instead the temporal and material becoming of the objects is now part of their design. These two characteristics apply to the objects themselves. The third characteristic applies to the whole style, to the way in which the single objects of apparel are combined with each other. The current era of fashion seems to have become a depository of styles, which is open to ever new configurations. Newness is not necessarily the invention of new forms anymore but a recombination of old elements. This variation also creates new silhouettes and forms but it also opens the possibility of mere repetition.

It is now possible that people choose their outfits completely from vintage stores and even make their hairdo and posture look as if they had just exited a time-machine. Even if a closer look reveals new elements or ruptures in the overall vintage silhouettes, it still gives the impression of seeing someone from another decade.

I am not as Vinken is sure that these elements should lead us to use the term of ›post-fashion‹. Surely such eclecticism is reminiscent of a rather cheap version of postmodern architecture. There is something about fashion in the last few decades that is different from the *mode de cent ans*, the fashion of the last hundred years, as Vinken puts it. But it has to be questioned whether this difference is a form of *post*-phenomenon. The prefix ›post-‹ usually suggests the end of some kind of development and the start of a time that lacks this form of development. It is true that the development of fashion has taken a different course since the 1980s. I would draw the temporal line between the 80s and the 90s because the 80s seem to have been the last decade to exhibit a recognizable style. As Andrew Benjamin points out in his essays on *Style and Time*, the temporality of fashion is complex and has to be thought of as a relation of three terms: appearance, recognition and identification. And furthermore: temporal development as a continuity is based on discontinuities, on differences created by variation. The question is how this change in the concept of fashion just described ought to be explained. The three elements that I have ascribed to what Vinken calls post-fashion might have existed in fashion before, but they have never been as important as they are now. What is now happening is not a complete rupture in the sense that fashion has stopped developing and is now just recycling; rather, we are confronted with a new, conscious form of production. Fashion has become more and more important since design has entered all parts of everyday life. There does not seem to be any single object in the cultural world that has not undergone a process of being designed in one way or the other. Now the fact that design is produced enters the design itself. Here, we find Friedrich Schlegel's idea of representing production by the product (Schlegel). This thought is one characterization of Romantic irony. Representation has always been a central topic in fashion, but what fashion mainly represented, at least until before the French Revolution, was external to fashion, namely social and gender distinctions. Then around 1800 the object of representation shifted from the external to the inner world of the subject, although the display of social status was still relevant. Today another form of representation has appeared. Fashion has started to represent *itself*, its conditions, its processes, and its temporality. This process of self-reflection can be regarded as the transition from fashion to art. In reflecting production by the product, and therefore in a material way, fashion creates objects that carry their meaning within themselves rather than being determined by an external objective or end. Fashion and its relation to art or its becoming art has been an issue at least since the 1970s. This is not a new topic but one that marks a quality in fashion that is quite recent. Schlegel understood irony as poetic reflection and with fashion becoming self-reflexive it can be understood as a form of Romantic irony because it creates objects that exhibit their temporal and material becoming, including its relation to the designer (author) and design (work).

A last thought I would like to mention has to do with the eclecticism that seems to characterize fashion today. Since the beginning of the 20th century, a completely new style of clothing has been developed with every new decade. The decades of fashion in the 20th century have become iconic for the historic face of this century. Today fashion seems to consist of a variation of these pre-existing iconic forms. As a result, there is a change in perception. Fashion has turned into a temporal medium in which we see something extraordinary – a temporal experience of a special character. The experience of time always involves the tenses of past, present and future and their combination makes, to use a phenomenological term, the extended present. The extended present always involves a kept-in-mind past, a present moment and an anticipated future. Tenses in the philosophy of time are always associated with a subject that experiences time. Ontologically tenses do not exist outside of the perceiving mind. In fashion (as well as in art, but there only if you are an expert) tensed time gains some objectivity because fashion gives visibility to temporal combinations. When Merleau-Ponty in his late writings speaks of the »flesh of time« (111) he describes the temporal aspects in the world of perception – the simultaneity of past, present and future in the visible world. In fashion today we can literally see the past and its productive opening to future forms. This kind of anticipation stems from the past and the past in turn does not vanish from the scene once it gives rise to new forms. Walter Benjamin wrote in his *Passages* that philosophy takes an interest in fashion because of its anticipations (112). The anticipations that can be drawn from fashion are nourished from the whole range of past forms and its vital connection to the present. But its predictions are never meant to be utopias; they never take themselves seriously. Although fashion is realized by serious thought and effort, it is always realized by material that never vanishes behind the reflections. There is a great deal of Romantic irony in serious fashion creation. The perception of style will not always have an intellectual or higher goal. But there is the possibility to see more – just like in a painting, where you can see apples on a plate or a history of perception. To see the whole in the parts and to envisage the lineage from the partial to the whole is a Romantic motif that has definitely not lost its contemporary relevance. In this article I have given a sketch of a relationship between concepts of Romanticism and the modern notion of fashion. Further investigations on different aspects of this relationship will undoubtedly have to follow.

Works Cited

Ackermann, Astrid. *Paris, London und die europäische Provinz. Die frühen Modejournale 1770–1830*. Frankfurt/M: Peter Lang, 2005.
Behler, Ernst. *Frühromantik*. Berlin/New York: de Gruyter, 1992.
Benjamin, Andrew. *Style and Time: Essays on the Politics of Appearance*. Evanston, IL: Northwestern University Press, 2006.
Benjamin, Walter. *Passagen-Werk*. Frankfurt/M: Suhrkamp, 1982.
Bertschik, Julia. *Mode und Moderne: Kleidung als Spiegel des Zeitgeistes in der deutschsprachigen Literatur (1770–1945)*. Köln: Böhlau, 2005.
Borchert, Angela/Ralf Dressel (eds.). *Das Journal des Luxus und der Moden: Kultur um 1800*. Heidelberg: Winter, 2004.
Deiters, Franz-Josef. »Poetisierung als kritisches Verfahren: ›Arbeit‹ in der Frühromantik«. *Limbus. Australisches Jahrbuch für germanistische Literatur- und Kulturwissenschaft* 2 (2009): 33–50.
Garve, Christian. »On Fashion« [1792]. *The Rise of Fashion*. Ed. Daniel L. Purdy. Minneapolis/London: University of Minnesota Press, 2004: 65–71.
Hegel, Georg Wilhelm Friedrich. »On Drapery« (from *Aesthetics* [1820]). *The Rise of Fashion*. Ed. Daniel L. Purdy. Minneapolis/London: University of Minnesota Press, 2004: 145–152.
Herder, Johann Gottfried. »Ideen zur Philosophie der Geschichte der Menschheit«. *Werke*. Vol. 6. Ed. Martin Bollacher. Frankfurt/M: Deutscher Klassiker Verlag, 1989.
Hoffmann, E.T.A. *Nachtstücke* [1817]. Stuttgart: Reclam, 1990.
Kawamura, Yuniya. *Fashion-ology*. Oxford/New York: Berg, 2006.
Landfester, Ulrike. *Der Dichtung Schleier. Zur poetischen Funktion von Kleidung in Goethes Frühwerk*. Freiburg i.B.: Rombach, 1995.
Lehmann, Ulrich. *Tigersprung. Fashion in Modernity*. Cambridge, MA/London: MIT Press, 2000.
Merleau-Ponty, Maurice. *The Visible and the Invisible* [1964]. Evanston, IL: Northwestern University Press, 1968.

Novalis. *Schriften*. Darmstadt: WBG, 1999.

Petersdorff, Dirk von. »Die Romantisierung der Ökonomie im ›Heinrich von Ofterdingen‹«. *Blütenstaub. Jahrbuch für Frühromantik* 2 (2009): 263–276.

Purdy, Daniel L. *The Tyranny of Elegance in the Era of Goethe*. Baltimore/London: Johns Hopkins University Press, 1998.

Rousseau, Jean-Jacques. »Discourse on the Arts and Sciences« [1750]. *The Rise of Fashion*. Ed. Daniel L. Purdy. Minneapolis/London: University of Minnesota Press, 2004: 37–48.

Schlegel, Friedrich. *Athenäums-Fragmente*. Stuttgart: Reclam, 1986.

Schmid, Werner (ed.). *Das Journal der Luxus und der Moden* (Teilnachdruck). Vol. 1–4. Leipzig: Edition Leipzig, 1967–1970. (*JLM*)

Simmel, Georg. »Fashion«. *American Journal of Sociology* 62 (1957): 541–558 (reprint of: *International Quarterly* X [1904]: 130–155).

Veblen, Thorstein. »Conspicuous Consumption« (from *The Theory of the Leisure Class* [1899]). *The Rise of Fashion*. Ed. Daniel L. Purdy. Minneapolis/London: University of Minnesota Press, 2004: 261–278.

Veblen, Thorstein. »Dress as an Expression of the Pecuniary Culture« (from *The Theory of the Leisure Class* [1899]). *The Rise of Fashion*. Ed. Daniel L. Purdy. Minneapolis/London: University of Minnesota Press, 2004: 278–288.

Vinken, Barbara. *Fashion Zeitgeist: Trends and Cycles in the Fashion System*. Oxford/New York: Berg, 2004.

Wieland, Christoph M./Schiller, Friedrich a.o. (eds.). *Journal für deutsche Frauen*. Leipzig, 1805f.

Witte, Samuel Simon. »An Answer to the Question: Would it Be Harmful or Beneficial to establish a National Uniform?« [1791] *The Rise of Fashion*. Ed. Daniel L. Purdy. Minneapolis/London: University of Minnesota Press, 2004: 72–78.

Andrew Benjamin (*Monash University*)

Hegel's Other Woman:
The Figure of Niobe in Hegel's *Lectures on Fine Art*

Zusammenfassung

In Hegels *Vorlesungen über die Ästhetik* repräsentieren Maria und Niobe zwei unterschiedliche Modalitäten der Liebe. Wenn sich aus ihrer Differenz eine genuin ethische Frage ergibt, dann handelt es sich um die Frage nach der Möglichkeit, Niobe zu lieben. Als solche wird Niobe zu *der* Figur des Ethischen. Das Ziel dieses Aufsatzes ist es, die ethischen Fragen zu verfolgen, die sich aus der unmöglichen Möglichkeit ergeben, Niobe zu lieben.

In a work written in 1789 of which only a few fragmentary pages still exist, a fragment now known as *Love*, Hegel wrote that a »pure heart [*ein reines Gemüt*] is not ashamed of love; but it is ashamed if its love is incomplete [*nicht vollkommen ist*]« (*ETW*, 306).[1] This allows for the following two questions to be posed: First, who can be said to have »*ein reines Gemüt*«? And second, whose continuity is defined by the enduring mark of shame? The question of »*ein reines Gemüt*«, as will be suggested, cannot be disassociated from a concern with Niobe. Moreover, her name will be given, from the outside, as an answer to the second question. Enduring as an inherently incomplete figure, Niobe is presented at the edge of assimilation. Not as the other *tout court*, but the other who, in standing in stone on the outside, complicates assimilation insofar as she is positioned outside any structure of recognition. In particular, those structures defined – to borrow the language of Hegel's *Phenomenology of Spirit* – in terms of »a loving recognition [*ein Anerkennen der Liebe*] in which the two sides, as regards their essence, do not stand in an antithetical relation to each other [*sich entgegensetzen*]« (*PS*, 466f.).
As such, given the possibility – if not the necessity – of exclusion, Niobe will have become an exemplary instance of the ethical. Integral to the argument presented here is the idea that her presence has a specificity that causes the ethical to be defined in relation to a projected, or refused, *being-at-one-with*

---

[1] The complete passage is: »[E]in reines Gemüt schämt sich der Liebe nicht, es schämt sich aber, daß diese nicht vollkommen ist« (*Hegels theologische Jugendschriften*, 380). See also references to ›the heart‹ in the Christian Bible; e.g. Matt. 8.5.

Niobe.² This is a definition that takes the setting of *being-at-one-with* and reworks its ontological basis in order to move from the singularity of relation, in which an initial affirmation of relationality is caused by its effacement within and by love, to the repositioning of relationality in terms of what can be described as the anoriginal relationality of a plural event.³ This move becomes, as a consequence, the actual site of philosophical contestation. What is at stake here is the relation between self and other in which forms of spacing play a fundamental role. This set up has already been gestured to by the use of the term ›incomplete‹ and the raised possibility (albeit in its negative presentation) of the complete.

In both stone and paint, Niobe's grief is clear. Her attempt to protect her children – especially the youngest child – finds its echo in both poetry and in sculpture. In the *Metamorphoses*, Ovid wrote: »[…] when six had been sent to death and suffered wounds, the last one remained, whom her mother with all her form (*toto corpore*), with all her robes concealed« (Ovid, 6.297ff.).⁴ The ›form‹ in question is, of course, her body. This is evidenced by the Uffizi statue, *Niobe Mother with Youngest Daughter*, in which Niobe attempts to surround her youngest with both body and clothes.⁵ And yet, despite being

---

[2] The expression *being-at-one-with* is used throughout this paper in order to signal what might be described as an abstract state of relationality. The relation is announced by the use of the term ›with‹. To the extent that *being-at-one-with* is defined in terms of unity or sameness – ›one‹ as either an original or a projected unity –, it signals a state of affairs in which being-with necessitates a relation defined in terms of an effaced internal spacing such that relationality is itself a form of identity relation. What is at work, therefore, is a projected unity of self and other. This is the structure, as will become clear, which is enacted within Hegel's conception of love. It is a structure that makes it impossible for Niobe to figure within a structure of relationality except as the excluded: i.e. once *being-at-one-with* is defined in terms of unity and sameness, Niobe exists within a state of enforced exclusion. What is enforced is the impossibility of relationality. What this opens up is the possibility of a different conception of *being-at-one-with*. However, once the ›one‹ is reconfigured in such a way that it defines a relation that maintains difference, and thus inscribes a spacing within it, what then occurs is the living out of this other position. This is the move from immediacy to mediacy. Once *being-at-one-with* is positioned such that both the ›one‹ and the ›with‹ are defined in terms of a founding plurality – i.e. a plural event that is itself a locus of activity – loving Niobe would entail a different conception of life.

[3] The ›plural event‹ is a term used to describe a state of original difference; a difference, that is, whose nature is ontological. It operates within a setting whereby both the ›one‹ and the ›with‹ within the idea of *being-at-one-with* are themselves defined in terms of a conception of difference that is taken to be original; hence it involves what can be described as ›anoriginal difference‹. Ontology is central to this argument: the ›plural event‹ concerns a mode of being present. Cf. Benjamin, *The Plural Event*.

[4] On Ovid's use of sources see Feldherr. On the positioning of Niobe in the *Iliad* see Hammer.

[5] For a detailed study of the statues in the Sala della Niobe at the Uffizi Gallery see Geominy.

enrobed by body and folds, the youngest girl still falls. Ovid, again: »And as she pleads the one she pleads for falls« (6.301). This failure to protect her daughter is integral to the figure of Niobe. »Fragment 161« from Aeschylus' *Niobe* positions ›Death‹ beyond any logic of appeasement. Neither pleading nor sacrificing, nor any other act, can diminish – let alone halt – the force of Death. The figure of Niobe continues to return as the site of an existence that is positioned in such a way that it cannot extricate itself from the hold of fate. Hegel, in comparing Mary and Niobe, writes of the former that even in her suffering her »complaint about the injustices of fate [*die Anklage der Ungerechtigkeit des Schicksals*]« will not be heard (*ETW*, 825f.). A question arises, however, at this precise point: Did Niobe thus complain? As she, and the Niobids, continue to appear in vase paintings, works of sculpture, literary texts, opera and – from the 17th century onwards – in both engravings and paintings, it is not as though she pleads for justice.[6] This opens up the further question: What would justice mean to Niobe? Perhaps – and this despite her failure, in Ovid's words, to »employ modest speech« (6.152), as well as her continual »haughty pride« (6.275) – there may not have been the expectation of justice; however, there could have been that which stemmed from friendship, namely that intermingling of respect and intimacy that any form of friendship would seem to demand.[7] The question of friendship – having befriended and having been befriended by the one who will turn upon her, a turning in which a structure of forgiveness is forestalled in advance by the imposition of a conception of justice in which justice is equated with retribution, an equation in which justice is denied – is, of course, the legacy of Sappho, »Fragment 142«.[8] Any fragment is enigmatic. Given what befell Niobe, and thus Leto's role within it, the enigma is compounded. »Fragment 142« reads as follows: »Λετω και Νιοβα μεν φιλαι ησαν εταιραι [*Leto and Niobe were beloved friends*]«.[9]

---

[6] All references to Sappho are to the Loeb Classical Library Edition. There is an impressive range of studies of the images of Niobe and the Niobids. See, amongst others, Keuls. In regards to the history of sculpture see Torso. For an operatic treatment of the ›story‹ see *Niobe, Regina di Tebe*, by Agostino Steffani (1654–1728).

[7] In regards to the failure to use »modest speech« see Aeschylus' *Niobe* (Cf. »Fragment 154a«; what needs to be noted is the use of the term θρασυστομειν).

[8] See also the use of κακογλωσσιο by Nonnos, *Dionysiaca*, II.161, to make a similar point.

[9] For a discussion of the complex problems posed by the word ηεταιραι see the Loeb edition of the source text: *Athenaeus*, 13.571d. For the translation of φιλαι as »friends« (as opposed to companions) see Carson.

The enigma is not located in the insistent form of friendship. On the contrary, it lies in the use of the imperfect form of the verb: They *were* (ησαν) friends. Hence the question is: What would it mean for a friendship to be over? Can friendships fail? Perhaps the fragment is wrong. Perhaps they were never friends or perhaps this positing of friendship is no more than a wish. In other words, this opens up as a domain of inquiry of the possibility of Niobe's position within a structure of friendship. (Ancillary to which is the question of the particularity of the structure of friendship within which Niobe could, in fact, have been located.) Hence, what is positioned as a question – though still as a yet-to-be-answered demand – is twofold: In the first instance, it is the possibility of *being-at-one-with* Niobe. In the second, it is the rethinking of what that ›one‹ entails within such a context. To bring both elements together, it is possible to ask the question more emphatically: What would it mean to love Niobe? Hence the project here has another title – a title that has its own sense of continuity: i.e. On loving Niobe. It is in terms of love and its presentation within works of art, from sculpture to poetry, that a return can be made to Hegel. From the early fragment *Love* (1797) – a fragment whose ostensible contents would be subsequently incorporated into his *The Spirit of Christianity* (1798/99) and then into the *Lectures on Fine Art* of the 1820s – ›love‹ was a continual concern. However, could love – that ›love‹, Hegel's ›love‹ – ever have concerned Niobe? Hence the title: On loving Niobe.

What first needs to be pursued is the way that love is presented within the *Lectures on Fine Art*[10], given that this is the text in which Niobe figures.[11] Presentation and figuration work together. The setting that is love's location is addressed in terms of the content matter of painting, content being presented here as an ›image‹. However, while the treatment of love is not reducible to its positioning within those concerns, a preliminary step remains necessary. One of Hegel's first engagements with the ›image‹, and thus with the question of its appropriate content, occurs in *The Spirit of Christianity*. The subject matter is what could be described as Jewish iconoclasm. He writes that the Jews have a specific relation to the presentation of images:

---

[10] Page numbers to the English and German editions of the text, respectively, are given in the body of the text. Unless otherwise signposted, all citations below derive from Hegel's *Lectures on Fine Art*.

[11] For other discussions of Hegel's treatment of love see Bernstein; and Ormiston.

> An image of God [*Götterbild*] was just stone or wood to them: »it sees not, it hears not,« *etc.*– […] they despise the image because it does not manage them and they have no knowledge of its deification [*Vergöttlichung*] in the intuition of the lover and in enjoyment of beauty [*in der Anschauung der Liebe und im Genuß der Schönheit*] (*ETW*, 192/284).[12]

The image of God therefore was, for Jews, nothing other than its material presence; it was »stone« or »wood«. They, the Jews, are not engaged by the image. The contrast, for Hegel, would be between the image and the word. The latter, the word understood as ›law‹, enjoins a necessary distance. It thus yields spacing at the heart of relationality; this spacing defers the closing and unifying processes that love, as Hegel will construe it, demands. In this distancing, the specificity of each – justice, love – would therefore need to be rethought in terms of actual difference, where difference exists as a question, rather than either an identity or an opposition. This intimates a fundamental distinction between love on the one hand and the opening up of law to justice on the other. Justice may involve the inherently incomplete, where the latter is understood as the spacing that constitutes relationality and in which activity – i.e. speaking – both sustains relationality and demands the furthering of the incomplete. Were it to do so then justice, bound up with spacing and speaking, what might be described as the placed finding of voice, would have distanced itself from the demands of love (as understood by Hegel).

The specific concern here is that the Jews cannot know that the image is able to acquire a content that is inherently spiritual. They remain distanced. This is, of course, the force of the image's »deification«. What they lack, as the passage makes clear, is the »intuition of the lover«. Even though the term »intuition« [*Anschauung*] will have acquired a more detailed and complex understanding by the time of Hegel's *Encyclopaedia* (cf. §449), at this stage what is central is the primacy of the lover where that primacy provides the setting in which the image is deified. Hence, the lover is at one with the image. This state, which is, of course, a specific determination of *being-at-one-with*, is central both to the operative presence of love, a presence that plays a central role in the construction of the figure of Niobe, and therefore is also providing the setting in which the figure's presence lends itself to philosophical contestation. A contestation centred on the ›one‹. Niobe, as with the Jew, is given an identity that is always established from the outside. What will always have been constructed is the figure.[13] Niobe's silence is

---

[12] In this instance the translation has been modified.
[13] See discussion of the ›figure‹ in my *Of Jews and Animals*.

integral to that figured existence. What endures therefore, precisely because it no longer endures, is the possibility of her talking. Thus there would be the presence of a voice coming not from stone but from silence, and thus into relation.[14]

In the *Lectures on Fine Art*, love emerges within Hegel's provision of the detail of the ›content‹ of painting (the content of the image). The content of painting is, for Hegel, initially dramatized by his juxtaposition of Egyptian and Greek images with what he describes as »the Christian mode of expression [*der christlichen Ausdrucksweise*]« (Hegel, *Lectures on Fine Art*, 22/801). In the image of Isis with Horus, for Hegel, »there is nothing maternal in her, no tenderness, no trait of […] soul and feeling« (21/800). This is not a claim about mere content; as Hegel has argued a few lines earlier, »in art the spiritual content is not separated from the mode of presentation« (21/800). What matters therefore, in the sense of that which finds material presence, is the spiritual content. Art's material presence is constrained to present that content. As a result, painting is then conditioned by having to present both the »inner soul« and »the depth of the heart«. At this point in the development of his argument, Hegel confronts the question that will always have to be encountered once art, and its presentation, are defined in terms of universality (given that both ›spirit‹ and ›soul‹ denote the presence of a universal). The question is the following: How, given the constraint imposed by universality, can the particular art work – be its content a face, a historical, a mythological or a natural setting – ever function as the appearance of the universal? The answer, which ties together particular and universal and, in addition, the one who sees and that which is seen, is that the presence of the particular has to allow for the presence of that which has universal hold, namely »inner spiritual life«. However, it must appear in its disappearing. In Hegel's terms, the »inner life« »can come into appearance in the external only as a retiring into itself out of it« (27/805). This mode of appearance demands its own form of comprehension. The mode in question is, of course, »intuition«. Hegel's argument, despite its complexity, introduces the central elements that occur in any response to the problem of the relationship between particularity and universality. What needs to be taken up is the relationship between this identification and recognition. Hegel does so in the following formulation, in which the spiritual becomes the locus of identification:

---

[14] This is of course the possibility that emerges in »Fragment 162« of Aeschylus' *Niobe*.

> So painting does indeed work for our intuition [*Anschauung*] but in a way in which the object that it presents does not remain an actual, total, spatial natural existence, rather it becomes a reflection of spirit [*Widerschein des Geistes*] in which it makes open its spiritual quality [*seine Geistigkeit*] in the sublation [*Aufhebung*] of its real existence and creating it such that it is a mere appearance in the realm of Spirit for the Spiritual [*bloßen Scheinen im Geistigen fürs Geistige*] (27/805).

In other words, the pretence of realism, which in this instance is identified with what might be described as actual particularity – e.g. the portrait is of an already determined face and which is nothing other than the person represented – is sublated. Sublation [*Aufhebung*], the process of cancelling yet retaining, is fundamental to Hegel's understanding both of development and the projected elimination of modes of internal spacing. Here there is a twofold movement. (That movement is both the process and the result of sublation.) First, there is the presentation of that which is always more than mere particularity; this is the »realm of Spirit«. In the second instance that to which the work presents itself is defined by »the Spiritual« (and is thus intuited on the level of Spirit). Intuition is the means by which *being-at-one-with*, defined in terms of Sameness, comes to be enacted. What the latter point establishes is that subjectivity is equally the location of simple particularity, the particular as what is defined by »real existence« as well as that which lifts the particular from its particularity, namely, the relationship between particular and universal. The latter is »he Spiritual«. While the art work cannot present Spirit in a state of the latter's self-actualized completion, hence the description of the presentation as »mere appearance«, it remains the case that once the connection between a work, its presentation and its reception is configured in terms of Spirit rather than material particularity, it then becomes possible to argue that the relation is best understood as a reiteration of a specific modality of *being-at-one-with*: that modality in which the site of recognition is defined in terms of the Spiritual and is thought in terms of Sameness. This conception of *being-at-one-with*, one in which particularity undoes itself, an undoing that is a form of retaining in and with the universal, is, for Hegel, the state of love. Hence,

> [l]ove is a matter of subjective feeling but, the subject which feels is *this* self-subsistent heart [*Herz*] which, in order to love, must desist from itself, give itself up [*sich aufgeben*], and sacrifice the inflexible focus of its self-defined particularity [*seiner Eigentümlichkeit opfern muß*] (43/818).

It will be essential to return to this logic of sacrifice after having clarified the sense of propriety that endures with and within painting.

For Hegel, painting's project is to make manifest »the innerlife of Spirit [*die Innerlichkeit des Geistes*]« (38/813). Painting is able to operate on both the level of the particular and the universal. In order for an authentic form of particularity to be present, particularity cannot show itself to be self-satisfied, and thus present as though it were merely given within its own naturalised setting. The »representation of the heart [*Darstellung des Gemüts*]« cannot be equated with an undetermined abstraction (40/815). For Hegel, this would amount to a de-historicization of Spirit. Hence, the

> depth and the profound feeling of the spirit presupposes that the soul has worked its way through its feeling and powers and the whole of its inner life [*inneres Leben*], i.e. that had overcome much, suffered grief, endured anguish and pain of soul and yet in this disunion has preserved its integrity and *withdrawn* out of itself into itself (40/815f).

The move from the ›natural‹ to the higher state presupposes this work. On having attained this higher state, Spirit could no longer revert to »unhappy consciousness [*unglückliche[s] Bewußtsein*]« (*PS*, 126–138/163–178). And yet happiness is not that which is there as the undoing of the unhappiness of »unhappy consciousness«. The move to the higher state is also the transformation of that which is given by »chance« namely »good fortune [*Glück*]« and »happiness [*Glückseligkeit*]«. They must be transformed into »bliss [*Seligkeit*]«. While it will be taken up at a later stage, it is vital to note that what is occurring here is the overcoming of the various permutations of *Glück*, and thus the sublation of the world, where the world is understood as the locus of a conception of both *Glück* and *Glückseligkeit* and in which both are configured as contingent. This occurs in the name of *Seligkeit* and thus the Spiritual. The sublation of the worldly, its sacrifice, thus sublation as a form of philosophical thinking needs to be understood, because of the necessary link between sublation and a determined end, as a logic sacrifice. Furthermore, that which is given the quality of a ›natural‹ setting also involves its being transferred into the »inner life of the spirit‹. The »soul« attains the state of bliss (*Seligkeit*) in its having overcome the hold of suffering. Hence, the »ideal subject matter« of painting is »the reconciliation of the individual heart with God [*die Versöhnung des subjektiven Gemütes mit Gott*] who in his appearance as a man has traversed the way of sorrows [*Weg der Schmerzen*]« (40/816). The »ideal« therefore, even if it functions at a distance from the modes of actualisation, cannot be disassociated from that state of *being-at-one-with* in which the process announced in the formulation is presented here in terms of an activity of reconciliation that is at the same time a sublation of »self-defined particularity [*Eigentümlichkeit*]« and which therefore needs to be understood as a form of sacrifice. The breaking of the natural world of human beings in which human being is no longer given within its subjection to natural being, but to its own transposition, opens up the possibility of a form of self overcoming in which worldly human being attains the level of Spirit and »oneness in and with God [*Einigkeit in und mit Gott*]«. As a result, »oneness in and with God« becomes the definition, in this context, of *being-at-one-with*. Equally, it defines the unicity of the one. This gives rise to the set up within which what Hegel identifies as »spiritual depth«, namely the »soul«, is positioned as that which »wills itself« (42/816). In willing itself, the soul is able to overcome its prior identification with particularity. Hegel's formulation is importantly precise. He notes that the »soul wills itself in an other«, then going on to argue that this act of willing, on the part of the soul, is defined by a form of externality. *Being-at-one-with* is the self-overcoming of the reduction of self to particularity. (It is present therefore as a form of self-sacrifice.) In Hegel's terms the soul »gives itself up in the face of God in order to find and enjoy itself in him« (41f/816). There is, therefore, an abandoning and recovery of the soul. This twofold movement is the »characteristic of love«. This love is »spiritual depth«. Moreover, it is love »without desire« and as such provides the spiritual in human being with the possibility of »reconciliation [*Versöhnung*]«; i.e. a return to self as a mode of completion that is at the same time that which becomes both a form of completion and thus enacted propriety. This possibility, a complex of modes of self-instantiation through sacrifice, is not worldly love, of course. Indeed, it involves a form of »death to the world [*abgestorben*]«. Moreover, the limitation at work within the move from the world, its sacrifice in the name of this love and thus a projected »reconciliation« is intrinsic to, if not definitional of, the very limitation of human being, when human being is defined initially in and by the absence of the »Spiritual«. Those limits have an intrinsic presence whose necessary imposition occurs because of the presence of »time« and the ineliminability of »finitude«.

Human being, thus construed, is essentially limited. And yet, it is these limitations that provide intimations of an »elevation into a beyond« (42/817). One works with the other, yielding a conception of finitude as dependent for its being what it is on the possibility of this »elevation« and thus on intimations of the infinite. Yet it may have been the case that the figures of Classical sculpture have brought with them a form of freedom and worldly overcoming – what Hegel refers to as »a trait of mourning [*Zug von Trauer*]« (42/817). However, this modality of »freedom« is not linked to »love«. The latter, the interconnection of freedom and love, involves a relation of »soul to soul« or »spirit to spirit«. The freedom of the Classical still retains a form of relationality that is incomplete. It is a sense of freedom without work and thus without the possibility of a form of reconciliation. Reconciliation involves the soul's work, and work is understood here as suffering. The soul suffers and »in suffering finds the sense of certainty and love and shows in grief that it has overcome itself within and by itself« (42/817). Suffering therefore has a necessary utility. While there is ›grandeur‹ within the forms of expression that mark the artistic presentation of both Niobe and Laocoon, their characters remain »empty [*leer*]« (42/817). Hence, the description of Laocoon's grief as merely »muscular«. In the context of their self-presentation, neither grief nor pain allow for their own self-overcoming. They endure as modes of presence without forms of reconciliation. As such, they endure – an endurance that for Hegel constructs their historicity – as incomplete. Hence, they are defined by the impossibility of that conception of *being-at-one-with*, which is itself determined by both completion and reconciliation. (Where both terms engender necessary forms of finality.) They are constructed as those with whom any form of reconciliation is impossible. They become figures that cannot be loved precisely because they are held outside a conception of love defined as the unity of self and other and therefore of *being-at-one-with* as determined by Sameness.

The question therefore is what does the presentation of the complete demand? Any attempt to answer this question has to begin with the recognition that the »authentic content« of painting, present as an »ideal«, is this state of completion. The ideal content therefore is »love reconciled and at peace with itself [*in sich versöhnte, befriedigte Liebe*]« (45/819). Hegel continues by defining the project of painting in terms of this reconciliation: »Painting has to portray spiritual subject matter in the form of actual and bodily human beings, and therefore the object of this love must not be painted as a merely spiritual beyond [*bloßes geistiges Jenseits*] but as actual and present [*wirklich and gegenwärtig*]« (45/819).

What is opened up by the location of painting and the attribution of a sense of propriety to the project of painting is the attempt to delimit painting's subject matter in terms of the presentation of that life »as actual and present«. That is, as a life in which love predominates, and thus one where neither life nor love can be disassociated radically from the reconciliation of universal and particular. The point of focus is the Holy Family. More specifically, however, it is the »Madonna's love for her child« which is for Hegel the »absolutely suitable ideal subject matter« (45/819). While it is always possible to present God in his singularity, were that to occur without the concession to God's real particularity, a particularity that occurs within and as the Trinity, then such a presentation is inherently inadequate. (Hence Hegel's identification of the limits of Van Eyck's *Ghent Altar Piece*. Limitations that are located in the presentation of God in his isolation.) Real particularity can only occur within the individuality and humanity of Christ. Not, however, Christ as presented »in his universality«, but Christ portrayed in his »appearance as man insofar as that appearance expresses the inner life of the spirit« (45/189). And yet, individuality and universality in their presentation in terms of a genuine separation open up the possibility, a possibility always there as a potential within the work, of their projected eventual reconciliation. The reconciliation is not, however, absolute. Hegel's comments on Raphael's *Sistine Madonna* (*The Madonna di San Sisto*) are central here. Hegel writes of the child, though this for Hegel is typical of Raphael's »pictures of the Christ-child« in general, that it

> has the most beautiful expression of childhood and yet we can see in them something beyond purely childlike innocence, something that makes visible the divine behind the veil of youth and gives us an inkling of the expansion of this Divinity into an infinite revelation [*unendlichen Offenbarung*]. And at the same time a picture of a child has a justification in the fact that in him the revelation stands as not yet complete [*noch nicht vollendet dasteht*] (49/823).

Here the formulation »not yet complete [*noch nicht vollendet*]« is decisive. What it opens up is the space of an imposed sense of finitude. However, the finite is delimited in terms of the particularity of the human on the one hand and, on the other, the possibility that particularity is conditioned by universality. Even if the revelation is not yet complete, this is importantly distinct from the setting in which the incomplete occasions shame. The Christ-child is not the locus of shame. Moreover, the locus of love, love as present such that what subjectivity contains is »love itself before us in what is loved« cannot pertain to Niobe (51/824). In addition, the suffering that follows the pure expression of love is the relationship between the mother and the child. This relation, which brings with it the centrality of Mary, reinforces further the identification of her inner being with love. If Mary is identified with love, then the other possibility for motherhood is the figure of Niobe. This possibility is accompanied by a conception of suffering defined by its enduring lack of reconciliation. It is thus distanced from that specific logic of love in which love is positioned, by the necessity of its accession, to a universality in which reconciliation, completion and self-sacrifice occur, and in which love demands the effaced retention of the specific particular within love. Niobe will always be there as Hegel's other woman.

And yet, within this setting, while Mary has become love personified, Niobe must remain without love. Niobe's entry, if only at the beginning, would seem to be cast in a positive light. She is described as confronting subjectivity in terms of her »pure sovereignty« and »unimpaired beauty« (53/826). That state however delimits her presence by defining it in terms of an irrecoverable distance occurring within a founding act of separation. She is given within and as a particular; a particular whose particularity is constructed by the necessary impossibility of relation. Her particularity is this beauty. Thus for Hegel she is only ever »this unfortunate one [*diese Unglückliche*]«. This formulation is of fundamental importance since it gives rise to a radical conjecture – i.e. possible confluence of the name Niobe with both *Glück* and *Glückseligkeit*. A confluence in which what would then open up as a possibility is the question of loving Niobe. Precisely because its initial presence is cast in the negative and therefore in terms of impossibility the question is how could such a connection be established. What would it mean to describe Niobe as *diese Glückliche*? (A description that would have the force of a radical transformation.) What will be suggested, in the guise of a conclusion, is that Pieter Clouwet's engraving of the figure of Niobe that accompanied Joost van de Vondel's 1703 translation of Ovid opens up the space in which the complex relation between love, *Glück, Glückseligkeit* and *Unglück* can be productively rethought.

Peter Clouwet. *Niobe* (1703).

In sum, one of the central concluding questions concerns the possibility of holding *Glückseligkeit* and *Seligkeit* apart. To do so would be to allow for the endurance of contingency and thus the spacing that maintains it. Allowing for the continuity of the contingent is to preclude, by definition, the possibility of both reconciliation and completion thought within a logic of sacrifice. Even though it will involve a form of reiteration it is essential that the details of Hegel's argument in this regard be noted. The accord between *Glückseligkeit* and *Seligkeit* occurs when there is a move away from a form of particularity. Overcoming »self-defined particularity [*Eigentümlichkeit*]«, what is given as particularity's self-definition, allows for the overcoming of what is described as »a natural form of serenity« (41/816). For Hegel, Hercules' labours, which were intended to bring an end to fated existence – an intention that foundered – nonetheless gave rise to a form of *Seligkeit*. However, the form in question was no more than »a blessed repose [*eine selige Ruhe*]«. »Repose« is not the overcoming of particularity; it is a remaining within it. Overcoming particularity, as it is formulated here, involves the move from *Glückseligkeit* to *Seligkeit*. The limitation of both *Glück* and *Glückseligkeit* is found in the necessity of their link to contingency. Hegel argues that this involves

> an accidental and natural correspondence between the individual and his external circumstances; but in bliss the good fortune [*das Glück*] still attendant on unmediated existence [*die unmittelbare Existenz*] falls away and the whole things is transferred into the inner life of spirit. Bliss is an acquired satisfaction and justified only on that account; it is a serenity in victory, the soul's feelings [*das Gefühl der Seele*] when it has eradicated from itself [*sich ausgetilgt*] everything sensuous and finite [*das Sinnliche und Endliche*] and therefore has cast aside the care that always lies in wait for us. The soul is blissful [*selig ist die Seele*] when after experiencing conflict and agony it has triumphed over its sufferings (41/816).

The sense of triumph here is the precise sense in which the soul incorporates *Glückseligkeit* as a condition of the soul determined as the site of universality rather than as a contingent possibility.

For Hegel, Niobe's beauty remains the outward appearance. Her particularity cannot allow for an overcoming in which her lack of fortune, thus her being »this unfortunate one [*dieser Unglücklichen*] would have its eventual incorporation into a state of »soulful bliss [*Seligkeit*]«. (Within this setting incorporation involves both reconciliation and completion.) Niobe loved her children. However that love is a mere attribute of her being. It does not define it. Here the comparison with Mary is fundamental. As Hegel writes in regard to Mary: »She does not only have love; rather her complete inner life is love [*ihr volles Inneres ist die Liebe*]« (53/826). Even though her heart breaks, Mary is not reduced to stone. There is that which »shines through her soul's suffering« (52/826). The »shining through« is a moving beyond, and thus sublation, as a form of self-sacrifice. Mary's beauty is not defined in terms of simple particularity in which beauty is reduced to an appearance. In contrast to mere appearance, and thus simple particularity, there is the »living beauty of soul« (52/826). The final aspect of the contrast that needs to be noted at this stage concerns the death of Mary. In her Assumption there is a return. A recovery of her youth and thus a set up that needs to be understood as the overcoming of the worldly: an overcoming that is a working through and thus is, at the same time, a retention of the worldly. Hegel's term here is *wiedererhalten*. A move that signals a recovery that is also a form of transcendence. Spirit is present. There has been a return in which there would then be the visible presentation of the relationship between inner and outer. The return is equally a coming into presence of that which has already been described as *being-at-one-with*. The process necessitates the distinction between the universal and particular such that the process can be repositioned as a coalescing; thus not as an actual identification, but as the potentiality for that sense of completion marked by a coalescing.

Niobe endures as stone. She has only ever been »unfortunate«. What does it mean to be unfortunate and thus to be condemned to the position that occurs at the limit and thus always endures outside? What is significant here is the positioning of Niobe. Such positioning has to be understood as given to Niobe. It creates her figured presence. This is the point at which Pieter Clouwet's engraving is central precisely because it is concerned with position and thus with place. Within the engraving the Niobids lie dead before Niobe. Her hands and face portray grief. Her clothing in its flow and fold suggests the possibility of the petrifaction to come. The realm from which the arrows were shot by Apollo and Artemis appears in the top of the engraving. Artemis' chariot can be seen, similarly, on top of the cloud. The domain of the Gods has been identified. The place on which she stands may have an indeterminate status, but what remains significant is its separation both from the defined place of the Gods and equally from the city that appears above and to the left of her head. Indeed it is possible to go further and define her position as subject to the Gods, and thus subject to fate, precisely because of her location outside the city. In writing about Niobe in *Either/Or*, Kierkegaard described her in the following terms:

[H]opeless she stands, turned to stone in recollection. She was *unhappy* [*ulykkelig*] for a moment; in the same moment she became *happy* [*lykkelig*] and nothing can take her *happiness* [*Lykke*] from her: the world changes but she knows no change, time comes, but for her there is no future time [*for hende er der ingen tilkommende Tid*] (227; emphasis A.B.).[15]

What is significant here is the reiteration of the complex logic of happiness. For Kierkegaard she endures within happiness, precisely because she will never be able to forget. Her being is delimited by a constant state of recollection. This provides the reason why, in Kierkegaard's terms, »for her there is no future time«. As a consequence, her suffering would be »useless«.[16] And yet, could it not be argued in response that the future is only possible when the constancy of memory is interrupted by that which calls on memory, namely the arrival of occurrences to be remembered; in other words, the arrival of that which is yet to acquire an image, thus the unpredicted or the unimagined. Being perpetually happy, precisely because it precludes the possibility of its cessation and reactivation is of course the same malaise that has already been identified in Hegel having named her as »this unfortunate one«. The key to the predicament to which Kierkegaard alludes is provided by the understanding that Niobe, within this setting, is condemned to perpetual existence without life. The lifelessness to which she is condemned is not her literal petrifaction. Hence, she is not pleading for justice. More significantly, she is not located in the place in which it is possible to make an appeal to justice – justice defined beyond its equation with retribution – i.e. the place of life: *being-in-place*.[17] Her separation from the city, her presence as subject to both the Gods and fate holds her apart therefore from both justice and life. And yet, in Clouwet's engraving she

---

[15] The original text reads: »Men intet Haab vinker hende, ingen Fremtid bevæger hende, ingen Udsigt frister hende, intet Haab uroliger hende – haabløs staaer hun forstenet i Erindring; hun var ulykkelig et Øieblik, I samme Øieblik blev hun lykkelig, og Intet kan tage hendes Lykke fra hende, Verden vexler, men hun kjender ingen Omskiftelse, og Tiden kommer, men for hende er der ingen tilkommende Tid« (Kierkegaard, *Enten-Eller*, 208).

[16] It is interesting to note Kierkegaard's use here of the expression »useless suffering« (Kierkegaard, *The Moment and Late Writings*, 295). It may be that Emmanuel Levinas' critique of theodicy is equally directed against this precise aspect of Kierkegaard's philosophical project. See Levinas.

[17] I have developed a concern with the relationship between being-in-place and justice in connection to Greek philosophy and literature in my *Place, Commonality and Judgment: Continental Philosophy and the Ancient Greeks*.

speaks. Hence, what endures is the possibility that contrary to the language of John Donne's *Epigram* she has not become her »owne sad tomb« (67).

Her lack of place is explicable in terms of a twofold process. In the first instance she is subject to fate. Subjectivization takes place therefore as an effect of fate she is determined by forms of externality. In the second, it is because her individuality, as constructed by her figured existence, is such that it is impossible for it to be sacrificed. She is constructed therefore outside the logic that her positioning maintains. She is particular; maintained as a form of particularity whose figured existence is such that she can only ever be particular. She has no place. Thus her silence is essential. Were she to speak, then another sense of particularity would have been possible. Her speaking is the extraordinary prospect opened up by Aeschylus' *Niobe*. In speaking – where speaking is understood as an act whose very possibility would be the refusal of fate, a catastrophe – she would have joined with Athena's project as present in Aeschylus' *Eumenides* of wresting a concern with human being away from the hold of fate and thus the equation of justice with both immediacy and violence.[18] Antigone chose her silence. In so doing, almost as an act of self-justification for that choice, Antigone declared herself the »same« (ομοιοταταν) as Niobe. She does not do this by naming Niobe. Her act of identification is with the »daughter of Tantalus« (*Antigone*, l, 823–829). By locating Niobe within the temporality of fate and aligning herself with her and with the conception of temporal continuity proper to fate, Antigone's actions, as a consequence, remain untouched, both by wisdom and by the domain of the world. Indeed, Haemon's admonition directed at Creon could have been just as easily and just as appositely have been directed at Antigone herself. At line 755 of the *Antigone* Haemon says: »If you were not my father [μη πατηρ] I would say that you had no wisdom [φρονειν]«.

Antigone's identification with Niobe comes undone at this precise point. Antigone condemns herself to silence. She is importantly not the »same«. Niobe has been condemned to a form of silence that cannot preclude the possibility of speech. Were Niobe to have spoken, then her voice would have entered into a realm in which there would be a play of voices and where conceptions of both *Glück* and *Glückseligkeit* would be mediated in advance by voiced presence. The abandoning of fate and the finding of voice therefore would occur within a setting that redefined both *Glück* and *Glückseligkeit*

---

[18] See the discussion of Athena in Chapter 1 of my *Place, Commonality and Judgment*, 8–28.

by having linked them to place; i.e. to the city rather than to the abnegation of place – i.e. to *Seligkeit* as that abnegation. The latter is premised on the already present sacrifice of the worldly (worldly particularity). It should not be forgotten in this context that Hölderlin in his Antigone translation translated ευδαιμονια as *Glückseligkeit*, a translation that stages the setting in which there is a necessary connection between ευδαιμονια and το φρονειν namely the city (*polis*). The setting provided by the polis as the locus of human being, thus *being-in-place*, will always distance ευδαιμονια as *Glückseligkeit* from *Seligkeit*. *Glückseligkeit* emerges in the spacing that occurs in its being held apart from projected endings.

This is the precise context in which it becomes possible to return to the structure that organized both the inclusion of Mary and the exclusion of Niobe, namely what has already been identified as that conception of *being-at-one-with*, which generates an understanding of relationality that began to define it in terms of particularity and universality. The lead here is provided by Walter Benjamin. While the context concerns a commentary on a poem by Brecht, Benjamin suggests, that what emerges within the structure of friendship, as that which defines its structure, is that it does not lead to the »overcoming of the spacing constituting human relationality, rather it brings it to life [*aufhebt den Abstand zwischen den Menschen, sondern lebendig macht*]« (Benjamin, *Gesammelte Schriften*, 1.2, 37/*Selected Writings*, 4, 248).[19]

What this means is that friendship is a holding apart. Friendship is a relation in which difference is maintained such that the condition of maintaining a »loving recognition« is that the elements constituting the relation remain both distanced as well as structured by founding an in-eliminable dissymmetry. With friendship, that distance is brought to life rather than overcome. The incomplete is maintained. Once Niobe is no longer positioned outside a relation in which her particularity would have been subsumed but within a relation of life instead, a fundamental transformation occurs. Not simply is she able to be loved, but allowing for a setting in which she could be loved – a space of allowing, allowing love – entails an enlivening of the world. An enlivening that would depend upon her location within the place of human being: that is, speaking as the sounding of *being-in-place*.

---

[19] Translation modified.

Works Cited

Aeschlyus, *Fragments*. Tr. and ed. Alan H. Sommerstein. Cambridge: Harvard University Press, 2008.
Benjamin, Andrew. *Place, Commonality and Judgment: Continental Philosophy and the Ancient Greeks*. London: Continuum, 2010.
Benjamin, Andrew. *Of Jews and Animals*. Edinburgh: Edinburgh University Press, 2010.
Benjamin, Walter. *Gesammelte Schriften*. Ed. Rolf Tiedemann/Hermann Schweppenhäuser. Frankfurt/M: Suhrkamp, 1980.
Benjamin, Walter. *Selected Writings*. Vol. 4. Tr. Howard Eiland. Ed. Marcus Paul Bullock/Michael William Jennings/Howard Eiland/Gary Smith. Cambridge, Massachusetts: Harvard University Press, 1996–2000.
Bernstein, J.M. »Love and law: Hegel's critique of morality«. *Social Research* 70.2 (2003): 393–432.
Carson, Anne. *If Not, Winter: Fragments of Sappho*. New York: Random House, 2002.
Donne, John. *Poetical Works*. Oxford: Oxford University Press, 1979.
Feldherr, Andrew. »Flaying the Other«. *Arethusa* 37.1 (2004): 77–87.
Geominy, Wilfred A. *Die Florentiner Niobiden*. Vol. I and II. PhD. Diss. Rheinische Friedrich-Wilhelms-Universität zu Bonn, 1984.
Hammer, Dean. »The Iliad as Ethical Thinking: Politics, Pity, and the Operation of Esteem«. *Arethusa* 35.2 (2002): 203–235.
Hegel, Georg Wilhelm Friedrich. *Early Theological Writings*. Tr. T. M. Knox. With an introduction and fragments. Tr. R. Kroner. Chicago: University of Chicago Press, 1948 / *Hegels Theologische Jugendschriften*. Ed. H. Nohl. Tübingen: J.C.B. Mohr, 1907. (*ETW*)
Hegel, Georg Wilhelm Friedrich. *Encyclopaedia of the Philosophical Sciences in Outline, and Critical Writings*. Tr. Arnold V. Miller, Steven A. Taubeneck and Diana Behler. Ed. Ernst Behler. New York: Continuum, 1990.
Hegel, Georg Wilhelm Friedrich. *Hegel's Aesthetics: Lectures on Fine Art*. Vol. 1. Tr. T. M. Knox. Oxford: Oxford University Press, 1975 / *Vorlesungen über die Ästhetik*. Frankfurt/M: Suhrkamp, 1986.
Hegel, Georg Wilhelm Friedrich. *Phenomenology of Spirit*. Tr. Arnold V. Miller. Oxford: Oxford University Press, 1997 / *Phänomenologie des Geistes. Werke 3*. Frankfurt/M: Suhrkamp, 1986. (*PS*)
Keuls, Eva. »Aeschylus' Niobe and Apulian Funerary Symbolism«. *Zeitschrift für Papyrologie und Epigraphik* 30 (1978): 41–68.
Kierkegaard, Soren. *Either/Or*. Part 1. Ed. and tr. Howard V. Hong/Edna H. Hong. Princeton: Princeton University Press, 1987. / *Enten-Eller*. Første halvbind. *Samlede Værker*. Vol. 2. Copenhagen: Gyldendal, 1962.

Kierkegaard, Soren. *The Moment and Late Writings*. Ed. and tr. Howard V. Hong/Edna H. Hong. Princeton: Princeton University Press, 2009.

Levinas, Emmanuel. »La souffrance inutile«. *Entre nous: Essais sure le penser-à-l'autre*. Paris: Grasset, 1991: 100–113.

Ormiston, Alice. »›The Spirit of Christianity and Its Fate‹. Towards a Reconsideration of the Role of Love in Hegel«. *Canadian Journal of Political Science/Revue canadienne de science politique* 35.3 (2002): 499–525.

Ovid. *Metamorphoses*. Tr. Z. Philip Ambrose. Newburyport: Focus Publishing, 2004.

Sappho and Alcaeus. *Greek Lyric: Sappho and Alcaeus*. (Loeb Classical Library). Tr. and ed. David Campbell. Cambridge: Harvard University Press, 1982.

Sophocles. *Antigone. Sophocles*, Vol 2. Tr. Hugh Lloyd-Jones. Cambridge: Harvard University Press, 1994.

Torso, Ian Balfour. »(The) Sublime Sex, Beautiful Bodies, and the Matter of the Text«. *Eighteenth-Century Studies* 39.3 (2006): 323–336.

Claudia Wirsing (*Friedrich-Schiller-Universität Jena*)

Friedrich Schlegel's Concept of Gender in his »Letter on Philosophy«

> Elle se détermine et se différencie par rapport
> à l'homme et non celui-ci par rapport à elle;
> elle est l'inessentiel en face de l'essentiel. Il
> est le Sujet, il est l'Absolu: elle est l'Autre.
>
> [She is defined and distinguished in relation
> to the man, but not he in relation to her.
> She is the inessential in contrast to the essential.
> He is the subject, the absolute; she the other.]
>
> (Simone de Beauvoir, 15)

Zusammenfassung

Der Aufsatz untersucht anhand von Friedrich Schlegels Brief *Über die Philosophie. An Dorothea* (1799), in welcher Weise Schlegel die Codierung des Weiblichen und Männlichen vornimmt. Dabei liegt der Fokus der Untersuchung vor allem auf der Grundspannung zwischen einer naturalisierten Festschreibung geschlechtsspezifischer Seinsweisen und der punktuellen Trangression fester Identitätsmuster des Männlichen und des Weiblichen. Damit soll das Grundproblem kategorialer, d.h. konstitutiver und vorbewusster Zuschreibungen von Geschlecht sowie die Frage nach der Bestimmbarkeit der Kultur/Natur-Grenze am Beginn der Moderne (Frühromantik) sichtbar werden.

I. Introduction: The romantic »theory of femininity«

During the years 1794–1800 Friedrich Schlegel dealt in detail with what he called his »theory of femininity«[1] (*KFSA*, II, 144), which he developed in his treatises about Greek femininity, in numerous *Lyceum*- and *Athenäum-Fragments*, in his letter *Über die Philosophie. An Dorothea (1799)* [*On Philosophy: To Dorothea*], and perhaps most notably in his novel *Lucinde*. However, his theory was hardly accepted by his contemporaries. While a few, notably

---

[1] Cf. the afterword by Menninghaus.

Schleiermacher[2], voiced their support for *Lucinde*, bourgeois circles seemed almost indignant. In a review in the *Jenaische Allgemeine Zeitung* for example, *Lucinde* was said to evoke »Langeweile und Ekel, Erstaunen und Verachtung, Scham und Traurigkeit [boredom and disgust, astonishment and disdain, shame and sadness]« (*KFSA*, V, L). Markus Schwering has summarized the political and social reasons for this rejection: »Der Skandal für viele damalige Leser besteht darin, daß *Lucinde* ein Sinnlichkeit und Geistigkeit zur Verbindung bringendes Liebesverhältnis darstellt, das auf die Sanktionierung durch den Ehering verzichtet, ja, gegen die konventionelle Ehe polemisch Stellung bezieht [The scandal for many readers at that time consisted in the fact that *Lucinde* envisages a romantic relationship that connects sensuality and intellectuality and renounces the sanctity of the wedding ring, indeed stands polemically against conventional marriage]« (Schwering, 535).

The much-discussed romantic principle of »symphilosophy« belongs to the practical dimension of this different image of women. »Symphilosophy«, among other things, means the abolition of hierarchical man-woman relationships and their transcendence in a common intellectual and social life. Friedrich Schlegel wrote programmatically in a letter about this concept of romantic friendship: it should »nie etwas andres seyn als ein heilsamer […] Antagonismus zu gemeinschaftlichen Zwecken und Werken [never be anything other than a salutary […] antagonism for common purposes and works]« (Schlegel on May 28th, 1798: *KFSA*, XXIV, 133). The climax of this early romantic friendship and this social attitude was reached in 1799 when A.W. Schlegel and his wife Caroline Böhmer, F. Schlegel and his partner Dorothea Veit, Tieck and his wife, Novalis, and Schelling all temporarily lived and worked together under one roof in Jena in order to embody the ideal of romantic poetry that is stated in the famous 116th *Athenäum-Fragment*: that of making »die Poesie lebendig und gesellig und das Leben und die Gesellschaft poetisch [poetry vivid and social, and life and society poetic]«.

Accordingly, animated by a desire for romantic fusion, Schlegel sought, as he put it in a letter to his brother August Wilhelm, a »Kunst, Individuen zu verschmelzen [art of fusing individuals]« (cf. Schleiermacher, XXXII):

---

[2] Cf. Schleiermacher's *Vertraute Briefe über Friedrich Schlegels Lucinde* (1800). Here Schleiermacher notes the socially explosive potential of the concept of love developed in Schlegel's work.

> Vielleicht würde eine ganz neue Epoche der Wissenschaften und Künste beginnen, wenn die Symphilosophie und Sympoesie so allgemein und so innig würde, daß es nichts seltnes mehr wäre, wenn mehrere sich gegenseitig ergänzende Naturen gemeinschaftliche Werke bildeten. [Perhaps a quite new epoch of the sciences and arts would begin if symphilosophy and sympoetry became so deeply engrained that it would be nothing unusual if several mutually complementing natures formed collective works] (XXXII).

Associated with this concept of symbiotic structures – and research has noted this time and again – is also an image of androgyny as a past as well as a future utopia of the wholeness of humanity: as Schwering puts it, Schlegel envisages »das Auseinanderfallen der Menschheit in zwei Geschlechter als Entfremdung von einem ursprünglichen Zustand harmonischen Einsseins und die Liebesvereinigung als Vorwegnahme einer Reunion, als ›Allegorie auf die Vollendung des Männlichen und Weiblichen zur vollen, ganzen Menschheit‹ [the dissolving of humanity into two genders as an estrangement from an original state of harmonious oneness and the union of love as an anticipation of reunion, as ›an allegory of the perfection of male and female in an entire, whole humanity‹]« (Schwering, 536f.).

Taking this into account, I would like to show that Schlegel's conceptual depth also has further dimensions, namely by considering his reflections on the category of gender in his letter to Dorothea, *Über die Philosophie*. The question of how sexuality and philosophical thinking are connected with each other is of special interest in this context: Schlegel expected from philosophy that it be able »das Ganze dar[zu]stellen [to express the whole thing]« (Schlegel, *Transzendentalphilosophie*, 93), and therefore to capture the extremely difficult and at the same time truly basic context as well as difference within sexuality. It is not a coincidence that in the *Athenäum* too there is a mostly overlooked programmatic text by Schlegel which brings together both questions in the title – namely: What is philosophy?, and What is gender?

In the following, I would like to concentrate on elaborating in detail the argumentative steps and strategies of *Über die Philosophie*. This approach is justified as it is only in this way that the full orchestration of Schlegel's reflections on gender and philosophy emerge, in which he allows changes of perspective to arise from difference – and precisely this determines important dimensions of the content.

The connection between philosophy and the concept of femininity in the title has of course a long Platonic tradition: The Diotima of Plato's *Symposium* (the only female figure who receives a speaking role in a Platonic dialogue) was seen as the embodiment of truth and wisdom.[3] And for some philosophers the myth of Diotima became a source of iconography for philosophy around 1800. For example, besides Friedrich Schlegel, Hölderlin similarly wrote about this »selig Wesen [blissful nature]« (Hölderlin, 172). Friedrich Schlegel's early writings *Über die weiblichen Charaktere in den griechischen Dichtern* [*On the Female Characters in the Greek Poets*] (1794) and *Über die Diotima* [*On Diotima*] (1795) are – precisely with regard to the image of women developed there – greatly influenced by the friendship he began in 1794 with Caroline Böhmer (who married his brother August Wilhelm two years later).

Nevertheless, I would like to show that Schlegel's letter to Dorothea exceeds this Platonic model of Diotima because Schlegel not only evokes the myth but also, and above all, devotes himself to the philosophical problems of regulating the relation between masculinity and femininity, deciding how this contrast ought to be conceived, and determining how it is connected with philosophy and poetry. In order to show this, I shall divide the text into three parts which correspond to Schlegel's three main steps of argumentation: I label the first part *Schlegel's analysis of the difference between masculinity and femininity*. The second part, which embodies the center of his argumentation, I shall caption: *Determination and nature: Schlegel's logic of the transgression of gender difference*. In the third part, which I shall call *Cultural media of transcendence*, Schlegel draws conclusions from his *deconstruction of gender difference* by deriving his concept of philosophy from it and linking it with the difference between male and female. Following the movements of the text's argumentation as closely as possible, it should become clear that the text itself produces and carries out a progressive search for, and rethinking of, gender difference.

First, though, I should issue a small methodological ›warning‹: My reading could in one sense be called deconstructive, since it transcends the text in places and thus crosses the borders of the text's signification. Although the text certainly has a central meaning, this exceeds the text's immediate self-awareness, namely what the text *says* or *means*; one must also take into account what it *does*. On the other hand, I do not assume that the text undermines itself. Rather, I shall try to distill structures of meaning from the text that do not immediately appear on the surface but rather lie deeper.

---

[3] Socrates reports to Agathon what he has heard from Diotima as follows: »And so I would like [to try to repeat to you] a speech about Eros that I once heard from a prophetess called Diotima who was very wise both in this matter and in others – yes, I would like to try to repeat to you the speech that she gave« (Platon, 129 [201d]).

II. Text exegesis 1: Schlegel's analysis of the difference between masculinity and femininity

At the very beginning of his letter to Dorothea, Schlegel evokes a contemporary ambivalence concerning femininity: on the one hand, he reproves various imputed bad female habits (for example, he writes, »Eitle Neugier ist Dein Hang zur Philosophie nicht [vain curiosity isn't your propensity to philosophy]« [*KFSA*, I, 41]); on the other, he highlights the lack of understanding that a philosophizing woman can cause (»Die Furcht vor dem, was die sogenannte Welt dazu sagen möchte [the fear of what the so-called world might have to say to that]« [41]). First and foremost, his work is a text that knows about gender images and gender expectations, but that cannot or will not discount them entirely. In keeping with this basic dynamic, the text is suffused on many levels by tensions: between, on one side, a Platonic assumption of the being and essence of individuals and genders (namely, when the text presupposes a stable, identical essence of the self in the case of Dorothea: »Dich mit einfacher Freimütigkeit zu zeigen, wie Du bist [To show you [...] with simple candor as you are]« [41]), and on the other, knowledge concerning the constructed nature of identity (individual, collective, and specific to a gender). Schlegel achieves a historical reworking of the gender scheme that incorporates the historical *construction* of gender identities: Femininity as ›moral innocence‹ is confronted with masculine learning as hard, rational thinking, in order to contrast feminine learning – which makes whole nations »weibisch [effeminate]« (41) – with male efficacy. But for the first time, Schlegel plays with loosening these *seemingly* fixed identity stereotypes by ›playing-off‹ their quite variously contextualized uses against one another. At the same time this philosophical method of a reflexive returning to gender identities and their own internal differences is implicitly identified with femininity because this is itself understood *as a reflexive* existence: »Denn wo einmal Weiblichkeit vorhanden ist, gibt's wohl keinen Augenblick, in dem sie nicht die Besitzerin an ihr Dasein erinnerte [For where femininity once exists, there is probably no moment in which it doesn't remind its owner of her existence]« (41).

Schlegel adds: »Sei es eine Einrichtung der Natur, oder eine Künstelei des Menschen; genug, es ist nun einmal so: das Weib ist ein häusliches Wesen [Be it a construct of nature or a human artefact; enough, that's the way things are: woman is a domestic being]« (42). At this point, within *one* sentence the established order of gender (»es ist nun einmal so [that's the way things are]«) is linked with the blurring of the origin and thereby of the scope of this order (»Sei es eine Einrichtung der Natur, oder eine Künstelei des Menschen [Be it a construct of nature or a human artefact]«). Schlegel strikingly reveals here the fundamental issue for gender which is the relationship between cultural and physical factors, i.e. between what is only made and hence is variable and what is biologically given and thought to be pre-determined. The origin of gender is indeterminable – gender identities are to be thought of equally as part of nature and culture because one cannot conceive of one of them without the other. The question whether specific qualities of the genders are natural and thus invariable or rather are the produced and thus revisable constructions of culture will remain unanswered at this point – and not only here – because for Schlegel it is a matter of revising the differentiations that are contained in the question. Accordingly, my paper will attempt to show how Schlegel implicitly develops a concept that – with reference to gender relations, based on the idea of androgyny and at the same time transgressing it – always thinks of the separation of natural and cultural determination with a view to overcoming it. Thus Schlegel reworks the stark opposition of culture and nature into a new configuration without merely reducing it to an androgynous unity.[4] My hypothesis is that he opposes two models in his letter to Dorothea: he neither reproduces the gender relationship in its binary oppositionality (whether naturally or culturally caused) nor abolishes the contrast in a third gender (as in an androgynous one). Instead, as we shall see, he develops *a concept of natural determination* in which the one part (man/woman) is always predisposed in a very specific way to transcendence in relation to the other. In addition, it is a matter of showing that this specific mode of transcendence toward the other gender also contains a genre-theoretical difference: gender and genre are made fluid and united in this project.

For even here where he speaks about the »Weib als häusliches Wesen [woman as a domestic being]«, Schlegel sees the gender-stereotyping that is contained in this very exactly, and he criticizes it in the name of the Dorothea addressed, whose absent reaction he anticipates here. The recurring strategy of this ›role speech‹ in the text should not be ignored – this is a text in which the male author Friedrich Schlegel speaks in the name of the imagined reader Dorothea and thus in the change of position between the

---

[4] The question to what extent the androgynous represents a pure unity or a unity of difference between man and woman (for in the end the androgynous is always from the one or the other side *in the direction of the other*) would need to be explored in various conceptual traditions but will not be treated further here.

genders simultaneously provides a dramatic representation of the transcendence he describes. The general strategy in dealing with gender difference that has already become visible is the following: Schlegel's criticism of these gender images and their limitations on individuality (which he always has understood as the highest value) does not take place simply as their negation, but as a revaluation and recasting. Schlegel sees that these images of masculinity and femininity are both wrong and necessary at the same time: on the one hand, there is the theoretical undecidability of what kind of basis they have, whether as a natural fact or as a cultural construction, but on the other hand, there is the obvious life-worldly fact that these images capture something that cannot be understood solely as a limitation and falsification. Thus Schlegel searches for another way to deal with this, for instance, by searching for ways to reinterpret the two sides, i.e. opening them up to the opposite of what they mean without effacing their meaning. So he more or less pursues a sort of deconstruction: he develops a destruction of gender images which knows that it must also construct these anew. The second part of the text, to which I turn now, will develop this idea further.

III. Text exegesis 2: Determination and nature: Schlegel's logic of the transgression of gender difference

At this point, the crucial passage of the whole text is given almost casually: »Nicht die Bestimmung der Frauen, sondern ihre *Natur* und *Lage* ist häuslich [Not the destiny of women, but their *nature* and *position* is domestic]« (43). This passage produces a differentiation at odds with those that mark gender difference traditionally. Here Schlegel confronts two kinds *of trans-individual necessity* with each other, i.e. two kinds of general determinants of the individual that are always already developed together within the individual and that at the same time are in conflict with each other: destiny and nature. The whole point of this argument in relation to the aforementioned blurring of the order and scope of the nature/culture difference is the following: Schlegel assumes here a second, still higher level of regulation *above* or beyond the nature/culture difference which can be used as a corrective because it precedes this nature/culture level. That is, even if it cannot be determined whether certain qualities of woman are natural or cultural, the power of these gender images can still be defused and relativized by assuming an even higher level of the causation of gender difference, which can then be used to claim the derivativeness of the nature/culture level. The difference of nature and culture is thus not the last determining cause of gender, because it provides an overarching level of difference that aims at quite different possible gender images and is able to mitigate or change the nature/culture difference over time. Schlegel does not simply negate certain images of the female; he does not even negate the idea that they possibly belong to the nature of woman; rather, he relativizes this nature by deriving it from an even more fundamental level of causation.

How exactly is this proposed level of destiny/nature to be understood? Destiny means here the divinely-controlled development of a person toward an entelechic purpose in education; therefore, *becoming* is the essential moment of destiny. On the other hand, the element of nature means the typical authenticity of people in their actual state of being. Schlegel's expression »nature and position« indicates furthermore that this »state of being« can be seen as either natural or historical, or rather cultural. Also noteworthy is the implied ambiguity of a ›second nature‹ that follows from the openness of the gender images, namely that of being either a natural or a cultural product with respect to the undetermined origin.

Regarding the difference between destiny and nature, one can say the following: both concepts are related in the form of their being (fixed state – becoming) in a hierarchical order of succession. The ›state‹ of nature can only be the basis for becoming something different and thereby for surpassing the fixed state of being. The ›becoming of destiny‹ is thus the overcoming of the ›state of nature‹ without thereby excluding the scope and necessity of the natural state. What men and women are ›by nature‹ – by the antecedent, categorical determinations of the ›first‹, biological, or ›second‹, cultural, nature – is not the last word in their determination and being; and it is also not their unsurpassable frame of being, even if it may be the cause that determines and limits specific traits of their essential character. Gender identities are therefore understood more as a mandate to attain a quite individual perspectival openness in the reflexive and practical appropriation of one's own gender structures.

The section that now follows within the second part of the text is characterized by a depiction of the constant change between the already-sketched perspectives of ›first‹ and ›second‹ nature, destiny and nature. Precisely the correlation between both levels is questioned, namely the relationship between the nature/culture and destiny/nature levels, and Schlegel alternates between the idea that the nature of women has to be regarded as something unnecessary and secondary which needs to be changed and stands in opposition to destiny, and the idea that natural femaleness is something essential and part of destiny and thus cannot be neutralized. For instance, he stresses, on the one hand, that the unambiguously social forces of a ›second nature‹ keep women locked within their so called natures: »Bedürfnisse, […] Ökonomie[,] Erde[,] Vorurteile[,] Gemeinheit[,] Mode[,] häusliche Moral [needs, […] economy[,] earth[,] prejudices[,] baseness[,] fashion[,] domestic morality]« (43). But on the other hand, the text immediately afterwards offers the following: »Die Lebensart der Frauen hat die Neigung, sie immer enger und enger zu beschränken, und ihren Geist noch vor seinem seligen Ende in den mütterlichen Schoß der Erde zu begraben [The way of life of women has the tendency to limit them more and more narrowly, and to bury their minds already before their blessed burial in the motherly womb of the earth]« (44). Schlegel's concept of the ›second nature‹ of the female becomes diffuse because he correlates a negative quality (»narrowness«) with the unambiguously biological definition of motherliness. This corresponds to the ambivalence of the plea that follows for women to escape from the prison of their nature (motherliness) in order to gain their destiny, namely the striving for the infinite, the divine. This striving for the divine is at the same time seen as something natural[5] (it is best for the citizen when one »der Entwickelung seiner Natur den freiesten möglichen Spielraum läßt [allows the development of his nature the greatest possible flexibility]« [44]) that cannot be controlled by art and education (everything aside from an education toward lawfulness and usefulness should »ganz allein ihm selbst überlassen bleiben [be completely left to himself]« [44]). The development of mind, morality, and individuality as the highest forces of man and as the basis of the engagement with the divine can only be effected by the natural social forces of friendship and love, and natural education hence develops from an equally natural sense of community. On the one hand, the task of mankind is to overcome the narrow natural borders of pure gender and

---

[5] The rationality of Schlegel's construction perhaps becomes clearer at a general level when one compares it with John McDowell's attempt to overcome the abstract opposition between nature and a »logical space of reasons«, and thereby to ground the possibility of real knowledge, namely by conceiving of a ›second nature‹ (McDowell, esp. 5, 84). In this ›second nature‹ the natural oppositions of the fields »nature/thought« (in Schlegel's case: masculine/feminine), which are conceived as excluding each other, are opened up to each other in such a way that they reveal a zone in which they are always already in transition, but without abolishing their difference (qtd. McDowell, esp. lecture 3, 46–65). In the light of such attempts to overcome categorical and quasi-natural oppositions like nature/thought, or nature/culture, and masculine/feminine without, on the other hand, abolishing their natural direction, Schlegel's suggestions appear considerably less strange than one might have supposed.

to progress toward the goal of destiny; on the other hand, this process of overcoming and becoming should itself be seen as natural and should match certain natural gender qualities of human beings.

Nevertheless, by the end of the second part of the text, Schlegel returns to the relativization of gender difference as has been established by his destiny/nature difference. He refers to gender difference as something external and posits reason as a higher power which unifies the difference of man and woman and points to and develops the structure of destiny. Schlegel criticizes once more the overemphasis and the fundamentalization of gender difference because it constrains destiny, i.e. the highest self-development of mankind. The limits of gender must not be the limits of the individual development of the person: the highest individual self-development aims at the transcendence of gender limits in order to reach the absolute unity of the self. The sexual characteristics of mankind here remain only within the realm of nature – are only nature, so to speak. On the other hand, it is nature itself that contains the disposition that overcomes itself: the nature of the female appears to be a frame that governs destiny and determines it because destiny is already shown within this nature. Schlegel therefore speaks of the »truth« of destiny to which the »hieroglyphs« (45) of nature are already pointing. The natural differences of gender already show traces of destiny which transcend the nature of gender and are at the same time determined and limited by this natural condition.

While destiny surpasses nature, destiny is at the same time bound to natural restrictions that cannot be ignored. Hence, the central dynamics of the text develop completely within the polysemic use of the term ›nature‹ with each of its two main meanings co-existing in a specific kind of tension: First, nature means both the opposite of destiny and is simultaneously consonant with it; nature is both corrected in the transcendence of destiny and preserved at the same time. Secondly, nature is first and second nature, namely biology as well as constructed culture. Within the tension between these differences, which react semantically to one another without either one being subordinated to the other, Schlegel tries to establish a complex concept of gender.

The last main idea in the second part of Schlegel's text can be established by an analysis of the set of natural purposes of the female:

1. Motherliness is now seen as the central, predominant purpose of woman. In this way, the female is understood as the medium of the reproduction of the species – a perspective that is contrary to Schlegel's idea of female individuality as the highest value of being. The male, on the contrary,

because he is determined by many small, limited purposes rather than by a global one, is now seen as having the more open, more undetermined, and therefore more versatile gender. At the same time, the female is identified with nature (as the male is with the artificial) and equated with the human because the female embodies unity and harmony. The female is therefore a being of singularization but at the same time of unification, harmony, and wholeness. By stating this, Schlegel possibly tried to conceive the dynamics of a relationship between destiny and nature in the following way: Natural purposes are single, limited, general characteristics of gender that are related to each other in contradiction. Destiny would then mean unifying this contradiction on a higher, more complete level of being, and thus would be interwoven with nature while at the same time surpassing it.

2. Sympathy as a natural purpose: Sympathy as the force of balance and harmony is now seen as typical of the female;[6] but this perspective comes into conflict with the natural purpose of motherliness and its form of singularization and limitation of the female. This must be understood as the crucial step of the argument. If one takes sympathy and motherliness together, the female encompasses oppositional natural purposes that produce a contradictory relation between destiny and nature *within* the nature of the female: because motherliness is the limited, fixed, natural purpose, and sympathy the open, dynamic purpose that is realized in the infinite becoming and surpassing of all natural boundaries. For the female, the basic contrast of nature and destiny reemerges *within* nature in the figure of oppositional natural purposes.[7] Following Niklas Luhmann, one could call this a »re-entry« structure. According to Luhmann, »re-entry« means the abstract structure of a re-entrance of a difference on one side of the difference: for example, consciousness is the reproduction of the system-environment difference within the side of the psychical system as a basic form of representation. In this context, Schlegel uses a similar theoretical pattern, but with the reverse aim: the aim is not to explain how representation of the outside world could be possibly given the closedness of systems, but on the contrary how this pattern of re-entry transcends any natural closedness of gender. At the same time, it becomes obvious that the theoretically much ›easier‹ model of the androgynous unity of gender is not an option for

---

[6] »Everything that tends toward absolute harmony, or a harmonic note, is related to the mystical, e.g. *femininity*. For its essence is inner homogeneity and striving for the most extreme unity« (*KFSA*, XVIII, 8 [fragment 46]).

[7] »Women are not at all passive but *antithetical*, physical and moral« (34 [fragment 164]).

Schlegel. The contradictory antagonism between the male and the female is not solved by a third category, but instead only indicates the uncertainty of its origin. As a contrast, it is limited because it is located within destiny-limited nature. The relationship of the natural gender difference to destiny as the space of human infinity is not an external relation: it takes place completely *within* the natural contrast of male and female through re-entry. Schlegel has made this clear before by indicating how destiny can already be traced within the natural differences. Thus nature and destiny re-emerge within gender difference in nature as a tension between natural purposes (limited motherliness – absolute sympathy): thus, nature and destiny enter into a constellation already *within* the side of nature and create a surpassing of natural gender *within* gender to indicate the direction of essential change that characterizes the limitations of gender. Schlegel's fundamental question of how the natural differences of typical gender images can be recognized in their control of our thinking and acting, but without accepting them as boundaries of absolute necessity for the idea and education of mankind,[8] has now already been answered: within the limitations of gender, the higher forces of the individual education of the human being toward his or her divine possibilities surpass the limitations of gender without destroying or deactivating them. The natural condition of the male/female difference is designed for its own internal surpassing: this means that the expansion of the natural limitations of gender is itself something natural because nature itself strives to be transformed into destiny. Schlegel thereby achieves the goal of combining the acknowledgment of gender difference and gender stereotypes with an idealistic transcendence towards the ideal of an absolute individuality that knows neither male nor female boundaries: gender images are critiqued not by ignoring them but by showing how they tend towards their own dialectical self-transcendence.

---

[8] Friedrich Schlegel: »One cannot determine a boundary unless one is this side of it and that side of it. Hence it is impossible to determine the boundary of cognition unless we can in some way (even if non-cognitively) reach beyond it« (521 [fragment 23]). The same basic idea occurs in Hegel: »It is therefore mere mindlessness not to realize that precisely the identification of something as finite or limited contains the proof of the *real presence* of the infinite, the unlimited, that knowledge of the boundary can only exist insofar as the unbounded lies *on this side* in consciousness« (Hegel, *Enzyklopädie der philosophischen Wissenschaften im Grundrisse (1830)*, 8, 144 [§ 60]). Concerning the idea of transcendence, see Schlegel's remarks on the logic of the work of art: »A work is cultivated [*gebildet*] when it is everywhere sharply bounded, but within the boundaries boundless and inexhaustible, when it is completely true to itself, everywhere similar, and yet raised above itself« (*KFSA*, II, 215 [fragment 297]).

Amongst the many problems of the text, two main issues stand out. Firstly, Schlegel doesn't show a consistent awareness of the problems with such gender-specific attributions. At no point does the text explicitly state why such a categorical ascription of male and female is deserving of criticism. Secondly, by sometimes naturalizing these attributions (instead of understanding them strictly as cultural constructions) – as the analysis has pointed out – a real tension arises in the text between the transgressive potentials of the gender codings and their biological determination.

IV. Text exegesis 3: Cultural media of transcendence

In the third part of the text Schlegel speaks directly about his concept of philosophy: his theory of the internal transcending of gender, specifically, is elaborated with regard to the cultural medium of its realization.
Schlegel understands religion in connection with Friedrich Schleiermacher's *Reden über die Religion* (1799) [*Speeches on Religion*] as an internal space (rather than as an ›institution‹) and as an exalted feeling for the harmony of the universe. Schlegel emphasizes over and over that the female has natural abilities for religion. Insofar as religion is the medium *of the whole* of thinking, knowledge, acting, and feeling, the female is by this affinity to religion always in the process of transcending the purely natural, limited purposes of being. Just as Schlegel attributes religiousness and religion to the female, he also ascribes to it the surpassing of the category and the reality of her singularity and limitation. Even love, according to Schlegel, is always directed to the whole within the particular, namely as a Platonic movement (»Eros«) to surpass the natural differences and limitations.[9] Love is the natural medium for the symbiosis of man and woman as their ›destiny‹ which transcends their natural individual characteristics (*KFSA*, I, 49). The harmony and unity of the universe is the purpose of destiny, so every individual must educate him- or herself to contain the whole of the universe in a single form. Unity and wholeness are reached culturally by poetry and philosophy as institutions and elements of the transcendence to metaphysical wholeness that are encountered again in religion at a higher level (50).

---

[9] See the Platonic conception of Eros as a force of transgression between the elements within a sphere of being (masculine/feminine) and between the spheres of being (material world/realm of ideas); Plato, 129–153 (201d–212c).

After the unity of religion, poetry is conceptualized by Schlegel as the female institution of transcendence (which is for the female more natural),[10] and philosophy as the male one.[11] Further on, he reflects on the method by which poetry and philosophy cause the transcendence to wholeness: the living *change* of the contrasts and *the compression* of the connection of all relations join together to become the living unity of the world (52). With this philosophy of living change, Schlegel follows Fichte und Schiller,[12] but he gives their theory of metaphysical interaction an independent twist which consists in the already-discussed logical internalization of the change as »re-entry«.

Philosophy and poetry surpass the borders of the contrast of individual and wholeness, nature and mind: the whole is created within the individual. Therefore, both are the »Geist und Seele der Menschheit [mind and soul of humanity]« (51):

> Poesie und Philosophie sind ein unteilbares Ganzes, ewig verbunden, obgleich selten beisammen, wie Kastor und Pollux. […] Aber in der Mitte begegnen sich ihre verschiedenen Richtungen; hier im Innersten und Allerheiligsten ist der Geist ganz, und Poesie und Philosophie völlig eins und verschmolzen. Die lebendige Einheit des Menschen kann keine starre Unveränderlichkeit sein, sie besteht im freundschaftlichen Wechsel [Poetry and philosophy are an indivisible

---

[10] Compare also Schlegel, *Ideen*, 257 [fragment 127]: »Women need the poetry of the poets less because their very essence is poetry.«

[11] »Let each thinking member of the organization feel its boundaries, but not without its unity in relation to the whole. For example, philosophy should be contrasted not only with unphilosophy but also with poetry« (248 [fragment 48]). »Poetry and philosophy are, depending on how one takes it, different spheres, different forms, or even factors of religion. For only try really to combine the two and you will end up with nothing other than religion« (247 [fragment 46]). »Religion is the centripetal and centrifugal force in the human mind and is what unites both« (245 [fragment 31]).»Whoever has religion will speak poetry. But philosophy is the tool for seeking and discovering it« (245 [fragment 34]). »The life and force of poetry consists in the fact that it transcends itself, seizes a piece of religion, and then returns to itself, appropriating it to itself. Exactly the same is true of philosophy« (244 [fragment 25]).

[12] In his *Grundlage der gesammten Wissenschaftslehre*, Fichte conceives the power of imagination as the ground of the exchange between mutually exclusive elements (I, non-I) that extends their boundary point, in which both absolutely exclude each other and at the same time connect, to a temporal moment in such a way that both pass over into each other in this transitory temporal space (qtd. Fichte, 352ff.) – a model of exchange that reappears in Schiller's *Briefe über die ästhetische Erziehung* at the point where the basic concepts of ›person‹ and ›condition‹ together with their mutually opposing forces coincide in aesthetic play (qtd. Schiller, 600ff. [13th and 14th Letters]).

> whole, forever bound, albeit rarely together, like Castor and Pollux. [...] But in the middle their different directions meet each other; here in the core and this ›holy of holies‹ the mind is complete, and poetry and philosophy are completely one and comingled. The living unity of the person cannot be rigidly immutable, it exists in amicable (ex)change] (52).

In the course of this, poetry (the female) is directed more towards the unity within limitation (poetry combines mind and nature), and philosophy (the male) is directed towards breaking free from finite harmony toward the infinite:[13] Again a conception that stands in contrast to Schlegel's identification of the female with religion as the medium of the highest unity of the finite and the infinite. Philosophy as »göttliche Gedanken [divine thoughts]« (51) raises the human being to the divinity of his or her destiny. Male and female need what is in each case contradictory to itself to become complete: because the female is naturally poetic, the counterbalance of philosophy must be acquired (51). Schlegel then gives further explanations of the meaning of philosophy: intellect (*Verstand*) and not reason (*Vernunft*) is the central organ of philosophy (54). Intellect is seen, on the one hand, as the organ of explanations, coherence, and infinite connection, and on the other hand, as the medium of a harmonic change of contradictions (54). Therefore, philosophical thoughts are in themselves complete, infinite individualities of the imagination. A truly social consciousness is seen as the intellectual environment of philosophy, because it is the organ of the unity of man and man and of god and man (55). Reflexivity is the necessary form of philosophy: philosophy is always philosophy of philosophy, meaning its own awareness of itself. Philosophy must be understood as a meta-science that elevates each single science to the divine by crossing its limitations and connecting it to the whole of knowledge (59). As the »Wissenschaft der Wissenschaften [science of the sciences]«, philosophy connects finite knowledge with its hidden infinite form and thereby figures as the true organ of metaphysical transcending. Philosophy therefore is not *content* but rather a *way* of thinking that makes finite contents infinite by adjusting them to a relation within the infinite.

In all these scattered remarks from the last part of the text about philosophy, religion, and poetry, Schlegel demonstrates a tendency to realize the abstract logic of contrast and transcendence in the form of a non-reductive

---

[13] Compare the following passage: »Only the man is capable of a cognition of nature. Women are not, but they should form religion within themselves and through them religion should be made revolutionary« (*KFSA*, XVIII, 160 [fragment 438]).

process of change, and at the same time to think about the cultural medium of this change (philosophy, poetry, etc.). The text admittedly delivers this only in the form of an attempt and, maybe on account of its shortness, not altogether conclusively. But it remains fascinating to see how Schlegel tries to handle philosophically the limitations and images of gender difference without denying its existence or abandoning it altogether.

V. Conclusion: Voice and writing

At the beginning of his text Schlegel speaks about male-female difference and uses the example of the relationship between himself and Dorothea Veit to show the analogous differentiation between ›voice‹ and ›writing‹: whereas the man is analogous to writing, the woman is an ›analogon‹ to voice. Then, the text continues:

> Ja, ich gestehe Dir, ich wundre mich, welche geheime Kraft in diesen toten Zügen [der Schrift, C.W.] verborgen liegt; wie die einfachsten Ausdrücke, die nichts weiter als wahr und genau scheinen, so bedeutend sein können, daß sie wie aus hellen Augen blicken, oder so sprechend wie kunstlose Akzente aus der tiefsten Seele. Man glaubt zu hören, was man nur liest […]. Die stillsten Züge scheinen mir eine schicklichere Hülle für diese tiefsten, unmittelbarsten Äußerungen des Geistes als das Geräusch der Lippen [Yes, I confess to you, I wonder which cryptic force lies hidden in these dead features [of writing, C.W.]; how the simplest expressions which appear nothing more than true and exact can be so meaningful that they seem to shine from bright eyes, or seem to speak with genuine accents from the deepest soul. One believes that one hears what one only reads […]. The most silent features seem to me a more proper casing for these deepest, most immediate expressions of the mind than the noise of the lips.] (42).

Schlegel here anticipates the internal change as a figure of immanent transcendence, because it is said that even in the lifeless exterior of written words there lies hidden a more intensive and purer life of the mind. However, voice and talk are only outwardly vivid, and are internally empty because their vividness is exhausted in the fleetingness of the expression itself. Regarding the ›masculinity‹ of writing, Schlegel conceives of a *male principle of motherhood*: like a mother, writing hides life in itself and is more alive precisely *because* it hides it. Against this, the voice »est ce grain sonore qui se désagrège et s'évanouit […] puisqu'elle est de ces objets qui n'ont d'existence qu'une fois disparus [is the trace of sound that dissolves and vanishes […] because it is one of those objects that only exist once they have disappeared]« (Barthes, 131), as Roland Barthes puts it in connection with Hegel's phrase concerning the »ausgesprochne[ ] Verschwinden [pronounced disappearance]« (Hegel, *Enzyklopädie der philosophischen Wissenschaften*, 115). It is also interesting to consider how Jacques Derrida reassesses this differentiation: 200 years later, he tries to think of the female as a figure of transcendence almost in the same way as Schlegel. Just as Schlegel conceives the feminine in relation to its transcendence of gender-identity – and thus in accord with Luhmann's model of »re-entry« –, Derrida also conceives of Woman as the unfixed, always elusive, self-transcending being, or non-being. In *Spurs: Nietzsche's Styles*, the transcending substance of the female is figured by her mixture of presence and absence, proximity and distance, being and becoming, nature and destiny – patterns that carry on the now familiar differentiations which were set up by Schlegel's theory of gender:

> Il n'y a pas d'essence de la femme parce que la femme écarte et s'écarte d'elle-même. Elle engloutit, envoile par le fond, sans fin, sans fond, toute essentialité, toute identité, toute propriété. Ici aveuglé le discours philosophique sombre – se laisse précipiter à sa perte. Il n'y a pas de verité de la femme mais c'est parce que cet écart abyssal de la vérité, cette non-vérité est la ›vérité‹. [...] Car si la femme *est* vérité, *elle* sait qu'il n'y a pas la vérité [There is no such thing as the essence of woman because woman distracts and distracts herself from herself. She engulfs, envelops fundamentally, without end, bottomless, every essentiality, every identity, every property. Blinded here, philosophical discourse sinks – falls to its ruin. There is no truth of woman, but that is because this bottomless distraction from the truth, this non-truth, is the ›truth‹. [...] Because if woman *is* the truth, *she* knows that there is no truth] (Derrida, 50f., translation modified).

But at the same time, Derrida identifies femininity with writing and not with the voice, in order to conceive the same logic of transcendence: this seems to be a characteristic of a medium-theoretical radical change that shows how culturally adjustable the medium of differentiation between male and female really is. However, that is another story.[14]

---

[14] I would like to thank Bonnie Broughton for helpful advice with this translation.

Works Cited

Barthes, Roland. *Fragments d'un discours amoureux*. Paris: Gallimard, 1977.
Beauvoir, Simone de. *Le deuxième sexe*. Vol. 6. Paris: Gallimard, 1949.
Behler, Ernst/Jean-Jacques Anstett/Hans Eichner (eds.). *Kritische Friedrich-Schlegel-Ausgabe*. 35 vols. Paderborn/Darmstadt/Zürich: Schöningh, 1958ff. (*KFSA*)
Derrida, Jacques. *Spurs/Éperons*. Ed. Stefano Agosti, trans. Barbara Harlow. Chicago/London: The University of Chicago Press, 1979: 33–143.
Fichte, Johann Gottlieb. *Grundlage der gesammten Wissenschaftslehre. Werke 1793–1795. Gesamtausgabe*. Ed. Reinhard Lauth/Hans Jacob. Vol. I/2. Stuttgart/Bad Cannstatt: Frommann Holzboog, 1965.
Hegel, Georg Wilhelm Friedrich. *Enzyklopädie der philosophischen Wissenschaften im Grundrisse (1830)*. Vol. 1. *Werke 8*. Frankfurt/M: Suhrkamp, 1986.
Hegel, Georg Wilhelm Friedrich. *Enzyklopädie der philosophischen Wissenschaften im Grundrisse (1830)*. Vol. 3. *Werke 10*. Frankfurt/M: Suhrkamp, 1986.
Hölderlin, Friedrich. »Diotima. Bruchstücke einer älteren Fassung«. *Sämtliche Werke und Briefe*. Ed. Jochen Schmidt. Vol. 1. Frankfurt/M: Deutscher Klassiker Verlag, 1992: 172–175.
McDowell, John. *Mind and World*. Cambridge, Mass: Harvard University Press, 1994.
Menninghaus, Winfried (ed.). *Friedrich Schlegel: Theorie der Weiblichkeit*. Frankfurt/M: Insel, 1983.
Platon. *Symposion. Sämtliche Werke*. Ed. Karlheinz Hülser. Vol. IV. Frankfurt/Leipzig: Insel, 1991.
Schlegel, Friedrich. *Ideen. Athenaeum. Eine Zeitschrift von August Wilhelm und Friedrich Schlegel*. Ed. Gerda Heinrich. Leipzig: Reclam, 1984: 242–262.
Schlegel, Friedrich. *Transzendentalphilosophie*. Ed. Michael Elsässer. Hamburg: Meiner, 1991.
Schleiermacher, Friedrich Daniel Ernst. *Schriften aus der Berliner Zeit 1798–1799. Kritische Gesamtausgabe*. Vol. 2. Berlin: de Gruyter, 1984.
Schiller, Friedrich. *Briefe über die ästhetische Erziehung. Theoretische Schriften*. Ed. Rolf-Peter Janz. Frankfurt/M: Deutscher Klassiker Verlag, 1992.
Schwering, Markus. »Romantische Theorie der Gesellschaft«. *Romantik-Handbuch*. Ed. Helmut Schanze. Stuttgart: Alfred Kröner, 1994: 508–541.

Klaus Vieweg (*Friedrich-Schiller-Universität Jena*)

Die romantische Kunst als ›Ende der Kunst‹[1]

Abstract

Hegel's infamous topos of the ›end of art‹ constitutes a key moment of his philosophy of art. This idea is based on the three facets of the ›natural‹, ›beautiful‹ and ›free‹ spirit as progress in the consciousness of freedom. The *freedom* of all individual particularities is described as the basis of human existence from which modernity can be conceived and forged. The ›end of art‹ includes the formation of the romantic, modern art and involves the exclusion of a further, and ›higher‹ historical form of art, a postmodern art. In no way it implies the demise of art, on the contrary: it implies the beginning of *free* art – »in its freedom beautiful art truly becomes truthful art« (Hegel). At the heart of Hegel's conception of modern (romantic-sceptical) art is therefore the elaboration of the cornerstone of *free* art.

Wenn man Hegels Charakterisierung der modernen Kunst als romantischer Kunst zum ersten Mal liest, ist man sicher erstaunt, ja verdutzt und traut den eigenen Augen nicht. Die Beweggründe Hegels für dieses Prädikat ›romantisch‹ sollen hier zur Debatte stehen. Als Ausgangspunkt soll folgende These von Friedrich Schlegel dienen: Die Skepsis sucht das *subjektive* Element der Philosophie *rein* darzustellen (vgl. Schlegel, 387). Darin stecken drei Dimensionen, die das Koordinatensystem für Hegels Überlegungen liefern: Negativität, Subjektivität und die Form der Darstellung. Die Freilegung dieses Zusammenhangs wäre Gegenstand für Monographien, hier nur ein Vorschlag für den Zugang zum Problem, und zwar anhand von Hegels Ästhetik und des dort explizierten Verständnisses der modernen, romantischen Kunst.

Bekanntlich galt der römische Gott Janus als Gott allen Ursprungs und Anfangs, zugleich als Gott mit einem doppelten Gesicht, als ein *amphi bios*, ein doppellebiges Wesen. Der pyrrhonische Skeptizismus zeigt ein solches Janusantlitz, er gleicht einer *Amphibie*, die in zwei Terrains zu leben bean-

---

[1] Der vorliegende Beitrag ist eine überarbeitete und verkürzte Fassung des Abschnitts »Freiheit und skeptische Phantasie – Die Romantische Kunst als Ende der Kunst« aus meiner Monographie *Skepsis und Freiheit*.

sprucht, sowohl im Terrestrischen des Logisch-Argumentativen, auf dem Lande des Urteils, als auch im Aquatischen der Erzählungen und Bilder, der Vorstellung und Phantasie. Diese *Sphinx* versucht gleichsam, die Brücke oder die Synthese zwischen Philosophischem und Literarischem zu bilden. Es geht um die Sprache der Skepsis, ihre Darstellungsform, ihre Mitteilungsweise, um die Frage nach der dem Skeptizismus angemessenen, adäquaten Ausdrucksart – um die These von der *philosophisch-literarischen Hybridnatur* des skeptischen Sprechens, sofern der Skeptiker sich zu diesem Ausdruck entschließt und nicht beim Schweigen und Lachen verharrt.

Zunächst soll ganz kurz auf die Wurzel des philosophisch-literarischen Doppelcharakters hingewiesen werden. Als Magna Charta der antiken Skepsis gelten bekanntlich die *Pyrrhonischen Hypotyposen* des Sextus. Auf der einen Seite verstehen sich die Pyrrhoniker als Prüfende, als gründlich Untersuchende und Abwägende, als *quaesitores et consideratores*. Unter Nutzung der berühmten Tropen wird die Isosthenia aufgewiesen und aus dieser Diagnose der Gleich-Gewichtigkeit der Urteile folgt die Zurückhaltung des Urteils, die Epoché – neben der Ataraxia ein Kernmoment des pyrrhonischen Unternehmens.

Diese Applikation von Tropen, besonders der fünf Tropen des Agrippa, erscheint auf den ersten Blick als ein klar und eindeutig logisch-argumentatives Verfahren. Mithilfe der Tropen wird die Unzulänglichkeit und Unhaltbarkeit des dogmatischen Philosophierens auf logisch-diskursive Weise offengelegt. Aber auf den zweiten Blick tritt die Crux ebenso deutlich hervor, die bereits in der Verwendung der Worte Hypotyposen und Tropen liegt. Im Anschluss an das traditionelle Verständnis der Hypotypose als rhetorischer Figur bedeutet diese für Sextus Entwurf oder Umriss, ähnlich wie bei Cicero das Vor-Stellen als ›Vor-Augen-Stellen‹, eine Veranschaulichung oder Vergegenwärtigung (repraesentatio), eine figürlich-bildliche Darstellung, eine Beschreibung, ein erzählendes Berichten.[2] Auch der Tropus hat seine Herkunft in der Rhetorik und gilt als ›Wendung‹, worin der eigentliche Ausdruck durch einen uneigentlichen ersetzt wird, z.B. ein Begriff durch eine mehrdeutige Metapher.[3]

---

[2] Diese Verbindung mit dem Erscheinenden und der Versinnlichung finden wir auch in Kants Gebrauch von Hypotypose im Kontext der Überlegungen zur ästhetischen Idee, der Vorstellung der Einbildungskraft, der kein Begriff adäquat sein kann.

[3] Die von manchen zu den Tropen gerechnete Ironie ist wegen ihres dezidiert negativen Charakters in besonderer Weise zur Darstellung des Skeptischen prädestiniert.

Auf jeden Fall verbinden sich in den Hypotyposen wie in den Tropen das Begrifflich-Argumentative und das Vorstellend-Bildliche, sie sollen im Zwischenreich situiert werden – wenn sie reine Argumente wären, so würde der Pyrrhoniker am von ihm bekämpften Spiel des Dogmatismus teilnehmen, wenn es sich hingegen um bloße Erzählungen handelte, könnte der Anspruch auf Destruktion des Dogmatismus und auf Philosophie schlechthin verloren gehen. Zwischen der Scylla des Urteils und der Charybdis der Urteilsenthaltung soll also gesegelt werden. Über den skeptischen Suspens, den Behauptungsverzicht, findet sich folgende neuralgische Stelle: »[...] daß ich von keinem der Dinge, die ich sagen werde, mit Sicherheit behaupte, daß es sich in jedem Falle so verhalte, wie ich sage, sondern, daß ich über jedes einzelne nur nach dem, was mir jetzt erscheint, erzählend berichte« (Sextus Empiricus, I, 4). Hier sind wichtige pyrrhonische Stichworte verbunden: 1) das Ich und das Einzelne, 2) das Hier und Jetzt, der Augenblick, 3) das Erscheinende und 4) das erzählende Berichten eines eigenen Erlebnisses (vgl. Niethammer, 198).[4] »Die Skeptische Schule hat zu ihrem Kriterium die Erscheinung, worunter sie eigentlich die *Vorstellung der Erscheinung* verstehen«. (209)[5] Der Skeptiker liefert einen *Bericht* über das von ihm hier und jetzt Erlebte, er teilt seine Erlebnisse in Form der *Erzählung seiner Vorstellungen* mit. Jeder Behauptung müsste so die Wendung ›wie es mir gerade hier und jetzt erscheint‹ vorausgeschickt werden. Erscheinendes (*phainomenon*), Vorstellung (*phantasia*), Negativität und pure Subjektivität verschmelzen in diesem Konzept.[6]

Das Kriterium des Skeptizismus – so Hegels grundlegende Einsicht – bildet das Erscheinende, worunter (in Übereinstimmung mit Sextus) *das Subjektive* (*phantasia auton*) zu verstehen ist – *phainesthai* und *phantasia*. Darin liegt der Gedanke der Subjektivität als Unabhängigkeit von jeglichem Gegebenen, die Unvoreingenommenheit – die Subjektivität als freie Seite der Philosophie. Die Erscheinung versteht Sextus als meine *Vorstellung*, das *phainomenon als pure Subjektivität (frei von jeglicher Objektivität), als bloß subjektive Vorstellung,*

---

[4] In der ersten deutschen Fassung dieser Passage von 1791 übersetzt Niethammer – ein vorzüglicher Kenner des alten Skeptizismus – wie folgt: »[...] meiner gegenwärtigen Einsicht gemäß« gebe ich »von allem, nur so wie ich es jetzt einsehe, bloß *historischen Bericht*«.

[5] Der Pyrrhonist fragt nach dem über das Erscheinende Ausgesagten, wobei Erscheinungen als Sachverhalte in der Form »einer *erlebnismäßigen Vorstellung*« gelten (Sextus Empiricus, I, 19).

[6] Was erscheint – so Sextus in seiner Schrift *Gegen die Dogmatiker* –, ist ›individuell und momentan‹, eine solche negative Position will bloß partikulare Subjektivität und Scheinen bleiben (vgl. Hegel, *Werke*, 2, 249).

phantasia, imaginatio, als mein inneres Bild. Als Medien des Pyrrhonismus erweisen sich so neben dem Argumentativen die Beschreibung, das Narrative, das Vorstellende, das Ästhetische und Poetische als *Versinnlichungen des Allgemeinen*. Die pyrrhonischen Hypotyposen nehmen so eine Zwischenstellung zwischen Argument und Erzählung ein, man kann sie sowohl als Argumente als auch als bloße subjektive Berichte lesen. Die pyrrhonische Mitteilungsweise oszilliert notwendig zwischen dem Begrifflichen und dem Bildlich-Anschaulichen, mit dem Trend zur poetischen Form. Diese Ambiguität wie auch die Syntheseversuche des Philosophischen und Literarischen, die Gedanken von Freiheit, Negativität und Subjektivität prägen wesentlich die Frühromantik – Stichwort Transzendentalpoesie. Hegel sieht eine *skeptische Grundverfasstheit moderner Kunst* schlechthin, die somit den Namen ›romantisch‹ zu Recht tragen kann, Schlegel versteht bekanntlich die Ironie als höchste und reinste Skepsis.

I. Die modern-skeptische Kunst als Ende der Kunst

> In ihrer Freiheit ist die schöne
> Kunst erst wahrhafte Kunst.
> (Hegel)

> Das Prinzip des Zweifels
> ist die Phantasie.
> (Montaigne)

In der Festlegung der verschiedenen paradigmatischen Synthesen von Bedeutung und Gestalt, die sich im Kunstwerk manifestieren, greifen die historisch-kulturelle Eingebundenheit und die logische Bestimmtheit, Inhalt und Form, ineinander. Der Kunst kommt eine Stellung in der ›Mitte‹ zwischen Natur und Geist zu, sie ist ›Vermittlerin‹, Medium im Sinne des vergeistigt Sinnlich-Natürlichen und des versinnlichten Geistigen. Der Geist hat in ihr sein ›schönes‹ Erscheinen. In der Kunst werde die konkrete Gestalt zum Zeichen der Idee erhoben, in der ›Idee der Schönheit‹ bestehe eine *Einheit von Idee und ihrer Gestalt*, die Hegel das Ideal nennt, die zur Gestalt gewordene Idee (vgl. *von der Pfordten*, 66). Die Bedeutung wird *sinnlich vergegenwärtigt*, ihr wird entsprechende *sinnliche Gegenwärtigkeit* gegeben, ein Gehaltvolles wird zu adäquater *sinnlicher Gegenwart* herausgestellt, die Wahrheit in sinnlicher Gestalt dargestellt (vgl. Hegel, *Werke*, 14, 272, 242; 16, 136).

Diese Position in der Mitte zwischen Natur und Freiheit wird von Hegel logisch wie historisch aufgewiesen. Im Aufstieg von der *natürlichen Geistigkeit* über die *schöne Geistigkeit* zur *freien Geistigkeit* korrespondieren das Systematische und das Geschichtliche. Die jeweilige Weise der Identität von Form und Inhalt, von Idee und Gestalt fungiert als Kriterium der Beurteilung und bestimmt den *Stufengang der historischen Kunstformen* wie auch den *Entfaltungsweg der paradigmatischen Darstellungsweisen oder Arten der Kunst*. Hegel unterscheidet drei Hauptstufen in der Formation menschlicher Freiheit und drei entsprechende Stufen der historischen Kunstentwicklung, *drei Grundtypen der schönen Einheit von Idee und Gestalt*: 1) Die orientalische Welt als Reich der *natürlichen* Geistigkeit; 2) die antike Welt als Reich der *schönen* Geistigkeit und 3) die moderne Welt als Reich der *freien* Geistigkeit. Konzipiert wird ein Weg von der Natur über die ›Brücke‹ der Schönheit hin zur Freiheit. Die zugeordneten geschichtlichen Stufen der Kunst sind 1) die symbolische im Orient, 2) die klassische in der Antike und 3) die romantische Kunst der Moderne.

Da es Hegel Dieter Henrich zufolge gelungen sei, die Grundzüge der neueren Kunst philosophisch zu bestimmen, sei sein Entwurf »unmittelbar der Gegenwart zugehörig« (Henrich, »Aktualität«, 300). Hegel hat Grundlinien fixiert, Grundbausteine geliefert, auf die eine heutige Kunstphilosophie aufbauen kann. Diese Ästhetik öffnet ein philosophisches Verständnis gegenwärtiger Kunstentwicklung. Ebenfalls soll Hegels Auffassung, dass *die Situation des Skeptikers das ›Hauptmoment‹ der modernen Poesie repräsentiert*, weiter fundiert werden (vgl. Hegel, *Werke*, 19, 362).[7] Hegel verknüpft auch in Hinsicht der romantischen Kunst seine außerordentlichen Kenntnisse von Kunstwerken mit dem Skalpell philosophischer Analyse, Sachkunde mit philosophischem Scharfsinn.

Der berühmt-berüchtigte Topos vom ›Ende der Kunst‹ folgt schlüssig aus der schon behandelten Triade historischer Stufen der Kunst, welcher der kulturfundierende Dreischritt *natürliche* Geistigkeit – *schöne* Geistigkeit – *freie* Geistigkeit zugrunde liegt. In diesem systematischen Aufbau kann keine qualitativ höhere ›*vierte*‹ oder *weitere* Stufe Platz haben, entsprechend der Triade der historischen Welten. Ende der Kunst bedeutet zunächst den prinzipiellen Ausschluss von weiteren, höheren Stufen von Kunst, den »*Verzicht auf eine Utopie* der zukünftigen Kunst« (vgl. Henrich, »Kunst und Kunstphilosophie«, 14; Hervorh. K.V.), den Ausschluss einer *Post-Moderne*. Mit der

---

[7] Zu Hegels Skeptizismus-Verständnis vgl. auch: Vieweg, *Philosophie des Remis* und *Skepsis und Freiheit*.

freien Geistigkeit hat die menschliche Existenz ein Fundament geschaffen, von dem aus sich Modernität, eigentliche humane Existenz erst zu entfalten beginnt. Ende der Kunst impliziert in keiner Weise den Untergang oder die Todesanzeige der Kunst, im Gegenteil: Es handelt sich um *den Anfang der Entfaltung freier Kunst* – »*in ihrer* [...] *Freiheit ist die schöne Kunst erst wahrhafte Kunst*« (Hegel, *Werke*, 13, 20, Hervorh. K.V.).

II. Das ›Hinausgehen der Kunst über sich selbst‹

Den Maßstab für die grundsätzliche Charakterisierung der historischen Kunstformen bildet die schon beschriebene Art und Weise der Synthese von Inhalt und Form, von Bedeutung und Gestalt. Die romantische Kunst hebt sowohl den orientalischen Typus der Nicht-Entsprechung oder Unangemessenheit sowie den antiken Typ der klassischen ›Harmonie‹ von Idee und sinnlicher Formierung auf und stellt »auf höhere Weise [...] den Unterschied und Gegensatz beider Seiten [...], der in der symbolischen Kunst unüberwunden geblieben war« (Hegel, *Werke*, 13, 111), wieder her und ›überschreitet‹ somit das klassische Ideal, geht über die klassische Kunstform und deren Ausdrucksweise hinaus. Dass die Kunst *über sich selbst hinausgeht* bedeutet, dass sie das Element der *versöhnten* Versinnlichung des Geistes verlassen hat, dass der sinnliche Schein, das Erscheinen des Absoluten, als dessen künstlerische Verbildlichung einen anderen Status erreicht hat, ein ›anderes Verhältnis‹ darstellt, in dem nicht nur Schönes, sondern auch *Un-Schönes* Ausdruck findet. Hegel spricht vom »Hinausgehen der Kunst über sich selbst, doch innerhalb ihres eigenen Gebiets und in Form der Kunst selber« (113). Die Kunst geht somit nicht unter, sie kann hingegen »immer mehr steigen und sich vollenden« (142), aber sie unterliegt ihrer *entscheidenden*, *ultimativen* Transformation hinsichtlich der Konstellation von Bedeutung und Gestalt, freie Geistigkeit beinhaltet das *Frei-Werden* und das *Ver-Geistigen der Kunst*.

III. Freiwerdung und Vergeistigung der Kunst

Wie mehrfach betont, kann das Absolute in angemessener und höchster Weise nur als *denkendes* Selbstverhältnis verstanden werden. Die Identität von Absolutem und Menschlichem kann adäquat – da sie selbst in ihrer Grundverfasstheit Denken ist – nur durch das *begreifende Denken* erfasst werden. Das Geistige findet »seinen Boden in sich selbst« (*Ascheberg*, 182), das Absolute als Eines »*entflieht der Kunst* und ist Gegenstand des Gedankens« (*Hotho*, 180). Der Geist entzieht sich letztlich einer entsprechenden vollendeten Vereinigung mit einem Äußeren. Das Geistige wird in sich frei, hat in sich seine Realität, insofern es *in sich selbst* ist und *nicht in einem Anderen* (vgl. 179).

Diese Einsicht gehört der modernen Welt an, es ergibt sich ein ›ungeheurer Unterschied‹ zur alten Welt. Es ist ein Inhalt gewonnen, der über die klassische Form wesentlich hinausgeht, denn die griechische Einheit von Absolutem und Menschlichem hat die Subjektivität nicht vordergründig als innerliches, subjektives Wissen, nicht dominant als Begriff, sondern wesentlich als *Vorstellung* – in der Mythologie als Erzählung, als Kunst-Religion. Der Geist der modernen Welt sei »über die Stufe hinaus, auf welcher die Kunst die höchste Weise ausmacht, sich des Absoluten bewußt zu sein«. – »Uns gilt die Kunst nicht mehr als die höchste Weise, in welcher die Wahrheit sich Existenz verschafft« (Hegel, *Werke*, 13, 24, 141). In den frühen Kulturen dominiert die *vorstellende* Selbstvergewisserung, die an sich seiende Einheit des Menschlichen und Absoluten, in der modernen Kultur hingegen das *denkende* Selbst-Verhältnis, das Wissen um die an sich seiende Einheit, um freie Subjektivität und freie Geistigkeit.

Das Geschäft der Philosophie bestehe darin, Begriffe an die Stelle von Vorstellungen zu setzen, der Geist könne nur »durch das Vorstellen hindurch und auf dasselbe sich wendend zum denkenden Begreifen fortgehen«. Freie Geistigkeit, freie Subjektivität als Grundprinzip der Moderne vermag nicht mehr *zureichend* durch ästhetische Imagination, nicht mehr hinlänglich *künstlerisch-mythologisch* dargestellt werden, dieser Grundgehalt bedarf wesentlich der *denkenden* Erfassung und des *begrifflichen* Ausdrucks, er muss auf den Begriff gebracht werden. Die Kunst bleibt eine der wesentlichen, absoluten Weisen der Vergewisserung des Absoluten, aber sie verliert ihre frühere Dominanz. Der Dichter ist eben nicht derjenige, der *allein* den Namen eines Weisen mit Recht führt (wie Novalis es behauptete), die Poeten sprechen Wahrheit, aber in einer bestimmten, in sich begrenzten Form. Hegels Philosophie inklusive der Philosophie der Kunst basiert auf der Erkenntnis, »daß die moderne Welt ihren Vernunftcharakter Zusammenhängen verdankt, die wesentlich nicht als ›schöne‹ beschrieben werden können« (Henrich, »Aktualität«, 300). Die moderne Welt der Freiheit von Denken und Wollen kann adäquat nur im begrifflichen Denken erfasst werden, denn es handelt sich um Verhältnisse, »deren Verfassung sinnlich erfahrbare Konkordanz ausschließt, die aber dennoch reicher in sich, differenzierter und im Hegel'schen

Sinne der Wahrheit somit die wahren sind: Die Verhältnisse des Rechts« (301). Als Nervenzentrum der Moderne gilt die freie Subjektivität, die ihrer angemessenen Darstellung durch die Kunst ›entflieht‹ – »der Gedanke und die Reflexion haben die Schönheit überflügelt« (Hegel, *Werke*, 13, 24). Der Kunst kann nur eine »partiale« Rolle (vgl. Henrich, »Kunst und Kunstphilosophie«, 15ff.) zugesprochen werden, sie hat ihre absolut verbindende und verbindliche Rolle verloren.[8] Welche Aspekte bestimmen weiterhin diese freie und vergeistigte, die romantische Kunst?

IV. Innerlichkeit und ›geistige‹ Schönheit

Das Prinzip des Romantischen besteht in der Freiheit des Geistes, der zur absoluten Innerlichkeit wird, der Mensch geht so in sich selbst zurück, steigt in die eigene Innerlichkeit hinab. Daraus folgen einige entscheidende Bestimmungen für die Kunst in der Moderne:

a) Von der ›plastischen Objektivität‹ zur poetischen Subjektivität
Die ›Innigkeit der Seele‹, die künstlerische Einbildungskraft als Vermögen der Kombination von Vorstellungen zu schönen inneren Bildern gilt als die Sphäre der ›*geistigen* Schönheit‹. In dieser Innerlichkeit hat das menschliche Gemüt seine Schönheit – die ›schöne Seele‹ als »innere[r] Raum und [...] innere[] Zeit der Vorstellungen und Empfindungen« (Hegel, *Werke*, 13, 123). Im Übergang von der klassisch-antiken zur modernen Kunst vollzieht sich der Dominanz-Wechsel vom ›schönen Körper‹ zur ›schönen Seele‹ (Jean Paul). Damit einher geht das Frei-Sein von einer Bindung an »äußerlich-sinnliche[s] Material« (123), die Idealität des Materials – der Vorstellungen.

b) Lebensläufe nach aufsteigender Linie
Die absolute Subjektivität verbleibt nicht in bloßer Innerlichkeit, sie hat notwendig ihr Erscheinen in der Subjektivität selbst als unmittelbarer, in der Ich-Heit als einzelnem Ich. Als das Dasein des Absoluten erscheint das *wirkliche, konkrete, einzelne, besondere* Subjekt. ›Ich bin der einzige Inhalt meines Buches‹ – mit diesem Slogan hatte Montaigne diese Grundform neuzeitlicher Literarizität begründet. Der Wesenszug von Kunst schlecht-

---

[8] Die Modernen sind darüber hinaus, »Werke der Kunst göttlich zu verehren und sie anbeten zu können [...]. Mögen wir die griechischen Götterbilder noch so vortrefflich finden und Gottvater, Christus, Maria noch so würdig und vollendet dargestellt sehen – es hilft nichts, unser Knie beugen wir doch nicht mehr« (Hegel, *Werke*, XIII, 140).

hin – ›Einzelheit des Gestaltens‹ – manifestiert sich in der Modernität in der Konzentration der Darstellung auf diese besonderen Einzelnen, ihres *Charakters* und *Schicksals*, der Darstellung der *Lebensformen* in Gestalt *literarischer Lebensläufe*. Theodor Gottlieb von Hippel hat mit dem Titel seines an Laurence Sternes *Tristram Shandy* orientierten Romans dieses Charakteristikum programmatisch fixiert: *Lebensläufe nach aufsteigender Linie*. Oscar Wilde brachte dies dann treffend auf den Punkt: »We live in an age when men treat art as if it were meant to be a form of autobiography« (Wilde, 18). Die literarischen Selbstgespräche, die poetischen Selbstporträts als Dialoge mit dem eigenen Ich bilden das neue Paradigma, es geht um die Darstellung des ›Lebens und der Taten‹ eines besonderen Individuums, um dessen ›Lehr- und Wanderjahre‹, um das Reisen und das Flanieren in der eigenen Subjektivität, um die Entdeckungsfahrten ins eigene Selbst mit seiner vielschichtigen Perspektivität und Dimensionalität, um individuelle Lebensvollzüge in ihrer Vielfalt und Zufälligkeit, um poetische Autobiographien als *phantasievolle Selbst-Konstruktionen* (vgl. dazu Vieweg, »Komik und Humor«), gemäß einem Satz von Laurence Sterne: »Alle Geschichten handeln von mir selbst.«

c) Frei-Werden der Kunst von einem bestimmten und begrenzten Gehalt
Der Gang in die Innerlichkeit impliziert das Frei-Werden von *aller festen Beschränkung auf einen bestimmten Kreis des Inhalts* – ein Grundpfeiler für die *Autonomie* der Kunst und des Künstlers. Die Kunst wird frei und unabhängig von allen bestimmten religiösen, politischen, nationalen, regionalen Gehalten, es vollzieht sich eine Ent-Tabuisierung, Kunst wird frei von jeder festen weltanschaulichen Determination und hat nur einen einzigen Orientierungspunkt: *Humanität*. In der Autonomie steckt das eminent *kritische* Potential der Kunst, das Vermögen des ungebundenen, vorurteilslosen Blicks auf die Welt. Ungeachtet der festgestellten Partialität der Rolle moderner Kunst leistet diese hier einen essentiellen Beitrag zur Modernität als einer *Kultur der Freiheit*. Kunst kann eine grundlegende Orientierungswirkung für die Menschen in der Weise sinnlicher Vergegenwärtigung des Menschlichen ausüben, Freiheit den Menschen ›an-sinnen‹. Aus dem universalen Prinzip der Subjektivität heraus kann eine Vielfalt von Ausdrucksformen entstehen, die vielschichtige Variationen freien Tuns offerieren. Mit der metaphorischen Vergegenwärtigung und der darin liegenden Anerkennung des ›Polytheistischen‹, der Mannigfaltigkeit der einen, freien Welt-Kunst kann die *Bildung zur Freiheit* werden.

V. Das Frei-Werden des Erscheinenden – Die Befreiung von bestimmten Gestaltungen

Die subjektive Innigkeit bedeutet den ›Triumph über alle Äußerlichkeit‹, eine Gleichgültigkeit gegen die äußere Gestaltung (vgl. Hegel, *Werke*, 14, 235). »Der Stoff hat jetzt nicht die Innerlichkeit *auszudrücken*, sondern in ihm soll die Innigkeit *erscheinen*, er soll *mit ausdrücken, daß das Äußerliche ein nicht Befriedigendes sei.* Die Innigkeit führt einen Gegensatz in sich gegen das äußerliche Dasein« (*Hotho*, 182). Die Subjektivität des Künstlers ist über seine Form erhaben, nicht durch sie bedingt (vgl. *Ascheberg*, 181). Der Stoff wird ›entlassen‹ und für sich frei, während in der Klassik der Inhalt die Form unterwarf. Mit der Freisetzung ihrer formellen Seite erhält die Kunst »eine ungeahnte Beweglichkeit und Freiheit; die Virtuosität des Künstlers kann sich immer stärker auf die formalen Elemente des Kunstwerks, auf das Verhältnis von Formen, Farben, Tönen und den diversen Sprachmöglichkeiten konzentrieren« (Büttner, »Hegels Prognose«, 54). Die heterogene Materie, das äußerlich-sinnliche Material ist freigegeben, *es darf jetzt auch ›unschön erscheinen‹* (vgl. *Hotho*, 182). Der Künstler wird in seinem Verhältnis zu historischen Stilformen zu einer *tabula rasa*, die gesamte Geschichte der Genres und Stile ist zur Adaptation freigegeben – die »Last des ›imaginären Museums‹« avanciert zu einem »Stigma der Freiheit des Künstlers« (Henrich, »Kunst und Kunstphilosophie«, 14).

Bedeutung und Gestalt werden entzweit, in sich seiende Subjektivität, absolut Innerliches und äußere Erscheinung trennen sich, fallen auseinander, werden kontrapunktisch. Diese *Unangemessenheit* von Idee und Formierung heißt, dass die Innigkeit in der Äußerlichkeit *erscheint* und »*in Zufälligkeit gegen ihre Bedeutung erscheinen darf*« (Hegel, *Werke*, 10, 370, § 562, Hervorh. K.V.). Die romantische Kunst tritt so als »ein Schweben und Tönen über einer Welt auf, die nur einen *Gegenschein* des Insichseins aufnehmen kann« (*Ascheberg*, 180). ›Gegenschein‹ meint, dass sich die Kunst ›selbst zum Scheinen bringt‹, dass sie selbst »ganz Schein« wird (180). Sie wird zum *Scheinen des Erscheinenden*, zur ›Form der Form‹. »Vom Schönen wird gleichsam das Scheinen als solches für sich fixiert« (Hegel, *Werke*, 14, 227). Die romantische Kunst geht so bis ins Formelle, bis in die Auflösung des ›Gegenständlichen‹. Der künstlerischen Kreativität steht der ›ganze Naturstoff‹ zur Formierung frei, die ganze Vielfalt des Darstellens wird geöffnet. Die alltäglichsten Themen werden zum Stoff der Imagination und des Ausdrucks, Hegel verweist hierbei besonders auf die holländische Malerei des goldenen Jahrhunderts und auf den modernen Roman.

VI. Die Nicht-Entsprechung von Bedeutung und Gehalt

Die der klassischen Kunst eigene ›versöhnte‹ Versinnlichung des Geistes, die Art und Weise des *eigentlichen, direkten* Ausdrucks hat ausgedient, die Bedeutung wird im Werk zugleich *formiert* und *de-formiert, ver-fremdet*. Damit kehrt die Modernität auf höherer Ebene zur Orientalität, zu Symbolik und Metaphorik[9] zurück. Die romantische Kunst muss auf einem Goethe'schen *West-Östlichen Divan* ›sitzen‹, eine Aufhebung von Orientalität und Klassizität vollziehen. Der in den Augen von Goethe, Hegel und Nietzsche *erste moderne* Romancier Laurence Sterne galt als der »grosse Meister der *Zweideutigkeit*« (Nietzsche, 424; Hervorh. im Original), sein deutscher Anhänger Jean Paul als ein Virtuose der Metaphorik (vgl. Vieweg, »Komik und Humor«). Bedeutung und Gestalt sind voneinander entfernt, sich unangemessen. In der romantischen Kunst dominiert das Symbolische und Metaphorische, die Dinge werden nicht direkt beim Namen genannt, sondern eben ›umschrieben‹. Symbol, Geheimnis, Rätsel und Entzifferung waren Hegels Stichworte für die *Orientalität*. Die romantische Phantasie gelangt wieder zur Präferenz des Metaphorischen, der uneigentlichen Äußerlichkeit, der Imagination vieler Welten, zur geistreichen und witzigen Weltkonstitution.[10]

---

[9] Die Metapher repräsentiert ein kurzes Symbol, das in ein Bild konzentriert ist, eine Bildlichkeit, durch welche der Gehalt ›hindurchscheint‹. Die Bedeutung wird in Form einer verwandten, ähnlichen Äußerlichkeit veranschaulicht. Die Ver-Bildlichung ergibt sich aus einer Übersetzung, einer Um-Schreibung. Es handelt sich um eine ins Kurze gezogene Vergleichung. Nur das Bild wird gezeigt, die gemeinte Bedeutung bleibt notwendig zwei- oder vieldeutig. Die sprachliche Form »ein Fluß von Tränen« ist vieldeutig, es kann in einem Befund des Augenarztes stehen oder in einem poetischen Text, wobei die Metapher für sich Trauer oder Freude ausdrücken könnte (vgl. Hegel, *Werke*, 13, 516–523).

[10] Die ungeheure Kraft der Metaphorik, welche die moderne Kunst mitprägt, liegt in folgenden drei Momenten: Erstens erfolgt eine Verstärkung von Bedeutungen sowohl durch sinnliche Vergrößerung des Tatbestandes als auch durch den Bezug zu vielfachen verwandten Erscheinungen, durch Formulierung von Analogien, durch Impulsgebung für mannigfache Assoziationen. Im poetischen Bild gelingt zweitens ein wichtiger Schritt zur Befreiung von der Gegenständlichkeit, in der Schönheit erfolgt eine ›Begeistigung des Äußeren‹. Im Metaphorischen zeigt sich schließlich drittens die freie Lust der Phantasie. Die Bedeutung, der Inhalt, der Begriff in seiner Bildlosigkeit verlangt nach Ausdruck in verwandten Anschauungen und Bildern, es ergibt sich die Möglichkeit origineller und überraschender Kombinationen. Im Humoristischen kehrt man gleichsam zum Symbolischen zurück, wo Bedeutung und Gestalt auseinanderfallen, nur dass es jetzt in der Moderne die bloße Subjektivität des Dichters ist, welche die fremdartige Ordnung frei konstituiert. Goethe und Hegel betonen unisono erstens den Genuss im Anschauen solcher Werke, man fühle sich – so Goethe – behaglich in der Nähe eines ›wohlmeinenden Mannes‹, dessen Gefühl uns sich mitteilt, der unsere Einbildungskraft erregt, unseren

Unangemessenheit, Symbolik und Metaphorik, das daraus sich gründende Rätselhafte, Geheimnisvolle fordern Dechiffrierung, Reflektieren und Denken heraus. Der Moderne muss sich üben in der Auflösung der »wunderlich aufgegebenen Rätsel« (Goethe, 3, 230), des Rätselhaften schlechthin. Der ethische Faden bleibt geheim, verdeckt, codiert, chiffriert, verschleiert. Der Geschmack wird notwendig auch verletzt, Hässlichkeit, Trivialität, Dissonanz, Amphibolik, Disharmonie, Verknüpfung von Erinnerungsfetzen, Kontrapunktik sind mögliche Züge. Das Enigmatische ruft nach Reflektiertheit und Wissen, infolge der Vergeistigung bedarf das Werk der Interpretation, die ihm zugehörig werden kann. Texte und Gemälde erschließen sich erst mit Hilfe von begleitenden Deutungen, eben nicht durch bloßes Lesen und Ansehen.

VII. Die Vergeistigung der Kunst

Dieser Trend zur Vergeistigung manifestiert sich auch im ›Material‹, in den Medien der Kunst, und zwar in der Weise der Tendenz hin zur ›Idealität‹ des Mediums, weltgeschichtlich *vom Stein hin zur Sprache*, vom Menschen in Gestalt der *Skulptur* bis hin zum Menschen als *poetisches Bild*. In der Optik Hegels dominieren Malerei, Musik und Poesie die romantische Kunst, im Aufstieg von der Farbe über den Ton hin zur Sprache, vom Mischen der Farb-Bilder über das Komponieren von Ton-Bildern hin zur Kreation von Sprach-Bildern. Heute stellt der Film eine wichtige und wirkungsmächtige Kombination dieser drei Gattungen dar.
Die Poesie gilt konsequenterweise als *geistigste* und *allgemeinste* Kunst. Sie basiert auf dem höchsten ideellen Zeichen, der Sprache, worin die negative Bedeutung des sinnlichen Elements kulminiert. Ihr innerliches Fundament besteht in der Vorstellung selbst, im Bild schlechthin, im ›Ein-Bilden‹ in geistigster und allgemeinster Form. Poesie ist eine Kunst, »welche jeden Inhalt, der nur überhaupt in die Phantasie einzugehen imstande ist, in jeder Form gestalten und aussprechen kann, *da ihr eigentliches Material die Phantasie selber bleibt*« (Hegel, *Werke*, 15, 233; Hervorh. K.V.).

Schwächen schmeichelt und unsere Stärken festigt, Hegel hatte von den ›Höhen und Tiefen des Gemüts‹ gesprochen.

VIII. Die Dichtkunst in der Moderne – Literarische Skepsis und moderner humoristischer Roman

Aus der Verknüpfung der bisher untersuchten Momente resultiert eine besonders herausragende Stellung der Poesie, innerhalb der romantischen Kunstform, für das Ende der Kunst. Auf diese Thematik soll hier nur kurz anhand eines Musterbeispiels hingewiesen sein. Dieses Exempel repräsentiert in der Sicht Hegels die erste Sternstunde der höchsten Stufe moderner Literatur, dieses Werk entspricht den drei Hauptkriterien, die Hegel für das höchste Level moderner (Dicht-)Kunst fixierte: a) Formelle Selbständigkeit und Freiheit des Charakters, der individuellen Besonderheit, b) Abenteuerlichkeit und freie Phantasie und c) Komik und Humor, Frei-Lassen im Welt-Verlachen, der Humor als das moderne, romantische Komische.

Den Inbegriff dieser Anforderungen *freier Geistigkeit* bildet der moderne humoristische Roman aus der Feder von Laurence Sterne. *Sentimental Journey* und besonders der *Tristram Shandy* gelten als Novum neuzeitlicher Literatur, als erste Romane *skeptischer Modernität*. Dieser Romantyp repräsentiert den entscheidenden Paradigmenwechsel in der modernen Dichtkunst, ist somit ›Vorbild‹ moderner Literatur schlechthin, *Paradigma moderner Kunst*. Im Anschluss an Hegels Lobpreis des wahren Humors bei Sterne mit seiner ›Tiefe und dem Reichtum des Geistes‹, lesen wir: »Hiermit sind wir bei dem *Schlusse* der romantischen Kunst angelangt, bei dem *Standpunkte der neuesten Zeit*« (Hegel, *Werke*, 14, 231, Hervorh. K.V.). Und an anderer Stelle heißt es: »[D]as Ende des Romantischen, ist, was wir Roman heißen« (*Ascheberg*, 179). Als geniale Vorläufer hebt Hegel Shakespeare und Cervantes heraus, als deutsche Nachfolger besonders Jean Paul, von Hippel und Goethe. Dieser Roman- und Dichtungstyp erfüllt die drei kardinalen Kriterien für die Modernität – a) *Freiheit des Charakters*, b) *Freiheit der Phantasie* und c) *Freiheit der komischen Subjektivität in Gestalt der Negativität des Welt-Humors*, die hier kurz rekapituliert werden (vgl. Vieweg, »Komik und Humor«).

Im Roman Sterne'scher Manier finden sich Charaktere in ihrer Bestimmtheit, Partikularität, Besonderheit dargestellt. Die Subjektivität gewinnt die Eigentümlichkeit des Individuellen, Unverwechselbaren. Der Roman wird vom Autor als ein ›witziger Dialog mit dem eigenen Ich‹ beschrieben, die Verfasser sind dem Montaigne-Credo ›Ich bin der einzige Inhalt meines Buches‹ verpflichtet. Es handelt sich um ein Flanieren, Promenieren und Vagabundieren des Selbst in sich, um Wanderungen des Ich im Ich, um die stete, nicht endende Suche des Selbst nach sich, um Entdeckungsreisen des Ich in sich selbst, somit um eine Verdopplung des Ich, die aber nicht zur

Identität gebracht wird.[11] Es geht um *fiktive Erzählungen von Lebensläufen der Individuen* mit ihren verschiedenen Interessen, Einstellungen, Weltsichten, Konflikten und Zerrissenheiten, in ihrer Tragik und Komik; um die Darstellung des eigentümlichen, kontingenten Individuellen, um die Schilderung der Lehr- und Wanderjahre, um poetische Selbstporträts mit allen Experimenten, Zufälligkeiten, Abenteuern, Originalitäten, Sonderheiten, Grillen, Marotten und ›Verrücktheiten‹ der Protagonisten, um die Darstellung von Gelingen oder Scheitern. Es geht also um Vorstellungen des einzelnen, unverwechselbaren Selbst von sich, um *Selbst-Verhältnisse in metaphorischer, bildlicher, erzählender Gestalt,* um *phantasievolle Selbst-Konstruktionen,* die höchste Weise der Darstellung von *Freiheit, Individualität und Selbstbewußtheit* in der Weise der modernen Dichtkunst.

Laut Sterne müsse man ›*jeden seine Geschichte auf seine eigene Art* erzählen lassen‹, es gehe darum, ›so zu schreiben, wie man selbst ist‹, und alle diese Geschichten – so fügt er dann ironisch an – ›seien wahr, *weil sie von mir selbst handeln*‹! Das ›Frei-Lassen‹ schließt die *Zufälligkeit* des Inneren und Äußeren ein, dem *Zufall und der Willkür als dem geistig Kontingenten* wird hier das volle Recht gegeben. Die ›Abenteuerei der Phantasie‹ gilt als Grundform des Romantischen, die abenteuerlich-offene Selbständigkeit der individuellen Begebenheiten und Handlungen. Daraus resultiert eine »*sich in sich selbst auflösende* und dadurch *komische* Welt der Ereignisse und Schicksale« (Hegel, Werke, 14, 216f.; Hervorh. K.V.), eine *Welt der subjektiven Heiterkeit.* Als Triumphator erweist sich die komische Subjektivität, in der ›verkehrten‹ und ›verrückten‹ Welt zeigt sich die produktive Macht der künstlerischen Kreativität über jeden Inhalt und jede Form. Im *Lachen,* in der alles durch sich und in sich auflösenden Individualität kommt der ›*Sieg der Subjektivität*‹ zur Erscheinung, die poetische und subjektive Anschaulichkeit freier Subjektivität. Dieser vernichtende Welt-Humor, der wahre ›höhere humoristische Weltgeist‹ (Jean Paul) gewährt in seiner Rolle als ›große Antithese des Lebens‹, als Welt-Narr und Welt-Narrheit *Freilassung.*[12] In der Moderne stellen sich laut Hegel in Gestalt des *objektiven Humors* sowohl die objektive Heiterkeit des Orientalen als auch der Aristophanische Geist und Grundton auf höherer Ebene wieder

---

[11] Siehe Starobinski/Müller-Funk, 72. Die »so vorgestellte Identität ist nicht mehr die sprachlose Zustimmung des Gleichen zum Gleichen, in der sich das Innerste stärkt und bekräftigt; sie schließt die Differenz ein und erhält sie aufrecht, sie nimmt die Gefahr des Scheins auf sich, die des Werdens und der Sprache« (52). Vgl. auch Zweig, »Montaigne ›wird zwei‹«.

[12] Jean Paul sieht schon im Orientalischen, in der Sakuntala-Dichtung, das Wirken des Narren.

her, »in vertiefterer Fülle und Innerlichkeit des Humors« (Hegel, *Werke*, 15, 572). Mit der geistig-humoristischen Schaffung einer Welt der subjektiven Heiterkeit versucht die Moderne sowohl die *antike Ataraxia* wie auch die *orientalisch-pyrrhonische Ruhe und Gelassenheit* wieder zurückzugewinnen, sich dieser zu er-innern.

In der modernen Kunst verbinden sich drei wesentliche Facetten der Freiheit: das Freisein der unverwechselbaren Charaktere, die freie künstlerische Einbildungskraft und die Freiheit der komisch-humoristischen Metaphorik. Der Humor ist seiner subjektiven Natur nach zu sehr auf dem Sprunge, in Selbstgefälligkeit, subjektive Partikularitäten und trivialen Inhalt umzukippen, heute verkehrt sich das Komische zur banal-dummen ›Comedy‹. Auch erwächst eine Tendenz zur Kuriosität, man beschreibt nicht mehr Lebensläufe oder Welt-Reisen, sondern Reisen um sein Zimmer oder Andachten über eine Schnupftabaksdose. Während der antike Dichter die ›Manier ohne alle Manier‹ verkörperte, der sein Ich in seinem Gegenstand verlor und die Rhapsoden als ›tote Instrumente der Rede‹ auftraten, die ›sich *von sich selbst fort* sangen‹, so singt der moderne Dichter sich *vollständig in sich hinein* und kann damit aber auch in die eigene Banalität und Trivialität fallen.

Die Kunst kommt bis zur Darstellung ihrer eigenen Auflösung, ihrer eigenen Gebrochenheit, ihrer ›*eigenen Entmündigung*‹ (A. Danto) und sie weiß von dieser und drückt sie aus, *Nichtigkeit* und *Sinnlosigkeit* kommen zur Darstellung. Aber mit dieser Reflektiertheit wird sie eben nicht ihrer Autonomie und Souveränität beraubt, nicht *per se* entmündigt. Sie gerät zum beständigen Abenteuer, ähnlich wie die Geschichte zu einem beständigen Spiel mit dem Feuer, sie kann in ihrem Wesen als ›An-Sinnen‹ zugleich ein Angebot für Freiheit und eine schwer aufzunehmende Zu-Mutung sein. Kunst wird von Hegel mit keiner Zeile totgesagt, nur ihre Bedrohtheit, ihre innere Spannung, ihr Oszillieren zwischen ›Abstraktheit‹ und ›Konkretheit‹, ihre Absurdität, ihre Ambiguität, ihre Zerrissenheit, ihre Kontrapunktik offengelegt.[13] Auf jeden Fall hat Hegel wichtige Tendenzen der Kunst des 20. Jahrhunderts schon andeutend vorweggenommen – Nicht-Gegenständlichkeit, Formalismus, Symbolismus, Manierismus, Impressionismus, Kontrapunktik, Verfremdung.

Mit seiner Unterscheidung zwischen objektivem und absolutem Geist fixiert Hegel die Differenz von Leben und Kunst, von Alltäglichkeit und ›Fest‹, von Werktag und Sonntag des Lebens. Die Kunst der Moderne kann in Hegels

---

[13] »Das Absurde, mit Geschmack dargestellt, erregt Widerwillen und Bewunderung« (Goethe, 18, 526).

Sicht eine neue *Kultur der Freiheit* befördern. Die Geschichte und die Kunst sind als ›Stufengang‹ am Ende. Wir stehen somit am Beginn des Wagnisses der humanen Gestaltung menschlicher Angelegenheiten und einer freien Vergegenwärtigung in der Kunst der Moderne. Hegels Philosophie der Kunst kann ungebrochene Aktualität beanspruchen, Grundlinien für eine moderne Ästhetik sind gezeichnet.[14]

Zitierte Literatur

Büttner, Stefan. »Hegels Prognose für eine künftige Kunstform und Thomas Manns Roman Joseph und seine Brüder«. *Unendlichkeit und Selbstreferenz.* Hg. Stephan Büttner/Andrea Esser/Gerhard Gönner. Würzburg: Königshausen und Neumann, 2002: 50–59.

Goethe, Johann Wolfgang von. *Berliner Ausgabe.* Bd 3. Berlin: Aufbau, 1965.

Goethe, Johann Wolfgang von. *Berliner Ausgabe.* Bd 18. Berlin: Aufbau, 1972.

Hegel, Georg Wilhelm Friedrich. *Werke in zwanzig Bänden. Theorie Werkausgabe.* Auf der Grundlage der Werke von 1832–1845 neu edierte Ausgabe. Redaktion Eva Moldenhauer/Karl Markus Michel. Frankfurt a.M.: Suhrkamp, 1969ff.

Hegel, Georg Wilhelm Friedrich. *Vorlesungen über Ästhetik. Berlin 1820/21* (Nachschrift Wilhelm von Ascheberg). Hg. Helmut Schneider. Frankfurt a.M.: Peter Lang, 1995. (*Ascheberg*)

Hegel, Georg Wilhelm Friedrich. *Vorlesungen über die Philosophie der Kunst* (Nachschrift Heinrich Gustav Hotho). Hg. Annemarie Gethmann-Siefert. Darmstadt: Wissenschaftliche Buchgesellschaft, 2003. (*Hotho*)

Hegel, Georg Wilhelm Friedrich. *Philosophie der Kunst. Vorlesung von 1826.* (Nachschrift von der Pfordten). Hg. Annemarie Gethmann-Siefert/Jeong-Im-Kwon/Karsten Berr. Frankfurt a. M.: Suhrkamp, 2005. (*von der Pfordten*)

Henrich, Dieter. »Zur Aktualität von Hegels Ästhetik«. *Hegel-Studien*, Beiheft 11 (1974): 295–301.

Henrich, Dieter. »Kunst und Kunstphilosophie der Gegenwart (Überlegungen mit Rücksicht auf Hegel)«. *Immanente Ästhetik – ästhetische Reflexion. Poetik und Hermeneutik II.* Hg. Wolfgang Iser. München: Fink, 1966: 11–32.

---

14 »Die Kunst, ihrem Begriffe nach, hat nichts anderes zu ihrem Beruf, als das in sich selbst Gehaltvolle zu adäquater, sinnlicher Gegenwart herauszustellen, und die Philosophie der Kunst muß es sich deshalb zu ihrem Hauptgeschäft werden lassen, was dies Gehaltvolle und seine schöne Erscheinungsweise ist, *denkend zu begreifen*« (Hegel, *Werke*, 14, 242; Hervorh. K.V.).

Müller-Funk, Wolfgang. *Erfahrung und Experiment: Studien zur Geschichte des Essayismus*, Berlin: Akademie Verlag 1995.

Niethammer, Friedrich Immanuel. »Probe einer Übersetzung aus des Sextus Empiricus drei Büchern von den Grundlehren der Pyrrhoniker«. *Beyträge zur Geschichte der Philosophie* 2. Hg. Georg Gustav Fülleborn. Chemnitz: Johann Carl Wesselhöft, 1792: 60–101.

Nietzsche, Friedrich. »Menschliches, Allzumenschliches II«. *Kritische Studienausgabe*. Hg. Giorgio Colli/Mazzino Montinari. München: Deutscher Taschenbuchverlag, 1999. Bd. 2: 367–704.

Schlegel, Friedrich. »Philosophische Fragmente«. *Kritische Ausgabe seiner Werke*. Bd. XVIII. Hg. Ernst Behler. Paderborn/München/Zürich: Ferdinand Schöningh, 1958ff.

Sextus Empiricus. *Pyrrhonische Hypotyposen*, Frankfurt a.M.: Suhrkamp, 1985.

Starobinski, Jean. *Montaigne. Denken und Existenz*. München/Wien: Carl Hanser, 1993.

Vieweg, Klaus. *Philosophie des Remis. Der junge Hegel und das ›Gespenst des Skepticismus‹*. München: Fink, 1999.

Vieweg, Klaus. »Komik und Humor als literarisch-poetische Skepsis – Hegel und Laurence Sterne«. *Skepsis und literarische Imagination*. Hg. Bernd Hüppauf/ Klaus Vieweg. München: Fink, 2003.

Vieweg, Klaus. *Skepsis und Freiheit. Hegel über den Skeptizismus zwischen Philosophie und Literatur*. München: Fink, 2006.

Wilde, Oscar. *The Picture of Dorian Gray*. London: Penguin, 1994.

Rezensionen/Reviews

Dimitris Vardoulakis. *The Doppelgänger. Literature's Philosophy.* New York: Fordham University Press, 2010. 329 pp. ISBN 978-0-8232-3298-7 (cloth), 978-0-8232-3299-4 9 (pbk), 978-0-8232-3300-7 (ebook).

The preamble to Dimitris Vardaloukis' bold and highly original study presents an intriguing proposition: »The doppelgänger overcomes the sovereign, self-identical subject by disrupting the nexus of knowledge and power. As such, the doppelgänger emerges as the other that literature has to grapple with in order to give philosophy a chance« (XIII).

At the same time, these lines indicate what must also be emphasized at the outset of this review: namely that this is *not* simply a treatise on that mysterious and often baleful literary figure familiar, for example, to readers of E.T.A. Hoffmann's *Die Elixiere des Teufels* or Poe's *William Wilson*. Instead, the focus is on modernity's response to the call for the construction of self-identity (XIII). The problematics of the relation between the (empirical) subject and (generalized) subjectivity are interrogated through the examination of a series of stagings in »the interstices of the literary, the critical, and the philosophical« (7). Under the heading of *self-reflection* (or its persistent failures), these are referred to as the doppelgänger.

Thus, while the German writer Jean Paul, who first coined the term in 1796 in his novel *Siebenkäs*, figures throughout the book, its central thesis is introduced with recourse to Oedipus as the *first* and the *last* man, whose self-reflective act of reason both initiates the humanist ideal of self-identity as self-knowledge and consigns the subject to isolation. The doppelgänger is presented as the *resistance* to all aspirations of *sameness* and to mere *presence*. Two vital aspects of the author's argumentation must be highlighted: Firstly, resistance should not be understood as negation of presence. Instead, »the subject persists through its resistance to both presence and absence, and, therefore, what matters is the manner in which it persists« (1). Secondly, the manner (or mode) of this »persisting« is *formal* and here, it is argued, we find the doppelgänger: It emerges as »an *operative* or *effective presence* to the extent that it effects the undoing of the framing of the subject by the opposition between mere presence and absence. Such an operation indicates a function of relationality – the various relations that structure the subject's ontology. This relationality is what is called here the doppelgänger« (1).

The keyword here is perhaps »operative«, as the doppelgänger is sought in the *enacting* of a ceaseless series of chiastic relations in the margins between the particular and the universal, the finite and the infinite, being created and being creative – a transformative process that refuses to privilege (let alone be subsumed under) any one of these poles and, perpetually resisting foreclosure, emblematically represents the »differential identity« (37) of the subject of modernity: the liminal subject. As the doppelgänger's ›interruptions‹ of the movements between all poles of totality inevitably include the dimension of the political, this leads to questions of self-interest and responsibility. Insofar as it contests the »logic of identity« (47), the doppelgänger is of itself a challenge to the autonomy of philosophy – but the book's focus is firmly on how reciprocities between discursive fields are forged.

While each of its five large chapters offers a separate framing of the problem, they represent the development of an overarching argument. This should not imply, however, that the literary readings are to be understood as elements of a »master narrative« (169), but rather as examples of historically determined sites where the doppelgänger's relations have unfolded (which entails that even Jean Paul's work is not of primary significance). These are generally arranged around a central text with a wide range of critics and philosophers (notably Derrida, Foucault, Lefebvre and Benjamin) as commentators. The following cannot aspire to do justice to the scope or detail of this complex study, but only to offer a sense of them by charting some of the intertwined questions, concepts and themes.

Chapter One, »The Critique of Loneliness«, introduces the doppelgänger as a function of Jean Paul's challenge to »the autonomy of reason that in turn underwrites the autonomy of the subject« (15), as posited by Idealism. A series of detailed readings of the writer's critique of Kant and in particular Fichte, which frame an excursion into Freud's study of the uncanny, lay the foundation of the rest of the book. Jean Paul's doppelgänger is contoured as the »*subject that cannot be denied*« (64), as its constitution is given through the differential relations that transform what seeks to deny it. If, as it is further argued, irony exposes the »trick« in Fichte's technique of installing literature where there is allegedly only philosophy (64), then this act effaces the independence of philosophy that it is intended to affirm, without reducing either to the other.

In Chapter Two, »The Subject of Modernity«, the figures of murder (as the foreclosure of the future) and confession, as »a rapprochement between divine and human law, a region that mediates between them« (76), serve to access the doppelgänger in Alexandros Papadiamantes' novella *The Murderess*. The hiatus between ›I‹ and ›You‹, as well as the ›to‹ and ›of‹ (implicit in the act of self-confession), leads into an analysis of temporality and of justice as a *penumbra* in the law. The vital distinction between denial and negation reveals the doppelgänger as »the element that gives the binding power to the *and*« (104).

It is in Chapter Three, »The Task of the Doppelgänger«, where the distinctive thrust of the study's approach truly comes to the fore. The figuration of the subject as the doppelgänger, it is argued, entails that this very figure »is operative not only in the literary work but also in the criticism addressing that work« (106). But if it is the medium of interpretation, then criticism will perforce have to »deal also with the author under the rubric of the doppelgänger« (106), and this move questions not only the subject, but subjectivity itself. In this manner »the expansion of the doppelgänger ineluctably leads from literature, to criticism, to philosophy« (107). The principle work chosen to pursue these questions is *L'arrêt de mort* (*Death Sentence*) by the French author, critic and philosopher Maurice Blanchot, whose writings mediate on the »boundaries between genres and discourses« (107), whereby the doppelgänger arises at the limit of each form of inquiry. The identification of Jean Paul as a background figure, never named but ever present, suggests a »rearticulation of the literary canon«, whereby the canonical author becomes the »collocational Other who collocutes (in) the text« (118).

Conjoining the concepts of the undoing of presence either in place or in time, Chapter Four pursues the »Politics of the Doppelgänger« in an interrogation of what it means to *write history*. Against the background of Walter Benjamin's writings on historiography, the equivocation inherent in the term »subject of history« (insofar as it can refer equally to the historical individual or the historian) serves to probe the »condition of the possibility of the subject's intervention in history« (137) – an act which manifests as judgement. The principle tool is the term *parataxis*, which evokes both the »agonistic and the conciliatory« (138) and by nature resists subjugation. The failure of its rival, *hypotaxis*, to determine the subject in Alasdair Gray's novel *Poor Things*, either by retrieving a foundational origin or by fixing a future (as a progression toward an ideal), reveals the doppelgänger.

Chapter Five, »Self-Inscriptions«, extends the investigation of authorship and criticism to the problem of *life* and *work*, chiefly by means of two signatories ideally suited to the task: Walter Benjamin and Franz Kafka. This discussion allows for a précis of the three main aspects of the doppelgänger's relationality, »a destruction of autonomous individuality, which leads to commonality; a retention of the subject as the capacity to interrupt the movement between completion and incompletion; and the responsibility to retain relationality as the exigency of the political« (225). In this sense, the doppelgänger's undercutting of »totalizing forms of presence« (234) necessarily occludes the (total) elimination of even what it opposes.

The concluding remarks summarize what can be regarded as one of the book's central tenets: Every attempt to deny the doppelgänger only »inscribes it in an even more central position in the discourse that seeks to deny it: the denial shows the blind spot – the unknown, the impossible, the under way, and hence the doppelgänger – operating in an essentialist discourse« (246). Philosophy *needs* the doppelgänger in order to avoid self-occlusion and find the openings to develop its ontology, and it is the literary and the critical which have served to highlight »the resistances proffered against the doppelganger« (247).

The demands of following the nuances of Vardoulakis' highly complex thesis are richly rewarded with a trove of original insights and stimuli for reflection. With its distinctive approach to some of the central tropes of modernity, as well as the consistency and coherence with which it pursued, this book will surely prove an important contribution to modernist criticism. What remains somewhat unclear (to this reviewer at least) is whether conditions exist for the emergence of the doppelgänger in a specific text. If, as is asserted at the end, the doppelgänger »figures as long as literature, criticism, and philosophy reflect each other« (246), and yet is enacted on specific sites, meaning that the »corpus of the doppelgänger is growing and diminishing depending on the responses offered to particular texts« (10), then the »as long« would seem to delimit its operations. Put another way: does the doppelgänger await the attention of the critic in any given text, or do texts exist that are unable to reflect philosophy? In this respect, the challenge to philosophy presented in this book can be read as an equally productive challenge to literary scholarship.

Dale Adams
(The University of Melbourne)

David Roberts. *The Total Work of Art in European Modernism.*
Ithaca, New York: Cornell University Press, 2011. 292pp. ISBN: 978-0-8014-5023-5.

In den ästhetiktheoretischen Diskursen des vergangenen Jahrhunderts besaß der Begriff des Gesamtkunstwerks nur einen sehr geringen Stellenwert. Ernst Bloch beispielsweise sprach vom Gesamtkunstwerk als einer »prinzipiell unkanonischen Kategorie«, die nur durch Wagners Genie als solche überhaupt in ein breiteres Bewusstsein rücken und lebensfähig werden konnte. Thomas Mann wiederum erblickte in der Vereinigung der Künste zum Gesamtkunstwerk nicht nur eine »lächerlich mechanische« Prozedur, sondern auch einen Abgrund an Dilettantismus. Die dezidierteste und vermutlich folgenreichste Kritik wurde von Theodor W. Adorno formuliert. Er lehnte das Gesamtkunstwerk als eine Form erzwungener ästhetischer Identität ab, die letztlich den Autonomiestatus der modernen Kunst untergrabe und auf die »Gleichschaltung« der Künste und Gattungen in den totalitären Systemen des 20. Jahrhunderts vorausweise. Auch wenn Adorno sein Verdikt später relativierte, wurde das Gesamtkunstwerk von einer professionellen Ästhetik lange als eine obskure und tendenziell präfaschistische Idee betrachtet, die quer zum Mainstream der modernen Kunst- und Kulturentwicklung zu stehen schien. Es ist vor diesem Hintergrund nicht weiter verwunderlich, dass das Phänomen des Gesamtkunstwerks, trotz der unbestreitbaren Faszination, die es auf die künstlerischen Avantgarden des späten 19. und frühen 20. Jahrhunderts ausgeübt hat, bis heute weitgehend ein Desiderat ästhetischer Theoriebildung und kunstwissenschaftlicher Analyse geblieben ist. Erst seit einigen Jahren scheint sich diese Situation langsam zu verändern, denn in jüngerer Zeit sind eine Reihe von Untersuchungen erschienen, darunter meine Studie *Die Sehnsucht nach dem Gesamtkunstwerk* (2004) sowie die Arbeiten von Anke Finger (*Das Gesamtkunstwerk der Moderne*, 2006), Marcella Lista (*L'ouvre d'art totale à la naissance des avant-gardes*, 2006) und Matthew Wilson Smith (*The Total Work of Art: From Bayreuth to Cyberspace*, 2007), in denen die Idee des Gesamtkunstwerks erstmals ohne ideologiekritische Blickverengungen zum Gegenstand systematischer historischer und theoretischer Explorationen wird. Dabei gelangten die genannten Untersuchungen insofern zu einer grundlegenden Neubewertung des Gesamtkunstwerks, als sie gegen den lange Zeit tonangebenden Deutungsansatz Adornos übereinstimmend den Modernitätscharakter dieses utopischen Projekts, in dem sich seit jeher künstlerische mit sozialen, kulturellen und religiösen Einheitssehnsüchten verbinden, in den Vordergrund rückten.

Mit der 2011 erschienen Studie *The Total Work of Art in European Modernism* hat der Melbourner Literatur- und Kulturwissenschaftler David Roberts nun die wohl materialreichste, historisch ausgreifendste und theoretisch avancierteste Analyse des Konzepts Gesamtkunstwerk vorgelegt. In ihr knüpft Roberts an die erwähnte Forschungsliteratur und ihre These von der Modernität des Gesamtkunstwerks an, er radikalisiert diese Position jedoch, indem er das Gesamtkunstwerk als »key concept« des europäischen Modernismus kennzeichnet und es dadurch gleichsam von der Peripherie des Moderne-Diskurses, wo es bislang seinen Platz hatte, in dessen Zentrum rückt. Auf dieser Grundlage entfaltet Roberts' Studie von Anfang an eine Erkenntnisperspektive, die die Grenzen der historischen und theoretischen Analyse des Gesamtkunstwerks überschreitet und darauf zielt, die ästhetische Moderne als Ganzes neu zu vermessen. Ausgehend von der Diagnose einer »far-reaching convergence between the idea of the total work and the spirit of avant-gardism« konzentriert sich die Studie auf drei zentrale theoretische Aspekte der Moderneproblematik: Sie rückt erstens die »dialectic of analysis and synthesis« in der Avantgardekunst in den Blickpunkt, wobei der bisher priorisierte Aspekt der Analyse, wie er sich in der »logic of differentiation and [in] the corresponding self-reflexive explorations of the formal und technical possibilities of each of the arts« manifestiert, und damit die modernetheoretischen Kernkonzepte der »separation« und der »autonomy of the arts« im Lichte des Gesamtkunstwerks und seiner ästhetischen Synthesebestrebungen eine deutliche Relativierung erfahren. Zweitens betont die Studie den »totalizing impulse of the avant-garde«, der nach Roberts auf der suggestiven »analogy between the reintegration of the arts and the reintegration of society« basiert und die Epoche der ästhetischen Moderne insgesamt maßgeblich prägt. Den inhaltlichen Schwerpunkt legt sie dabei auf metaphysisch inspirierte Visionen des Gesamtkunstwerks, wie sie z.B. in den Welterlösungsprojekten der »romantisch-idealistischen Avantgardekunst« exemplarisch zum Ausdruck kommen. Nicht zuletzt über solche Gewichtungen stellt die Studie drittens eine weitere »key assumption of aesthetic modernism« grundlegend in Frage: »the neat equation of avant-gardism with progress« und damit einhergehend »the familiar left-right divide between revolution and reaction, or between the modern and the antimodern«.

Auch im Hinblick auf die lange Zeit umstrittene oder schlichtweg ungeklärte Definition des Begriffs ›Gesamtkunstwerk‹ beschreitet Roberts neue Wege. Dabei stützt er sich zunächst auf meinen Versuch einer Begriffsbestimmung aus dem Jahr 2004, wonach ein Gesamtkunstwerk durch vier verschiedene Komponenten charakterisiert ist: eine inter- oder multimediale Struktur, einen Begriff von der idealen Vereinigung der Künste, ein ideelles Bild vom Ganzen sowie ein ästhetisch, sozial, kulturell, technisch oder religiös-eschatologisch dimensionierter Utopieentwurf, als dessen Realisierungsmedium das Gesamtkunstwerk zugleich fungiert. Während meine Studie jedoch den explizit ästhetischen Charakter des Gesamtkunstwerks hervorhebt und dieses mithin auf Kunstwerke sowie künstlerische Projekte und Entwürfe beschränkt, sieht Roberts in diesem ein Phänomen, das die Grenzen des Ästhetischen sprengt und auf die Sphären von Politik und Religion ausgreift. Diese Ausweitung des Gesamtkunstwerkbegriffs führt Roberts zu zwei bedeutsamen Neuperspektivierungen: Zum einen fügt er der theatralen und architektonischen Traditionslinie des Gesamtkunstwerks, wie sie in meiner Arbeit anhand von modernen Fortschreibungen und Neukonzeptualisierungen der griechischen Tragödie und der gotischen Kathedrale herausgearbeitet wurden, eine dritte – festivalische – Linie hinzu, die ihr historisches Grundmuster in den Festen der antiken Stadtrepubliken Sparta und Rom besitzt. Mit ihr rückt – und dies ist sicherlich eines der Hauptverdienste der Studie – der bislang in der Forschungsliteratur noch kaum thematisierte französische Strang der Gesamtkunstwerksentwicklung ins Blickfeld, der von Rousseaus Idee der Zivilreligion ausgeht und eine Vielzahl von Modellen und Projekten umfasst, diese Idee in die ästhetische Form öffentlicher Festveranstaltungen zu überführen. Bereits in Rousseaus eigener Festkonzeption wird dabei eine »unacknowleged tension« zwischen dem Typus eines utopisch-kommunitären Volksfests auf der einen Seite und dem einer staatlich gelenkten Massenveranstaltung auf der anderen Seite sichtbar, die in der Form eines internen Widerspruchs zwischen (emanzipativer) »Antistruktur« und (repressiver) »Struktur« die Ästhetik des Gesamtkunstwerks insgesamt bestimmt. Zum anderen dehnt Roberts den Begriff des Gesamtkunstwerks auf den Totalitarismus des 20. Jahrhunderts aus und zieht so eine direkte Linie von den Einheitsentwürfen des modernen Gesamtkunstwerks zu den staatsästhetischen Großvisionen Mussolinis, Hitlers und Stalins. Auch wenn Roberts nicht der Erste ist, der das Gesamtkunstwerk mit dem totalitären Staat faschistischer, nationalsozialistischer oder stalinistischer Prägung gleichsetzt – vor ihm haben etwa Jean Clair in *Der Hang zum Gesamtkunstwerk* (1983) und Boris Groys (*Gesamtkunstwerk Stalin. Die gespaltene Kultur in der Sowjetunion,* 1988) Blaupausen für eine solche Engführung geliefert –, so geht seine Argumentation doch in eine gänzlich andere Richtung als die seiner Vorgänger, insofern er zum ersten Mal die gemeinsame Genealogie beider Phänomene über eine gründliche Aufarbeitung ihrer ideengeschichtlichen Bezüge u.a. zu Nietzsche, Le Bon, Sorel, d'Annunzio oder Jünger freilegt. Es sind jedoch nicht nur diese historisch-genetischen Gesichtspunkte, die eine Identifikation von Gesamtkunstwerk und totalitärer Politik nahelegen; für Roberts liegen deren Konvergenzen noch auf einer anderen Ebene, nämlich in ihrem utopischen Bezug auf den Erfahrungsraum eines nietzscheanisch zu verstehenden ›Sublimen‹, in dem alle gesellschaftlichen Distanzverhältnisse in der unmittelbaren Präsenz einer kollektiven sozialen Aktion aufgehoben sind, die unweigerlich zwischen Terror und Ekstase, Annihilation und Entgrenzung changiert. Als ästhetisches Korrelat des Ausnahmezustands und der mit ihm verbundenen Suspension politischer, rechtlicher und sozialer Normen bildet dieser Raum des Sublimen den, wie Roberts formuliert, »abyssal ground« der säkularen Moderne, »which refers on the one hand to [...] the destination or ›end‹ of (aesthetically differentiated) art, and on the other to [...] the destination or ›end‹ of (functionally differentiated) politics«. Roberts' Studie liefert indessen nicht nur bemerkenswerte theoretische

Neuansätze, sie gibt auch erstmals einen systematischen Überblick über die Theorie- und Konzeptgeschichte des Gesamtkunstwerks von der Französischen Revolution bis zur Gegenwart, den sie in drei chronologisch verfahrenden Großkapiteln entfaltet. Im ersten Teil dieser historischen Gesamtschau wird zunächst die primär politisch perspektivierte französisch-festivalische (Ursprungs-)Linie der Gesamtkunstwerksentwicklung betrachtet, wobei neben Rousseaus »antitheatrical ideal of the popular festival« vor allem die Massenfeste der Französischen Revolution und die utopischen Ideen des Saint-Simonismus zu einer industriegesellschaftlichen Kultfeier examiniert werden. Die Studie verschiebt dann den Fokus auf den zweiten Entwicklungsstrang des Gesamtkunstwerks, indem sie zeigt, wie »Rousseau's German disciples from Schiller to Hegel, from Hölderlin to Schelling« die politische Idee einer »new religion of humanity« aufnehmen und sie in die ästhetische Idee einer neuen Mythologie übersetzen, die von einem revitalisierten »public drama« getragen werden soll. Es ist schließlich Richard Wagner, der in seinen Züricher Manifestschriften (1848–1852) die beiden Modelle des »revolutionary festival« französischer und des »festival drama« deutscher Prägung in der Utopie einer mythopoetisch fundierten Synthese von Kunst, Religion und Politik zusammenführt, die in ihren entscheidenden Zügen dem »organischen« Gesamtkunstwerk der antiken griechischen Tragödie nachkonstruiert ist. Wagners epochemachender Versuch einer Rückkehr zu den kunstreligiösen Ursprüngen des Theaters in seinem Bühnenweihfestspiel *Parsifal* bildet den Ausgangspunkt des zweiten Kapitels, das die Um- und Neuformatierungen des theatralen Gesamtkunstwerks in den romantisch-idealistischen Avantgarden seit den 1880er Jahren untersucht. Im Rahmen eingehender Analysen symbolistischer, expressionistischer oder surrealistischer Theaterentwürfe legt die Studie dabei nicht nur den elementaren Zug ins Irrationale frei, der diese Entwürfe ausnahmslos bestimmt und mit den gängigen Theorien und Definitionen avantgardistischer Kunst kaum in Einklang zu bringen ist; sie gelangt am Ende des Kapitels überdies zu einer Typologie des theatralen Gesamtkunstwerks, in der drei Grundmodelle unterschieden werden: ein spirituelles Modell, in dem das Gesamtkunstwerk als Symbol eines synästhetisch dimensionierten Geistigen auf Prozesse der Abstraktion und Vergeistigung hinwirken soll (Mallarmé, Skrjabin, Kandinsky, Schönberg); ein primitiv-orgiastisches Modell, in welchem das Gesamtkunstwerk in therapeutischer Perspektive auf seine magischen und rituellen Wurzeln im Rahmen eines alle Grenzen nivellierenden Totalspektakels zurückgeführt wird (Stravinsky, Artaud); sowie ein Verfremdungsmodell, das auf die ironisch-distanzierende »de-fusion« der szenischen Ausdrucksmittel setzt, nichtsdestoweniger aber als Medium einer resakralisierenden »re-fusion« des Theaters fungieren kann (Claudel, Brecht). Das dritte Kapitel schließlich charakterisiert die totalitäre Variante des Gesamtkunstwerks, wie sie von den »aktivistischen Avantgarden« in Italien, Deutschland und der Sowjetunion nach den Erfahrungen des Ersten Weltkriegs als Versuch einer (Wieder-)Vereinigung von Kunst und Leben mit z.T. beträchtlichem Erfolg realisiert wurde. Danach basiert das von d'Annunzio und den italienischen Futuristen um Marinetti getragene faschistische Gesamtkunstwerk auf einer Idolatrisierung des Krieges, die als »heroic, sacrifice antithesis to the decadence of the bourgeois society« vornehmlich zwei ästhetische Prinzipien involviert: die Sakralisierung und die Theatralisierung militärischer und politischer Macht. Innerhalb des nationalsozialistischen Gesamtkunstwerks mündet diese Tendenz in eine »religion of death«, die sich in Hitlers Faszination für den zeitlosen Monumentalismus von Pyramiden und Totenburgen oder Speers Ruinenwerttheorie ebenso manifestiert wie in den Kultritualen der Nürnberger Parteitage, in denen die Subjekte ihre Selbstannihilation in den endlosen Kolonnen der marschierenden Massen lustvoll zelebrieren. Demgegenüber zeichnet sich die sowjetische Version des Gesamtkunstwerks durch einen prometheisch übersteigerten Utopismus aus, der sich vor allem darin zeigt, dass ihre wichtigsten künstlerischen Trägergruppen – vom Futurismus über den Suprematismus bis hin zu den konstruktivistischen Organisationen des Proletkults und des LEF – übereinstimmend auf die totale Neukonstruktion von Mensch, Erde und Kosmos mit ästhetisch-technischen Mitteln zielten. Es ist vor diesem Hintergrund kein Wunder, dass die Allianz von ästhetischer und politischer Avantgarde in der Sowjetunion bald zerfiel und erstere liquidiert oder in die innere oder äußere Emigration getrieben wurde, denn Roberts' Engführung von Gesamtkunstwerk und Totalitarismus verdeutlicht, dass Lenin und besonders Stalin in den futuristischen und konstruktivistischen Künstlergruppen vor allem eines sehen mussten: Konkurrenzunternehmen, deren ästhetische Totalprojekte mit ihren eigenen staatskünstlerischen Großutopien um das Recht auf Realisierung stritten. Wenn dabei, wie Roberts in einer ingeniösen Lesart der Moskauer »show trials« in den späten 1930er Jahren nahelegt, noch die Auslöschung der bolschewistischen Kunst- und Polit-Avantgarden durch Stalin als eine »sinister form of Dionysian theatre« und damit als Teilstück jenes stalinistischen Staatsgesamtkunstwerks gedeutet werden kann, das in einer »grotesque fusion of utopia and dystopia« den gleichermaßen materiellen wie ideellen Totalumbau des Sowjetreichs voranzutreiben suchte, dann illustriert dies die eminenten Zerstörungspotentiale, die die Träume von einer künstlerischen Umschöpfung des Ganzen freizusetzen vermochten. Es sind historische Erfahrungen dieser Art, die dazu geführt haben, dass das Gesamtkunstwerk als aktivistisch betriebenes Projekt künstlerischer Weltvereinheitlichung zumindest in der westlichen Hemisphäre seine Attraktivität verloren hat. Wie Roberts zum Abschluss seiner Arbeit betont, bedeutet dies jedoch kein Ende der Gesamtkunstwerksentwicklung insgesamt, sondern nur den Beginn einer neuen postmodern-kapitalistischen Phase, die sich einerseits durch das Fehlen utopischer Metanarrative, anderseits durch eine zunehmend weitgreifendere Ästhetisierung, Festivalisierung und Kommerzialisierung der Alltagswelt auszeichnet. Entsprechend liest Roberts Hollywood als postmoderne Fortführung des mytho- und musikdramatischen Projekts von Richard Wagner, Museen, Einkaufszentren, Themenparks oder die Simulationskapitale Las Vegas als postmoderne Reformulierungen des modernen Architekturgesamtkunstwerks und Disneyland »as rebirth of the total work of art [...] that exchanged the monumental German sublime for the ›monumental American ridiculous‹«. Ihren Höhepunkt erreicht diese postmoderne Variante des Gesamtkunstwerks in der virtuellen Realität des Cyberspace, in dessen Utopie einer »totalen Immersion« in die entortete Sphäre digitaler Poiesis Roberts nurmehr eine ironische Reminiszenz an die emphatischen Erwartungen erblickt, die Richard Wagner einst mit der Praxis kollektiver Kunstproduktion verband. Roberts' Studie ist in mehrfacher Hinsicht beeindruckend: Sie ist nicht nur auf der Grundlage einer stupenden Kenntnis moderner Kunst und Kunsttheorie erarbeitet, sondern legt auch virtuos die historischen und konzeptionellen Leitlinien der Gesamtkunstwerksentwicklung in der ästhetischen Moderne frei. Darüber hinaus fördert sie eine Vielzahl von Aspekten zutage, die, obschon von eminenter Bedeutung für die Problematik des Gesamtkunstwerks, in der Forschungsliteratur noch keine ausreichende Beachtung gefunden haben. Ebenso neu wie produktiv ist etwa die Thematisierung Saint-Simonistischer Einflüsse, die Akzentuierung performativer Gesichtspunkte oder die Gegenüberstellung von »absoluter Kunst« (Hans Belting) und Gesamtkunstwerk als komplementäre Versuche zu einer Restituierung des Ästhetischen als sozialer und religiöser Vereinigungsmacht. Auch die entschiedene Neubeschreibung des Gesamtkunstwerks als Produkt der Französischen Revolution oder die Idee, mithilfe der Kategorie des Sublimen dessen utopische Erfahrungswelten zu markieren, wird der Forschung mit Sicherheit neue Impulse liefern. Bedauerlich ist hingegen die mit der Konzentration auf festivalische und theatrale Formen einhergehende weitgehend fehlende Beleuchtung des architektonischen Gesamtkunstwerks, das in der Studie lediglich in einem Kapitel über die expressionistische Kristallkathedrale abgehandelt wird. Gerade im Hinblick auf die Architekturutopien der Französischen Revolution, die sich, wie etwa Boullées Entwürfe zu einem *Kenotaph für Newton* oder einem *Tempel der Vernunft*, in ihren zivilreligiösen Intentionen an die Seite von Rousseaus Festmodell stellen ließen, dessen Agenda aber nicht performativ, sondern auf der Ebene symbolischer Repräsentation einlösen, wären neue Einsichten zu erwarten gewesen. Eine Geschichte des architektonischen Gesamtkunstwerks bleibt so bis auf Weiteres ein Forschungsdesiderat. Nicht ganz verständlich ist auch, warum die musikalisch und bildkünstlerisch inspirierten Theoreme und Projekte zu Synästhesie und Gesamtkunstwerk, wie sie in der deutschen Romantik, etwa von Philipp Otto Runge, Ludwig Tieck, Novalis oder den Brüdern Schlegel entwickelt wurden, in der Studie keine Rolle spielen; ein vollständiger Überblick über die Geschichte des Gesamtkunstwerks hätte ihrer Einbeziehung wohl bedurft. Zuletzt stellt sich die Frage, ob Roberts These von der postmodernen Ironisierung des Gesamtkunstwerks in der Gegenwart vor dem Hintergrund seines Theoriemodells nicht möglicherweise vorschnell formuliert ist. Hierfür spricht etwa das Beispiel Nordkorea, wo jene, die an der totalitären Version des Gesamtkunstwerks interessiert sind, noch heute die von Kim Il Sung erdachte politische Religion des ›Chuch'e‹ in Form von Monumentalbauwerken und Massenfestivitäten studieren können; oder die Existenz des radikalen Islam – einer tendenziell totalitären Bewegung, die nicht nur über ein »grandios-theatralisches ›Weltbild‹« und eine »berauschende utopische Schlußvision« in der »Wiederaufrichtung des Weltemirats« (Peter Sloterdijk. *Zeit und Zorn. Ein politisch-psychologischer Versuch*) verfügt, sondern der es auch gelungen ist, sich mit den Anschlägen vom 11. September 2001 – einem terroristischen »Total-Event«, in dessen massenmedialer Dauerrepräsentation ästhetische Inszenierung und reales Ereignis längst ununterscheidbar geworden sind – in die Annalen des Gesamtkunstwerks einzuschreiben. Es passt ins Bild, dass die Zerstörung des World Trade Centres, die der Wagner-Adept Karl Heinz Stockhausen nicht von ungefähr als größtes Kunstwerk aller Zeiten bezeichnet hat, von weiten Teilen der zeitgenössischen Kulturphilosophie als Ende der Postmoderne betrachtet wird.

Auch wenn gerade im Hinblick auf das politisch-totalitäre Gesamtkunstwerk noch weiterer Klärungs- und Differenzierungsbedarf besteht – der Leistung von Roberts' Studie tut dies keinen Abbruch. Das breite Spektrum der behandelten künstlerischen Projekte, der Reichtum der Verknüpfungen und Querverweise, die überzeugende theoretische Anlage – all dies erschließt nicht nur neue und produktive analytische Horizonte, es demonstriert überdies die beträchtliche, zumeist noch immer unterschätzte ästhetiktheoretische Relevanz des Gesamtkunstwerks. David Roberts hat ein großartiges Buch geschrieben. Gleichermaßen theoretische Grundlagenreflexion, konzeptgeschichtliches Großpanorama und Neukonstruktion der ästhetischen Moderne markiert es einen kategorialen Sprung: Es promoviert das Konzept Gesamtkunstwerk erstmals vom Erkenntnisgegenstand zum Erkenntnismedium und damit von einer nur deskriptiven zu einer vielseitig einsetzbaren operativen Kategorie, die für die Analyse ästhetischer, politischer und religiöser Grenzphänomene insgesamt fruchtbar gemacht werden kann. Roberts' Studie bedeutet einen vielversprechenden Anfang in dieser Hinsicht. Es steht zu hoffen, dass sie weitere Forschungsarbeiten in diesem Feld inspirieren wird.

Roger Fornoff
(Universität Belgrad)

Petra Rüdiger/Konrad Gross (eds.).
Translation of Cultures.
Amsterdam/New York: Rodopi, 2009. 306pp. ISBN 978-90-420-2596-7.

The 2009 edited volume *Translation of Cultures* sets out to explore so-called ›cross-boundary communication‹ through mutual exchange, open dialogue, enforced process, misunderstanding, or even violent conflict. Contributors in this volume, assembled out of the 28th Conference of the Association for the Study of the New Literatures in English in 2005, address the notion of ›translation of cultures‹ from a variety of distinct angles, with an overarching emphasis on attempting to subvert the Western focus of concepts such as equivalence, as well as broadening the postcolonial approach to translation studies. In their introduction the editors welcome the current state of the ›globalized present‹ as one that presents translation as an »inevitable requirement in order to ease the flow of disinterested and unbiased cultural communication« (IX). Volumes such as these play an important role in extending one of the most fervently-explored areas of translation studies, following Mary Snell-Hornby's coining of the so-called ›cultural turn‹ of the early 1990s. This move, which saw translation reach beyond ›the word‹ and towards a text's cultural environment, created a boom into studies on the varying impacts of culture/s on translation. Research into notions of power and translation included feminist writing and translation, translation and colonisation, and translation as re-writing. This volume tackles many of these cognate areas in great detail, including the translatability and untranslatability of cultures, travel and translation in the contact zone, translation of the transcultural self, and postcolonial multilingualism. The editors have assembled an impressive and diverse range of contributions from all corners of the globe including Australia, New Zealand, the Indian sub-continent, South Africa, Germany and Canada. Contributors have unlocked some valuable and innovative insights into the distinct cultural identities of diasporic Indian women writers and the Māori people of New Zealand, as well as looking at the cultural-linguistic experiences of Nigerian women writers, and Bible translation in Papua New Guinea. With thinking around cultural translation ever-evolving and ever-expanding, this volume is a timely reminder of the potential for the notion of cultural translation to extend into diverse and eclectic new cultural environments.

The volume begins with the topic of ›translatability and untranslatability of cultures‹, calling to mind notions of rewriting and adaptation, which, for particular target audiences, convey particular cultural perceptions of ›the other‹. For example, Omotayo Oloruntoba-Oju tackles the way in which classical texts are ›translated‹ and ›adapted‹ in Africa, thus questioning the application of these very terms within such contexts. This chapter provides an illuminating study on African playwrights who create new African texts (via the sometimes murky route of ›*apparent* translation‹), foregrounding the African socio-political situation and abrogating the hegemonic claims of the source. The examples presented by the author are particularly interesting. Ursula Kluwick's exploration of the way in which the ›mysterious East‹ is packaged by publishers to Western readers unearths some vital connections between the commodification of certain literatures (i.e. postcolonial) and the global literary market. Using Genette's notion of paratextuality (which is, pleasingly, gaining increasing attention within the paradigm of translation studies), Kluwick argues that certain ›marked‹ features of the physical book play an important role in the way in which texts are received (i.e. as emblems of the ›exotic‹ East). In the second section on ›travel and translation in the contact zone‹, Joanna Collins casts aside the more traditional approach to translation analysis (i.e. an interlingual one), looking at the ›translation‹ of colonial Australia for European audiences, as »a failure of transposed Western conceptions of landscape to describe Australia, [...] communication of the landscape is also a form of acclimatization and, in this sense, a translation« (117). Given the interest in translation and transnationalism, the third section has particular force, with explorations such as Michaela Moura-Koçoğlu's raising issues to do with language and identity (hers relate specifically to indigenous languages and identity in contemporary Māori writing). Christine Vogt-William addresses the connection between the translational and the transnational in the works of two diasporic poets (Ramabai Espinet, an Indo-Trinidadian-Canadian, and Sujata Bhatt, an Indian-American-German). In the closing section on ›postcolonial multilingualism‹ a more linguistic approach is provided in the featured case studies, including a report on immersion teaching in Germany.

Overall, the case studies are highly revealing and cast new light on translation in these various contexts.

Leah Gerber
(Monash University)

Gaby Pailer. *Hedwig Dohm.*
Hannover: Wehrhahn, 2011. 125 Seiten.
ISBN 978-3-86525-237-1.

In der erst im Jahr 2010 im Hannoveraner Wehrhahn-Verlag gestarteten und von Alexander Košenina, Nikola Rossbach und Franziska Schößler herausgegebenen Reihe »Meteore« ist mit einer Einführung in das Leben und Werk der Schriftstellerin Hedwig Dohm nun bereits der siebente Band erschienen. Hedwig Dohm (1831–1919) – Berlinerin jüdischer Abstammung und eine der ersten, die in Deutschland bereits 1873 das Stimmrecht für Frauen forderten – wurde zur Vordenkerin und Gallionsfigur der deutschen Frauenbewegung. Im 19. Jahrhundert war die erste deutsche radikale Feministin eine der bekanntesten Schriftstellerinnen und Publizistinnen, danach war sie weitgehend vergessen, bis zu ihrer Wiederentdeckung durch die zweite deutsche Frauenbewegung in den 1970er Jahren. Dann allerdings wurde die Großmutter Katia Manns zu einer in feministischen und genderkritischen Kontexten vielzitierten Ikone. Die Anerkennung, die Hedwig Dohms Schreiben zukam, galt dabei lange Zeit ihrer scharfzüngigen Essayistik und weniger dem literarischen Werk, dessen genderkritisches Potenzial sich erst dem konsequent ästhetisch fragenden Blick erschließt.

Einen solchen Blickwinkel nimmt Gaby Pailer in ihrer eben erschienenen Einführung ein, deren erklärtes Ziel es deshalb auch ist, Hedwig Dohms »Platz innerhalb der literarischen Genrediskurse von Essayistik, Dramatik und Narrativik neu zu bestimmen« (7), »indem erstmals eine literatur- und kulturwissenschaftliche Kontextualisierung von Dohms Lebenswerk unternommen wird« (9). Dementsprechend beginnt die Darstellung von Hedwig Dohms Leben und Werk mit einem Abriss der literarischen »Anfänge« (11–28) im Kontext einer Beschreibung von Dohms Familiengeschichte und sozialer Herkunft.

Dabei wird auch deutlich, wie viel aus genuin philologischer Perspektive »auch nach mehr als dreißigjähriger Beschäftigung mit Dohm« (8) noch zu erarbeiten und zu entdecken geblieben ist: Bis heute ist ein Archiv mit Sammelschwerpunkt ›Hedwig Dohm‹ – und das heißt auch, der Versuch Hedwig Dohms Nachlass systematisch zusammenzutragen – ein Desiderat im institutionalisierten kulturellen Gedächtnis zum deutschsprachigen Schriftgut. Zu Dohms Frühwerk gehören neben der 1867 erschienenen Darstellung *Die Spanische National-Literatur in ihrer geschichtlichen Entwickelung* auch Märchen und Gedichte, darunter ein Sonett an Dohms persönlichen Bekannten Ferdinand Lassalle sowie eine Stanze an den dänischen Dramatiker Henrik Ibsen. Dohms literarisches Frühwerk verweist bereits auf das spätere Interesse an gesellschaftskritischen Themen. Allerdings stehen zu diesem Zeitpunkt »Geschlechterfragen […] noch nicht deutlich im Zentrum ihrer Überlegungen. Das soll sich erst in den 70er Jahren radikal ändern« (28). Diese radikale Wendung zeigt sich deutlich in Dohms essayistischem Schreiben, das Pailer, in ›Polemik‹ und ›Journalismus‹ unterteilt, im Kapitel »Essayistik« vorstellt (29–43). Dabei ließe sich das ästhetische Prinzip von Dohms literarischem Schreiben – das collagenhafte Übereinandermontieren von Anspielungen, Zitaten und eigenen Ideen und Formulierungen – bereits erkennen, indem Dohm selbst theoretisch ausführt, »dass kulturelle Entwicklung ebenso wie die Identität des Einzelnen ›Palimpseste‹ bilden, deren Einschreibungen es zu entziffern gilt«, so dass »ein Seelen-Palimpsest zu entziffern [sei], das von Jahrtausenden und von allen Völkern der Erde überschrieben worden ist« (31). In ihren polemischen Schriften wie *Was die Pastoren von den Frauen denken* (1872), *Der Jesuitismus im Hausstande* (1873), *Die wissenschaftliche Emanzipation der Frau* (1874) oder auch *Gesichtspunkte für die Erziehung zur Ehe* (1909) wende sich Dohm vehement gegen theologische und pädagogische Konzepte einer dichotomen Geschlechterordnung und plädiere für die konsequente Gleichbehandlung von Mädchen und Jungen bzw. Frauen und Männern in allen Bereichen des privaten und öffentlichen Lebens wie Bildung, Politik, Rechtsordnung und Arbeitswelt. Zu den interessantesten Aspekten der Essayistik – das wird in Pailers knapper Darstellung doch recht deutlich – gehört sicherlich die verblüffende Avanciertheit von Dohms Argumentation über die »soziale und rhetorische Konstruiertheit von Geschlecht […], des Herstellungs- und Aufführungscharakters geschlechtlicher Identität […] wie ihn wesentlich später die feministische Debatte der 1990er Jahre unter dem Begriff des ›Gender‹ diskutieren wird« (36). Dabei wird in der Essayistik bereits eine Grundtendenz von Dohms literarischem Stil deutlich, nämlich Anspielungen so zu montieren und anerkannten Gelehrten wie Friedrich Nietzsche »ihre Weisheiten im Munde umzudrehen« (42), dass der sexistische Original-Sprecher in einem witzigen, durch die Rezeption zu leistenden Kombinationsspiel letztlich mit seinen eigenen Worten widerlegt wird. Pailers Kapitel zur »Dramatik« (44–63) widmet sich Hedwig Dohms Lustspielen und szenischen Dialogen. Bisher von der Forschung noch kaum berücksichtigt, zeigt Pailer anschaulich, wie gut die dramatische Form zu Dohms Auffassung passt, »dass literarische Werke grundsätzlich in einem Dialog mit der Tradition, auf der sie aufbauen, stehen« (44). Sämtliche der von Dohm in den 1870er Jahren verfassten Lustspiele sowie der zwischen 1911 und 1914 verfassten szenischen Dialoge legen weniger Gewicht auf die Handlung, sondern zeichnen sich durch den Dohm'schen Wortwitz aus, mit dem die Autorin verschiedene Thematiken um das Problem der zeitgenössischen Geschlechterrollen, etwa weibliche Bildung und bürgerliche Konvenienzehe, thematisiert. Das umfangreichste Kapitel der Einführung widmet sich – und darin spiegelt sich Dohms eigene Gewichtung bei der Wahl des literarischen Genres – Dohms »Narrativik« (64–94). Während die bisherige Forschung zu Dohms literarischem Schaffen sich vor allem auf die Novelle *Werde die Du bist* aus dem Jahr 1894 und ihre Romantrilogie konzentrieren, wird in der vorliegenden Einführung – davon ausgehend, dass »die neuere Forschung […] erhellen [konnte], wie Dohm in ihrem erzählerischen Werk Verschränkungen von Kreativität, Bildung und Geschlecht gestaltet und durch ein genuin intertextuelles Verfahren die gesellschaftliche Konstruiertheit von Geschlechterrollen und -barrieren sichtbar macht« (67) – »die Narrativik in ihrer Entwicklung von den Anfängen bis zum *Fin de siècle* vorgestellt und im Kontext der zeitgenössischen Gattungsdiskurse von Novelle und Roman untersucht« (67). Auch hier vermag Pailer auf relativ wenigen Seiten sehr anschaulich darzulegen, dass bei den genrebezogenen Überlegungen Dohms intertextuelle Anspielungen und Bezüge auf die Werke von berühmten Zeitgenossen wie Theodor Fontane, Friedrich Nietzsche, Émile Zola und Richard Wagner, aber auch Vertreter der klassischen Literatur wie Goethe, Kleist, Hoffmann und Eichendorff eine zentrale Rolle spielen. Dabei gibt Pailer auch zu bedenken, Dohms Texte könnten nicht nur auf den Schulkanon bezogen werden, denn »zu Dohms Zeit schreibt eine Vielzahl von Autoren und Autorinnen Belletristik, die mittlerweile aus dem kulturellen Gedächtnis verschwunden ist« (82). Geht es in sämtlichen literarischen Werken Hedwig Dohms um die Gestaltung der zeitgenössischen Geschlechterverhältnisse und die problematische weibliche Rolle, so ist an der hier vorliegenden ästhetisch argumentierenden Einführung in die Novellen und Romane besonders erhellend, dass die Überlegungen zur literarischen Gestaltung durch Verweise auf briefliche Äußerungen ergänzt werden, in denen Dohm den Literaturbetrieb ihrer Zeit kommentiert und ihr eigenes Schaffen so indirekt selbst poetologisch verortet. Dohms literarischer Bezug auf Zolas Kritik der bürgerlichen Geschlechterökonomie wird so zum Beispiel außerpoetisch-empirisch zusätzlich abgesichert. Hedwig Dohms Bedeutung hinsichtlich der Entwicklung des modernen Romans wird vor allem durch die Betrachtung von ihrer Romantrilogie im Genrekontext der Zeit deutlich. *Schicksale einer Seele* (1899), *Sibilla Dalmar* (1896) und *Christa Ruland* (1902) erzählen von der Entwicklung jeweils einer Frau aus einer Generation des 19. Jahrhunderts, gestaltet in der Form des im 18. Jahrhundert über englische Vorbilder in Deutschland aufgekommenen Briefromans. Spielt in *Sibilla Dalmar* Nietzsches *Zarathustra* eine besondere Rolle, so ist es in *Schicksale einer Seele* die Referenz zu Goethes *Wilhelm Meister* und in *Christa Ruland* der ambivalente parallele Bezug auf die »Philosophie des Egoismus und Solipsismus« (93) von Max Stirner einerseits und die altruistischen ethischen Implikationen von Lev Tolstojs Dichtung andererseits. Auf die Trilogie als Ganzes bezogen betonen Pailers Ausführungen, »dass die frühe autobiographische Lesart besonders der ersten beiden Romane grundfalsch ist« (94). Liest man die für Dohms Gesamtwerk zentrale Romantrilogie dagegen mit konsequent ästhetisch fragendem Blick in Bezug auf die Genreentwicklung des Romans im 19. Jahrhundert, so wird deutlich: Dohms »Romantrilogie gestaltet, thematisch wie strukturell, die ›andere Moderne‹ der Frau und ihre entsprechend andersgearteten Krisen« (94). Entsprechend einer chronologisch verfahrenden Einführung in Leben und Werk schließen die Erläuterungen zu Dohms »Spätwerk« (95–109) das Bändchen ab. Zusammenfassend verweist Pailer noch einmal auf Dohms stark intertextuelle und selbstreflektive Schreibweise, die sich auch in der schriftstellerischen Betätigung zahlreicher Dohm'scher Heldinnen selbst widerspiegele und dazu führe, dass die Autorin – nach der Auseinandersetzung mit den poetischen Programmen von Klassik und Romantik und von Realismus und Naturalismus – in ihrem Spätwerk ein eigenes ästhetisches Konzept demonstriere. Dabei lasse sich Dohms Ästhetik durchaus »in Anlehnung an die ›progressive Universalpoesie‹ der Romantiker [...] als ›progressive Genderpoesie‹ bezeichnen« (96), zeige sie doch deutlich, wie fortschrittlich Hedwig Dohm die Vorstellung der Ausbildung personaler und kollektiver Identität mit Sprach- und Literatursozialisation verbindet. So begreift Hedwig Dohm (und das zeigen, wie Pailer anschaulich darstellt, eben gerade auch ihre literarischen Werke) Geschichte als Geschlechtergeschichte – lange bevor die

Kategorie ›Gender‹ als sozio-kulturelle Konstruktion Einzug in feministische und geschlechterkritische Debatten hält.

Die nun vorgelegte ästhetisch argumentierende Einführung in das Werk Hedwig Dohms bietet einen gelungenen Kontrast zu den bisher vorliegenden Überblicksdarstellungen. Nicht nur weckt Pailer mit ihrer Argumentation Neugier auf die Lektüre der Primärtexte und Lust zum intertextuell sensibilisierten, genauen Hinsehen. Deutlich wird auch, wie sehr zu Unrecht Dohms Werk nach wie vor in der germanistischen Forschung und Lehre vernachlässigt wird. Nicht zuletzt ist die angenehme Lesbarkeit und Unterhaltsamkeit von Gaby Pailers Beitrag zu Wehrhahns »Meteoren« hervorzuheben.

Birte Giesler
(The University of Sydney)

Leith Passmore. *Ulrike Meinhof and the Red Army Faction: Performing Terrorism.* New York: Palgrave Macmillan, 2011. XII + 212 pp. ISBN 978-0-230-33747-3.

The Red Army Faction or RAF existed from 1970 to 1998 when its remaining members declared somewhat cynically that they would end their ›project‹. While the so-called second and third generations of the RAF continued to murder high profile business leaders, US soldiers, police officers, and state representatives, after the RAF founders were captured in 1972, the public was always most outraged and fascinated by this first generation of RAF terrorists, which included the former journalist Ulrike Meinhof; the daughter of a Protestant minister and fellow of the prestigious *Studienstiftung des deutschen Volkes* Gudrun Ensslin; and the social misfit Andreas Baader. Leith Passmore's book understands the activities and writings of this group as a performance that radically reconfigured and transformed public discourse in the Federal Republic in the 1970s. In his view, terrorism has to be understood as a communicative practice, because dismissing terrorist acts as meaningless, senseless, and irrational precludes historical understanding and analysis.

The study analyses the statements, proclamations, and treatises of the RAF in the underground, which can be mostly attributed to Ulrike Meinhof. But Passmore moves beyond a purely textual analysis of the group's written communications and tries to understand the social and cultural significance of the terrorist acts. Drawing on Mark Juergensmeyer's study of religious terrorism, he argues that RAF terrorism can be best understood as »performative violence«. While RAF violence had symbolic aspects in that the group's targets signified the political and economic structures of the Federal Republic as the RAF saw them, the performative violence of the RAF also profoundly transformed public discourse. According to this conception, terrorism is a »discursively constituted phenomenon that is created, and continually recreated, by performative acts of violence, acts of imagery, and acts of texts« (6). Violence, images, and texts all refer to each other and can therefore not be read in isolation.

The author explores the transformative aspect of RAF violence in relation to the group's war narrative. This narrative was already important in the protest movements of the 1960's, which in part perceived the Federal Republic as a fascist state. For many student protesters, skirmishes with police and incidents such as the killing of the student Benno Ohnesorg by a police officer during a 1967 protest against the visit of the Shah of Persia confirmed readings of the FRG as a state with fascist tendencies. This perception justified political opposition as well as violent acts as ›resistance‹. Ulrike Meinhof explained attacks on the US army with reference to »the strategists of extermination« to suggest similarities between the Vietnam War and Nazi extermination policies. The RAF tried to align its activities with the military campaigns of the Vietcong and sympathizers published images of the arrested terrorists alongside images of captured Vietcong.

Initially, German politicians and main stream media rejected the RAF's war narrative, but, as Passmore claims, they eventually accepted this model for understanding terrorism, mostly because of the RAF bombing spree that changed official perceptions of the group. In his view, the »bombings were able to perform war by inserting the Federal Republic into that visual space in the West German consciousness occupied by the conflict in Vietnam« (48). In this way, »RAF words and images worked together to align the mainstream discourse of terrorism with the alternative narrative of war« (48). This interpretation is innovative but also to some extent problematic. While it is certainly possible to interpret RAF terrorism as form of performative violence that transformed official understandings of political order and security, the implication that state officials and mainstream media may have accepted central aspects of the RAF war narrative is not very convincing. As Passmore himself notes, the judges in the Stammheim trial consistently rejected the legitimacy of the war narrative by refusing the claims of the accused to be treated as prisoners of war. This is not to deny that the response of the state to the terrorist acts might have validated the RAF's war narrative in the eyes of its supporters and sympathizers.

By contrast, Passmore's interpretation of the ideological elements of RAF texts is highly sophisticated. RAF treatises were often framed by quotations of Socialist and Communist luminaries such as Marx, Mao, and Lenin. In using such quotes, Ulrike Meinhof did not articulate a coherent ideological framework based on a theoretical understanding of different forms of Marxism. As Passmore shows, these quotes constituted a »pictorial ideology« that used Marxist thinkers as signposts that tapped into the emotions and dominant narratives among sympathizers of the RAF. This essentially visual ideology evoked themes of sacrifice, loyalty, treachery, martyrdom, and glorious violence to bind people to the group. The RAF favoured action and practice (Praxis) over theory. It did not develop a sophisticated theoretical critique of capitalism.

Despite a few shortcomings, this is an excellent study that uses a sophisticated theoretical framework to analyse the intricate relationships between violence, imagery, and texts. In doing so, Passmore explores social and cultural functions of violence in political discourse, which will be of interest to scholars in many academic fields.

Michael Hau
(Monash University)

Albrecht Dümling. *Die verschwundenen Musiker. Jüdische Flüchtlinge in Australien.* Köln/Weimar/Wien: Böhlau, 2011. 444 Seiten. ISBN 978-3-412-20666-6.

In seinem neuesten Werk legt der deutsche Musikwissenschaftler und Journalist Albrecht Dümling einen umfangreichen und schön gestalteten Band zum australischen Musikexil vor. Anhand von knapp 100 Künstlerbiografien, einzeln nochmals in einem Anhang angeführt, sucht der Autor dem deutschsprachigen Publikum neue Facetten des australischen Exils nahezubringen, einem in der Exilforschung seit den 1980er Jahren bearbeiteten, aber in der breiteren Öffentlichkeit immer noch relativ unbekannten Themengebiet. Die Stationen des in 18 Kapitel unterteilten Werks folgen einem chronologischen Verlauf, beginnend mit der Stellung der Musik für das jüdische Bildungsbürgertum und der Ideologisierung und Kriminalisierung des Jazz in den 30er Jahren, und umfassen die unterschiedlichen Einwanderungswege. In den Blickwinkel rücken hierbei Tourneen – so blieben beispielsweise die klassischen Pianisten Jascha und Tossy Spivakovsky ebenso wie die Jazztruppe *The Weintraubs Syncopaters* in Australien ›hängen‹ (die Wiener Mozart-Sängerknaben und Stephan Haag erwähnt Dümling nur am Rande) – sowie die Deportation der »Dunera Boys« aus England und deren Internierung in Tatura und Hay (in diesem Zusammenhang ist ein eigenes Kapitel der Musikrevue *Sergeant Snow White* gewidmet). Dümlings weiter Musikbegriff erlaubt es ihm, sich sowohl auf Jazz als auch auf klassische Musik, auf Kammermusik – am Beispiel der Gründung der heute noch bestehenden Gesellschaft für Kammermusik *Musica Viva* – wie auf Synagogenmusik zu beziehen. Den Abschluss bildet ein Ausblick auf den Einfluss der exilierten Musiker auf unterschiedliche Sparten des australischen Musiklebens (vom Dirigenten bis zur Synagoge) in der Nachkriegszeit.

Für ein breites deutsches Publikum bietet dieser Band eine gute Einführung und einen Überblick über das australische Musikexil. Die umfangreiche Recherche zu den Einzelbiografien – der Autor bezieht sich hier auf Interviews sowie auf diverse Akten in australischen Archiven – machen die meisten Kapitel des Bandes zu einer anregenden Lektüre, und die Stimmen der Betroffenen werden durch zahlreiche Zitate aus persönlichen Dokumenten zum Leben erweckt. Hier liegt Dümlings Stärke, der sich durch seine Kuratortätigkeit für Ausstellungen wie ›Entartete Musik‹ und Symposien zum Exil einen Namen gemacht und reichhaltige Erfahrung als Wissensvermittler hat. Aus historischer Perspektive lassen sich jedoch einige methodologische wie inhaltliche Einwände vorbringen. Es stellt sich beispielsweise die Frage, ob die chronologische Struktur des Bandes ebenso wie der Umstand, dass wesentlich die Perspektive der im Band zitierten Emigranten vertreten wird, dem Leser ein wirklich umfassendes Bild vermitteln. Gerade aufgrund der unterschiedlichen im Exil vertretenen Musiksparten hätte ein disziplinärer Blick die Unterschiede fruchtbar zur Geltung gebracht und eine andere Diskussionsebene ermöglicht. Stattdessen sucht der Autor die Erzählung in eine allgemeine Erzählung des Exils einzugliedern, was weder neu ist, noch immer gut gelingt. So argumentiert Dümling beispielsweise, dass sich die österreichischen Emigranten in Australien deswegen ungebrochen auf ein österreichisches Musikgedächtnis beziehen konnten, weil sie ihr Heimatland »als erstes Opfer der faschistischen Aggression« (248) wahrnahmen. Dieser Opfermythos entspricht wesentlich der österreichischen staatlichen Erinnerungspolitik, hat jedoch für die Situation in Australien relativ geringe Bedeutung. Der Bezug auf das Wienerlied und die Wiener Operette lässt sich wohl eher auf den verhältnismäßig hohen Anteil österreichischer Emigranten an der australischen Gesamtemigration zurückführen. Diese war ein Resultat historischer Bedingungen, da die jüdische Bevölkerung Österreichs nach der Annexion, den damit in Zusammenhang stehenden Pogromen und aus Furcht vor der deutschen Expansionspolitik bereit war, auch weit entfernte Emigrationsziele wie Australien in Betracht zu ziehen. Aufgrund der demografischen Situation Österreichs und der historisch gewachsenen Konzentration der jüdischen Bevölkerung in Wien kann davon ausgegangen werden, dass auf den Herkunftsort bezogen die Mehrheit aller australischen Emigranten aus Wien stammte (gefolgt von Berlin) und deswegen ein Bezug auf eine Wiener Musiktradition, die zumindest im Kabarett im Gegensatz zu einer österreichischen Tradition empfunden wurde, naheliegend war.

Auch die Kontrastierung des Musikexils mit anderen Bereichen des australischen Exils wäre durchaus sinnvoll gewesen. In diesem Zusammenhang berücksichtigt Dümling einige zentrale Werke der Forschungsliteratur nicht (so u.a. den 1985 von Konrad Kwiet und Joseph A. Moses herausgegebenen Sonderband des *Australian Journal of Politics and History* mit dem Titel *On Being a German-Jewish Refugee in Australia*, Kay Weintraubs Artikel zur Kriegserfahrung der Weintraub Syncopaters sowie die zahlreichen Arbeiten der Rezensentin zum australischen Exil, insbesondere dessen Kabarett- und Theatergeschichte). Die Ausblendung der Rolle der Musik für das australische Exilkabarett erscheint besonders bedauernswert, da zahlreiche Beziehungen zwischen der Musik- und der Theater- und Kabarettszene bereits nachgewiesen sind. Auch trifft die von Dümling konstatierte Entprofessionalisierung der Musiker im australischen Exil ebenso für die Theatermacher zu, wobei letztere ihre Anstrengungen auf die eigene Community konzentrierten – und in diesem Zusammenhang die ›eigenen‹ Musiker durchaus einspannten.

Trotz solcher Schwachpunkte ist Dümling ein lesenswerter Gesamteindruck des australischen Musiklebens im Exil gelungen. Das Buch kann als biografisches Grundlagenwerk des australischen Musikexils Geltung beanspruchen, und auch der Einblick in die zahlreichen Ego-Dokumente stellt sowohl für ein breites Publikum als auch für das Fach eine Bereicherung dar. Die Hauptthese des Buches, dass ein einheitliches Gesamtbild nicht existiere und sich eine Tendenz zur Entprofessionalisierung in den Einzelbiografien nachweisen lasse, erscheint jedenfalls überzeugend.

Birgit Lang
(The University of Melbourne)

Nadine Helmi/Gerhard Fischer. *The Enemy at Home: German Internees in World War I Australia.*
Sydney: University of New South Wales Press, 2011. 288 Seiten. ISBN 9-781-742232645.

Ein erstaunlicher Fund liegt diesem Buch zugrunde. 2004 entdeckte die Forscherin Nadine Helmi einige eindrucksvolle Fotografien, die 90 Jahre zuvor in australischen Internierungslagern von einem gewissen Paul Dubotzki gemacht worden waren. Helmi ging den Spuren Dubotzkis nach. Es gelang ihr, Kontakt mit seinen zwei in Deutschland lebenden 80-jährigen Töchtern aufzunehmen. Sie legten Dubotzkis umfangreiche Sammlung von Fotografien offen, einschließlich Hunderter, die das tagtägliche Leben in den Internierungslagern eindringlich zeigen. Nun sind diese Fotografien einer breiteren Öffentlichkeit zugänglich

– im Jahre 2011 fand eine Ausstellung unter dem Namen *The Enemy at Home* im Sydneyer Museum statt, zudem sind die Lichtbilder in einem gleichnamigen Buch veröffentlicht worden, begleitet von anderen Fotografien dieser Periode und mit einem Kommentar zum geschichtlichen Hintergrund von Gerhard Fischer. Das Buch ist keineswegs bloß ein Katalog zur Ausstellung, sondern hat seinen eigenständigen Wert als historische Dokumentation der Zustände in australischen Internierungslagern während des Ersten Weltkrieges.

Zwischen 1914 und 1918 wurden 6890 »feindliche Ausländer« (*enemy aliens*) in Australien interniert. 80 Prozent von ihnen wurden von den australischen Behörden als Deutsche klassifiziert und eine kleine Gruppe als Staatsbürger des schon untergehenden Habsburgerreiches Österreich-Ungarn. Die groben Vorgehensweisen der Behörden und die Gerichtsprozesse, die zur Internierung führten, waren Folge der Kriegshysterie dieser Epoche. Die Umstände der Betroffenen wurden im Einzelnen nicht untersucht und eine äußerst dünne Beweislage reichte aus, um sie zu internieren – es herrschte eine pauschale Schuldvermutung bei diesen in Gewahrsam genommenen Personen. Gegen die einseitigen Gerichtsbeschlüsse durften die Inhaftierten keinen Einspruch erheben. 4500 der Internierten waren schon lange vor Kriegsausbruch in Australien ansässig – viele von ihnen lebten seit Jahrzehnten im Lande und mehr als 700 waren bereits australische Staatsbürger. Die meisten Inhaftierten waren Männer, aber auch 150 Frauen und Kinder kamen hinter Gitter. Es gab viele beklagenswerte Geschichten von Personen deutscher Abstammung, die aus ›Rassenhass‹ seitens ihrer Nachbarn oder wegen geschäftlicher Rivalitäten von Konkurrenten denunziert worden waren. Die Feindseligkeit gegen Deutsche war so groß, dass sich 1500 Personen freiwillig internieren ließen – ihnen war das Lagerleben lieber als die ständigen Anfeindungen und erzwungene Arbeitslosigkeit außerhalb des Lagers.

Dubotzkis Fotografien zeigen nun erstmals im Detail, dass die Inhaftierten ein tatsächlich reges und vielseitiges Lagerleben geführt haben. Kurz nach ihrer Einweisung in das damals größte Inhaftierungslager Holsworthy bildeten die Häftlinge kleine Selbsthilfegruppen und Arbeitskollektive, um sich den Repressalien des Lagerkommandos zu widersetzen. Langsam gewannen sie dabei ein beträchtliches Maß an Selbstständigkeit und Eigenverwaltung. Schließlich wurden von den Internierten gewählte Repräsentanten für fast alle Aspekte des tagtäglichen Lebens innerhalb des Lagers verantwortlich und konnten somit viele Aktivitäten für sich selbst organisieren. Im Lager Holsworthy gab es sogar eine Volkshochschule. Unter den Dozenten war ein gewisser Dr. Peter Pringsheim, Schwager von Thomas Mann. Als der Krieg ausbrach, befand er sich auf einem wissenschaftlichen Fachkongress in Melbourne und wurde umgehend inhaftiert.

Als ausgebildeter Fotograf hatte Dubotzki ein scharfes Auge für das Leben im Lager. Als offizieller Fotograf begleitete er 1913 eine Expedition nach China und Sumatra. Danach ging er nach Australien und nach Kriegsausbruch wurde er interniert. Da die Lager ihr eigenes und relativ selbstständiges Wirtschaftsleben hatten, beschloss Dubotzki, ein Fotogeschäft aufzumachen. Ironischerweise hatte er im Lager mehr Freiheit zu fotografieren als außerhalb des Lagers, da feindliche Ausländer draußen in der australischen Gesellschaft auf offener Straße keinen Fotoapparat benutzen durften.

Beim Fotografieren ging Dubotzki sehr sorgfältig vor, mit einem Blick für eine gelungene Aufstellung und Inszenierung seiner Bilder. Als Internierter hatte er zweifelsohne diverse freie Stunden, die er sich mit dem Aufnehmen von durchdachten und künstlerisch gelungenen Szenen vertrieb. Auch das Malen lernte er in der Lagermalerschule. Dubotzki verbrachte den Großteil seiner Internierungszeit in dem Lager Trial Bay. Dort war es im Vergleich zu anderen Lagern verhältnismäßig behaglich. Die wohlhabendsten unter den Internierten wohnten dort – Schiffspersonen, die immer noch ihre Einkommen beziehen konnten, und deutsche Kolonisten, die von den Südseeinseln vertrieben worden waren.

Trial Bay liegt an der zentralen Küste von New South Wales (der Name ›Trial Bay‹ geht zurück auf eine alte Schiffbruchsgeschichte, nicht auf die spätere Gründung des dortigen Gefängnisses). Dubotzkis Fotografien zeigen die Strandcafés, die die Internierten neben dem Lager aufgemacht hatten. Sie durften zu bestimmten Zeiten im Ozean baden und Sport treiben – darunter Turnen, was bei vielen besonders beliebt war. Theaterliebhaber schufen Bühnenbilder aus Abfallmaterial und produzierten Plakate, um Aufführungen einem wahrhaft gefangenen Publikum bekanntzumachen.

The Enemy at Home leistet einen wichtigen Beitrag zu drei Fachbereichen. Erstens erinnern uns Dubotzkis Bilder an die Kunst der Dokumentarfotografie – 90 Jahre nach dem Ersten Weltkrieg bringen seine Fotografien diese verschleierte Welt hinter den Lagermauern wieder ans Licht. Zweitens erinnert uns das Buch an ein wichtiges und verdrängtes Kapitel in der Geschichte der Deutschen und Österreicher in Australien. Gerhard Fischer beschreibt dieses Kapitel der Geschichte der deutschsprachigen Einwanderung auf dem fünften Kontinent als »die Zerstörung der deutschaustralischen Gemeinschaft«. Drittens sind diese während des Ersten Weltkrieges enstandenen Lager ein erstes Beispiel für eine Internierungspraxis seitens der australischen Einwanderungsbehörden, die leider auch noch heute Bestand hat: Auch im 21. Jahrhundert sitzen noch Tausende Asylbewerber oder, je nach politischem Sprachgebrauch, ›illegale Einwanderer‹ in Internierungslagern hinter Stacheldraht. Eine oft jahrelange Internierung mit ungewissem Entscheidungsausgang hat äußerst schädliche Auswirkungen auf das physische und psychische Wohlbefinden der Betroffenen, wie in vielen öffentlichen und nichtstaatlichen Gutachten festgestellt worden ist. Betrachtet man Dubotzkis Fotografien, kommt man leicht zu dem Schluss, dass ein höherer Grad an Selbstständigkeit und Selbstverwaltung zu einem etwas erträglicheren oder halbwegs ›humanen‹ Leben für die Insassen führen dürfte.

Auch noch Monate nach dem Ende des Ersten Weltkrieges blieben die Internierten in den Lagern hängen, weil man kein Interesse an ihrer (Re-)Integrierung in die australische Gesellschaft hatte und ihr weiteres Bleiben im Land sowieso unerwünscht war. Fast alle wurden nach Deutschland zurückgeschickt, sobald Schiffe bereitstanden. Für manche Internierte war dies eine willkommene Freilassung aus der Haft. Für andere bedeutete es eine tragische, permanente Trennung von ihren Familien. Einzelne wie William Meyer, der noch Frau und Sohn in Sydney hatte, leisteten Widerstand gegen ihre Abschiebung aus Australien, allerdings vergebens, da die Abschiebung mit rechtlichen Mitteln nicht anfechtbar war.

Paul Dubotzki wurde 1919 nach Deutschland abgeschoben, aber nicht ohne ein bemerkenswertes Bild seiner Abreise gemacht zu haben. 1918 wurde das Lager in Trial Bay plötzlich geräumt und die Internierten zu einem anderen Lager, Holsworthy, im Landesinneren geschickt, weil das Gerücht umging, das gefürchtete deutsche Kriegsschiff ›Wolf‹ nähere sich der australischen Ostküste. Dubotzki machte ein Bild von dem Chaos der Abreise, welches ein unerwartetes Detail enthält – ein Hut steht klar und deutlich auf einem Leitungsmast. Er wurde vom Fotografen mit Absicht dort hingestellt. Mit dem hängengebliebenen Hut wollte Dubotzki vermutlich sagen: »Ich habe hier gelebt und ich werde nicht verschwinden, ohne ein Zeichen meiner Präsenz hier zurückzulassen.« In der Tat hat er viele Fotografien hinterlassen, die in diesem beeindruckenden Buch zu beschauen sind.

Glenn Nicholls
(Swinburne University of Technology)

Rüdiger Görner/Angus Nicholls (eds).
In the Embrace of the Swan. Anglo-German Mythologies in Literature, the Visual Arts and Cultural Theory.
Berlin/New York: De Gruyter, 2010. 408 pp. ISBN 978-3-11-173363-0.

This handsomely produced collection of essays is the outcome of a 2007 Conference in the Centre for Anglo-German Cultural Relations, University of London, which was preceded and prepared by a two year graduate colloquium on myth. Lack of space precludes more than a summary overview of this rich and stimulating essay collection. The comparative interest of the volume is evident in a certain division of labour, in which theories of myth remain a largely German affair. The opening essays by Christoph Jamme, »Mythos zwischen Sprache und Schrift«, and Herwig Gottwald, »Gegenwärtigkeit des Mythos nach der Aufklärung?« and the final essay by Kurt Hübner, »Rationality in Myth and Science« frame the collection through their re-visiting of key terms of the German discourse of modernity since the late eighteenth century but of lesser consequence in the British reception of myth. The confrontation of enlightenment and myth no longer possesses the virulence it once did. Jamme and Gottwald deconstruct the old oppositions in productive fashion. The distinction between myth and mythology is for Jamme already a product of the Axial Age (800–200 B. C.) in both East and West. Greek mythology since Homer and Hesiod announces the beginning of a modern reception of (oral) myth, that is, a process of enlightenment which makes mythology a record of the ongoing work on myth in art and in theory. For Gottwald, the concept of myth can only be thought differentially, that is, in terms of (the unity of) the difference myth/non-myth. Gottwald is accordingly sceptical of the idea of the enduring presence of myth favoured by such theorists as Leszak Kolakowski, Mircea Eliade, Paul Veyne and Hübner. Hübner for his part reads the clash between enlightenment and romantic attitudes towards myth in the light of the twin dangers of a naïve faith in science and of a return of the repressed. He therefore argues that the task of civilization lies in finding a balance between the enlightenment assumption of an evolution from mythos to logos and the romantic sense of the ongoing presence of myth. Hans Blumenberg's version of this balance is directed, as Robert Segal shows, against the assumptions underlying both positions. If myth has an ongoing relevance, it lies neither in the Enlightenment view that myth arose to satisfy intellectual curiosity nor in the Romantic view that myth arose spontaneously. Rather, it lies for Blumenberg in the ongoing work of re-interpretation that myths provoke.

Segal's comparison of E.B. Tylor and Blumenberg in »From Nineteenth to Twentieth Century Theorizing about Myth in Britain and Germany« brings the respective theoretical traditions into closer focus, complemented by the essay of Myrian Richter and Bernd Hamacher on the Third International Congress for the History of Religion held in Oxford in 1908 with its opposed anthropological models of historical evolution and the historicist emphasis on the individuality of cultures and religions and by the essay of Christoph Benne comparing reception of the Dionysus myth in Germany and England. The crucial period for the modern reception of myth belongs, however, to the threshold of modernity in the second half of the eighteenth century. Thus Benne ties the return of Dionysus to the impact of the French Revolution that made Dionysus for Hölderlin the »god of revolution«. Lucas Gisi relates the development of the comparative study of myth to the emergence of a historical consciousness in the later eighteenth century that recognized the parallels between ancient cultures and contemporary primitive societies. Ritchie Robertson takes a completely different tack by highlighting the dangers of modern mythmaking as indicated by paranoiac theories of conspiracy that saw in the French Revolution the hand of secret societies. Freemasons now took the place that Jesuits had hitherto occupied in the conspiratorial imaginary. Henceforth Jesuits, Freemasons and Jews were allotted the role of dangerous outsiders in the new post-revolutionary landscape of nationalist myth. In Isaiah Berlin's reading of European Romanticism, Hamann is identified as the father of irrationalism, a reading, as Timo Günther demonstrates, that is guilty of a reductive and undialectical distinction between the Enlightenment and Romanticism.

The modern tensions between Enlightenment and Romanticism form the recurrent thread of the *theoretical* work on myth. When we turn to the contribution of art and literature, however, we enter the sphere of a romantic modernism in which the tension between mythos and logos appears in the (negative) interplay between the naïve and the sentimental. Maike Oergel explores the ›dialectic of modernity‹ around 1800 in English and German literature with reference to ›The Bard as Original and Future Poet‹. Rüdiger Singer compares the formal and mythical parallels between Goethe's elegy *Euphrosyne* and the poems of Ossian, the very type of the original bard of modern, ›sentimental‹ invention. Sybille Erle juxtaposes Blake's and Lavater's search for the lost original, the divine likeness of Christ. Wilfried Barner documents the (self-) mythicizing of Byron in poetry, painting, even sculpture, crowned by his death in the struggle for Greek independence that elevated him to a European figure. The essays on the reception of myth in twentieth-century art and literature reveal the ascendency of syncretic, mystical mythologies in Yeats and D.H. Lawrence (Maria Thanassa), political and psychoanalytic in Broch and Thomas Mann (Monika Ritzer), and highly personal and private in the iconography of Max Ernst and Leonora Carrington (Ernst Schonfield). The contemporary intrudes more directly in Petra Rau's survey of the mythical overtones present in the fascination of British observers with the Nazi cult of the body and in Volker Mergenthaler's analysis of Durs Grünbein's response to 9/11 in which Coventry and Dresden function as mythical coordinates of the poet's search for meaning. Whether we regard myth and mythology as present or past, the present collection shows that it is not a theme facing exhaustion. Not only does this volume open up a new field of comparative research, it makes at the same time a larger gap visible, the need for comparative studies in myth and mythology that embrace the diverse but interrelated cultures of European modernism since the French Revolution.

David Roberts
(Monash University)

Anhang / Appendix

Richtlinien für die Gestaltung deutscher Manuskripte

Die Aufsätze können in englischer oder deutscher Sprache verfasst werden. Im Deutschen ist die neue Rechtschreibung (Stand August 2006) zu verwenden. Die Aufsätze sollten einen Umfang von etwa *15 Druckseiten* (etwa 35.000 Zeichen, mit Leerzeichen gerechnet) haben.
Zwecks Einheitlichkeit sollten die Manuskripte in einer leicht abgewandelten MLA-Version eingereicht werden (siehe unten). Bitte *nicht* mit Endnote oder vergleichbaren Programmen arbeiten.

1. Zur *Unterteilung des Textes* in größere Sinnabschnitte dienen römische Ziffern mit Punkt (I.) bzw. Zwischenüberschriften mit römischer Ziffer und Punkt (I. Zur Methode).
2. *Hervorhebungen* sind im Manuskript einheitlich kenntlich zu machen, sie erscheinen im Druck kursiv. Bitte keine Unterstreichungen, keinen Fettdruck und keine unterschiedlichen Schrifttypen und -größen verwenden.
3. *Zitate* im laufenden Text werden in doppelte, Zitate innerhalb von Zitaten in einfache Anführungszeichen gesetzt. Auslassungen in Zitaten werden durch drei Punkte in eckigen Klammern gekennzeichnet. Einfügungen, d.h. eigene Kommentare oder Erläuterungen, stehen ebenfalls in eckigen Klammern.
4. *Zeichensetzung bei Zitaten* sollte folgendermaßen aussehen: Enzensberger zufolge schwört der Westdeutsche »auf sein Lufthansa-Weltbürgertum«, während sich der Ostdeutsche fühlt, als wäre er »moralisch allemal der Größte« (471). Bei Blockzitaten bitte keine Anführungszeichen verwenden und den Literaturverweis in Klammern vor das Satzzeichen stellen.
5. *Anmerkungen* sollen im Manuskript durch hochgestellte Ziffern ohne Klammern gekennzeichnet werden. Die Anmerkungsziffer steht nach dem Satzpunkt oder dem Doppelpunkt, aber vor dem Komma oder dem Semikolon. Anmerkungen sollen für inhaltliche Ergänzungen verwendet werden. Literaturverweise in Anmerkungen werden wie Literaturverweise im fortlaufenden Text behandelt (siehe 6), d.h. beschränkt auf eine Kurzreferenz. Die vollständige Literaturangabe findet sich dann im anhängenden Literaturverzeichnis.
6. *Literaturhinweise* sollen in den Text durch Klammerverweise auf das Literaturverzeichnis eingearbeitet werden (hierbei wird bei Eindeutigkeit auf Vornamen verzichtet). Der Literaturhinweis enthält also Autorennamen, Kurztitel und eventuell Seitenangabe: (Luhmann, *Kunst der Gesellschaft*, 65). Der Kurztitel entfällt bei Eindeutigkeit des Verweises (Luhmann,

65). Bei fortlaufender Mehrfachzitierung eines Werkes und Eindeutigkeit des Verweises entfällt auch der Autorenname (65f.) (65-68). – Bei Werken, die häufig zitiert werden, können der Einfachheit halber auch Siglen benutzt werden (*LW*, 24). Diese sollten im Literaturverzeichnis folgendermaßen aufgeführt werden: Ransmayr, Christoph. *Die letzte Welt*. Frankfurt a.M.: Fischer, 2004. (*LW*) – In den Klammerverweisen steht zwischen verschiedenen Autoren verschiedener Werke (Huizinga; Elias) bzw. bei Zitierung mehrerer Werke desselben Autors ein Semikolon (Agamben, *Homer sacer*; *Auschwitz*) oder auch (Agamben, *Homo sacer,* 66; *Auschwitz,* 130-134). Bei zwei Autoren desselben Werkes steht zwischen den Autorennamen ein Schrägstrich (Böhme/Böhme, 299), bei mehr als zwei Autoren ist nach dem Erstautor »et al.« anzuführen (Klibansky et al.). Romantitel und Titel von Monographien und Aufsatzsammlungen werden kursiv gesetzt (Luhmann, *Soziale Systeme*), während Titel von Artikeln, Essays und Gedichten in Anführungsstrichen stehen (Rilke, »Der Panther«).

7. Das *Literaturverzeichnis* steht unter »Zitierte Literatur« am Ende des Manuskripts. Die bibliographischen Angaben sollen in der nachstehenden Reihenfolge erfolgen: Autor (Zu- und Vorname). *Titel*. Erscheinungsort: Verlag, Erscheinungsjahr. Vgl. auch die unten angeführten Beispiele. In das Literaturverzeichnis sind die ausgeschriebenen Vornamen der Autoren sowie die Verlagsangaben aufzunehmen. Hervorhebungen in kursiv gesetzten Titeln sind mit einfachen Anführungsstrichen zu kennzeichnen. Bei Herausgeberschaften werden alle Herausgeber namentlich aufgeführt.
8. *Tabellen und Illustrationen* sind dem Manuskript auf gesonderten Blättern beizulegen und fortlaufend zu numerieren. Im Manuskript ist die Stelle zu kennzeichnen, an der die Tabelle oder die Abbildung eingefügt werden soll.
9. Bei anderen Werken entnommenen Zitaten wird cit. benutzt.

Beispiele zum Literaturverzeichnis

Monografien

Simmel, Georg. *Philosophie des Geldes. Gesamtausgabe.* Hg. Otthein Rammstedt. Bd. 6. Frankfurt a.M.: Suhrkamp, 1989.

Freud, Sigmund. *Gesammelte Werke.* Hg. Anna Freud. Frankfurt a.M.: Fischer, 1999.

Streim, Georg/Peter Sprengel. *Berliner und Wiener Moderne. Vermittlung und Abgrenzung in Literatur, Theater, Publizistik.* Wien/Köln/Weimar: Böhler, 1998.

Sammelbände

Fohrmann, Jürgen (Hg.). *Systemtheorie und Literatur.* München: Fink, 1996.

Klibansky, Raymond/Erwin Panofsky/Fritz Saxl (Hg.). *Saturn und Melancholie. Studien zur Geschichte der Naturphilosophie und Medizin, der Religion und der Kunst.* Übers. Christa Buschendorf. Frankfurt a.M.: Suhrkamp, 1992.

Reichert, Klaus/Fritz Senn (Hg.). *Materialien zu James Joyces ›Ein Porträt des Künstlers als junger Mann‹.* Frankfurt a.M.: Suhrkamp, 1975.

Aufsätze aus Sammelbänden

Merton, Robert K. »Sozialstruktur und Anomie«. *Soziologische Theorie und soziale Struktur.* Berlin: de Gruyter, 1995: 115-154.

Stichweh, Heinz Rudolf. »Wissenschaftliche Beobachtung der Kunst. Ästhetik, Kunstwissenschaft und Kunstgeschichte in der Ausdifferenzierung des Kunstsystems«. *Systemtheorie und Literatur.* Hg. Jürgen Fohrmann. München: Fink, 1996: 115-154.

Schuller, Marianne. »Gesang vom Tierleben. Kafkas Erzählung ›Josefine, die Sängerin oder Das Volk der Mäuse‹«. *Singularitäten. Literatur – Wissenschaft – Verantwortung.* Hg. Marianne Schuller/Elisabeth Strowick. Freiburg: Rombach, 2001: 219-234.

Zeitschriftenaufsätze

Witte, Bernd. »Bilder der Endzeit. Zu einem authentischen Text der ›Berliner Kindheit‹ von Walter Benjamin«. *DVjs* 58 (1984): 570-592.

Tietz, Udo. »Ästhetik und Geschichte. Eine philosophisch-ästhetische Analyse des Frühwerks von Georg Lukács«. *Weimarer Beiträge* 35.4 (1989): 560-580.

Style Guidelines for Manuscripts in English

Articles can be in English or German. Articles in German should adhere to the rules of the German Writing Reform (August 2006). Articles should be approx 15 pages long (approx. 35,000 characters, including spaces). To ensure uniformity please use our style sheet which is a slightly modified version of the MLA-style. Please do *not* use endnote or comparable programmes.

1. *Subdivisions* of the text are to be marked in roman numerals followed by a full stop, e.g. (I.) or by section titles preceded by a roman numeral and a full stop (I. On Method).
2. *Emphases* should all appear in italics. Please do not use bold, underlining, different fonts, or font sizes.
3. *Citations* are to appear in double quotation marks, quotations within quotations in single quotation marks. Omissions in quotations are to be indicated by three points in square brackets. Authorial insertions within quotations are likewise to appear in square brackets.
4. *Punctuation with citations* should be used as follows: »The pastoral symphony«, concludes Meeker, »is a thoroughly domesticated score« (90). Please do not use quotation marks with indented quotations. Here the bibliographic reference should be in brackets and should precede the full stop.
5. *Footnotes,* which should be numbered and in superscript, should be reserved for supplementary arguments or commentaries. Footnote numbers should follow full stops and colons but should precede commas and semicolons. Bibliographic references in footnotes should follow the same conventions as in the text (see point 6), i.e. with a short reference. The full reference should be listed in the bibliography.
6. *Bibliographic references* should be included in brackets in the text – first names of authors should be omitted unless the reference is not clear – and must clearly point to specific sources in the list of works cited. The bibliographic reference should contain the author's surname, an abridged title, and the page number if necessary (Luhmann, *Kunst der Gesellschaft*, 65). The title does not need to be included if the reference is unambiguous, e.g. (Luhmann, 65). When referencing the same work continuously the author's name should be omitted (65f.) (65-68). – If referencing the same work frequently abbreviations can be used (*LW*, 24). This abbreviation should be included in the bibliography: Ransmayr, Christoph. *The Last World*. Tr. John E. Woods. New York: Grove

Press, 1990 (1988). (*LW*) - In case that two or more references are cited at the same time they should be separated by a semicolon, e.g. (Huizinga; Elias), or (Agamben, *Homer sacer*; *Remnants of Auschwitz*), or (Agamben, *Homo sacer*, 66; *Remnants of Auschwitz*, 30). If a cited work has two authors, the names are separated by a forward slash (Böhme/Böhme, 299). If a work has more than two authors please use the first name followed by »et al.« (Klibansky et al.). Titles of novels, monographs or titles of scholarly collections are in italics (Luhmann, *Soziale Systeme*), while titles of essays, articles and poems are in quotation marks (Rilke, »Der Panther«).
7. The *list of works cited* is to appear at the end of the manuscript. Bibliographical details should appear in the following order: Author's full name. *Title*. Place of publication: Publisher, year of publication. See the examples given below. If in a title an emphasis is given or another title is quoted these will appear in single quotation marks. If more than two editors are responsible for a scholarly collection all names are listed.
8. *Tables* and *pictures* are to be submitted with the manuscript on individual pages and should be numbered continuously. The point in the manuscript where the table or picture is to be inserted should be clearly marked.
9. Please use Australian English (-ize not -ise/ honour not honor)
10. When citing indirectly please use: qtd.

Examples of Works Cited

Monographs

Jacobson, Roman/Linda R. Waugh. *The Sound Shape of Language*. Bloomington: Indiana University Press, 1979.

Ricoeur, Paul. *The Rule of Metaphor*. Tr. Robert Czerny. London: Routledge, 2003.

Simmel, Georg. *Philosophie des Geldes. Gesamtausgabe*. Ed. Otthein Rammstedt. Vol. 6. Frankfurt/M: Suhrkamp, 1989.

Freud, Sigmund. *Gesammelte Werke*. Ed. Anna Freud. Frankfurt/M: Fischer, 1999.

Anthologies

Fohrmann, Jürgen (ed.). *Systemtheorie und Literatur*. Munich: Fink, 1996.

Klibansky, Raymond/Erwin Panofsky/Fritz Saxl (eds.). *Saturn und Melancholie: Studien zur Geschichte der Naturphilosophie und Medizin, der Religion und der Kunst*. Tr. Christa Buschendorf. Frankfurt/M: Suhrkamp, 1992.

Reichert, Klaus/Fritz Senn (eds.). *Materialien zu James Joyces ›Ein Porträt des Künstlers als junger Mann‹*. Frankfurt/M: Suhrkamp, 1975.

Articles in Anthologies

Merton, Robert K. »Sozialstruktur und Anomie«. *Soziologische Theorie und soziale Struktur*. Berlin: de Gruyter, 1995: 115-154.

Olschner, Leonard. »Poetic Mutations of Silence: At the Nexus of Paul Celan and Ossip Mandelstam«. *Word Traces: Readings of Paul Celan*. Ed. Aris Fioretos. Baltimore: Johns Hopkins University Press, 1994: 369-386.

Articles in Periodicals

Hallin, Daniel C. »Sound Bite News: Television Coverage of Elections, 1968-1988«. *Journal of Communication* 42.2 (1992): 5-24.

Roberts, David. »Towards a Genealogy and Typology of Spectacle: Some Comments on Debord«. *Thesis Eleven* 75 (2003): 54-68.

Beiträger / Contributors

Dale Adams, PhD. Lecturer in German Studies at the University of Melbourne.
Postal address: The University of Melbourne. School of Languages and Linguistics. Parkville Campus, Arts Building, Parkville, VIC 3010, Australia.
Email: adamsd@unimelb.edu.au

Andrew Benjamin, PhD. Professor of Critical Theory and Philosophical Aesthetics at Monash University, FAHA.
Postal address: Monash University. School of English, Communications and Performance Studies. Clayton Campus, Robert Menzies Building, VIC 3800, Australia.
Email: Andrew.Benjamin@monash.edu

Ralf Beuthan, Dr. phil. Assistant Professor in Philosophy at Myongji University.
Postal address: Myongji University, Department of Philosophy, 50-3 Namgajwa-dong, Seodaemun-gu, Seoul, Korea (120-728).
Email: beuthan@googlemail.com

Yvonne Förster-Beuthan, Dr. phil. Juniorprofessorin für Philosophie an der Leuphana Universität Lüneburg.
Postanschrift: Leuphana-Universität Lüneburg, Institut für Kulturtheorie, Kulturforschung, Künste, Scharnhorststr. 1, 21335 Lüneburg, Deutschland.
Email: yvonne.foerster@leuphana.de

James Hodkinson, PhD. Associate Professor in German Studies at the University of Warwick.
Postal address: University of Warwick, Department of German Studies, Coventry CV4 7AL, United Kingdom.
Email: j.r.hodkinson@warwick.ac.uk

Johannes Friedrich Lehmann, Dr. phil. habil. Privatdozent für Neuere Deutsche Literaturwissenschaft an der Universität Duisburg-Essen.
Postanschrift: Universität Essen-Duisburg, Institut für Germanistik, Universitätsstr. 12, 45141 Essen, Deutschland.
Email: Johannes.Lehmann@uni-due.de

Ruth Pullin, PhD. Art Historian and Curator at the National Gallery of Victoria.
Postal address: National Gallery of Victoria, Department of Australian Art, 180 St Kilda Road, Melbourne, VIC 3004, Australia.
Email: Ruth.Pullin@gmail.com

Kate Rigby, PhD. Associate Professor in Comparative Literature at Monash University, FAHA.
Postal address: Monash University. School of English, Communications and Performance Studies. Clayton Campus, Robert Menzies Building, VIC 3800, Australia.
Email: Kate.Rigby@monash.edu

Ritchie Robertson, PhD. Taylor Professor of German at the University of Oxford, FBA.
Postal address: Faculty of Modern Languages, University of Oxford, 47 Wellington Square, Oxford OX1 2JF, United Kingdom.
Email: Ritchie.Robertson@mod-langs.ox.ac.uk

Klaus Vieweg, Dr. phil. Professor für Philosophie an der Friedrich-Schiller-Universität Jena.
Postanschrift: Friedrich-Schiller-Universität Jena, Institut für Philosophie, Zwätzengasse 9, 07743 Jena, Deutschland.
Email: Klaus.Vieweg@uni-jena.de

Claudia Wirsing, M.A. Doktorandin in Philosophie an der Friedrich-Schiller-Universität Jena.
Postanschrift: Friedrich-Schiller-Universität Jena, Institut für Philosophie, Zwätzengasse 9, 07743 Jena, Deutschland.
Email: Claudia.Wirsing@yahoo.de

Herausgeber / Editors

Franz-Josef Deiters, Dr. phil. habil. Associate Professor of German Studies at Monash University, FAHA.
Postal address: Monash University, Melbourne. School of Languages, Cultures and Linguistics, Clayton Campus, Robert Menzies Building, Clayton, VIC 3800, Australia.
Email: Franz-Josef.Deiters@monash.edu

Axel Fliethmann, Dr. phil. Senior Lecturer in German Studies at Monash University.
Postal address: Monash University, Melbourne. School of Languages, Cultures and Linguistics. Clayton Campus, Robert Menzies Building, Clayton, VIC 3800, Australia.
Email: Axel.Fliethmann@monash.edu

Birgit Lang, Dr. phil. Senior Lecturer in German Studies at the University of Melbourne.
Postal address: University of Melbourne. School of Languages and Linguistics, Parkville Campus, Babel Building, Parkville, VIC 3010, Australia.
Email: langb@unimelb.edu.au

Alison Lewis, PhD. Professor of German Studies at the University of Melbourne, FAHA.
Postal address: The University of Melbourne. School of Languages and Linguistics, Parkville Campus, Babel Building, Parkville, VIC 3010, Australia.
Email: lewisa@unimelb.edu.au

Christiane Weller, PhD. Senior Lecturer in German Studies at Monash University.
Postal address: Monash University, Melbourne. School of Languages, Cultures and Linguistics, Clayton Campus, Robert Menzies Building, Clayton, VIC 3800, Australia.
Email: Tina.Weller@monash.edu